Legal
First
Aid

Legal
First
Aid

by Henry Shain

Funk & Wagnalls
New York

Manufactured in the United States of America

Library of Congress Cataloging in Publication Data

Shain, Henry.
  Legal first aid.

  1. Law—United States—Popular works. I. Title.
KF387.S45 1975   340′.0973   75-12737
ISBN 0-308-10201-0

1 2 3 4 5 6 7 8 9 10

to J.W.

Contents

PART III
THE FAMILY

PART IV
INJURY CLAIMS

PART V
CONSUMER PROTECTION

PART VI
CONSTITUTIONAL FREEDOMS

FOREWORD

As a practicing attorney who deals mainly with the problems of the individual and the family, I find it appalling that most people have so little knowledge of the laws which guide their everyday lives. Because of fear which is bred through ignorance, many laymen are afraid of judges, lawyers and the law in general. The lack of a basic legal education has reduced many laymen's knowledge to a few brief, untrue cliches as "possession is nine-tenths of the law".

The real loser in this educational crisis is the American middle class citizen, who fears that high attorney fees will impoverish him. Those who know and understand the legal system best reap the most benefits from it, and the middle class citizen, acting both as consumer and taxpayer, is able to harvest precious little because of his limited knowledge and experience with the law. Hopefully, this book will alleviate some of these problems by providing practical information about the law.

Just as we learn preventive medicine and dentistry, we should learn some basic law for preventive purposes -- call it "Legal First Aid." Respect for the law should come from knowledge -- not from fear of lawyers and judges. And knowledge of general laws which directly affect the citizen can alert him to many needed changes which he can help to accomplish as an interested voter.

This book is designed to give the reader a good general background in the laws which govern his everyday life. My goal in writing the book is to provide enough general knowledge to make rational, intelligent legal decisions. You will find chapters covering everything from marriage and divorce to injury claims -- from consumer rights to the rights of the criminally accused -- from wills and estate planning to the rights and obligations of juveniles and their parents.

WARNING! This book cannot replace your lawyer. Modern technology has created many machines which replace men, but no machine or book can replace a lawyer.

This book is designed to give you some general knowledge of the law. It is not a do-it-yourself guide, and it should not be read as such. It should alert you to the need for an attorney. And, if legal counsel is necessary, hopefully you will be able to find a good lawyer; you will know what to expect from your lawyer and the legal system and you will be able to discuss your problem with your attorney on an intelligent level.

The law is dynamic; it can change at a moment's notice. Lawyers must supplement their law books yearly to keep up with the changes. It must be remembered that certain passages could be rendered obsolete by legislation or court decision. However, the book is written in generalities, and it is not intended as an exact treatise. Therefore, its usefulness should remain intact for many years to come.

Since I live and practice in San Francisco and I am a member of the California Bar, I have written about the laws of the state with which I am most familiar. But the laws and jurisprudence of the states are so similar that, indeed, this book is useful everywhere in America.

At the end of many of the chapters I have compiled charts to show what the laws on subjects within the chapter are in the 50 states and the District of Columbia. I obtained the chart information from legal digests, professional publications and articles from the general media. The charts represent only a brief summary of the law as it was when the book was prepared. In reading these charts one must take cognizance that the laws are far more complicated and subject to many more interpretations than are shown on the charts.

Much of the ignorance of the average person in understanding the law stems from use of unfamiliar terms and phrases. In writing this book, I have attempted to use non-technical words for better understanding. Where legal phraseology is used, I have made an explanation of its meaning, and there is a glossary of legal terms at the end of the book.

Most of the examples in the book are fictional situations. The names of the persons in the fictional examples are not real persons, and any resemblance to real persons, living or dead, is purely coincidental.

Now is the time for public acknowledgement and appreciation to those persons and institutions without whose aid this book would have been impossible: I wish to thank my mother and father whose genes, encouragement, push and money provided me with an opportunity to pursue a higher education; the University of California at Berkeley, which gave that higher education; my local draft board whose threats drove me to the draft-exempt sanctuary of law school; Barbara Bayley Ambrosio, who typed much of the original manuscript; Professor Peter Donnici, who scrutinized the chapters on constitutional law; Jean Brewer and Marilyn Hill of the University of California Extension School in San Francisco, who allowed me to teach my course, "The Individual and His Legal Affairs," which provided a writing discipline; Jo Ann Webb, who gave valuable editorial assistance and advice; and my many clients who gave me the confidence, experience and fees which were necessary for the writing of this book.

Henry Shain
San Francisco

PART I

THE ORIGIN AND STRUCTURE OF THE LAW

CHAPTER 1

Establishment of
Law in the United States

IN THE BEGINNING

A basic understanding of American law demands some knowledge of the origin of the law and the basis for American jurisprudence. How is it that a court can nullify an Act of Congress? Why can a judge order a man to jail for failing to support his children or his wife? How is it that one judge can order a labor union composed of thousands of men to continue working after they have voted to strike? These and other powers of the American judiciary did not evolve overnight. The whole nature, power and function of our judicial system has evolved slowly and continuously for thousands of years.

But where does one begin in a discussion of the origin of the law? Certainly the laws of Moses, the Greeks, the Romans, and Jesus have contributed. There is no point where law begins and the subjects of anthropology, history, and theology end.

Our legal institutions can be traced to those of the countries which ruled our nation before its independence. There have been sizable contributions from the French and the Spanish. Most of our legal traditions come from the English common law. With all due respect to earlier contributors, this discussion of the origin of American jurisprudence will begin around the year 600 A.D., which is the time of the first English Code.

Aethelbert, King of the Kentings, ordered the laws of his people to be put in writing. Aethelbert had just embraced the Christian faith, and these written laws were his gesture to emulate the Roman Code. The primitive laws consisted of just 90 brief sentences. For example, one of them reads as follows: "If one man strike another with the fist on the nose -- three shillings."

Aethelbert's statutes, known as Kentish Law, were supplemented by additional laws imposed by subsequent rulers until 1066, the year of the Norman Conquest of England.

During this 500 year period England was passing from a period of barbarism and tribalism to feudalism. There was little power behind the Kentish laws except for a brief period between 1017 and 1035 when Kanute was able to enforce the statutes instead of treating them as mere wishes, as his predecessors had. The courts could not compel their edicts and judgments; the rules of self-help and vengeance were much more commonplace. The English tradition of the rule of law and order had to be arduously and laboriously won over the centuries.

The Kentish laws originally imposed fines for the commission of crimes. The fines were payable to the victims of the crime, or in the case of a homicide, to the families of the victims. The courts were not strong enough to impose criminal penalties on the perpetrators of a crime. The law's last weapon was to put a criminal offender outside the peace; he became the foe of his society, and it was the duty of the law-abiding to waste his land, burn his home, and to hunt him down as though he were a beast of prey. As the state grew stronger, forms of criminal punishment could be imposed. But even at the time of the Norman Conquest, the crime of murder could still be atoned by the payment of money.

The Normans were, in a sense, less civilized than the people they conquered, for the Normans had no written laws. William the Conqueror let his new English subjects keep their old laws, and the small changes he did make were negligible. During the period of the early Norman rule, the great bulk of justice was done by the small local courts. The King's own court protected only royal rights and the causes of the barons. In fact, the King's Court was French-speaking, and its members thought of themselves as Frenchmen, not Englishmen.

Henry II (1133-1189) had the most profound influence on the system of English jurisprudence. He concentrated the entire judicial system of English justice in a central court of professional judges who were experts on the law. He thereby won power and control of the judiciary, and he provided an avenue of appeal for the peasants to plead their petty affairs. By concentrating the courts at Westminster, Henry II unified and stabilized the laws of his country.

Every decision of this new national court was written and recorded for posterity. A judgment became precedent, binding on future courts. The written memoranda of the courts would explain the logic of their decisions. While the Kentish laws were still in force, they were too brief and vague to be of any great consequence. The judges would determine the issues of each individual case before them, weigh the logic of the arguments presented by both sides of the issue, and render judgment accordingly. The powers of the throne backed up the court and thereby established the power of the courts to act. The judges made the laws; there was no active legislative body to govern the lives of the English people at that time.

As the structure of the court system changed to meet the needs of the people, the common law of England did not change appreciably because the decisions of the law-making courts were recorded for posterity. A court was bound by tradition to follow the rules of law and precedents of earlier courts. It was only when the logic of an argument which determined a legal issue was no longer applicable that a court would upset a precedent and change the law. Furthermore, it was the highest judicial tribunals or courts of last resort which would change rules of law. Indeed, it was extremely rare that a lower court would take it upon itself to upset a law which had been established in years past. This concept, established by Henry II of judge-made law or law by logic and experience is known as the common law.

These written judicial decisions were stored in books and categorized by the court which gave the judgment. The cases were also identified by the names of the disputing parties. (For instance, *Natali vs. Shain,* 12 King's Bench 139 meant that the decision in the case where Natali was suing Shain can be found in the twelfth volume of the King's Bench series of recorded cases at page 139.) This sysem of identifying precedent-setting cases is still used throughout the United States and the United Kingdom.

Henry II also made the procedure of trial by jury available to all the people in civil matters. Prior to this time, a procedure which was tantamount to trial by jury had been established in royal courts. Henry II gave litigants the option of trying their cases in the King's Court where 12 men were chosen to decide the better right. If the dispute was over the ownership of land, the jury consisted of 12 knights, not just ordinary men. However, the trial by jury was optional. The claimant still had the alternative of battling his opponent to determine a dispute, and both the claimant and the respondent could hire professional pugilists to represent them at the duel.

Originally, jurors did not determine questions of fact, but they acted as witnesses. Most legal transactions were done in public, such as the conveyance of land, and the neighbors of the litigant were called to testify to what they had witnessed. The verdict was the sworn testimony of the countryside. The trial by jury as we know it today eventually evolved from this form.

At this time the tradition of a grand jury and the indictment for criminal offenses was established. In the beginning of this system, the same jury which indicted the man could also try him. The accused had to consent to trial by jury. He had the option of death by pressing. The advantage to this morbid alternative was to escape the obloquy of conviction as a felon.

We must take the reforms of Henry II in their historical and social perspective. England had become a feudal state. Most of the benefits of the judicial system inured to royalty and the landowning classes. But some benefits did trickle down to the masses. Whatever the improprieties and shortcomings of the system were, the tradition, the power, and the independence of the judiciary were established, as was the institution of trial by jury and other due process guarantees.

For many in the United States who are so used to looking at one supreme body of law, the Constitution, and the myriads of subordinate laws, neatly codified into volumes known as codes and enacted by legislative bodies, the concept of the common law is a difficult one to grasp and comprehend. At the time of the institution of the royal courts and the common law, there was no great body of law to which the judges could look for reassurance. One reason why judicial precedence acquired exclusive authority was the absence of any one source of law capable of competing with the judiciary. Legislation was still exceptional and occasional, and there was no independent learned class.

By 1272 (after Henry II died) there were, for all practical purposes, only four statutes or documents on the books. The Kentish laws and the law books of the Norman ages were forgotten. It was the common law established by the King's Court which ruled. District customs were giving way to the general customs established by these courts. Therefore, the King's judges did more than end the strife of disputing parties; they established law for similar cases in the future. The judgment of one of these English courts not only looked backward but looked forward as well.

From the period 1300 to 1600, Parliament dealt in trifling matters. Henry VIII upset some of Parliament's inertia, but still left the law-making to the people he considered professionals in that area -- the judges. Henry VIII precipitated many changes in the law, most growing out of his thoughts on his break with Roman Catholicism. Also, the force of statute was given to the King's proclamations. Henry's Parliament made some major changes in the laws of property and crime. During this period the judges did make some vague claim that they could disregard the statutes which were directly at variance with the common law or the law of God or the royal prerogative; but these claims were few and far between, and little came of them.

During the period 1600 to 1688, the common law had taken permanent shape. There were a multitude of reported cases and definite legal principles that had been ascertained. Also, the court of equity had acquired its own jurisprudence and some definite standards, as the power of royal prerogative had been diminished. The Parliamentary Revolution brought many reforms to the legal system. Kangaroo courts and other inequities were terminated. Parliament began to exercise its law-making powers by supplementing and improving existing common law.

The Parliamentary Revolution restored energy and vigor to the Parliament by subordinating the Crown. The right of the people to govern their destiny without the interference of the Crown had been firmly established even though the English did restore their monarchy after the reign of Oliver Cromwell.

While the new unified and energetic Parliament passed many new statutes, it did little to abrogate or change the common law. The courts still drew upon the logic and experience of the past to make decisions on cases presently before them.

JUDICIAL REVIEW

Since the American colonies were settled by British citizens, disputes among the colonists were decided by courts which used the English common law as the foundation for their decisions. But the American colonists had fewer rights than British citizens, as the colonists were more subject to the prerogatives of the Crown. The absence of just laws and the tyranny of the monarchs of England brought revolution and independence to America. However, independence did not bring a whole new body of law and legal institutions to the former British colonies.

After independence was won, representatives from the colonies renamed them states and established a loosely knit confederation bound together by the Articles of Confederation. After the establishment of the Articles, the individual states still used court systems patterned after the English common law.

The Articles did not provide for a strong federal government to give the states cohesion, nor did they provide for the states to honor the laws and judgments of the sister states. A redress of grievances between inhabitants of two states could best be achieved through violence. Law and order and the integrity of the judicial system proved to be chaotic.

The shortcomings of a loosely knit confederation was soon rectified by the Constitution. The Constitution, in establishing stronger central government, gave the federal judiciary the power to decide disputes arising over matters of federal law enacted by Congress and the power to decide disputes between residents of two different states. The Constitution also provided that each state give "full faith and credit" to the judgments of its sister states. Thus, in theory, the Constitution gave the judiciary the power it needed to maintain law and order.

The Constitution created the Supreme Court and the federal judiciary as a separate, independent branch of government. The function of this branch was to "interpret" the law. The word "interpret" is vague. Most would assume that the function of the courts would remain that of deciding disputes between conflicting litigants. There is nothing in the Constitution which explicitly gives the Supreme Court the power to nullify Acts of Congress, statutes duly enacted by state legislatures, and executive action by the President of the United States or governors of the individual states. In fact, the Supreme Court did not attempt to make any such daring decisions in the early years of its tenure.

The real power and influence of the Supreme Court did not begin until 1801 when John Marshall assumed the position of Chief Justice. Marshall was a Federalist. He felt that a strong federal government was necessary to maintain the cohesion and integrity of the nation. The anti-Federalists were against this. Their feelings were engendered by a general skepticism about central authority after the bitter experience with the English monarchs. They also had economic reasons. Thomas Jefferson was the leader of the anti-Federalists, and his administration was in power at the time of Marshall's momentous decisions.

John Marshall believed in a strong federal government, and the strength of his convictions was certainly expressed in his decisions. In 1803 Marshall's Court invalidated an Act of Congress (*Marbury vs. Madison*). The power of the judiciary to scrutinize the validity of the acts of other branches of the government is known as the power of judicial review and is considered a necessary part of a check-and-balance system of government. The power of judicial review makes the judiciary equal and independent to the executive and legislative branches.

But how is it that a body of nine men, who are not even elected by the people they serve, can nullify legislation enacted by the representatives of the people? Marshall felt that any nation which was created by a document must hold that document supreme. In our case, the document was the Constitution of the United States, and Marshall felt that any legislation which was in contravention to the letter or spirit of the Constitution was objectionable. It is the duty of the Supreme Court to interpret any situation with reference to the Constitution. The Constitution is supreme, and any governmental act which is repugnant to it must be declared unconstitutional and void. Therefore, in later years when Congress passed the National Industrial Recovery Act and it was signed into law by President Roosevelt, the Supreme Court had the right to nullify this legislation when it found that certain aspects of it were irreconcilable with the Constitution. Likewise, when the state of Alabama enacted legislation authorizing and enforcing segregated public facilities, the U.S. Supreme Court had the power to nullify this law on the grounds that it was incompatible with the Fourteenth Amendment.

The judiciary does not pass on every piece of congressional and state legislation. The U.S. Supreme Court established a precedent in 1793 when it decided not to give an advisory opinion. The courts will only decide actual cases or controversies which arise from lawsuits; they will not give advisory opinions on pending legislation.

The decisions of the Marshall Court were accepted and complied with. While later Supreme Courts heard cases with similar issues, the common law principles and power of precedent and the logic of Chief Justice Marshall's opinions were affirmed. Today, there is no question over the power, authority and jurisdiction of the U.S. Supreme Court.

But the Supreme Court does not have dictatorial powers. The final word is still in the hands of the people through their elected representatives. If the people are unhappy with a decision of the Supreme Court, the change which they desire can be effected by amending the Constitution. Amendment is a long arduous process involving Congress and state legislatures but, nevertheless, the Constitution does provide for change by the people.

It is not the function of the judiciary to enact laws, but the practical effect of many judicial interpretations is the making of new law. The courts, especially the U.S. Supreme Court, have come under heavy criticism for judicial activism -- unnecessarily encroaching on the legislative branch of government. But these decisions have been based on sound legal principles. Whenever there is a check-and-balance system of government, there has to be some overlap of function in its branches.

Proponents of judicial activism argue that the courts have finally assumed the responsibilities they had avoided for so many years. The active courts and the increased use of the initiative process have certainly filled the vacuum left by inefficient, unresponsive legislatures.

The preceding paragraphs should not leave the impression that all the laws of the United States have been created through judicial decisions. Our laws fall into a three-tiered structure: the fundamental law found in the U.S. Constitution and the constitutions of the 50 states; the statutes enacted under the authority of the various constitutions by the Congress, the state and local legislative bodies, and the initiative process; and, lastly, court decisions interpreting the various statutes and ordinances.

FEDERALISM AND THE APPLICATION OF
THE BILL OF RIGHTS TO THE STATES

The Bill of Rights recognizes individual freedom, and it places limits on any governmental authority which limits it. Prior to the Civil War, the Bill of Rights only applied to the exercise of power by the federal government. In fact, the Supreme Court decided in 1833 that the Bill of Rights did not apply to state action.

The real battle of states' rights versus federal rights was born out of the skepticism of those who feared the tyranny of the federal government. States' rights were supposedly demanded for the protection of individuals, but when the states abused individual rights, the term lost its significance.

The Thirteenth, Fourteenth, and Fifteenth Amendments to the Constitution were designed to protect the individual from the encroachment on his basic rights by the states. The Thirteenth Amendment forbade slavery; the Fifteenth

Amendment prevented the states from abridging the right of a citizen to vote on account of race, color or previous condition of servitude. The Fourteenth Amendment provided in part: "... nor shall any state deprive any person of life, liberty or property without due process of law; nor deny to any person within its jurisdiction the full protection of the laws ... ".

The reasoning behind the adoption of the Fourteenth Amendment would lead to the conclusion that the Bill of Rights should be applied to the states in the same uniform degree it is applied to the federal government. However, the terms "due process of law" and "equal protection of the laws" are ambiguous and the Fourteenth Amendment was not interpreted to mean that *all* of the provisions of the Bill of Rights applied to the states. The Supreme Court originally took a position that the Fourteenth Amendment only demanded that the states meet the requirement of fundamental fairness in the treatment of citizens. The states did not have to meet the same high standards as the federal government.

The fundamental fairness doctrine has eroded in favor of a "selective incorporation" viewpoint. The court now feels that some, not all, provisions of the Bill of Rights are incorporated in the Fourteenth Amendment and apply to the states to the same degree that they apply to the federal government. This means that the minimum federal standards are now minimum state standards -- a state court cannot diminish or reduce the standards, but it can establish even higher standards for its own state.

CHAPTER 2

The Courts

INTRODUCTION

There are 52 separate and distinct court systems in the United States; one for each of the 50 states, one for the District of Columbia and then there is the federal system. While no system is exactly the same, all have similar structures and procedures. All are divided into trial courts and appeals courts.

The trial courts, whether by jury or judge alone, listen to testimony, weigh evidence, and make a decision, usually called a judgment. The appellate courts hear cases appealed from the lower trial courts or from a lower appeals court. The appellate courts usually do not listen to new evidence; they review the evidence which was before the trial court and pass upon the legitimacy and legality of the decision reached by the trial court. The decisions of the appellate courts are recorded for posterity, and they become binding law in future situations unless and until they are overruled by courts with equal or higher jurisdiction.

All trial courts and some appellate courts are divided into criminal and civil departments. While, technically, a criminal complaint against a citizen is a "lawsuit" of the state against that person (The State of North Carolina vs. Jones), a criminal matter is infinitely more serious than a civil lawsuit. In a criminal matter, the defendant is arrested before he is tried. If he is found guilty, he can be sent to prison. Criminal charges are always prosecuted by government agencies. In the federal system, the U.S. Attorney or the Attorney General's Office is the prosecuting attorney. In the state courts, it is the district attorney or state's attorney. The state prosecutes its case against the accused in the name of society to seek punishment or redress.

Civil lawsuits are concerned with the legal rights of disputing individuals including living persons, corporations and governmental bodies. Civil lawsuits are only involved with property and carry no threat of imprisonment or fines. Civil litigants can obtain punitive damages in some cases if they can prove malice, oppression, fraud or recklessness. (Criminal actions and civil lawsuits will be discussed extensively in chapters 4 and 5.)

In addition to the basic trial courts, there are also administrative agencies which can hold hearings and make decisions which are legally binding upon the disputing parties before them. The special administrative agencies are established by legislative action. For instance, Congress has created such agencies as the Food and Drug Administration, the Federal Power Commission and the Federal Trade Commission. In the states there are agencies like the Alcoholic Beverage Control Commission, the Department of Motor Vehicles and the Industrial Accident Commission. All of these agencies must adhere to the constitutional requirements of due process of law. Decisions they render are appealable to a regularly constituted appellate court.

Throughout this chapter and other chapters of this book, the term jurisdiction is used, and now is a good time to explain it. Jurisdiction means the legal right of courts to exercise their power and authority. Courts obtain jurisdiction through specific legislative statutes or from a specific clause in the Constitution. Courts can only decide disputes which fall within the areas of their jurisdiction and if a court attempts to exercise authority beyond its jurisdiction, its decision must be reversed upon appeal.

THE FEDERAL COURTS

Congress has established a federal system of courts to hear cases involving federal law. These courts also hear cases involving litigants from different states where the amount in controversy is more than $10,000. Their role in these "diversity of citizenship" cases was designed to prevent a litigant from being "hometowned"—that is, put at a disadvantage because he must bring an action in the state court of his opponent.

All federal judges, including Supreme Court justices, are appointed by the President of the United States with the advice and consent of the Senate. Federal judges may serve for life or until impeachment by Congress for gross misconduct.

The basic federal trial court of general jurisdiction is the U.S. District Court. There is at least one court in every state of the union. Besides hearing trials, this court will also entertain writs of habeas corpus, which are tantamount to appeals from the decisions of the state court. The writs must allege an unconstitutional denial of rights and will only be entertained after a criminal defendant has exhausted all of his remedies in his own state's courts.

The second tier of the three-tiered federal court system is the Circuit Court of Appeals. Congress has divided the United States into ten judicial circuits, and each one of these circuits has its own appellate court. Washington, D.C., also has its own circuit court. Each circuit court hears appeals of decisions from federal district courts within its circuit. The circuit court also hears appeals of decisions of federal administrative agencies and appeals from the U.S. Tax Court.

The court of last resort is the U.S. Supreme Court which has nine justices and meets in Washington, D.C. The Court has original jurisdiction to hear trials between disputing states, but most of its business is hearing appeals of federal questions which either originate in the federal courts or may be appeals of state court decisions involving federal questions of law. Unlike other courts, the Supreme Court does not have to consider all of the appeals which are brought to it for a decision. The Court only wants to decide cases which are of major importance and, therefore, at least four justices must agree that a case should be heard before the entire Court will rule on it.

The decisions of the U.S. Supreme Court have profound effects on our society. Since our jurisprudence is based upon precedents and this is the court of last resort, its decisions can last indefinitely. It is true that the court may rehear a case or an issue and decide it in a different manner from a previous court, but prior decisions are an extremely persuasive argument in any subsequent litigation.

> A classic example of the Court reversing itself occurred in the area of segregated public facilities. In 1896, in a case called *Plessy vs. Fergueson*, the Supreme Court decided that segregated public facilities were equal if the quality of the facilities was equal among the users. Thus, the doctrine of separate but equal was established. It provided the legal basis for segregated school systems and other segregated public facilities. Finally, 58 years later, in 1954 the court reversed itself in a case called *Brown vs. the Board of Education of Topeka, Kansas*. In that case, the Supreme Court emphatically stated that separate facilities were inherently unequal, and ordered all officially segregated school districts to desegregate with all due deliberate speed.

THE STATE COURTS

State court systems are patterned after the federal court system. The state courts of general trial jurisdiction may be called superior courts, circuit courts, county courts or district courts. (New York calls its general trial court the State Supreme Court.) These courts are generally divided into departments or divisions to deal with specific aspects of the law — criminal, civil, domestic relations, probate and juvenile. The states also have lower courts to deal with smaller matters such as traffic violations, misdemeanors (petty crimes) and civil disputes involving a limited amount of money. They may be called municipal courts, justices of the peace, magistrate courts and police courts.

Decisions of courts of general trial jurisdiction are appealable to an intermediate appellate court in the more populous states. Decisions from intermediate appellate courts (or from state courts of general trial jurisdiction where there are no intermediate appellate courts) are appealed to a state supreme court. If a decision of a state's highest court involves only state law, the case can go no further.

The selection of judges varies greatly. Most state judges are selected by appointment by the governor sometimes with the approval of a legislative body or judicial qualifications commission. (In some states mayors or town councils can select judges for courts of more limited jurisdiction.) In other states judges must be voted into office by the people. Still other states provide for the appointment of judges, but these judges must run for re-election when their terms expire.

If justice is truly blind, then the judges who administer it should be impartial. Unfortunately, the system of choosing judges leaves much to be desired. The appointment of judges is fraught with political manipulation, payoffs and cronyism.

The democratic process is not the best way to select judges because the office is one which requires a great deal of technical proficiency, and the voters have very little way of determining which candidate is the most qualified. Another drawback is the very nature of the modern political process as we have come to know it in recent years. That is, running for office requires a great deal of money, which is all too often donated for favors, not civic improvement.

The state of Missouri has a plan which allows local bar associations to choose qualified candidates for a judgeship, and the governor must select from this list. The problem with this plan, sometimes called the "Merit Plan", is that local bar associations in large cities are often controlled by the large corporate firms — the fat cats of the profession. This could prevent qualified sole practitioners from judgeships.

Confidence in the courts, as with most other public institutions, has been waning over the years. Judges have been clamoring for lower work loads, more courtrooms, more attaches and more proficient attorneys. But judicial reform has a higher priority, and it could be accomplished through qualification tests and judicial qualification commissions to pass upon prospective appointments and to discipline judges accused of misconduct in office.

SMALL CLAIMS COURTS

All states have a Small Claims Court or a small claims procedure in their lower courts. It provides an informal procedure for trials of small claims, and a few states allow a landlord to get a judgment for back rent and *eviction* of a tenant.

The key feature to Small Claims Courts is the saving of time and money. The time saving comes with the informal procedures and early trial dates. The saving of money comes with the lack of a need for an attorney at the trial. To keep the

Small Claims Courts as people's courts, no lawyer should be allowed, but unfortunately, only four states follow this rule. (California, Idaho, Minnesota and Nebraska). Most states make the use of an attorney optional, and some states force corporations to appear at trial with a lawyer.

Only a defendant can appeal from a judgment in Small Claims Court. The appeal usually results in a new trial in a higher court, where both parties can be represented by an attorney.

Getting a judgment in Small Claims Court, as in all other courts, does not mean that you are going to be paid off automatically. Check the chapter on credit to see the legal methods which a judgment creditor can use to collect a debt, and for that matter, the legal methods which a judgment debtor can use to avoid paying a debt.

ALTERNATIVES

Before leaving this chapter on the structure of the court system, other methods of settling disputes besides dueling and threats of violence should be mentioned. Arbitration is a term we hear a lot when talking about labor disputes. It is also a method disputing parties can agree to use to present their case to an arbitrator and abide by his decision. Many state legislatures have enacted enabling laws which give an arbitration award the full force and effect of a judgment rendered by a court of law.

In order to implement arbitration, the disputing parties must either have contracted to arbitrate disputes instead of bringing them in a court of law or mutually agree to arbitrate. The American Arbitration Association (AAA) is a non-profit national organization which has its own set of rules and procedures. When parties agree to arbitrate their matter before the AAA, they agree to abide by its rules.

Because of overcrowded calendars, the courts are always looking for innovative ways to administer and expedite justice. They have used court commissioners instead of judges to deal with many less demanding, more perfunctory matters. Some courts have begun to use experienced trial attorneys to sit as judges or arbitrators in individual cases where all the parties to a lawsuit agree to this.

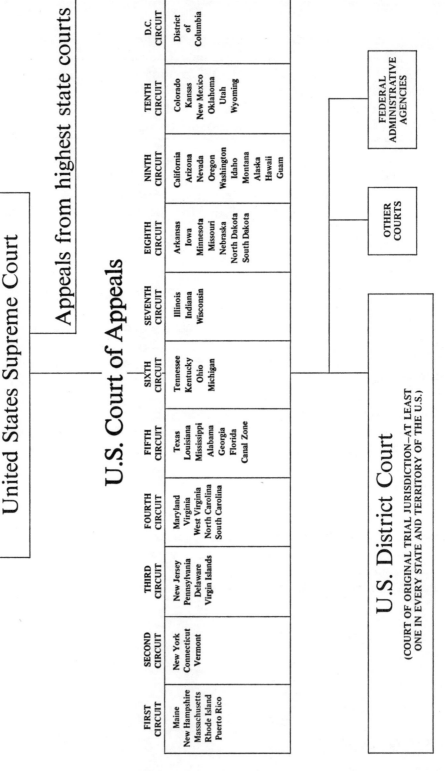

FEDERAL COURT SYSTEM

United States Supreme Court

Appeals from highest state courts

U.S. Court of Appeals

FIRST CIRCUIT	SECOND CIRCUIT	THIRD CIRCUIT	FOURTH CIRCUIT	FIFTH CIRCUIT	SIXTH CIRCUIT	SEVENTH CIRCUIT	EIGHTH CIRCUIT	NINTH CIRCUIT	TENTH CIRCUIT	D.C. CIRCUIT
Maine New Hampshire Massachusetts Rhode Island Puerto Rico	New York Connecticut Vermont	New Jersey Pennsylvania Delaware Virgin Islands	Maryland Virginia West Virginia North Carolina South Carolina	Texas Louisiana Mississippi Alabama Georgia Florida Canal Zone	Tennessee Kentucky Ohio Michigan	Illinois Indiana Wisconsin	Arkansas Iowa Minnesota Missouri Nebraska North Dakota South Dakota	California Arizona Nevada Oregon Washington Idaho Montana Alaska Hawaii Guam	Colorado Kansas New Mexico Oklahoma Utah Wyoming	District of Columbia

U.S. District Court

(COURT OF ORIGINAL TRIAL JURISDICTION–AT LEAST ONE IN EVERY STATE AND TERRITORY OF THE U.S.)

FEDERAL ADMINISTRATIVE AGENCIES

OTHER COURTS

STATE COURTS

	Small Claims Court Limits	Court of General Trial Jurisdiction	Intermediate Appellate Court	Highest State Court
ALABAMA	$300	Circuit Court	Court of Appeal	Supreme Court
ALASKA	$1,000	Superior Court	NONE	Supreme Court
ARIZONA	$500	Superior Court	Court of Appeal	Supreme Court
ARKANSAS	$500	Circuit Court	NONE	Supreme Court
CALIFORNIA	$500	Superior Court	Court of Appeal	Supreme Court
COLORADO	$500	District Court	Court of Appeal	Supreme Court
CONNECTICUT	$750	Superior Court	NONE	Supreme Court
DELAWARE	$1,500	Superior Court	NONE	Supreme Court
D. C.	$750	Superior Court	Circuit Court of Appeals	U.S. Supreme Court
FLORIDA	NO COURT	Circuit Court	District Court of Appeals	Supreme Court
GEORGIA	Varies from county to county	Superior Court	Court of Appeals	Supreme Court
HAWAII	$300	Circuit Court	NONE	Supreme Court
IDAHO	$200	District Court	NONE	Supreme Court
ILLINOIS	$1,000	Circuit Court	Appellate Court	Supreme Court
INDIANA	$500	Superior Court	Court of Appeals	Supreme Court
IOWA	$300	District Court	NONE	Supreme Court
KANSAS	$100	District Court	NONE	Supreme Court
KENTUCKY	$500	Circuit Court	NONE	Court of Appeals
LOUISIANA	$500	District Court	Court of Appeals	Supreme Court
MAINE	$200	Superior Court	NONE	Supreme Judicial Court

	Small Claims Court Limits	Court of General Trial Jurisdiction	Intermediate Appellate Court	Highest State Court
MARYLAND	$1000	Circuit Court	Court of Special Appeals	Court of Appeals
MASSACHUSETTS	$400	Superior Court	Appeals Court	Supreme Judicial Court
MICHIGAN	$300–$500	Circuit Court	Court of Appeals	Supreme Court
MINNESOTA	$300–$500	District Court	NONE	Supreme Court
MISSISSIPPI	$200	Circuit Court	NONE	Supreme Court
MISSOURI	Varies from county to county	Circuit Court	Court of Appeals	Supreme Court
MONTANA	$300	District Court	NONE	Supreme Court
NEBRASKA	$500	District Court	NONE	Supreme Court
NEVADA	$300	District Court	NONE	Supreme Court
NEW HAMPSHIRE	$300	Superior Court	NONE	Supreme Court
NEW JERSEY	$200	Superior Court	NONE	Supreme Court
NEW MEXICO	$2,000	District Court	Court of Appeals	Supreme Court
NEW YORK	$500	Supreme Court	NONE	Court of Appeals
NORTH CAROLINA	$300	Superior Court	Court of Appeals	Supreme Court
NORTH DAKOTA	$200	District Court	NONE	Supreme Court
OHIO	$150	Court of Common Pleas	Court of Appeals	Supreme Court
OKLAHOMA	$400	District Court	Court of Appeals Court of Criminal Appeals	Supreme Court
OREGON	$500	Circuit Court	Court of Appeals	Supreme Court
PENNSYLVANIA	$500	Superior Court	NONE	Supreme Court
RHODE ISLAND	$300	Superior Court	NONE	Supreme Court

	Small Claims Court Limits	Court of General Trial Jurisdiction	Intermediate Appellate Court	Highest State Court
SOUTH CAROLINA	$200 – $1000	Circuit Court	NONE	Supreme Court
SOUTH DAKOTA	$500	Circuit Court	NONE	Supreme Court
TENNESSEE	$3,000	Circuit Court	Court of Appeals Court of Criminal Appeals	Supreme Court
TEXAS	$150–$200	District Court	Court of Appeals Court of Criminal Appeals	Supreme Court
UTAH	$200	District Court	NONE	Supreme Court
VERMONT	$250	County Court	NONE	Supreme Court
VIRGINIA	$3,000	Circuit Court	NONE	Supreme Court of Appeals
WASHINGTON	$100–$200	Superior Court	Court of Appeals	Supreme Court
WEST VIRGINIA	$300	Circuit Court	NONE	Supreme Court of Appeals
WISCONSIN	$500	Circuit Court	NONE	Supreme Court
WYOMING	$100	District Court	NONE	Supreme Court

FOOTNOTES

1There is a small claims procedure in District, Municipal, Superior and Justice Courts.

CHAPTER 3

You and Your Attorney

INTRODUCTION

There are 375,000 lawyers in the United States. Unfortunately, they all cannot be good, and fortunately, they are not all bad. Attorneys picture themselves as knights in shining armor, righting the wrongs in our society through the art of advocacy (which is an indefinable combination of intelligence, knowledge, guile and luck.) Their detractors call them thieves, jackals, hypocrites, and other epithets. Since attorneys are only human, their conduct is subject to the same excellence and shortcomings of other members of the species. The purpose of this book is to arm its reader with an intelligent knowledge of the law so that he can make rational decisions concerning the legal aspects of his life. The purpose of this chapter is to arm him with some knowledge of the legal profession so that he can make a wise decision in selecting an attorney.

EDUCATION AND ADMISSION TO THE BAR

Each state through its legislature and state bar controls its lawyers. The fact that one is admitted to practice law in one state does not automatically provide him with a license to practice law in another state. Every member of a bar must pass a bar examination or other qualification test before he can be admitted to practice. Oddly enough, there is no similar qualification test for judges to pass before they can assume the bench.

Most attorneys have the advantage of at least some college education and, more than likely, a college degree. The traditional method of obtaining a license to practice law is graduating from an accredited university, and then passing a full time law school program in three years and, finally, passing the state bar examination.

There are also part-time night law schools which require little or no college education in order to gain enrollment. The record of these schools in the results of the bar examination is not as good as the law schools of major universities. Some states also allow an applicant to gain his education under the tutelage of a practicing attorney in the state, and this education is scrutinized by the bar.

Law school is an arduous, tedious struggle. It presents more of a test for perserverance than intelligence. Law teaching methods are slow and plodding but are supposed to train you to think as a lawyer. The prospect of a three-day bar examination comes as a welcome relief after years of study. If an applicant fails a bar examination, he may keep taking subsequent bar examinations until he passes.

THE FUNCTION AND METHODS OF A LAWYER

The function of the lawyer is to represent his client. His services may take place strictly within the office as he prepares a letter, will, partnership agreement, corporate merger papers or other drafting service.

The legal services may be performed in the courtroom in the form of pretrial arguments, actual trial or oral arguments before an appellate court.

Whatever the task, the function of the attorney is usually the same. He must analyze the needs of his client, marshal the relevant facts and determine and apply the law to the particular situation. Some situations will dictate easy solutions; other problems will dictate extensive legal research, paper work, and court appearances.

An attorney may not legally cheat, lie, suborn perjury or in any other way deceive the court for the benefit of his client or himself. Nor is it his duty to accept the case of every person who comes to him.

Anything said to an attorney by a client or a prospective client in a private consultation is strictly privileged. These confidential conversations or communications cannot be divulged unless the client expressly authorizes it. This rule is designed to protect the attorney-client relationship and promote full disclosure of facts between them.

This chapter deals extensively with the duties of the attorney, but mention must also be made of the duty of the client to reveal all of the facts surrounding his case to his attorney. It is the job of the attorney to sift the relevant from the irrelevant—the client should withhold nothing for his own protection. Many an attorney has lost a trial or become severely embarrassed because his client has foolishly been less than candid.

CONTROLLING THE LAWYER

The practice of law is strictly regulated by the individual states. The American Bar Association (ABA) is a national, voluntary organization of lawyers; it has no power to prevent a person from practicing law. The ABA does publish a code of ethics, and most states use this code to establish minimum standards of professional conduct for the legal profession. If an attorney violates a rule of professional conduct of his state, the violation can result in public or private censure, probation, suspension of his license for a limited period of time or outright revocation of a license.

The attorney is an officer of the court, and he must conduct himself with dignity and respect for the judicial process when he is in the courtroom. Disrespect by attorneys in the courtroom usually results in stern admonitions by judges or citations for contempt. A gross or repeated violation can result in disbarment of the attorney.

Some illegal conduct by an attorney outside of his practice can result in the loss of his license. If he commits an act of moral turpitude (such as larceny, forgery, burglary and receiving stolen property), he is subject to disbarment proceedings. A few crimes which do not involve moral turpitude and do not reflect on the attorney's ability to practice law are assault and battery and possession of marijuana. As a general rule, minor crimes of passion are not considered as serious as economic crimes.

The solicitation of clients by attorneys is strictly prohibited by the canons of ethics. Attorneys are supposed to conduct themselves as professionals, not as merchandisers. Attorneys are supposed to build a clientele through word of mouth about their capabilities. (Usually it is the attorney who must spread the word to promote his private practice.)

Attorneys who solicit clients too intensely are subject to punishment by the state. Ambulance-chasing (discussed in the chapter on injury litigation) is the most flagrant form of unlawful solicitation. Attorneys are also supposed to avoid the use of large signs, direct advertising or unreasonable promises of results of performance. The client who accepts the services of the unethical soliciting attorney is not committing a crime, but he is perpetuating a blight on the profession, and the client will reap the just fruits of an unethical attorney-client relationship. If you are hustled by an unethical attorney or his agent, contact the state bar immediately; do not wait to get burned before making the report.

The commingling, misuse or embezzlement of clients' funds by an attorney is strictly prohibited. Attorneys—by virtue of the position of trust and confidence placed in them by clients in handling their financial affairs—are constantly exposed to opportunities to misuse their clients' funds. Only a very small number of them yield to the temptation of misuse or outright embezzlement, and the record of the state bar in disbarring these scoundrels is extremely good.

When attorneys keep the funds of their clients for professional reasons, the money must be kept in a separate trustee account. The commingling of clients' funds in personal or business accounts is strictly prohibited. Even if the commingled funds are not misused, embezzled or otherwise neglected, the state bar will still punish an attorney who is foolish enough to commingle his client's assets with his own.

The disbarment of an attorney who goes south with his clients' money does little to placate the victim. To alleviate this problem, many states provide for a client security fund to reimburse a victim for all or part of these losses, a mandatory assessment on all of the active members of the bar provides this fund.

The preceding paragraphs should not leave the impression that all, or even a majority, of dishonest, incompetent and unethical lawyers are properly penalized. The state bars have a very poor record in disciplining attorneys except in cases of outright theft. This is a result of lawyers insisting on policing themselves. There are no "public, non-professional" persons on disciplinary committees or on the policy making boards of state bar associations, government bodies whose organizations are shrouded in mystery and aloofness from public representation and participation.

FINDING A LAWYER

The rich have personal lawyers, and they have no trouble in obtaining the names of other needed attorneys through business and family contacts, the poor use neighborhood legal aid offices in the large cities or the rural legal assistance foundations in the smaller communities.

But the great majority of middle class citizens who may need the services of an attorney once or twice in their lifetime may have a great deal of trouble in selecting an attorney. The traditional method is by personal knowledge of the attorney by the client or through a referral from a friend of the client. If a friend or relative gives you an attorney's name, be sure you know why he recommends the lawyer.

You can also go to the local county bar association to get the name of a lawyer from its referral panel. The normal procedure is for the prospective client to make an appointment through the bar association. This usually consists of a thirty-minute consultation for a nominal fee payable to the bar association. If you are satisfied with the lawyer, hire him. If he is not suitable, you are not obligated to retain him. You can always go back to the referral panel for another name.

Many people believe that specialists are needed to handle specific legal problems. This is untrue—most problems can be handled by general practitioners If the problem is so complicated that a specialist is necessary, then the general practitioner can always refer the case at no extra cost to the client.

The public has few ways of finding out which attorneys specialize in what fields, as the bar prohibits them from listing themselves as specialists except in the case of patent attorneys. There is no qualification test to license a lawyer to hold himself out as a specialist. (The only state which makes an exception to this is California, which has a specialization program in the fields of taxation, workmen's compensation and criminal law.)

Even though most attorneys cannot list themselves as specialists, the referral panels ask member attorneys to list the particular fields of law in which they have the most experience and to list the fields of law in which they have no interest. A prospective client will tell the panel what type of problem he has, and they can send him to the proper attorney.

The selection of an attorney is a matter of individual taste, personality and financial capability. I always maintain that one must like his attorney in order to respect and trust him. The attorney-client relationship is based on trust and confidence—without it a change of attorneys is in order. (Although this can be expensive and time consuming.) Also, remember that attorneys are slow to take another lawyer's case and, in most instances, the second attorney will try to convince you that the first lawyer is doing a credible job.

The selection of an attorney is a very personal choice and no precise standards can be stated. Important factors may include reputation, personal contacts, and office location. There are some situations, however, about which the consumer should be warned:

1. Beware of the attorney who boasts that he is the best available. There is no such thing. There are bad attorneys and good attorneys, but there is no best attorney. A client who wins his case may feel his attorney is "best," but the "best" for one is not necessarily "best" for all.
2. Ask the prospective attorney if he is knowledgeable and capable in the field of law in which you have a problem.
3. Beware of an attorney who will take a case "on the side." If he already has a full time job with a large law firm or a governmental agncy, he owes his first duty to his employer, and he probably cannot devote enough time to your problem.
4. Watch out for the attorney who illegally solicits a case himself or through a representative or agent. If he is unfaithful to his code of professional ethics, he can also be expected to be unfaithful to you.

FEES

Lawyers' fees cause a great deal of consternation and apprehension to consumers. The fear of excessive fees prevents many people from seeking legal advice when it is sorely needed.

The attorney, as a small businessman, is on his own when it comes to determining fees for his services. The amount not only depends on the time involved, but also on the ability of the client to pay and the lawyer's case load. Remember that an attorney has a large amount of overhead expense - about half of all his fees go toward running a legal office properly and efficiently.

Local bar associations may print a suggested minimum fee schedule, but remember that this schedule is only suggested and not binding upon attorneys or their clients. My experience with these schedules is that they tend to run higher than the going rate. Minimum fee schedules are now under attack as illegal price fixing and a restraint of trade.

Attorneys have various methods of charging fees. Some charge a flat fee for a job—such as $25 for a will, $350 for a divorce, or $275 for an adoption. Sometimes when an attorney charges a flat fee for a routine job, complications will arise causing him to ask for more money. The client should be aware of all the procedures the attorney will go through to accomplish the job so that he can recognize a legitimate complication and understand who caused this complication to arise.

In probate matters, the court sets fees and they are based on a percentage of the estate which the attorney is handling. Neither the attorney nor the client will have much control over the amount of the fee, as it is normally based on some statutory amount. This method of payment is not always fair and equitable, as the attorney who handles a $100,000 estate may work much harder than one who arranges the final affairs of a millionaire. This also works an injustice for the client who ends up paying on the basis of the size of his estate, not on the basis of work performed by the attorney. In the cases of large estates, attorneys have been known to make fee arrangements which are less than the statutory amount. The lawyer may also petition the court for extraordinary fees for extraordinary work performed.

In accident cases and other tort cases, the attorney usually collects his fee by taking a percentage of the entire amount obtained after a judgment or settlement. This contingent fee arrangement normally means the lawyer advances all court costs necessary to pursue the claim, but the client will eventually pay these costs out of his final settlement. Attorneys claim that the contingent fee arrangement allows the poor to retain the services of a lawyer to properly represent them.

The point of consternation over the contingent fee contract has been some exhorbitant percentages taken by attorneys. The percentages range from 25 per cent and less to 50 per cent of the net settlement. Competition among lawyers in the personal injury field is the most cut-throat in the entire profession. They will bargain over the percentage which they will take in personal injury cases especially where severe injury or death is involved.

Usually the percentage charged in an accident case will depend on the degree of the injuries and the degree of the liability for the accident. In cases of clear liability, many attorneys will charge only 25 per cent and, in no event, should the injured client pay more than 33⅓ per cent.

Contingent fees are most unjust to a client in the kind of case where there is a minimal amount of insurance but a severe injury—a $15,000 minimum insurance policy coupled with the loss of a leg, for instance. In this type of case, the insurance company will normally pay the limits of its policy after determining the liability for the accident and the extent of the injuries, and getting this settlement might only require a few letters and a few phone calls from the attorney. For this service he could collect $5,000 on a 33^1/$_3$ per cent contingent fee contract. An attorney who handles a case such as this should significantly reduce his fee to make it commensurate with the work he has performed.

Even with the percentages that attorneys charge in contingent fee types of cases, the client is still better off with the aid of legal counsel.

The last method an attorney may use to charge a fee is the hourly rate. Such rates may range from $20 to $200 per hour. Most business attorneys charge their clients this way. Others will charge a flat fee against an hourly charge or use some other combination of methods to determine the fee.

Whatever method the attorney uses to ascertain his fee, the client should be absolutely sure of the fee arrangement at the time he retains the attorney.

Since an attorney's fees can be financially ruinous, new methods of financing legal fees are being studied. There are plans for legal insurance where you pay premiums into a non-profit organization (similar to Blue Cross and Blue Shield medical insurance). Also private insurance companies are writing legal insurance policies. In the foreseeable future legal insurance will be given employees as a fringe benefit, as medical insurance now is.

Some states have approved a plan where organizations can retain an attorney to handle legal matters for their members. Labor unions, consumer cooperatives, and employee organizations are now utilizing such plans.

Lawyers' fees are generally too high. Add to this the bill padding and make-work practices of many attorneys, and you have a system of justice which the average man cannot afford to enjoy. That businessmen put up with this only increases the cost of doing business, and this is passed on to the consumer in higher prices. There are many legal functions (uncomplicated divorces, title searches, and probates) which the consumer could accomplish himself, if the legislatures would only simplify the laws, but this is unlikely because so many legislators are also practicing attorneys. These same politicians refuse to lower state imposed attorneys' fees in probate administrations and municipal bond offerings to make the fees match the worth of the legal services. The consumers' best chance for reform in controlling lawyers and their fees is through the initiative process if their representatives are unwilling to do the job.

AMERICAN BAR ASSOCIATION
CODE OF PROFESSIONAL RESPONSIBILITY
FOR ATTORNEYS

CANON 1
A lawyer should assist in maintaining the integrity and competence of the legal profession.

CANON 2
A lawyer should assist the legal profession in fulfilling its duty to make legal counsel available.

CANON 3
A lawyer should assist in preventing the unauthorized practice of law.

CANON 4
A lawyer should preserve the confidences and secrets of a client.

CANON 5
A lawyer should exercise independent professional judgment on behalf of a client.

CANON 6
A lawyer should represent a client competently.

CANON 7
A lawyer should represent a client zealously within the bounds of the law.

CANON 8
A lawyer should assist in improving the legal system.

CANON 9
A lawyer should avoid even the appearance of professional impropriety.

CODE OF JUDICIAL CONDUCT

CANON 1
A Judge should uphold the integrity and independence of the judiciary.

CANON 2
A Judge should avoid impropriety and the appearance of impropriety in all his activities.

CANON 3
A Judge should perform the duties of his office impartially and diligently.

CANON 4
A Judge may engage in activities to improve the law, the legal system, and the administration of justice.

CANON 5
A Judge should regulate his extra-judicial activities to minimize the risk of conflict with his judicial duties.

CANON 6
A Judge should regularly file reports of compensation received for quasi-judicial and extra-judicial activities.

CANON 7
A Judge should refrain from political activity inappropriate to his judicial office.

SURVEY OF MINIMUM FEES

(Actual schedule of a large metropolitan area)

CIVIL MATTERS

	MINIMUM RANGE

OFFICE TIME

1. Basic hourly rate for consultation, research and general preparation. — $ 50 - $ 75

2. For periods of time of less than one hour including office visits, telephone calls, and correspondence, a proportion of the hourly rate is charged with a minimum charge of $25 for any original consultation. — 25

TIME AWAY FROM OFFICE (Include Travel Time)

1. Time away from office is charged at the hourly rate. However, a reasonable and equitable downward adjustment is made for travel time. — 50 - 75

TRIAL TIME AND PER DIEM RATES

1. Municipal Court
   (a) Per diem, unless on retainer or contingent basis. — 250 - 300
   (b) Less than one day a proportionate charge with a minimum of — 125 - 150
   (c) Preparation and filing of complaint or cross-complaint. — 150 - 250
   (d) Preparation of answer with general denials. — 75 - 125
       With special defenses. — 150 - 250

2. Superior Court
   (a) Per diem, unless on retainer or contingent basis. — 300 - 500
   (b) For less than one day, a proportionate charge with a minimum of — 175
   (c) Preparation and filing of complaint or other original pleading. — 250 - 500

3. Default Suits requiring publication (e.g. quiet title action). — 500 - 750

PERSONAL INJURY, WRONGFUL DEATH, MALPRACTICE, ETC.

1. Plaintiff's cases:
   (a) If settled prior to pre-trial hearing. — 33-1/3%
   (b) If tried or settled after pre-trial hearing. — 40%
   (c) If case appealed, or new trial granted. — 50%
   (d) For willful misconduct or intoxication in motor vehicle guest cases, wrongful arrest, false imprisonment and malpractice cases. — 40%-50%
   (e) Minor's cases (governed by Court Rules).

   (NOTE: This field is so varied and the degrees of liability so important that it can only be pointed out that each case depends upon its own facts. Contingent fees vary from 33-1/3% to 50%, depending upon whether the client or the attorney advances the costs and whether the claim is settled, suit filed or the case tried, and the difficulty of establishing the liability.)

ADOPTION PROCEEDINGS

1. Agency adoptions, not requiring publication, citation, etc. — 225 - 300

2. Non-agency adoptions, not requiring publication, citation, etc. — 275 - 500

3. Stepparent adoption, not requiring publication, citation, or other extraordinary services. — 225 - 300

4. Where two or more children of the same parentage are involved in one petition, add $50 to $100 for each additional child.

5. For abandonment hearing pursuant to citation add $250-$500.

6. For abandonment hearing pursuant to publication, default, add $125-$200.

7. For petition for order for sole custody. — 250 - 500

CHANGE OF NAME

1. Court proceeding to effect change of name. — 250 - 350

---

2. Where two or more persons of the same family are involved, add $50 for each additional name.

ESTABLISH BIRTH

1. Court proceeding to establish birth. — $ 200 - 300

DOMESTIC RELATIONS

(NOTE: To determine the appropriate fee, you should consider the various individual charges listed below, in accordance with services rendered; this procedure is adopted because of the frequency with which proceedings are begun but abandoned by the litigants at an early stage.)

(a) Default Dissolution, Nullity, Separation, Paternity, Independent Action for child support (without O.S.C.) — 350 - 400
(b) Original OSC — 200 - 250
(c) OSC, cited spouse — 200 - 250
(d) Any other OSC or motion — 200 - 250
(e) Property Settlement Agreement — 200 - 250
(f) Review of Property Settlement Agreement, only service. — 75 - 100
(g) Contested case - per diem — 350 - 500
(h) Final Judgment of Dissolution, only service. — 50 - 75
(i) Order for Publication (additional) — 75 -

BUSINESS TRANSFERS AND SALES

1. Sale, including preparation of Agreement of Sale, Notice of Sale, Assignment of Lease, and incidental papers, 2-1/4% to 4% of purchase price, in any event a minimum of --- — 250 - 500

   (a) Holding escrow, additional 1% to 2% of amount held with a minimum of -- — 100 - 200
   (b) Lease, additional. — 50 - 150
   (c) Mortgage, Pledge of Stock, Deed of Trust, etc. additional. — 50 - 100

2. Partnership Agreement or other form of business organization for buyer, additional. (See Schedule on Partnership.)

BUSINESS TRANSFERS AND SALES

3. Liquor License Transfer to include supporting documents and coordination with investigation, additional. — $250 - 500

PARTNERSHIP

1. Partnership Agreement, simple. — 250 - 400

2. Partnership Agreement, limited, including Certificate (without Permit) — 400 - 750

3. Partnership Agreement, with purchase and sale or reciprocal insurance provisions. — 400 - 750

4. Partnership Dissolution, by agreement. — 250 - 500

5. Partnership Agreement with Permit. — 1000 - 1500

CORPORATIONS

1. Preincorporation Agreement. — 200 - 250

2. Formation of Corporation through organizational meeting of Directors and first Minutes of Board of Directors including issuance of stock by notification. — 500 - 750

3. For issuance of stock requiring a Permit. — 750 - 1000

4. Transfer of Securities from Escrow to Legend. — 75 - 150

5. Release of Securities from Escrow or Legend. — 250 - 500

6. Amending Articles of Incorporation. — 200 - 250

7. Transfer of Legend stock. — 50 - 75

8. Dissolution of corporation (voluntary) — 300 - 600

9. For organization of non-profit corporations where lawyer is contributing his time 1/2 of normal corporate rates - (This is intended to cover the lawyer's out-of-pocket overhead costs).

10. For Buy and Sell Agreements:
    (a) Agreement for corporate purchase of decedent's stock — 250 - 500

CORPORATIONS

	MINIMUM RANGE
(b) Buy-sell between stockholders.	$250 - 500
(c) If insurance is used add---	100 - 200
11. Drafting trust agreement for pension or profit-sharing plan.	750 - 1500

(a) No actuarial or accounting work but qualification of plan with Internal Revenue.

COLLECTIONS

Retail Accounts:

On all accounts where suit is not filed	33-1/3%
Claims already reduced to judgment, "skips", out-of-town claims that must be forwarded to another attorney, claims against bankrupts, and all claims upon which suit is filed.	50%

(NOTE: All of the foregoing fees are contingent upon collection.)

Wholesale Accounts:

A contingent fee equal to:	20% of the first $750 collected; 15% of the next $750 and 13% on the excess of $1500.

BANKRUPTCY AND INSOLVENCY

1. Per diem, Superior Court rates.

2. Involuntary.	350 - 1250

3. Voluntary:

(a) Petition, Schedule and first meeting of creditors (no asset case)	300 - 500
(b) If both husband and wife, add	100 - 200

4. All other matters should be charged at Superior Court rates or Office Hourly rates.

REAL ESTATE DOCUMENTS (With use of forms)

1. Deeds, simple.	$ 25 -
2. Deeds with Life Estates or other restrictions or reversions.	50 - 100
3. Promissory note with deed of trust or mortgage.	50 - 150
4. Request for notice of sale or default.	25 - 50
5. Substitution of Trustee.	25 - 50
6. Rescission of Notice of Default.	25 - 50
7. Declaration or abandonment of Homestead.	50 - 75
8. Deed of Reconveyance or Satisfaction of Mortgage.	25 - 50
9. Assignment of Deed of Trust & Endorsement of Note.	25 - 50
10. Examination of any document together with Opinion.	50 - 100
11. Power of Attorney.	25 - 75
12. Lease, simple, residential.	50 - 100

REAL ESTATE SALES

1. Examination of instruments, escrow instructions together with advice and opinion.	100 - 200
2. If negotiation or special drafting involved, 1% of sale price with a minimum of	150 -

UNLAWFUL DETAINER (Municipal Court)

1. Notice.	35 - 50
2. Commence Suit.	150 - 250
3. Secure judgment.	100 - 200
4. Sheriff's eviction.	100 - 200

(NOTE: This does not include any compensation for collection of rent which should be a separate service.)

CONDEMNATION

1. Non contingent: Use basic time rate for preparation, and per diem rate for trial in Superior Court.

2. Contingent: On settlement or on trial 5% of total amount paid, or 50% of net recovery over the amount originally offered by condemning authority, whichever sum is greater, reimbursement of costs advanced, including expert witness fee.

MECHANICS AND MATERIALMEN'S LIENS

	MINIMUM RANGE
1. Preparation of any notice, or Lien, or release of Lien, Notice of non-responsibility or any other notice.	$ 50 -
2. Foreclosure of Mechanic's or Materialmen's Lien, Superior Court Rates.	

MORTGAGE AND LIEN FORECLOSURES

1. Notice of default.	Statutory Fee
2. Foreclosure of real property by power of sale.	250 - 500
3. Foreclosure by Suit - see Superior Court Rates.	

TERMINATION OF JOINT TENANCY INTEREST

	MINIMUM RANGE

1. 1/3rd of the statutory probate fee, commencing in every instance at the primary rate, and not less than:

(a) When handled in a Court proceeding to establish facts of death, or as a part of the general administration of an estate. $150 - 350

(b) When handled without Court proceedings of either sort.

ESTATE PLANNING

1. Consultations and Analysis (At basic hourly rate).

(a) Office consultations to gather facts and client's objectives of wills, trust agreements, deeds, securities, insurance policies, business agreements, tax returns.

(b) Tax planning.

2. Drafting of Documents:

(a) Ordinary wills.	50 - 75
(1) Reciprocal wills	75 - 100
(b) Will with trust or other special provisions.	150 - 250
(1) Reciprocal wills with trust provisions.	200 - 400
(c) Reciprocal wills between spouses, with trusts for spouse and children.	250 - 500
(d) Inter vivos trust.	250 - 500

The charges for inter vivos trust are merely for drafting the documents and do not cover any fee for transferring the assets which are charged separately.

CRIMINAL MATTERS

1. Preliminary examinations.	$300 - 350
2. Misdemeanor defense-retainer.	300 - 500
3. Defense Felony Drunk Driving (Retainer)	750 - 1000
4. Defense Misdemeanor Drunk Driving	500 -
5. Felony defense (Retainer)	$750 - 1000
6. Arraignment and plea.	100 - 200
7. Probation and sentence	200 - 350
8. Appeals to Superior Court	500 - 550
9. Appeals to D.C.A. and Supreme Court	1000 - 1500
10. Bail writs.	100 - 125
11. Motion to Suppress Evidence	200 - 250
12. Motion to Dismiss	200 - 250

PART II

CRIMINAL ACTIONS AND CIVIL LAWSUITS

CHAPTER 4

Anatomy of a Civil Lawsuit

THE COMPLAINT -- THE FIRST DOCUMENT

Whenever you feel wronged, and want to seek redress in the courts, you must file an initial document with the court stating the basis for grievances. The person filing this document is called the plaintiff (although in some situations he may be called the petitioner, applicant, or contestant).

The document which must be filed with the clerk of a court is called a complaint, and it must clearly state the factual basis for the plaintiff's claim. If the complaint is defective or lacking in some respect, it can normally be amended.

The person or persons named in the complaint as causing the plaintiff damages are known as defendants (although in some cases they are called respondents).

The plaintiff's complaint must be filed with the clerk of the county or district where the defendant lives or where the grievance took place. The place where a court action is heard is called *venue.*

The complaint must be filed within a certain period of time in order to avoid the statute of limitations which prevents the prosecution of stale claims. Statutes of limitations differ from state to state, and they differ with the type of claim. If you fail to file a complaint within the prescribed statute of limitations, you are barred forever from obtaining a court judgment in the matter.

SUMMONS

When a complaint is filed with a clerk of a court, he also issues a summons. (In some jurisdictions the plaintiff's lawyer issues the summons.) This document directs the defendants to respond to the complaint within a certain period of time—usually 30 days. It should advise the defendants to seek the aid of a lawyer and tell them that if they do not respond to the complaint within the prescribed time period, the plaintiff may take a default judgment against them.

SERVICE—LETTING THE OTHER SIDE
KNOW ABOUT THE LAWSUIT

It is not enough for a plaintiff to file a complaint and obtain the issuance of a summons in order to get the matter before a court. Defendants must receive the proper notice, and it is not the job of the clerk of the court to inform them.

The job of giving defendants notice of a lawsuit belongs to a process server, who may be a sheriff, local constable or private party. Generally, the plaintiff cannot act as his own process server.

It is only necessary for the server to deliver the summons and complaint in such a way that the defendant has an opportunity to read these documents. It is not necessary for the defendant to sign for the papers—they do not even have to touch him. The process server only needs to drop the papers in the conscious presence of a defendant.

Irate defendants sometimes assault process servers which is stupid, since he is an innocent party and legal complications can follow such assaults.

Defendants also feel that they can avoid a lawsuit by ducking the process server—which is also foolish since there are alternative methods of service for hidden defendants. Substitute service can be made at a defendant's place of employment or at his home or.through publication in a newspaper.

Many states also allow service by mail. The plaintiff's attorney merely mails the summons and complaint to the defendant, and the defendant acknowledges receipt by return mail to the plaintiff's attorney.

ANSWER AND DEFAULT

If a defendant is properly served with summons and complaint, and he does not answer it within the prescribed period of time, the plaintiff may take a default judgment against him. This means that the plaintiff can go to court and obtain a judgment without the presence of the defendant. These default judgments are as valid as those reached after a contested hearing where both parties are present. Although there are methods to vacate a default judgment on very specific grounds, any defendant who is served with a summons and complaint should seek the advice of an attorney immediately instead of waiting until the last moment to answer the complaint.

The normal response of a defendant to the complaint is an answer. This is a document which normally denies most of the allegations of the complaint and it must be filed with the clerk of the same court in which the complaint has been filed. (A copy of the answer is sent to the plaintiff's attorney.)

SETTING THE CASE FOR TRIAL

Once all of the defendants have been served by the plaintiff, either party to the law suit can file a memorandum with the court clerk to set the case for trial. The time it takes to obtain a trial date depends on the congestion of the calendar and the length of time estimated for a trial. In a large city with a congested calendar, you can expect it will take anywhere from two to four years after the date of filing a memorandum to get a jury trial.

At the time a civil matter is set for trial, the parties must decide if they want the case to be heard by a jury or a judge sitting without a jury. In some cases, this type of decision is not necessary for neither party will have the right to a jury trial. However, litigants in most civil cases are entitled to a jury if they request it. The decision for or against a jury trial is normally a tactical maneuver for an attorney. (Even if you ask for a jury, you can always waive it at a later date.)

DISCOVERY—FINDING OUT ABOUT
THE OTHER SIDE'S CASE

All states have some civil discovery procedures so litigants may discover important facts about their cases while they are waiting for a trial date. The purpose of discovery is to avoid surprise during a trial, promote fairness and to make attorneys more fully aware of the realities of their cases to encourage pre-trial settlements. The scope of discovery varies from state to state. (If you don't obey the discovery statutes, your case may be dismissed.)

The most widely used tool of discovery is the deposition -- that is, testimony of a party or other witness under oath. This is obtained largely through a question-and-answer process between the attorneys and the person testifying. All parties and their attorneys have a right to be present at a deposition (normally taken in the office of one of the attorneys.) All must be given fair and adequate notice of the date and time of a deposition. All of the attorneys have an opportunity to cross-examine the witness on any relevant matters.

Deposition testimony is taken down by a shorthand reporter who later transcribes it. The person who gave the testimony may later read it to correct any transcription mistakes.

If a witness gives trial testimony which differs from his deposition testimony, he will be asked to account for the discrepancy. The witness at a deposition is under oath; if he tells any lies, he is subject to prosecution for perjury.

The deposition preserves testimony so that if someone who has been deposed cannot appear at trial, his deposition may be read into evidence.

Other methods of discovery include interrogatories, admissions, orders for the production of documents, inspection of premises, blood tests and medical examinations.

TRIAL

If a jury is requested, it must be selected just before the trial starts. Each prospective juror is questioned for possible bias. If it is found (for instance, "I hate insurance companies" or "I know the plaintiff, and I don't believe a thing he says"), then the juror is excused. The attorneys can also eliminate a limited number of prospective jurors for no specific reason (pre-emptory challenges). This is when the lawyers practice amateur psychology.

Prior to any testimony being given at a trial, both the attorneys for plaintiff and defendant have the right to make opening statements to explain what facts they intend to prove in their cases. The plaintiff goes first and the defendant may give his opening statement immediately after the plaintiff or wait until his turn to give evidence.

The plaintiff or defendant can force the attendance of a witness at trial by properly serving the witness with a subpoena. If a person properly served with a subpoena does not appear at a court proceeding, he can be held in contempt of court with the sentence depending upon the jurisdiction of the court and the severity of the contempt.

After the plaintiff has submitted his case, it is the defendant's turn to offer evidence. When the defendant submits his case, the plaintiff may offer rebuttal evidence, to which the defendant may offer re-rebuttal evidence. When both sides have completed their presentations, the matter is submitted and is ready for final argument.

Since the burden of proof is on the plaintiff, he gives his final argument first. When the plaintiff is finished, the defendant may make a rebuttal argument. The plaintiff's attorney then has the right to make a closing argument. After the closing arguments neither attorney speaks again.

Nothing of what either attorney says in his opening or final statements can be considered as evidence. Their statements familiarize a judge or jury with the case and/or persuade them to find in their favor.

If a judge is hearing the trial, he will retire and make a decision after the arguments are given. If a jury is hearing it, the judge must instruct them on the applicable law in the case and once these instructions are read, the jury retires to reach a verdict.

In most states at least three-fourths of a jury (normally composed of 12 persons) must agree before a verdict can be reached. If they fail to do this, there is a mistrial and the case must be retried. In the federal system, a jury must be unanimous in order to reach a verdict.

If an error of law has been committed at the trial and the plaintiff or defendant is unhappy with the results, either party may make a motion before the judge for a new trial, and either party may appeal the decision or judgment to an appellate court.

SUING THE GOVERNMENT

In merry old England there was a saying that "the King can do no wrong." History tells us that just the opposite was true, but this saying became a legal truism at common law, for no citizen could sue the government. This theory of sovereign immunity crossed the Atlantic and became a part of American jurisprudence. It means that no citizen can sue the government—federal, state or local—unless there is specific legislation allowing him to. As a practical matter the federal government and all states have laws which allow citizens to sue in specific situations.

The preceding paragraphs in this chapter have dealt with the procedures one can expect when suing other individuals or corporations. When one sues a government, the procedures and the applicable statutes of limitation may vary considerably. If an individual feels he has a grievance against a governmental body, he should consult with an attorney immediately to protect his rights.

APPEAL

If you are unhappy with a decision of a trial court — judge or jury — you can appeal to a higher court. In order to win the appeal, you must prove that the judge made an error of law and that error *substantially* affected the outcome of the case. (Many times judges will make mistakes, but these errors are so harmless that the appeals court will not reverse the judgment.)

Before starting an appeal, you can make a motion for a new trial before the trial judge. These motions are based on essentially the same grounds as the appeal, but this motion does allow a judge to make a review of his earlier decision. (These motions can also be used to increase or decrease a jury verdict for money damages.) Motions for new trial and appeals must be made within a statutory period of time, set by each state.

In order for an appeals court to determine if an error has been made at a trial, a transcript of the trial testimony must be prepared by the shorthand reporter who has been taking a verbatim account of the trial. Their rates are very high — so high that they inhibit many appeals which might otherwise be taken.

STATUTES OF LIMITATION FOR FILING A CIVIL LAWSUIT[1]

(IN YEARS)	BREACH OF WRITTEN CONTRACT	CONVERSION	FRAUD	BATTERY	DEFAMATION	FALSE IMPRISONMENT	MALICIOUS PROSECUTION	PERSONAL INJURY	WRONGFUL DEATH	DAMAGE TO PERSONAL PROPERTY	MEDICAL MALPRACTICE
ALABAMA	4	6	1	1	1	1	1	1	2	6	2
ALASKA	4	6	2	2	2	2	2	2	2	6	2
ARIZONA	4	2	3	2	1	1	1	2	2	2	2
ARKANSAS	4	3	5	1	3[7]	1	5	3	3	3	2
CALIFORNIA	4	3	3	1	1	1	1	1	1	3	1
COLORADO	4	6	3	1	1	1	1	1	2[2]	6	2
CONNECTICUT	4	3	3	2	2	3	3	2	2[2]	2	2
DELAWARE	4	3	3	2	2	2	2	2	2	2	2
D. C.	4	3	3	1	1	1	1	1	1	3	1
FLORIDA	4	3	3	2	2	2	2	4	2	3	4
GEORGIA	4	4	4	2	1	2[3]	2[3]	2	2	4	2
HAWAII	4	6	6	2	2	6	6	2	2	2	2
IDAHO	4	3	3	2	2	2	4	2	2	3	2
ILLINOIS	4	5	5	2	1	2	2	2	2	5	2
INDIANA	4	6	6	2	2	2	2	2	2	2	2
IOWA	2	5	5	2	2	2	2	2	2	5	2
KANSAS	4	2	2	1	1	1	1	2	2	2	2
KENTUCKY	4	5	5	1	1	1	1	1	1	5	1
LOUISIANA	1	1	1	1	1	1	1	1	1	1	1
MAINE	4	6	6	2	2	2	6	6	2	6	2
MARYLAND	4	3	3	1	1	3	3	3	2	3	3
MASSACHUSETTS	4	6	2	2	2	2	2	2	2	2	3
MICHIGAN	2-10[4]	3	3	2	1	2	2	3	3	3	2
MINNESOTA	4	6	6	2	2	2	2	2	3[2]	6	2
MISSISSIPPI	4	6	6	1	1	1	1	6	6	6	6
MISSOURI	4	5	5	2	2	2	2	5	1	5	2
MONTANA	4	2	2	2	2	2	2	2	3	2	2

STATUTES OF LIMITATION FOR FILING A CIVIL LAWSUIT

	BREACH OF WRITTEN CONTRACT	CONVERSION	FRAUD	BATTERY	DEFAMATION	FALSE IMPRISON-MENT	MALICIOUS PROSECU-TION	PERSONAL INJURY	WRONGFUL DEATH	DAMAGE TO PERSONAL PROPERTY	MEDICAL MAL-PRACTICE
NEBRASKA	5	4	4	1	1	1	1	4	2	4	2
NEVADA	6	3	3	2	2	2	2	2	2	3	2
NEW HAMPSHIRE	6	6	6	2	2	2	2	2[4]	2	6	2
NEW JERSEY	6	6	6	2	1	6	6	2	2	6	2
NEW MEXICO	6	4	4	3	3	3	3	3	3	4	3
NEW YORK	6	3	6	1	1	1	1	3	2	3	3
NORTH CAROLINA	3	3	3	1	1[8]	1	3	3	2	3	3
NORTH DAKOTA	6	6	6	2	2	2	6	6	2	6	2
OHIO	15	4	4	1	1	1	1	2	2	2	1
OKLAHOMA	5	2	2	1	1	1	1	2	2	2	2
OREGON	6	6	2	2	1	2	2	2	3[2]	6	2[6]
PENNSYLVANIA	6	6	1	2	1	1	1	2	1	6	2
RHODE ISLAND	6	6	6	6	6[7]	6	3	2	2	6	6
SOUTH CAROLINA	6	6	6	2	2	2	6	6	6	6	6
SOUTH DAKOTA	6	6	6	2	2	2	6	3	3	6	2
TENNESSEE	6	3	3	1	1[6]	1	1	1	1	3	1
TEXAS	4	2	2	2	1	1	1	2	2	2	2
UTAH	6	3	3	1	1	1	1	4	2	3	4
VERMONT	6	6	6	3	3	3	3	3[5]	2	3	3
VIRGINIA	5	5	2	2	2	2	2	2	2	5	2
WASHINGTON	6	3	3	2	2	2	3	3	3	3	3
WEST VIRGINIA	10	2	2	2	2	2	2	2	2	2	2
WISCONSIN	6	6	6	2	2	2	2	3	3	6	3
WYOMING	10	4	4	1	1	1	1	4	2	4	4

FOOTNOTES:

1 Time for filing suits for fraud or malpractice are from the date of discovery; for wrongful death on the date of death; for other torts on the day the tort was committed; and for breach of contract on the day the breach was committed.

2 Time runs from the time malpractice occurred; also runs from the date the act causing death occurred.

3 Injuries to person, 2 years; injuries to reputation, 1 year.

4 The limit is one year for skiing injuries.

5 Time runs from the date of discovery, and is never more than 7 years from the date of the negligent act.

6 Libel 1 year, slander 6 months.

7 Libel 6 years, slander 1 year.

- 39 -

CHAPTER 5

"You are Under Arrest"— The Rights of the Criminally Accused

Fifth Amendment: "No person shall be held to answer for a capital, or otherwise infamous crime unless on a presentment or indictment of a Grand Jury, except in cases arising in the land or naval forces, or in the Militia, when in actual service in time of war or public danger; nor shall any person be subject for the same offense to be twice put in jeopardy of life or limb; nor shall be compelled in any criminal case to be a witness against himself, nor be deprived of life, liberty, or property without due process of law; nor shall private property be taken for public use, without just compensation."

Sixth Amendment: "In all criminal prosecutions, the accused shall enjoy the right to a speedy and public trial, by an impartial jury of the State and district wherein the crime shall have been committed, which district shall have been previously ascertained by law, and to be informed of the nature and cause of the accusation; to be confronted with the witnesses against him; to have compulsory process for obtaining witnesses in his favor, and to have the Assistance of Counsel for his defense."

Eighth Amendment: "Excessive bail shall not be required, nor excessive fines imposed nor cruel and unusual punishments inflicted."

INTRODUCTION

"You are under arrest." This is one of the most frightening sentences in our language. The suspect may be innocent or guilty of a crime; he may be convicted or acquitted on the criminal charge; he may be sentenced to prison at a later date or be placed on probation and fined without serving jail time. No matter what the eventual outcome, when you are arrested you usually must go to jail immediately and stay there until you obtain bail or a release from the court.

Once arrested, you will be booked, photographed, fingerprinted and placed in a cell with a variety of persons who may be drunks, transvestites, murderers or sadists. The purpose of this chapter is not to advise the reader on methods to evade the law or protect himself from arrest but rather to advise you of your constitutional rights after an arrest and of the legal significance of the steps you must go through.

SUSPICION

Police officers may stop and detain citizens without actually placing them under arrest. They have the right to investigate suspicious circumstances and may stop citizens and ask them questions concerning their identity and these circumstances. The policeman also may frisk you for weapons in order to protect himself from harm.

ARREST

An arrest occurs when you are effectively within the custody and control of a policeman, a peace officer or a private person making a citizen's arrest. The officer will usually tell you that you are under arrest, but these exact words are not necessary. An officer can make an arrest without a warrant if he has reasonable cause to believe that you have committed a felony (reasonable cause means more than just actually seeing someone commit a crime; it can also mean seeing the suspect running from the scene of a crime, holding a smoking pistol or other similar indications that the suspect has committed a felony). Most felony arrests are made without a warrant because the officer does not have the time to go before a judge. If there is time, then serving a suspect with an arrest warrant is the proper way.

An officer can only make an arrest for a misdemeanor if it is committed in his presence or with an arrest warrant. If a misdemeanor has not actually been committed in the presence of an officer and he still wants to make an arrest, he must present the results of his investigation to a judge and ask for an arrest warrant. A private citizen can make an arrest or file a criminal complaint against the suspect, which will result in an arrest warrant.

If a policeman comes to your home to make an arrest, he must knock at the door, allow you a reasonable time to answer his knock and announce his authority and intentions. This restriction on the police can only be excused if the policeman has *reasonable* cause to believe that his life is in danger, the suspect is escaping or valuable evidence is being destroyed. Only *reasonable* force to overcome resistance from a suspect can be used to make an arrest.

Immediately after the arrest you can expect to be informed of some constitutional rights:

1. You have a right to remain silent.
2. Anything you might say can be held against you in a trial.
3. You have the right to an attorney.
4. If you cannot afford an attorney, one will be provided for you free of charge.

The reading of these constitutional rights is commonly called the Miranda warnings since the practice stems from the 1966 Supreme Court decision, *Miranda vs. Arizona.* The Court decided in that case that before statements could be taken from the arrested suspect and used against him in court, he had to be advised of his constitutional rights and, further, he had to voluntarily and intelligently waive them. If the accused does not want to speak with the police after he has been arrested, then they can no longer question him.

While everyone has accepted the provisions of the Fifth Amendment right to remain silent and the Sixth Amendment right to an attorney, the application of these rights has been hotly disputed. The traditional view was that the right to remain silent and the right to an attorney could be used by a defendant at the time of his trial, but the police could extract confessions and admissions without advising him of his rights before the trial.

Through a long series of cases (the last of which was *Miranda vs. Arizona*) the Supreme Court took the position that the Fifth and Sixth Amendments could only have real meaning if they applied at the time of arrest -- not just at the time of trial. The right to remain silent (the right not to testify against yourself) and the right to an attorney are of little help at the time of trial if the prosecutor can introduce a confession made after arrest.

The privilege against self-incrimination goes back further than the adoption of our Constitution. In the 17th century John Lilburne, a Puritan dissenter, was brought before the British Star Chamber and charged with "sending factitious, scandalous books" to England. Lilburne felt that he was entitled to notice, indictment and a trial under the laws of England. He felt he had the privilege against self-incrimination.

When Lilburne refused to respond to any questions, he was tied to a cart and whipped as he rode through the streets of London. He was eventually placed in a public pillory. Even after this treatment, Lilburne continued to urge all who would listen to resist the kind of tyranny which had brought about this horrible treatment. Since he would not be silent, Lilburne was dragged to solitary confinement where his hands and legs were bound in irons and he was not given anything to eat for ten days. This case became a cause celebre in England, and it brought about many reforms in the judicial system. Thereafter the criminally

accused could refuse to testify and incriminate himself.

The U.S. Supreme Court did not consider the constitutionality of confessions in state criminal trials until *Brown vs. Mississippi* in 1936. In that case, a black was hung upside down and tortured in his prison cell by local police in a small Mississippi town. He eventually confessed and the confession was used against him at a later trial. The defendant's attorney objected to the confession, but the conviction was upheld in the Mississippi courts. The U.S. Supreme Court reversed Brown's conviction on the grounds that any confession or admission obtained through torture was unconstitutional. The Court felt that it was far better to release a man, even if he were actually guilty of a crime, than to dignify the practice of torture by any governmental agency.

It must be remembered that the Supreme Court in the Brown case did not punish the torturers. It merely excluded the tainted confession from evidence. Despite the torture, if the state could produce other evidence which would convict the defendant, then the conviction would be upheld.

After the Brown decision, the Supreme Court made many more decisions involving the rights of an accused to remain silent and to an attorney. Confessions obtained through the use of torture were considered unreliable and thus inadmissible in court. For many years the test for the admissibility of a confession was its trustworthiness. Eventually the test of trustworthiness gave way to the test of voluntariness. If a confession was obtained through coercion—physical or mental—it was excluded because it was not voluntarily given by the accused. Along with this position came decisions giving the accused the right to an attorney immediately upon being arrested. All of these decisions culminated in *Miranda vs. Arizona* in 1966.

There have been many decisions since then which have further interpreted the Miranda ruling, but the basic obligation of the police to explain to you your constitutional rights before a confession or statement can be taken is still intact. Furthermore, not only is any statement or admission taken from an accused without an intelligent waiver of his rights inadmissible, but also any evidence which is the fruit of this statement is excluded.

Many suspects complain that their Miranda rights were not read to them and they feel that the entire case should be dropped and charges dismissed because of this. But this is not the case. The police can always gather evidence and obtain a valid conviction without the use of a confession or admission. They only have to give Miranda warnings if they want to take statements from the accused.

The practical effect of the Miranda decision is the elimination of any form of police coercion. The so-called third degree, threats and intimidation have hopefully been eliminated. The police can still obtain confessions, but now such state-

ments are under the close scrutiny of a court. If the prosecutor wants to use a confession in a criminal trial, there must be a prior hearing to determine if it was properly obtained.

STATION HOUSE

The normal procedure after an arrest is to take the accused to the police station for booking, photographing, and fingerprinting. (Even if charges are dropped or the accused is later acquitted, his arrest record and fingerprints will generally remain on file for posterity with the state and the FBI.) The right to remain silent only involves words uttered from the lips of an accused; it does not include physical evidence taken from him including fingerprints, voice prints, fingernail clippings and hair samples.

In drunk driving cases the police may want to take blood, urine or breath tests to determine the blood alcohol content of a suspect driver. In many states when an individual is arrested for driving under the influence of alcohol or drugs, he can refuse to take these tests, but the refusal will result in the loss of his driver's license for six months—despite his guilt or innocence. The driver has no right to an attorney at the time of the test, but most states give him the right to have a doctor administer the blood test. All constitutional objections to this law have been upheld, as the courts have taken the position that driving a car is a privilege granted by the state, not a constitutional right.

After the booking procedure has been completed you are entitled to two telephone calls (at your own expense). Some police and sheriffs will give you free unlimited use of the phone to reach a lawyer, a bailbondsman, a relative or a friend in need.

There is an alternative to the traditional arrest and booking procedure. Many communities allow a policeman to issue a citation rather than take the suspect to the police station for booking. This procedure is the same as the one which is employed for traffic violations. The accused signs the citation and promises to appear in court at a later date.

Citation release programs have a dual function: (1) They protect the rights of defendants who are legally presumed innocent until proved guilty. (2) They relieve the police of the odious clerical duties involved in taking in and booking an accused. The police can then use more of their time to protect the community. Citation release is generally used for misdemeanors which do not involve violence (a misdemeanor is a crime which is punishable by not more than one year in a county jail and/or a fine.)

The New York Police Department uses this citation release procedure and it has proved to be an enormous financial success. During the first two years of its use, the New York City Police saved 2.5 million dollars and eliminated 368,000 man-hours of work.

BAIL

The first thought on your mind when you have just been arrested is getting out of jail quickly -- this is normally accomplished through bail.

The right to bail in federal cases is guaranteed by the Eighth Amendment, but it has not been incorporated to apply to the states.

The right to bail is not absolute, and balancing techniques can be employed. Since due process requires that an accused be considered innocent until proved guilty, he should not have to stay in jail pending his trial. However, experience tells us that some defendants will run rather than face the charges, and keeping such risky cases in jail until the end of the trial is a valid action by the state. Refusal to grant bail is only done in very grave cases.

Recent federal legislation allows a judge to deny bail if the prosecution can make a proper showing that the accused will be a threat to society if he is released. This occurs only after a hearing where both sides may present evidence. The constitutionality of this law has not been tested yet.

To make bail you must post cash or a redeemable bond with the clerk of the court to guarantee you will appear in court at all stages of the proceedings. If you fail to appear, a bench warrant for your arrest will be issued, and the bail will be forfeited.

A judge determines the amount of bail for each offense, and it depends on the gravity of the offense, the ability of the accused to post bail, his past criminal record and his ties in the community where he has been charged. For many criminal offenses there is a set bail schedule so that a special order by a judge is not necessary. Once bail is set, either by a schedule or a judge, it can be reduced or increased at any time during the proceedings if circumstances warrant the change.

In almost every jailhouse there is a list of local bondsmen who will provide bail if you cannot raise the cash. You will be allowed to phone a bondsman as well as an attorney to arrange for release. The bondsman can speak with an accused after he has been booked. The bondsman will investigate to determine if the man is a good risk, for if the accused does not appear in court, the bondsman will lose the entire bail. His fee is generally 10% of the bail -- the fee on a $5,000 bail is, therefore, $500. The fee is not returnable to the suspect if he is acquitted.

There are alternatives to this bail procedure. One is known as release on your own recognizance, often called "OR." With the police using advanced electronic technology, it is becoming increasingly difficult for a suspect to escape the reach of the law. Courts have come to recognize that many defendants are a good risk to return to court to face charges without bail, and many defendants are too poor to afford bail. So judges may now OR a defendant depending on the gravity of the charges and the status of the defendant's employment, family, residence and prior criminal record. If the accused has a job and a family, it is a pretty good bet that he will be released on OR. But if he is a transient without a job and he has been charged with a serious felony, an OR is unlikely.

An OR release is more desirable than bail because of the financial savings involved, but bail is a lot quicker procedure. If you are arrested at night, an order for an OR release usually cannot be obtained until at least the next morning or afternoon, while bail will produce an immediate release.

In the federal courts a defendant may be allowed to post only 10% of the bail, and this sum will be kept by the court clerk until the matter is finally determined, after which the defendant will receive the deposit back from the clerk, despite his guilt or innocence.

THE RIGHT TO AN ATTORNEY

The right of the accused to have a lawyer is guaranteed by the Sixth Amendment and this right has been incorporated to apply to all the states. This right requires that the state or federal government supply an attorney if the defendant is too poor to hire one. And, as discussed earlier in the section under arrest, the police must advise anyone under arrest that he has a right to an attorney. This right to counsel in all criminal prosecutions is considered incident to due process of law and a fair trial.

The Supreme Court did not begin to apply this right to counsel rule until 1932 when it decided that in cases involving the death penalty the state must provide an attorney if the defendant was too poor to afford one. In 1963 the court held that persons accused of serious crimes had the right to counsel. Then in 1972, the Supreme Court culminated this trend of opinions by stating that the accused has the right to an attorney at all stages of the proceedings against him when he is charged with any criminal offense which could cost him a loss of liberty.

That the Constitution now guarantees the right to counsel in criminal cases does not necessarily mean that the defendant must employ an attorney. He may voluntarily and intelligently waive this right, including the right to a free lawyer. The defendant can enter a plea of guilty without the help of an attorney and he can also conduct a trial without a lawyer. However, any course of action by an individual in a criminal matter is inadvisable without, at least, the advice if not the full representation of a lawyer. (Some states now have laws which force a person accused of a felony to use an attorney.)

It has been estimated that over 60% of today's criminal defendants are too poor to afford their own attorney. In many states and counties this presents a tremendous burden on the local bar and upon the taxpayers, since private attorneys are often assigned by judges to represent an indigent defendant. Most counties pay a nominal sum to these volunteers, but others pay nothing.

The large counties use institutionalized public defender systems. The public defender may be an elected or appointed county official, who has a staff of attorneys whose job it is to represent the indigent in criminal matters. Defendants often complain that public defenders do not do an adequate job, but in most cases this is not true since these lawyers are specialists in criminal law. Public defender offices do suffer from a lack of funds and investigators, and since they deal with so many cases public defenders normally cannot give the defendant the individualized special treatment he might like.

You do not have to be unemployed to qualify for a public defender. Many persons are employed but still too poor to afford an attorney. It is up to the public defender and the judge to determine who is eligible. In a marginal case, the judge should decide in favor of the use of a public defender to insure that the defendant receives a fair hearing at all stages of the proceedings. The accused does not have a right to a particular public defender or a particular private attorney on an indigent panel, but he does have the right to fire his court-appointed counsel and hire a private attorney.

In retaining a private attorney, one should always make sure of the exact fee arrangement. Some charge by the hour but, in criminal cases, most attorneys charge on a lump sum basis. Fee arrangements should be made on the basis of appearances made, work performed, and results accomplished. One should make sure that he has an exact fee arrangement before he retains a lawyer. In other words, find out what the attorney's fee will be for each court appearance, for a court trial, for a jury trial, for appearance at sentencing and for any other legal work which he might perform. He might charge a lump sum fee which must be paid prior to his appearing in court. If the criminal charges are dropped entirely or the case is settled in just one court appearance, the attorney can keep the entire lump sum, so a wise defendant arranges for payment on a work performed basis.

Before hiring an attorney in a criminal matter, make sure that he is well versed in the law. With all of the recent Supreme Court decisions interpreting criminal laws and procedures, the field of criminal law has become highly specialized. One does not have to limit his practice to just criminal matters to be proficient in this category of law, but it is wise to determine that a lawyer is knowledgeable before hiring him.

An attorney simply sells his time and services, and he cannot guarantee the outcome of a case. A defendant who hires a lawyer on the basis of a guaranteed outcome is foolish.

The attorney who charges the highest fee is not necessarily the best one for a particular situation. Many attorneys have been fortunate enough to receive a lot of publicity, but publicity and reputation are not necessarily proportional to proficiency, though they may be proportional to fees. There are many aggressive young lawyers whose rates are lower than their older counterparts in the field. If you cannot find a good criminal lawyer, check with the referral panels of the local bar associations.

Due process of law means that the person accused of a crime cannot be convicted unless the state proves that he is guilty beyond a reasonable doubt and to a moral certainty. It is the duty of an attorney who represents an accused to safeguard his constitutional rights and to generally provide that kind of representation and defense that forces the public prosecutor to meet this heavy burden of proof. Even if the accused confesses to his attorney in a private consultation, the lawyer still has this obligation to protect his client's rights. For instance, the accused may have valid defenses such as insanity or diminished mental capacity and, too, the confession may be untrue.

ARRAIGNMENT

Arraignment is the procedure in which an accused is personally advised by a judge or a magistrate of the exact nature of the charges pending against him, and he is also re-advised of most of his constitutional rights including the right to a jury trial, the right against self-incrimination, the right to confront witnesses, the right to compel the attendance of witnesses at a trial and the right to an attorney. Arraignment satisfies the Sixth Amendment right to be informed of the nature and cause of the accusation.

In federal cases the accused must be brought before a magistrate or judge as soon as practicable for arraignment. Each state has its own arraignment procedure, but it must be fair and must prevent the accused from languishing in jail without knowing the exact nature of the criminal charges against him. (For instance, in California a man must be brought before a magistrate or judge within two days of his arrest, but if the second day falls on a Saturday, Sunday or holiday, he must wait until the following court day for arraignment. If arraignment does not occur within two days, the charges must be dropped. In the case of a felony, the accused must be re-arrested and re-charged, but in a misdemeanor, he cannot be re-charged for the same offense. Other states have similar procedures.)

At the arraignment the accused may make an application for a free court-appointed attorney, or he may ask for a reasonable continuance to obtain his own attorney.

The court will normally ask the defendant to plead to the charges at the time of the arraignment, although a reasonable continuance may be granted for a plea. The length of any continuance depends upon the circumstances, the waiver of a right to a speedy trial, and the patience of the court. The defendant may plead not guilty, guilty, not guilty by reason of insanity and nolo contendere (no contest), which is tantamount to pleading guilty. The latter plea is not admissible against the defendant in a civil matter involving the same set of facts. A plea of no contest may be used by someone involved in an automobile accident who does not want his criminal plea to be used against him in a later civil trial. If a defendant pleads not guilty by reason of insanity, the court will appoint a psychiatrist to examine him to render an opinion at a later date.

GRAND JURY INDICTMENT OR INFORMATION

The Fifth Amendment right of an accused who is charged with a capital or infamous (felony) crime to be indicted by a grand jury is only a federal right and does not apply to the states. But the states must have some procedure to guarantee that there is reasonable cause to hold a man to answer for a felony. They can use grand juries or preliminary hearings.

Preliminary hearings are held before magistrates or judges who hear evidence from both sides. The defendant has the right to have a lawyer at the hearing, and he can cross-examine the witnesses who testify against him. Constitutional defenses involving unreasonable searches and seizures and coerced confessions can be used by a defendant at these hearings. If the presiding magistrate or judge feels that there is reasonable and probable cause to hold the defendant to answer after the preliminary examination is over, then a document known as an information will be filed charging the defendant with one or more specific felony offenses.

A grand jury usually meets at specified times, or it can be called into a special session. Only the prosecutor appears before the grand jury; neither the defendant nor his attorney have a right to be present. The prosecutor does not have to present all of his evidence, just enough to give the grand jury reasonable cause to believe the defendant committed the felony for which he is charged. If a majority of the jurors find there is reasonable cause, then they will return an indictment, and the accused must answer for these specific charges.

The grand jury system has been challenged, but the courts have long upheld its validity. Critics say the grand jury is composed of people who are seldom of the race, national origin, or age as the persons they are indicting. But remember that the grand jury only indicts, it does not convict and the validity of an indictment is appealable.

Indictments and informations protect the accused in that they prevent him from being brought to trial before there has been a preliminary determination that there is enough evidence to justify his standing trial for a felony. Neither an indictment nor an information can be considered evidence of guilt.

THE RIGHT TO A SPEEDY AND PUBLIC TRIAL

The principle of the speedy trial dates back to the Magna Carta and was designed to protect the accused from prolonged imprisonment while he is awaiting trial. The constitutional clause which guarantees a speedy trial does not give exact guidelines. Each state has specific laws to meet this constitutional obligation. (For instance, in California, a defendant charged with a felony must be brought to trial within 60 days after the indictment or information. A person charged with a misdemeanor must be brought to trial within 30 days of the date of the filing of the complaint if he is in custody and within 45 days if he is not being held.)

The right to a speedy trial may be waived, and this is often done by defendants who are not in custody while they are waiting for a trial or by those in custody who need more time to prepare a defense. The waiving of time is normally in the best interests of a defendant.

The right to a public trial is also a well established tradition of American and English jurisprudence, and it protects a defendant from any secret use or abuse of judicial power. A judge does have authority to limit the number of spectators in the courtroom, and, in a very few cases, to keep the general public out. (This is done in sex cases involving young children.) He also has the right to bar the use of cameras or broadcasting equipment in the courtroom.

DISCOVERY

In many states and in the federal courts a defendant has a statutory right to discovery in a criminal case. For instance, he has a right to see the police report about his case. This right of discovery is very limited in most states and in the federal court system, as it is not a constitutional right.

In some states the defendant can obtain the names and addresses of all of the witnesses the prosecution plans to use. The defense can also inspect notebooks of the arresting policemen and view other documentary and demonstrative evidence of the prosecution. The prosecutor has a much more limited right to discovery.

The purpose of this discovery statute is to make both sides put their cards on the table without infringing upon the defendant's constitutional rights. By knowing the strength and weaknesses of each other's case, the two sides are more likely to get together and negotiate a plea rather than go to the time and expense of a trial.

THE RIGHT TO A JURY TRIAL

The constitutional right to a jury trial is guaranteed in all criminal cases. Federal rules call for a 12 member jury which must reach a unanimous verdict before finding a man guilty or not guilty.

The states do not have a constitutional obligation to use the same number of jurors, nor do juries have to reach a unanimous verdict, although most states follow the federal example.

The right to a jury trial can be waived by a defendant. Jury waiver is a tactical matter (a defendant may have a precise technical defense which a judge will more easily understand). It is also, unfortunately, a financial consideration, since lawyers generally charge more to try a case before a jury.

If the jury cannot reach a verdict, then there is a mistrial, and the case will have to be tried again in front of another jury or dismissed.

Jurors are selected from voter registration rolls. They are first questioned by the prosecutor and the defense attorney to determine if they have any bias; in federal cases a judge conducts this examination. A biased juror can be removed for cause. A certain number of jurors may also be excused from duty by the prosecutor and the defense attorney without any reason being stated.

Members of racial or ethnic minorities cannot be systematically excluded from jury service. A guilty verdict from such an unbalanced jury will be reversed even though the evidence clearly shows guilt because such verdicts are in violation of the due process and fairness guarantees of the Constitution.

THE RIGHT TO CONFRONT WITNESSES

The Sixth Amendment right of an accused to confront the witnesses against him has been incorporated to apply to the states through the Fourteenth Amendment and it applies at all adversary proceedings except at the grand jury level.

This right of confrontation allows a defendant or his attorney to cross-examine prosecution witnesses, and it protects the accused from false, incomplete or misleading testimony.

THE RIGHT AGAINST SELF-INCRIMINATION

We have already discussed the privilege against self-incrimination after arrest. This section will deal with the Fifth Amendment right during a trial.

The right against self-incrimination means a defendant cannot be forced to testify against himself. It can be exercised in all civil and criminal cases, before a legislative investigating committee or in any other proceedings where testimony is compelled under oath. The right is also protected by the constitutions and statutes of all of the states. It may be invoked whenever an answer directly incriminates a person to a crime or furnishes a link in the chain of evidence of a crime.

The federal government and the states now have immunity laws which force a witness to answer all questions propounded to him even though the answers may be incriminating. The immunity laws circumvent the Fifth Amendment because they immunize the witness against any criminal prosecution which might result from his incriminating answers. By granting immunity the prosecution may lose its right to convict and punish a criminal, but the information which the witness can supply is thought to be more important than a single conviction. If a witness refuses to answer even after he has been given immunity, he can be punished for contempt.

The right against self-incrimination is personal to the individual and he cannot use it to protect a corporation, labor union or any other organization. For instance, a man who keeps business records cannot refuse to divulge the records after he has been properly subpoenaed to testify. The right only applies to testimony which would implicate you in a criminal offense, and it does not protect you from testifying to facts which could lead to an embarrassing or compromising situation.

The defendant does not have to testify at all, and the prosecutor cannot call a defendant to the witness stand to force him to assert his right against self-incrimination. Nor can the prosecutor comment on the exercise of this constitutional right during the trial.

The right against self-incrimination can be waived at any time. However, before a judge can accept a waiver, he must determine that it has been made intelligently and voluntarily. The right is also lost if a defendant takes the witness stand and testifies in his own behalf. After a defendant assumes the witness stand in his own criminal trial, he must answer all proper questions propounded to him on cross-examination by the prosecutor. Once a defendant has intelligently and voluntarily waived his right against self-incrimination, he can no longer claim it.

The decision to allow a defendant to testify in his own behalf is an important tactical choice. In most cases it is a good idea, as the jurors have a natural inclination to want to hear him speak. But it is not advisable if he has a past criminal record which can be used to impeach him or if he has an abrasive or highly excitable personality.

NEGOTIATED PLEAS

American courts process thousands of criminal cases daily. To relieve congested court calendars and aid in the administration of criminal justice, the process of negotiated pleas has been accepted and dignified by our highest courts. A negotiated plea normally consists of either (1) a plea of guilty with an agreement on the sentence, or (2) a plea of guilty to a less serious criminal charge. (For instance, trespass is a less serious charge than burglary.)

Negotiated pleas allow a prosecutor to dispose of cases in which he is not sure he can get a conviction, and it allows him to dispose of less serious matters and devote more time to severe, violent crimes.

Once you plead not guilty, it is relatively easy to change the plea to guilty or no contest. Before pleading guilty, the court must re-advise you of all constitutional rights and tell you that a plea of guilty is a waiver of these rights.

The court is under an obligation to make sure that a plea of guilty is entered intelligently and voluntarily. If the plea has been negotiated, the details of the negotiations, including the sentence, must be spelled out in court for the protection of the defendant, his attorney, the prosecutor and the judge. The judge should also tell the defendant the maximum sentence he could receive by pleading guilty.

Note -- once you plead guilty, it's very hard to withdraw it and reinstate a plea of not guilty.

SENTENCING AND THE RIGHT AGAINST CRUEL AND UNUSUAL PUNISHMENT

Once you plead guilty or are found guilty by a judge or jury, it is up to the court to sentence you .

Prior to the sentencing, the judge may ask for a pre-sentence investigative report which is normally conducted by the adult probation department which produces a probation report. The report will not only go into the details of the crime but will also go into family background, past record and rehabilitative prognosis of the defendant. While judges consider probation reports, they are not bound by their findings or recommendations.

A criminal sentence may include any one or a combination of the following: jail, a fine or probation. As part of the probation, the court may impose certain restrictions and conditions including a prohibition on the use of alcohol or drugs. If a sentenced defendant violates the conditions of his probation, a judge may re-sentence him to serve any suspended part of his jail term.

There is a statutory maximum to a judge's sentence. For many misdemeanors, the maximum is one year in the county jail. For felonies, the judge will state a prescribed period of time or the law will call for indeterminate sentencing.

Indeterminate sentencing means that the prisoner is put in the custody of the state prison department for the period prescribed by law. Once he is in the penitentiary, it is up to the prison personnel and the parole board to determine when he gets out. For instance, for a crime which draws a one to ten year sentence, the prisoner must serve a minimum of one year and a maximum of ten. But the actual time which the prisoner serves will depend on his rehabilitation and his conduct in prison. Therefore, a prisoner who is cooperative and unobtrusive will be released sooner than a prisoner who has been contemptuous and obdurate even though both men have been convicted of the same crime and sentenced to serve the same time. Many penologists feel that indeterminate sentencing is a major prison reform. Some critics feel it is open to a great deal of abuse.

Parole is the conditional release of a prisoner—technically he is still doing his time outside the prison even though he is still in the legal custody of the parole board acting through a parole officer. The prisoner has to report to his parole officer regularly and abide by the conditions of parole. (Keeping a steady job, staying away from alcohol, drugs and firearms and regular testing for use of narcotics.) Once parole is granted, it cannot be taken away unless there is good cause, and even then the parolee must be given a hearing with due process guarantees which makes the state prove that he has been a willful violater of parole.

The governor of the state can grant a reprieve (stay of execution), a commutation of a sentence (reduction of a criminal sentence such as reducing a death penalty to life imprisonment), and a full pardon. The President can grant reprieves, commutations and pardons of federal crimes only.

The constitutional limitation on the right of a judge to sentence a defendant is found in the Eighth Amendment which prevents the cruel and unusual punishment. The definition of cruel and unusual punishment changes with a changing society. Torture, mutilation, and public humiliation are now cruel, unusual, and illegal, but jail sentences, reasonable conditions of probation and confinement to mental institutions are not.

The death penalty for crimes of murder, rape and kidnapping was considered constitutional if the execution was accomplished as swiftly and as painlessly as possible until 1972.

> In 1947 Willie Francis was due to be electrocuted in Louisiana. He was placed in the chair, and the switch was turned on, but the current was not strong enough to kill him. He was taken back to his cell, and when they attempted to execute Francis again, he petitioned the Supreme Court for relief on the grounds that the second execution would be cruel and unusual punishment. The court rejected his argument, and he was executed.

In 1973, the Supreme Court decided everyone in America then facing the death penalty would be saved, and all laws which instituted this penalty were invalid insofar as the sentence was concerned. (The case was called *Furman vs. Georgia,* and the vote was five-to-four.)

Two justices who voted with the majority felt that the death penalty was unconstitutional, and it was cruel and unusual in light of the values of our present society. They felt that it was no longer a valid deterrent to crime, and even if it were a deterrent, the harm to society far outweighed any of the benefits the death penalty might bring.

The other three majority justices felt that the death penalty was unconstitutional because of the method in which it was administered, for it was not applied under the equal protection of the laws requirement of the Fourteenth Amendment. Statistics proved that only the poor or the minorities were executed; the rich rarely paid with their lives. This was especially true in the South where rape was a capital crime.

The four dissenting justices felt that only the individual state legislatures could eliminate the death penalty.

Since three of the justices who voted for abolition did not find that the death penalty itself was cruel and unusual, the states can reinstate it with laws which would strip a judge or a jury of any discretion in sentencing. The new laws would have to make death mandatory for certain crimes.

EXTRADITION

Each state can only enforce its own penal laws for crimes which have been committed within its borders, and too, federal courts only hear criminal cases involving federal laws which have been broken within the United States, its territories and possessions. Sometimes the same act can be a crime against the state and the federal government, in which case both state and federal courts have jurisdiction. This is called "concurring jurisdiction."

Even though a crime may have been committed in a state or in the United States, an accused can only be held for trial if he is in the custody of the court with jurisdiction. Extradition is the surrender by one state or nation to another of a person accused of a crime. The Constitution puts the duty of interstate extradition on the state governors. This means that if you are charged with a crime in one state and found in another, you cannot be brought back to the original state without a formal order of extradition. This is accomplished after a governor has determined that you have been legally charged with a crime and are a fugitive from justice. You can waive formal extradition.

The right of a foreign country or of the United States to demand extradition exists only when that right is given by a formal treaty. Without a treaty the United States will not surrender a fugitive to a foreign government.

DOUBLE JEOPARDY

Double jeopardy means that a person can only be tried for the commission of a crime once. If he is acquitted, then he can never be tried for the same crime in the same jurisdiction again. If there is a mistrial, then he can be retried. If he is convicted but later appeals and wins his appeal, then he can be retried. The government cannot appeal an acquittal after a trial.

Jeopardy attaches when there is an actual trial. If an accused is arrested but the charges are dismissed before a trial, he can be rearrested and tried for the same crime without violating the Constitution.

If the same act is a crime against the state and the federal government and you are acquitted in the state court, you can still be held for trial in the federal court. For instance, when the persons accused of murdering three civil rights workers in Mississippi in 1964 were acquitted in their own state court, their later conviction in federal court for violating the civil rights of the same deceased people was legal.

DUE PROCESS OF LAW

The Fifth Amendment's due process of law clause guarantees fairness of treatment to the criminally accused. Just what is considered fair depends on other constitutional clauses, the history of American and English jurisprudence and the circumstances of the case.

Since the designers of the Constitution could not possibly cover all of the areas of freedom in one document, the due process of law clause has been used to define and identify rights which are not specifically listed. For instance, this clause has been used to identify your rights to a fair trial and to the presumption of innocence until proven guilty beyond a reasonable doubt.

The due process clause also ameliorates situations where there is a conflict between clauses in the Constitution. An example of how this clause is applied follows:

> Dr. Sam Sheppard, a prominent osteopath in the city of Cleveland, was accused of murdering his wife in 1954. His arrest was precipitated by articles in the Cleveland press. The murder attracted national attention, and the trial developed into a Roman holiday for the press. The prosecutor spoke to the papers about the case, and they printed many false misleading articles. In effect, the newspapers had convicted Sam Sheppard before his trial even began. He was convicted of murder, and he appealed many times. Finally in 1966 the Supreme Court reversed the conviction on the grounds that the undue amount of pretrial publicity and the circus atmosphere surrounding his trial denied Dr. Sheppard due process of law. This theory of pretrial publicity and due process of law also caused the reversal of one of the convictions of Billie Sol Estes and the conviction of Jack Ruby for the murder of Lee Harvey Oswald. Dr. Sheppard was later retried for his wife's murder and acquitted.

In the Sheppard case the court had to balance the right of an individual to receive a fair trial against freedom of the press and the right of the public to know. The court felt that if there was a conflict between these freedoms, then the right to receive a fair trial should prevail. The Sheppard decision did not enjoin the press from publishing material about pending trials, but it put an obligation on the courts to control pre-trial publicity by ordering everyone associated with a case -- including prosecutors, police, defense attorneys and the defendants -- to refrain from speaking about the matters publicly. If they talk to the media, they can be held in contempt of court.

If a defendant feels that he has received so much publicity that it will prejudice his case, he can move to change the venue of the trial to another county. A hearing will be held, and the defendant must show newspaper articles or other publicity which he feels has prejudiced him to the point where he could not possibly receive a fair trial in the county. The defendant may also move his case from state to federal court if he can show that he cannot get a fair trial in the state courts.

There are many critics of the recent wave of court decisions which have increased individual rights and reversed some criminal convictions. They point to an increasing crime rate and a low apprehension and conviction rate. But this criticism must be tempered by the meaning and spirit of due process of law and, for that matter, the Fourth, Fifth, Sixth and Eighth Amendments to the United States Constitution. The motivation behind due process of law is the fear that innocent people will go to jail or even be executed for crimes which they did not commit. Due process of law protects the innocent and the guilty from the abuse of power by government officials—and it preserves human dignity. It is true that some of the guilty may go free, but this is a small price to pay to guarantee a fair and scrupulous judicial system which is dedicated to protecting the innocent.

PART III

THE FAMILY

CHAPTER 6

Marriage—Divorce—
Annulment—Separation

MARRIAGE AND DIVORCE GENERALLY

Before discussing divorce, some paragraphs should be devoted to its pre-requisite -- marriage. The regulation of marriage and divorce is strictly within the powers of the individual states to control. The principle behind this power is the interest of the state in preserving and protecting the integrity of the family unit and society in general. Since there is no uniform law on these matters, legislation varies from state to state.

Couples may be required to obtain a license before they can legally enter into a ceremony of marriage, and they may be compelled to wait a short period of time between the issuance of a license and the ceremony. Most states require both to take blood tests to make sure neither has a venereal disease before the wedding.

Minimum age requirements may also be set. Most states allow a man and a woman to marry without their parents' consent at age 18.

Bigamous and incestuous marriages are forbidden everywhere. However, the degree of blood relationship between prospective bride and groom differs from state to state.

The Supreme Court has outlawed the prohibition of interracial marriages.

Wedding ceremonies differ greatly around the world. The states generally recognize the validity of a marriage which was *legally* performed in another state or in a foreign country.

COMMON LAW MARRIAGES

When a couple lives together as man and wife without the benefit of a marriage license and ceremony, this is called a common law marriage. They are legally recognized in 13 states. If a state does not recognize a common law marriage, neither party to it can acquire property or support rights from the other as a result of this relationship. (They can contract with each other or put their property in joint tenancy.)

> Heather and Herman met each other at a jazz concert and soon found an apartment together in San Francisco, where they lived as husband and wife. In fact, they told their friends and business associates that they were legally married. They lived this way for 20 years, during which Herman was able to accumulate $50,000 in stocks and bonds – all of which were in his name alone. While they were still living together, Herman died without a will. His only living relative was a cousin in New Jersey. Since Herman and Heather had lived in a state which did not recgnize common law marriages, the entire estate passed to his cousin. Herman could have avoided this by (1) naming Heather as a beneficiary in a will, (2) adding her name as a joint tenant on his property, or (3) marrying her.

Although they receive a lot of publicity, homosexual marriages are not recognized in any state of the union and homosexual couples cannot acquire property rights in each other's accumulations in the absence of a contract, nor can they maintain a divorce proceeding against each other.

RESIDENCE

A marriage can be dissolved in a state where at least one of the parties resides immediately before filing for divorce. The individual states decide how long you must reside within its borders to meet the residence rule. Some states also require a person to live in one county for a period of time before filing for divorce. The shortest residence requirement is still in Nevada and Idaho -- only 6 weeks. It is up to the individual court hearing a domestic relations matter to determine if the residence requirement has been properly met.

Since divorce laws vary markedly among the states, one partner may move into another state, even temporarily, in order to take advantage of its divorce laws. (The Supreme Court has ruled that each party takes his marriage, but not necessarily his children and property with him.) But, although the court may be able to grant a divorce, it may not be able to settle property rights or the issues of child custody, child support and alimony -- unless the court acquires jurisdiction over both parties, the children or the property. Out of state divorces can cause many problems, and it is best to settle domestic differences in your home state.

This brings us to the validity of divorce decrees obtained in foreign countries. Many are obtained in places like the Dominican Republic where the residence requirement is only 24 hours—you can even obtain a divorce by mail.

If both husband and wife agree to submit to the jurisdiction of a foreign country, this divorce decree can be valid. Such divorces are normally accomplished with the parties entering into a marital settlement agreement before consenting to foreign jurisdiction. However, a wife who wants alimony and child support payments is foolish to do this, since she would have a difficult time enforcing her rights. If a husband or wife does not comply with the marital settlement agreement in a foreign divorce, the other spouse must start new legal proceedings in his home state.

If one spouse obtains a "quickie" foreign divorce without the consent of the other, the decree is invalid in the United States.

GROUNDS FOR DIVORCE

All 50 states and the District of Columbia have grounds which must be proved in order to sever the bonds of matrimony. Most states still require one partner to give proof of specific acts of misconduct by the other -- such as sexual incapacity, adultery, cruelty, drunkenness, desertion, insanity, fraud, bigamy, non-support and sexual perversion. This introduces an element of recrimination and rancor into the courtroom, and judges must watch and listen as attorneys air all this dirty laundry. These states also require coroboration -- that is, it is not enough for a partner to testify of specific acts of misconduct; another witness must be brought to court to attest to them.

Many states purposely make it hard to obtain a divorce, feeling it is the duty of the state to preserve the family unit. Most states have taken the position that it is impossible for a state to tell two members of its adult population to love and live with each other. If they cannot make a go of it, they should be allowed to dissolve the marriage with dignity and fairness. These states allow a partner to dissolve a marriage without proving fault for the breakup.

The grounds for a "no fault" divorce are irreconcilable or irretrievable differences. Some of the states have substituted the word dissolution for divorce, and this dramatically emphasizes the major change in concept. Now either party can testify that there are irreconcilable or irretrievable differences. No corroberating witness is necessary. One spouse cannot prevent the other from obtaining a divorce. A judge need only be convinced that the marriage is beyond reconciliation to grant the divorce.

A few states have added the no fault ground for divorce but still retain the old specific grounds of misconduct. These states give the spouses a choice, and the choice has some bearing on the division of property and alimony.

Some states provide reconciliation services, and either party to a divorce proceeding may request this help. The court will order a husband and wife to speak with members of the reconciliation staff, but, obviously, a court cannot force them to reconcile.

Once residence and grounds for divorce have been established the parties must agree or the court must rule on the following issues: (1) division of property and debts, (2) child custody and visitation, (3) child support, (4) alimony and (5) attorneys fees and costs.

DIVISION OF PROPERTY

Under the old English common law whatever property was earned or acquired by a husband was his separate property, and whatever property was earned or acquired by the wife was also *his* separate property. So much for history. All states allow spouses to own property in their separate names, but the method of dividing property which has been acquired during marriage varies among the states.

In non-community property states (42) anything a husband earns in his own name is his separate property. The likewise is true for a wife. This means that if the husband is the sole wage earner of the family and he keeps his savings and other property (including the home) in his name alone, this is his separate property before, during and after a divorce — a most unfair law to women, who, with the consent and at the urging of their husbands, have spent their time raising children and keeping a home in good order.

Husbands and wives who live in non-community property states can avoid these harsh rules by acquiring property jointly. They can do this as joint tenants or *tenants by the entirety.* The latter is a form of ownership reserved for married persons, and it means that both spouses own the whole property, that neither can transfer ownership without the consent of the other and that upon the death of one, the entire property goes to the survivor. Since tenancy by the entirety is reserved for married persons only, a divorce would necessitate dividing the property in half.

Community property laws are in effect in California, Arizona, Idaho, Louisiana, Nevada, New Mexico, Texas and Washington. The theory behind them is that the husband and wife, bound together in matrimony, form a community. Everything that both do—including earning income, cooking meals, raising children, accumulating property and incurring debts -- contributes in some way to that community. If one partner earns all of the income this does not detract from the other's homemaking contribution to the community. Both must share in the burdens and benefits of the marriage partnership.

All the two accumulate together is their community property. In fact, if the husband and wife accumulate it in another non-community property state, bring it to a community property state and establish residence, the property is considered community.

Traditionally, community property laws make the husband the sole manager of the community property. Therefore, any gains he accumulates in his own name or in the name of both spouses is still community property, and conversely, any losses he incurs are a loss to the entire community. (If the husband is a drunk or a poor gambler, the wife loses: if the husband is a successful businessman, she wins.) These old laws are obviously out of touch with present reality, and they are of questionable constitutional validity. In California, Texas and Washington both spouses are co-managers of the community property—neither one can contract for a substantial debt without the written consent of the other. None of the community property states allows the husband to give away community assets without the wife's consent. Furthermore, any property which the wife accumulates in her own name with the husband's consent is her separate property, not part of the community.

> Phil and Beatrice were married in 1965. Prior to this Beatrice owned her own home in Texas, and she and Phil moved there after the marriage. Both worked during the marriage, and Phil used the savings for extensive repairs and additions on the home. In 1971 Phil filed for a dissolution. The only major asset was the home, and it was awarded to Beatrice because it was her separate property before the marriage. Phil had absolutely no financial interest since, as the manager of the community property, his repairs and improvements were considered gifts to Beatrice. This same result would have occurred in a non-community property state.

Not all things accumulated during a marriage are marital or community property. If one spouse receives a gift or inheritance, then it is his or hers separately. Property owned before the marriage remains separate afterwards, and earnings from this property are also considered separate. For instance, if a husband inherits stock, its dividends are his separately.

Separate property loses this status if you add your spouse's name to the ownership or otherwise commingle it with community or marital property. Therefore, if a husband sells the stock he has inherited and reinvests the proceeds in marital property investments, the separate property is commingled and loses its separate status.

> Ken and Angela married while Ken was a dental student. After he received his license, they settled in Sacramento, California. After five years, the dental practice was appraised at $150,000. Angela filed for a dissolution of the marriage, and the practice was properly listed as a community asset.
>
> If Ken had not married Angela until after he had established his practice to this point, then it would have been his separate property. If Ken had a small practice, married Angela and then developed it so it was worth more, he might argue that the practice was still his separate property — although a court in this situation could very easily find that it was commingled to such a point that the entire practice should be considered community property. In non-community property states there would be no question that Ken's practice, no matter when it started or flourished, would be his separate property.

In all states if a wife acquires a debt in her own name, this is her own separate debt. The husband is not liable to pay for the debts of a wife taken in her own name except for the necessities of life — food, clothing and medical/dental care. This is the reason why so many businesses refuse to give a married woman credit in her own name — they know they cannot collect against the husband if the wife fails to pay.

Normally any assets or debts which either party accumulates after they have separated but before a divorce decree are considered separate. However, if one spouse leaves the other one's name on a credit card, any future charges on that card become the debts of both persons — the creditor doesn't care who pays, and he can go after both persons despite a divorce decree or property settlement agreement.

If a husband and wife cannot agree on the division of their property, the matter must go to trial for a judge to decide who will get what. In making the division, the judge must consider the net amount of assets, that is, he must subtract the debts from the assets. If the husband and wife have accumulated more debts than assets, each party may be responsible for a share of the net deficit. All states are supposed to fairly divide property, but fundamental fairness and justice are vague terms, and there are many disgruntled veterans of divorce who will take exception to the application of these terms in their specific cases.

Courts consider the following factors in dividing marital property: (1) contribution of each spouse; (2) the value of each piece of property; (3) the economic circumstances of the family, i.e. who has custody of the children and needs a home and other property for their proper maintenance. In those states which require specific grounds for divorce, the courts can also consider the factor of fault in dividing the property. For instance, if a wife can prove that her husband treated her with extreme cruelty, then a court could justify awarding her a disproportionate share.

Generally, in the no fault states, the courts do not consider fault in dividing community property — it's usually divided 50-50.

In making the division a judge must consider the net amount of assets. That is, he must subtract the debts from the assets. If the husband and wife have accumulated more debts than assets, each party may be responsible for a share of the net deficit.

The duty of a judge to award substantially one-half of the property to each spouse is a fair and equitable rule; but it sometimes presents difficult situations:

> Tony and Pamela were married for ten years when they decided on divorce. They had two children, ages 8 and 6. Tony worked as a carpenter and Pamela was a secretary. During the 10-year marriage they did not accumulate much cash, but there was a home with an equity of $12,000. They agreed that Pamela should have custody of the children, and she wanted to maintain

the home instead of moving to an apartment. But Tony wanted his one-half equity in cash immediately. The court can award possession of the home to the wife and order her to make monthly payments to the husband until his one-half equity was repaid. Or it could award Tony his half but allow Pamela to stay in the home for a reasonable period without making payments; she could then either obtain a loan to pay Tony or sell the home and find housing elsewhere.

Tim and Patricia married after their high school graduation and Tim started his own plumbing business which, 15 years later, was valued at $100,000. Patricia sued Tim to dissolve the marriage and for a division of the community property which, of course, included the plumbing business. Since the two had put all of their money and efforts into the business, it was the only substantial asset they had. Patricia wanted her value of the business in cash immediately. but it would be unfair to force Tim to sell in order to pay her off. If Tim could not arrange for a loan to pay her, a judge woud probably award the business to Tim with the provision that he pay Patricia with monthly installments.

A husband and wife can divide their property without a judge's approval through marital settlement agreements. They should be in writing, and they should be made a part of a divorce decree.

A man and a woman can enter into contracts before marriage in which either party can bargain away property or alimony rights. But no court will uphold these agreements unless they appear fair to both sides. This means that the party giving up a substantial legal right should be represented by an attorney and be financially compensated in a fair amount. It should be obvious from the paragraphs in this section that anyone with substantial property holdings should consult an attorney before entering into marriage.

CHILD CUSTODY AND VISITATION

Traditionally, after a divorce the mother gets custody of the children, especially small children. But lately, the courts are eschewing tradition and awarding custody to the father.

Custody laws differ from state to state. In some states a mother will automatically receive custody unless the father can prove that she is an unfit parent -- a very difficult task. In most states judges have a wide degree of latitude in deciding what is in the best interest of the children. If there is a contest the judge must look at the circumstances of both parents and decide who can provide a better home.

If there is a contest over child custody, the court will order an investigation by a trained investigating officer who will interview the parties, close relatives, friends and the children themselves. He will also investigate charges of misconduct and submit his findings and recommendations to the trial judge in a written report. (A copy will be sent to the attorneys, and they have the opportunity to cross-examine him at the trial.) The trial judge is not bound by this recommendation, but it will obviously weigh heavily.

While it is a general rule in no fault states that neither spouse can bring up specific acts of misconduct against the other, there is an exception to the rule in child custody cases where these acts have some bearing on how children will be raised.

Under the best interest tests, children of tender years are normally placed with the mother. As the age and maturity of the child progresses, the father has a better chance for custody. The children may voice their preference but it is not binding on a court, although it is persuasive.

When one parent gets custody of the children, the other is normally entitled to visit them. Even in those cases where bitter fighting has occurred between the husband and wife, they should be mature enough to realize that the children should not be used as pawns in their dispute. Judgments of dissolution and divorce usually grant reasonable visitation rights without spelling out the exact times and days. The court leaves this matter to the parents but where there is a dispute, the court will intervene and define the exact visitation rights. These rights depend on the availability of the parent to see the children and their ages. They often include overnight visits of the children and visits of one week or more during the summer and Christmas vacations. A court will seldom prevent a parent from seeing the children altogether.

Grandparents also have some visitation rights, and they can go to court to enforce these rights if the parent refuses to grant them.

The states are divided on the issue of whether non-parents can have custody of children over the objection of the natural parents. Under the best interest test some states will award custody of a child to foster parents, grandparents, aunts and uncles or brothers and sisters if they can provide a better home than the natural parent. These states' courts respect the natural right of a parent, but feel that the paramount interest is the welfare of the child. Other states cling to the tradition that a natural parent has superior rights to child custody over all others and will not interfere with this inviolate right.

Court orders on child custody and visitation are never final. A parent can always go back to court to modify the order even though it was contained in an interlocutory or final judgment of divorce. The courts recognize that family life is dynamic, and that circumstances may change which may warrant a change in custody or visitation privileges.

CHILD SUPPORT

Parents must financially support their children. Failure to do so is a crime, and it can bring on contempt of court charges.

If there are children, support is always a divorce issue. The amount of child support depends on the needs of the children, their sources of income and the ability of the parents to pay. If there is a court hearing, the parent with custody offers evidence showing expenses for child rearing and his ability to pay for the child support. The other parent submits a statement showing his net worth, income and monthly living expenses. From this data the judge makes a child support award. Judges consider child support a primary obligation, and other debts are considered subordinate to it.

Both parents have a support obligation but when the father retains custody, it is rare that a mother is ordered to make child support payments. If payments are ordered, they are usually nominal.

A parent must support his children until they reach the age of majority -- 18 in most states. If a minor child marries, joins the armed services or leaves home and assumes his own support, the law considers him emancipated and his parents no longer have to support him.

Orders for child support are never final. While they appear in interlocutory and final judgments of dissolution and divorce, either party can go back to court at a later date to modify the payments because of a change in circumstances. But this must be major to get the court to change its order. Such circumstances could occur when a father has lost his job or suffered a serious loss of income since the time of the order. Increases in child support are ordered after a major inflationary period or after a long period of time when the financial need of the children appreciably increases.

A parent who contributes over 50% to the support of a child can claim that child as an exemption on his or her federal and state income tax returns. A father who contributes $100 per month is presumed by the IRS to have given that 50%, but a mother with custody can rebut this presumption by proving that she contributes more than the father. If the divorced or separated parents both claim the child as a dependency exemption, they are sure to be audited by the taxman.

When Charles and Sandra were divorced in 1965, they had two children, ages 5 and 8. Charles was employed by the federal government, earning $8,500 per year. The two agreed, and the court ordered that Charles pay $75 per month per child to Sandra for child support. Sandra remarried in 1970, and in 1972 she asked Charles for a support increase. He refused, and Sandra petitioned the court for a modification of the support order. Sandra told the court that the circumstances had changed remarkably since 1965; the cost of raising children, ages 12 and 15 was considerably higher than it had been

7 years previously, and inflation had seriously eroded the value of the $75 payment. Charles' salary had increased to $12,000 per year. Charles cited that it cost him more to live since 1965 and that Sandra's new husband should bear some of the cost of raising the children. The judge recognized the increased financial needs of the children, declared that Sandra's new husband had no obligation to support Charles' children and raised Charles' payment to $150 per month per child.

It is normal for a father to also provide his children with medical insurance. He may also name them as life insurance beneficiaries as long as they are minors.

ALIMONY OR SPOUSAL SUPPORT

The word "alimony" is anathema to thousands of bitter ex-husbands and women's liberationists across this land. Alimony is part of our legal heritage, and all states provide for it when the need arises. A few states have substituted the phrase "spousal support" for alimony; but that is just a horse of the same color.

Not all divorces include an award of alimony. It is the husbands who are usually ordered to pay it, but circumstances can arise where a wife would have to pay her husband alimony -- a very rare situation indeed. (For the sake of simplicity, I shall assume in the remainder of this section that the husband is the giver of alimony and the wife is the recipient.)

Judges have a wide degree of discretion in awarding alimony. It depends on these factors: 1) The length of the marriage, 2) the ability of the wife to work without hurting the children (ability means physical ability as well as proficiency in a trade or profession), 3) age of the wife, 4) the style and manner in which she is accustomed to living and 5) the man's financial ability to pay.

Alimony awards are given to a wife for her lifetime or for a prescribed period of time, depending on the circumstances. If alimony is awarded for a definite period, the wife no longer has any right to support after the period has elapsed. In any event, a husband has no duty to pay alimony if the wife remarries or lives with another man as his wife.

Just like child support orders, awards for alimony can be modified by either husband or wife at a later date if there is a substantial change in circumstances. Many times a wife is able to support herself at the time of the divorce, but the court recognizes that she was married for so long that she has some right to alimony if she were unable to work. In these cases, the court will award a nominal amount of alimony, perhaps $1 per year, for a certain length of time or indefinitely to keep the issue of alimony open. If no alimony is awarded, the issue is closed, and neither spouse can come back to court at a later date to ask for it.

Alimony is taxable income to the party receiving it and a tax deduction to the party paying it.

Mark and Christine were married in 1961 when Mark was a junior executive with a large corporation and Christine was a school teacher. She continued to work for two more years, but retired to begin raising a family. By 1971 Mark was earning $35,000 a year and the two had a $50,000 home in the suburbs; they also had three children, ages 9, 5 and 6 months. In 1972 Christine filed for a dissolution, and she and Mark agreed on child custody, division of the marital property and child support. They could not agree on the the amount of alimony or the duration, and they left the matter in issue for a judge to decide. Christine stated that she was physically able to go back to work as a school teacher with some upgraded training, but she did not want to resume working until her youngest child was in school. The judge ordered Mark to pay Christine the sum of $900 per month for alimony for six years, after which it dropped to $50 per month.

Alimony and child support are debts which are not dischargeable in bankruptcy.

ATTORNEY'S FEES AND COSTS

In domestic relations cases, the courts may order the husband to pay the wife's attorney's fees if the wife cannot afford to pay herself. The amount of the award should be commensurate with the time spent by the attorney, but many couts have awarded fees on the basis of the husband's net worth. This is most unfair since it has nothing to do with the time spent by an attorney on a domestic relations case. In the many states which still have a fault concept of divorce, the husband is ordered to pay the wife's attorney on the basis that he is the guilty party, and the one who has caused the litigation.

MISCELLANEOUS

Judges in domestic relations cases may make other appropriate orders and injunctions. For instance, a court may enjoin the parties from disturbing, molesting or annoying each other, or from making disparaging remarks about each other in the presence of the children. A court may prevent one party from claiming one or all of the children as dependents on an income tax return, and it may order a party to sign a document necessary to transfer title pursuant to a division of property.

A wife can obtain an order from the court reinstating her maiden name. This is a matter of personal choice, not a legal obligation.

INTERIM ORDERS

In most instances where a family separates and there are children, the wife needs temporary support for herself and the children. Since it takes some time for parties to get to trial on the merits of their action, the courts have established a domestic relations department to hear pleas for temporary support and other temporary orders, pending the final outcome of the case. These departments also entertain motions to award attorney's fees, temporary custody of the children, and visitation rights. They may also enjoin and restrain parties to prevent them from disposing of or wasting property; molesting or annoying one another, or removing the children from the county, the state or the country.

The parties can reach an agreement and stipulate to an interim order, or they can let a domestic relations judge hear the evidence and make a ruling.

DEFAULT OR CONTEST

If the defendant or respondent spouse does not respond to the petition for dissolution or complaint for divorce within the time prescribed by law (usually 30 days) after it has been properly served, then the petitioning spouse can obtain a judgment by default without the presence of the other. If the defendant files a response within the allotted time after service, the matter is at issue, and it is incumbent upon one of the attorneys to set it for trial.

INTERLOCUTORY AND FINAL JUDGMENTS

Once a divorce is settled (or there is a default) one of the spouses must go to court to obtain a divorce or dissolution judgment. If the two cannot reach an agreement, they must ask a judge to decide the issues to obtain this decree, which not only severs the bonds of matrimony but also spells out the rights and liabilities of the two parties on division of property, child custody and the other issues previously discussed.

Some states provide for both interlocutory and final judgments, and they require some time to pass between the filing for a divorce and the final judgment or between the date of the interlocutory decree and the final judgment. The reason behind this is that the state wants to give the parties time to pause and reflect on their actions and possibly consider reconciliation. All too often a person files for divorce without giving careful thought to the decision, and he is prohibited from divorcing or remarrying immediately so that he can have some time to think it over. If a husband and wife reconcile after an interlocutory judgment but before a final judgment, they do not need a new marriage ceremony since they are still legally husband and wife.

After an interlocutory decree is entered, the two may act as single persons in every respect except they cannot remarry until the final judgment is entered. Also during this time between judgments, the parties may still file joint federal income tax returns.

ENFORCEMENT

All orders of the court in domestic relations cases are enforceable by contempt proceedings. One party can bring the other who has not obeyed an existing order into court to show cause why he should not be held in contempt. The penalty can be jail and/or a fine. In the case of payment of child support and alimony, the defaulting party can relieve himself of contempt by showing that he could not afford to make payments, but this showing will not relieve him of the liability of paying some time in the future -- it simply relieves him from a contempt finding.

Orders for child support and alimony in one state are enforceable in others. If an Illinois court orders child support and/or alimony, the obligated party cannot escape his obligations by moving to Ohio. All of the states (except Iowa) have enacted the Uniform Reciprocal Enforcement of Support Law, which allows district attorneys or private attorneys to institute proceedings to enforce child support and alimony orders in another state.

The sheriff can execute on wages and other assets to enforce support payments.

ANNULMENTS

Annulments (also known as nullities and invalidities of marriage) differ from divorces and dissolutions in that they declare marriages void from their beginning instead of severed. The common grounds are bigamy, insanity, incest, under age, fraud, force or duress and sexual impotence. They must exist at the time of marriage.

Even though the marriage is considered void from the beginning, a few states allow an annulled spouse to have a right to alimony, marital property and attorney's fees. This protects a wife who may be married for many years to a man who is a bigamist.

> Bill and Peggy discussed their future life extensively before marrying. Peggy wanted children badly, but Bill, in agreeing to have them, prevailed upon her to wait at least a year. They enjoyed a normal married life for one year. Then Peggy started asking about raising a family but Bill procrastinated. Six months later, Bill declared that he never wanted children, and Peggy immediately stopped sleeping with him. She filed for an annulment and won on the grounds of fraud in that Bill had deceitfully induced her into marriage by promising to have children.

LEGAL SEPARATION

Since many people still have compunctions about terminating a marriage, the law provides for them to legally separate and accumulate separate property. These proceedings are known as actions for legal separation, separate maintenance or some similar title.

The grounds for a legal separation are usually the same as the grounds for a divorce or dissolution. The only real difference is that the legally separated parties cannot remarry. The issues of child support and custody, alimony, division of property and attorney's fees must also be dealt with in a legal separation.

STATE MARRIAGE LAWS

| | MINIMUM AGE FOR MARRIAGE | | | | COMMON LAW MARRIAGES RECOGNIZED | BLOOD TEST REQUIRED | LENGTH OF WAITING PERIOD FROM APPLICATION TO ISSUANCE OF LICENSE TO MARRY |
| | WITH CONSENT OF PARENTS | | WITHOUT CONSENT OF PARENTS | | | | |
	MALE	FEMALE	MALE	FEMALE			
ALABAMA	17	14	21	18	yes	yes	none
ALASKA	18	16	19	18	no	yes	3 days
ARIZONA	18	16	18	18	no	yes	2 days
ARKANSAS	18	16	21	18	no	yes	3 days
CALIFORNIA	18	16	18	18	no[13]	yes	none
COLORADO	16	16	21	18	yes	yes	none
CONNECTICUT	16	16	18	18	no	yes	4 days
DELAWARE	18	16	18	18	no	yes	none[10]
D. C.	18	16	21	18	yes	yes	3 days
FLORIDA	18	16	21	21	no[1]	yes	3 days
GEORGIA	18	16	18	18	yes	yes	3 days[7]
HAWAII	18	16	18	18	no	yes	none
IDAHO	18	16	18	18	yes	yes	none
ILLINOIS	18	16	18	18	no	yes	none
INDIANA	18	16	18	18	no	yes	3 days
IOWA	18	16	19	18	yes	yes	3 days
KANSAS	18	18	18	18	yes	yes	3 days
KENTUCKY	18	16	18	18	no	yes	3 days
LOUISIANA	18	16	18	18	no	yes	none[11]

| | MINIMUM AGE FOR MARRIAGE | | | COMMON LAW MARRIAGES RECOGNIZED | BLOOD TEST REQUIRED | LENGTH OF WAITING PERIOD FROM APPLICATION TO ISSUANCE OF LICENSE TO MARRY |
	WITH CONSENT OF PARENTS MALE–FEMALE	WITHOUT CONSENT OF PARENTS MALE–FEMALE				
MAINE	16	18	18	no	yes	5 days
MARYLAND	18	21	18	no	no	2 days
MASSACHUSETTS	18	18	18	no	yes	3 days
MICHIGAN	18	18	18	no	yes	3 days
MINNESOTA	18	21	18	no[2]	no	5 days
MISSISSIPPI	17	21	18	no[3]	yes	3 days
MISSOURI	15	21	18	no[4]	yes	3 days
MONTANA	18	18	18	yes	yes	5 days
NEBRASKA	18	19	19	no	yes	none
NEVADA	18	21	18	no	no	none
NEW HAMPSHIRE	14	20	18	no[5]	yes	5 days
NEW JERSEY	18	18	18	no	yes	3 days
NEW MEXICO	17	18	18	no	yes	3 days
NEW YORK	16	21	18	no	yes	none[10]
NORTH CAROLINA	16	18	18	no	yes	none
NORTH DAKOTA	18	21	18	no	yes	none
OHIO	18	21	21	yes	yes	5 days
OKLAHOMA	18	18	18	yes	yes	none[8]
OREGON	18	21	18	no	yes	7 days
PENNSYLVANIA	16	18	18	yes	yes	3 days

| | MINIMUM AGE FOR MARRIAGE | | COMMON LAW MARRIAGES RECOGNIZED | BLOOD TEST REQUIRED | LENGTH OF WAITING PERIOD FROM APPLICATION TO ISSUANCE OF LICENSE TO MARRY |
	WITH CONSENT OF PARENTS MALE–FEMALE	WITHOUT CONSENT OF PARENTS MALE–FEMALE			
RHODE ISLAND	18 16	18 18	yes	yes	none
SOUTH CAROLINA	16 14	18 18	yes	no	1 day
SOUTH DAKOTA	18 16	21 18	no[6]	yes	none
TENNESSEE	16 16	18 18	no	yes	none[9]
TEXAS	16 14	19 18	yes	yes	none
UTAH	16 14	21 18	yes	yes	none
VERMONT	18 16	21 18	no	yes	none[12]
VIRGINIA	18 16	18 18	no	yes	none
WASHINGTON	17 17	18 18	no	yes	3 days
WEST VIRGINIA	18 16	18 18	no	yes	3 days
WISCONSIN	18 16	18 18	no	yes	5 days
WYOMING	18 16	19 19	no	yes	none

FOOTNOTES:

1 Recognized if marriage consummated before Jan. 1, 1968.
2 Recognized if marriage consummated before Apr. 26, 1941.
3 Recognized if marriage consummated before Apr. 5, 1956.
4 Recognized if marriage consummated before Mar. 31, 1921.
5 Recognized if marriage consummated before Dec. 1, 1939.
6 Recognized if marriage consummated before July 1, 1950.
7 No waiting period if both parties are 21 or if under age female signs an affidavit of pregnancy.
8 If either party is below age of consent, 3 days is required.
9 If both parties are under 21, 3 days is required.
10 Parties must wait 24 hours after issuance of license to marry.
11 Parties must wait 72 hours after issuance of license to marry.
12 Parties must wait 5 days after issuance of license to marry.
13 A recent judicial decision has recognized common law marriages in very limited circumstances.

STATE RESIDENCE REQUIREMENTS AND GROUNDS FOR DIVORCE

STATE	RESIDENCE REQUIREMENT	NO FAULT	ADULTERY	ATTEMPTED MURDER OF SPOUSE	BIGAMY	CRUELTY	DESERTION	DURESS	FELONY CONVICTION	FRAUD	HABITUAL DRUG USE OR DRUNKENNESS	INCOMPATIBILITY	INSANITY	LENGTHY SEPARATION	LIFE IMPRISONMENT	PERSONAL INDIGNITIES	VENEREAL DISEASE	Wife Pregnant at Marriage by Another Man Without Knowledge of Husband	WILLFUL OR GROSS NEGLECT	SEXUAL INCAPACITY	NON SUPPORT	PHYSICAL DEFECT
ALABAMA[1]	6 Months	✓	✓			✓	✓	✓	✓	✓	✓	✓	✓	✓	✓		✓	✓	✓	✓	✓	✓
ALASKA	1 Year[2]	✓	✓			✓	✓		✓	✓	✓	✓	✓	✓					✓	✓	✓	
ARIZONA	3 Months	✓	IRRECONCILABLE OR IRRETRIEVABLE DIFFERENCES																			
ARKANSAS	2 Months	✓	✓	✓		✓	✓		✓		✓								✓	✓		
CALIFORNIA	6 Months[3]	✓	IRRECONCILABLE OR IRRETRIEVABLE DIFFERENCES OR POST-MARITAL INSANITY																			
COLORADO	3 Months	✓	IRRECONCILABLE OR IRRETRIEVABLE DIFFERENCES.																			
CONNECTICUT	1 Year[2]	✓	✓			✓	✓		✓	✓	✓	✓		✓	✓							
DELAWARE	1 Year[4]	✓	✓			✓	✓		✓	✓	✓	✓	✓	✓						✓		
D.C.	1 Year	✓				✓	✓		✓			✓		✓								
FLORIDA	6 Months	✓	IRRECONCILABLE OR IRRETRIEVABLE DIFFERENCES.		✓							✓	✓									
GEORGIA	6 Mos.[18]	✓	✓		✓	✓	✓	✓	✓	✓	✓	✓		✓			✓					
HAWAII	1 Year[3]	✓	IRRECONCILABLE OR IRRETRIEVABLE DIFFERENCES.											✓								
IDAHO	6 Weeks	✓	✓			✓	✓		✓	✓	✓	✓	✓	✓						✓		
ILLINOIS[6]	1 Year[5]	✓	✓	✓		✓	✓		✓	✓	✓					✓						
INDIANA[7]	1 Year[18]	✓	✓	✓		✓	✓		✓	✓	✓		✓							✓		
IOWA	1 Year	✓	IRRECONCILABLE OR IRRETRIEVABLE DIFFERENCES																			
KANSAS	6 Months	✓	✓			✓	✓	✓	✓	✓	✓	✓	✓	✓						✓		
KENTUCKY	6 Months	✓				✓			✓			✓					✓				✓	
LOUISIANA[8]	2 Years		✓		✓	✓	✓	✓	✓	✓		✓		✓								
MAINE	6 Months	✓	✓		✓	✓	✓		✓	✓	✓		✓	✓					✓	✓		
MARYLAND	1 Year		✓	✓		✓	✓	✓		✓		✓	✓	✓								
MASSACHUSETTS	2 years[9]		✓		✓	✓	✓		✓	✓	✓		✓				✓		✓	✓		
MICHIGAN	1 Year[2]	✓	IRRECONCILABLE OR IRRETRIEVABLE DIFFERENCES											✓								
MINNESOTA	1 Year[10]	✓	✓			✓	✓	✓	✓	✓	✓	✓		✓					✓	✓		
MISSISSIPPI	1 Year	✓	✓		✓	✓	✓		✓	✓	✓	✓		✓			✓			✓		
MISSOURI	1 Year	✓	✓		✓	✓	✓		✓	✓	✓	✓		✓	✓		✓			✓		
MONTANA[11]	1 Year	✓	✓		✓	✓	✓		✓	✓	✓	✓							✓	✓		
NEBRASKA	1 Year	✓																				
NEVADA	6 Weeks	✓	✓			IRRECONCILABLE OR IRRETRIEVABLE DIFFERENCES OR POST-MARITAL INSANITY																
NEW HAMPSHIRE[13]	1 Year[12]	✓	✓			IRRECONCILABLE OR IRRETRIEVABLE DIFFERENCES.																
NEW JERSEY	1 Year	✓	✓		✓	✓	✓		✓		✓	✓		✓					✓	✓		
NEW MEXICO	1 Year	✓	✓		✓	✓	✓		✓		✓	✓		✓			✓		✓	✓		

-78-

STATE RESIDENCE REQUIREMENTS AND GROUNDS FOR DIVORCE (Cont'd)

STATE	RESIDENCE REQUIREMENT	NO FAULT	ADULTERY	ATTEMPTED MURDER OF SPOUSE	BIGAMY	CRUELTY	DESERTION	DURESS	FELONY CONVICTION	FRAUD	HABITUAL DRUG USE OR DRUNKENNESS	INCOMPATIBILITY	INSANITY	LENGTHY SEPARATION	LIFE IMPRISONMENT	PERSONAL INDIGNITIES	VENEREAL DISEASE	Wife Pregnant at Marriage or Marriage by Another Man Without Knowledge of Husband	WILLFUL OR GROSS NEGLECT	SEXUAL INCAPACITY	NON SUPPORT	PHYSICAL DEFECT
NEW YORK[14]	2 Years		✓			✓	✓		✓					✓	✓						✓	
NORTH CAROLINA	6 Months	✓	✓			✓							✓	✓						✓		✓
NORTH DAKOTA	1 Year	✓	✓		✓	✓	✓		✓		✓		✓				✓	✓	✓	✓		
OHIO	1 Year[3]	✓	✓		✓	✓	✓		✓	✓	✓						✓	✓	✓	✓		
OKLAHOMA	6 mos.[15]	✓	✓		✓	✓	✓		✓	✓	✓	✓	✓					✓	✓	✓		
OREGON	6 months	✓																				
PENNSYLVANIA	1 Year		✓		✓	✓	✓	✓	✓	✓			✓				✓				✓	
RHODE ISLAND	2 Years		✓		✓	✓	✓	✓	✓	✓	✓		✓	✓						✓		✓
SOUTH CAROLINA	1 Year		✓			✓	✓	✓		✓	✓								✓			
SOUTH DAKOTA	1 Yr.[3,2]		✓			✓	✓	✓	✓	✓	✓	✓	✓		✓		✓			✓		
TENNESSEE	1 Year[17]		✓	✓	✓	✓	✓	✓	✓	✓	✓		✓							✓		✓
TEXAS	1 Year[18]	✓	✓	✓		✓	✓		✓			✓	✓	✓								
UTAH	3 mos.[3]		✓		✓	✓	✓	✓	✓		✓	✓	✓	✓		✓				✓		
VERMONT	6 Months	✓	✓			✓	✓		✓				✓	✓			✓					
VIRGINIA	1 Year	✓	✓			✓	✓		✓				✓	✓			✓					
WASHINGTON	6 Months	✓	✓			✓	✓		✓													
WEST VIRGINIA[16]	1 Year		✓			✓	✓		✓	✓	✓		✓		✓					✓		
WISCONSIN	6 Mos.[15]		✓		✓	✓	✓		✓	✓	✓		✓							✓		
WYOMING	60 days[2]		✓		✓	✓	✓		✓		✓		✓	✓	✓		✓			✓	✓	✓

IRRECONCILABLE OR IRRETRIEVABLE DIFFERENCES. (Oregon)

FOOTNOTES

1Other Grounds: (1) Crime against nature, (2) separation agreement for two years.
2If plaintiff is resident and marriage ceremony performed in state, residence requirement is fulfilled. Also 10 days in county.
3Three months in county.
4Suit for adultery or bigamy may be brought anytime.
5If grounds occurred in Illinois; then requirement reduced to six months.
6Other Grounds: Communication of veneral disease.
7Other Grounds: Neglect of conjugal duty.
8Other Grounds: (1) Public defamation; (2) fugitive from justice.
9Parties must also be living apart for thirty days unless court grants waiver of this requirement.
10No requirement if ground is adultery while complaining party resided in state.

11Other Grounds: Repeated false public charges as to chastity of wife.
12If both parties are residents, then no requirement.
13Other Grounds: (1) Refusal to copulate for six months; (2) membership in religious sect which prohibits copulation.
14Requirement only one year if parties married in state, reside in state, or grounds arose in state.
15Thirty days in county.
16Other Grounds: Wife was a prostitute before marriage and husband did not know this prior to marriage.
17If plaintiff is a resident and grounds for divorce occurred in state, residence requirement waived.
18Also six months in county.

TIME LIMITATIONS ON MARRIAGE AFTER DIVORCE

State	Time Required Between Filing or Service of Divorce Suit and Final Judgment	Time Required Between Interlocutory and Final Judgment of Divorce
ALABAMA	none[2]	none[2]
ALASKA	30 days	none
ARIZONA	20 days	none
ARKANSAS	30 days	none
CALIFORNIA	6 months	none
COLORADO	90 days	none
CONNECTICUT	none	none
DELAWARE	none	1 month
D.C.	none	none
FLORIDA	20 days	none
GEORGIA	none	none
HAWAII	none	none
IDAHO	none	none
ILLINOIS	none	none
INDIANA	none	none
IOWA	none	none[4]
KANSAS	60 days	none[5]
KENTUCKY	none	none
LOUISIANA	none	none[6]
MAINE	none	none
MARYLAND	none	none
MASSACHUSETTS	none	6 months
MICHIGAN	none	none
MINNESOTA	none	none[7]
MISSISSIPPI	none	none
MISSOURI	none	none
MONTANA	none	none[8]
NEBRASKA	none	6 months
NEVADA	none	none
NEW HAMPSHIRE	none	none
NEW JERSEY	none	none
NEW MEXICO	none	none
NEW YORK	none	none
NORTH CAROLINA	none	none
NORTH DAKOTA	none	none
OHIO	none	none
OKLAHOMA	none	none[9]
OREGON	none	none[7]

STATE	Time Required Between Filing or Service of Divorce Suit and Final Judgment	Time Required Between Interlocutory and Final Judgment of Divorce
PENNSYLVANIA	none	none
RHODE ISLAND	none	6-7 months
SOUTH CAROLINA	3 months	none
SOUTH DAKOTA	none	none
TENNESSEE	none	none
TEXAS	none	none [3]
UTAH	none	3 months

STATE	Time Required Between Filing or Service of Divorce Suit and Final Judgment	Time Required Between Interlocutory and Final Judgment of Divorce
VERMONT	none	3 months
VIRGINIA	none	none
WASHINGTON	90 days	none
WEST VIRGINIA	none	none
WISCONSIN	none	6 months
WYOMING	none	none

FOOTNOTES:

[1] Notwithstanding the absence of a time requirement between the interlocutory and the final, there may be a state imposed time limit after the interlocutory judgment in which time either party may notice an appeal of the interlocutory judgment.

[2] Both parties cannot remarry for 60 days after the final judgment.

[3] Both parties must wait 1 year after the final judgment to remarry if the grounds for divorce were cruelty.

[4] Both parties cannot remarry for 1 year after Final unless the Court grants a shorter time.

[5] Both parties must wait for 60 days after the final to marry.

[6] The female must wait 10 months after the final to remarry; the defendant cannot marry the correspondent if the ground for divorce is adultery. This law is probably unconstitutional.

[7] Both parties must wait 6 months after the final to remarry.

[8] Divorce proceedings may be delayed for 90 days if there are minor children and the court feels there is a chance for reconciliation.

[9] At the court's discretion after the final judgment.

GROUNDS FOR ANNULMENT

	IMPOTENCE	WIFE PREGNANT BY ANOTHER MAN	STERILITY	VENEREAL DISEASE	INSANITY	FRAUD	UNDER-AGE	BIGAMY	NOT SOLEMNIZED BY PROPER AUTHORITY	INCEST	FORCE OR DURESS
ALABAMA					✓	✓	✓	✓		✓	✓
ALASKA		✓			✓	✓	✓	✓	✓	✓	✓
ARIZONA	✓				✓					✓	
ARKANSAS					✓	✓	✓	✓		✓	✓
CALIFORNIA	✓				✓	✓	✓	✓		✓	✓
COLORADO					✓	✓	✓	✓		✓	✓
CONNECTICUT						✓		✓	✓	✓	
DELAWARE	✓	✓		✓	✓	✓	✓	✓	✓	✓	✓
D.C.	✓				✓	✓	✓	✓		✓	✓
FLORIDA											
GEORGIA					✓	✓	✓	✓		✓	✓
HAWAII	✓				✓	✓	✓	✓		✓	✓
IDAHO	✓		✓		✓	✓	✓	✓		✓	✓
ILLINOIS		✓			✓	✓	✓	✓		✓	✓
INDIANA					✓	✓	✓	✓		✓	
IOWA	✓				✓		✓	✓		✓	
KANSAS	✓	✓	✓		✓	✓	✓	✓	✓	✓	✓

GROUNDS FOR ANNULMENT

	IMPOTENCE	WIFE PREGNANT BY ANOTHER MAN	STERILITY	VENEREAL DISEASE	INSANITY	FRAUD	UNDER-AGE	BIGAMY	NOT SOLEMNIZED BY PROPER AUTHORITY	INCEST	FORCE OR DURESS
KENTUCKY	✓	✓	✓		✓	✓	✓	✓	✓	✓	✓
LOUISIANA		✓	✓		✓	✓		✓		✓	✓
MAINE					✓			✓	✓	✓	
MARYLAND					✓		✓	✓	✓	✓	
MASSACHUSETTS		✓		✓	✓	✓	✓	✓		✓	
MICHIGAN	✓	✓	✓		✓	✓	✓	✓		✓	✓
MINNESOTA					✓	✓	✓	✓		✓	✓
MISSISSIPPI	✓	✓			✓	✓	✓	✓		✓	✓
MISSOURI					✓			✓		✓	✓
MONTANA	✓				✓	✓	✓	✓		✓	✓
NEBRASKA	✓				✓	✓	✓	✓		✓	✓
NEVADA					✓	✓	✓	✓		✓	
NEW HAMPSHIRE								✓		✓	
NEW JERSEY	✓				✓	✓	✓	✓		✓	✓
NEW MEXICO							✓	✓		✓	
NEW YORK	✓				✓	✓	✓	✓		✓	✓
NORTH CAROLINA	✓				✓		✓	✓		✓	

GROUNDS FOR ANNULMENT

STATE	IMPOTENCE	WIFE PREGNANT BY ANOTHER MAN	STERILITY	VENEREAL DISEASE	INSANITY	FRAUD	UNDER-AGE	BIGAMY	NOT SOLEMNIZED BY PROPER AUTHORITY	INCEST	FORCE OR DURESS
NORTH DAKOTA	✓				✓	✓	✓	✓		✓	✓
OHIO					✓	✓	✓	✓		✓	✓
OKLAHOMA					✓		✓	✓		✓	
OREGON					✓	✓	✓	✓		✓	✓
PENNSYLVANIA					✓		✓	✓		✓	
RHODE ISLAND							✓	✓		✓	
SOUTH CAROLINA					✓		✓	✓		✓	
SOUTH DAKOTA	✓		✓		✓	✓	✓	✓		✓	✓
TENNESSEE					✓	✓	✓	✓		✓	✓
TEXAS	✓				✓	✓	✓	✓		✓	✓
UTAH	✓			✓	✓	✓	✓	✓	✓	✓	✓
VERMONT	✓		✓	✓	✓	✓	✓	✓	✓	✓	✓
VIRGINIA	✓				✓	✓	✓	✓	✓	✓	✓
WASHINGTON						✓	✓	✓		✓	✓
WEST VIRGINIA	✓	✓		✓	✓	✓	✓	✓		✓	✓
WISCONSIN	✓				✓	✓		✓		✓	✓
WYOMING	✓			✓	✓	✓	✓	✓		✓	✓

CHAPTER 7

Adoptions

INTRODUCTION

Adoptions are court orders which make a complete substitution of a parent or parents. After the decree of adoption, the child assumes all of the rights of a natural child of his adopted parent, and the rights and obligations of his former parent or parents are extinguished. When a former father allows his child to be adopted by his ex-wife's new husband, the father loses the right to visit or obtain custody, and he no longer has to support the child. Adopted persons receive legal inheritance rights through their new parents and usually lose any right to inherit through their natural parents—unless specifically named in a will.

No one other than an approved agency of the state may take a fee for arranging an adoption. If an attorney is involved in the adoption, his fee is generated by services in representing the adopting parents, such as the preparation of petitions and consents, aid in the investigation and court appearances. Any payment to natural parents for the adoption of their children is illegal.

Each state has its own laws on adoption, but they are all similar in substance. The states generally provide for four kinds of adoptions: (1) independent adoption of minors, (2) agency adoption of minors, (3) step-parent adoptions and adoption of adults. You must be at least 10 years older than the person you adopt.

All adoptions of children are checked out by investigating arms of the court, such as a welfare department or similar agency. That agency will issue a report of its findings and recommendations, which the court may or may not follow. Adoption is only granted if it is in the child's best interests, and the courts have the final say in this matter.

THE INDEPENDENT ADOPTION OF A MINOR

It is possible to adopt a child directly from the natural parents without any intervening state agency by filing a petition in court which contains the consent of your spouse (if you are married), the child's consent if he is over 12 years old (the age differs among the states) and the consent of the natural parents. If the child is illegitimate (born out of wedlock), only the consent of the natural mother is necessary although a recent U.S. Supreme Court decision has put the necessity of the natural father's consent in question.

After the consent of the natural parents has been signed and filed, it cannot be withdrawn unless there is court approval, except in those few states where the law specifically allows a natural parent to regain the child within a certain time period (New York). The ability of natural parents to withdraw their consent is one of the most important questions in the minds of the adopting parents. Each state has its own law on the subject, but most state courts will only allow a natural parent to withdraw his consent if it is in the best interest of the child. The factors the court will consider are the age of the child, the age of the adopting parents, the age of the natural parents and the general environment for the child in the home of the adopting parents versus the home of the natural parent, and the circumstances which led to the natural parent giving consent. Some states make it easy for natural parents to revoke their consent before a decree of adoption (Michigan, New York and Louisiana); other states make the consents irrevocable (Florida and Illinois). Once a court has made an order or a judgment for adoption, it is virtually impossible for the natural parents to regain custody (except in Louisiana).

No consent from the natural parents is necessary when : (1) the parents have already lost custody of the child to the state, (2) the natural parent has deserted the child without provision for its identification or (3) the natural parent has surrendered the child for adoption or lost it for adoption in another state.

After the adoption petition and consents have been filed and the investigative reports have been considered, the court holds a private hearing with the adopting parties to make a final determination. Once a judge has signed the order, all the filing papers are sealed and a new birth certificate which changes the child's last name to the name of the adopting parents is prepared. The old birth certificate is also sealed from public view.

> Adopting parents always fear the ability of the natural mother to withdraw her consent. The last notorious case involving this subject occurred a few years ago in New York and Florida. A childless couple from New York adopted a young girl in that state. The natural mother had given her consent to the adoption. After the child had lived with her new parents for a few months, the natural mother withdrew her consent, and the New York courts allowed her to do so.

The adopting parents moved from New York to Florida and started a legal action to validate the adoption there. Since Florida does not allow a natural mother to withdraw consent, the Florida courts granted the adoption decree. Florida did not have to give full faith and credit to the New York decision once the adopting parents and the child declared their residence to be Florida, as each state has the jurisdiction to decide the rights of minor children who reside within its borders. The New York order regarding this adoption is still valid, but only in New York. If the child ever returns to New York, she would have to be returned to her natural mother.

THE AGENCY ADOPTION

The only difference between an independent adoption and an agency adoption is that, in the latter case, the custody of the child has already been relinquished to an agency licensed by the state which is responsible for the custody and control of the child. The agency will place him temporarily (six months to one year) in the home of the adopting parents. The agency can retake the child before a petition for adoptions is filed but cannot afterwards unless there is court approval after due notice to all parties.

The agency will also report to the judge on the suitability of the home of the adopting parents. The agency can ask for fees to cover hospital expenses of the natural mother and other administrative costs, but these fees can be waived or reduced at the discretion of the agency.

STEP-PARENT ADOPTIONS OF A MINOR

A step-parent can petition to adopt his step-child. You must have the consent of the natural parent who no longer has physical custody of the child (unless this parent has willfully abandoned the child for one year or more). Of course, the consent of the natural parent with custody is also necessary. Step-parent adoptions are also investigated by the court.

ADULT ADOPTIONS

Most states permit an adult to adopt another adult as his natural child. Only an agreement between the adopting and adopted adults is needed. There is no investigation, but there is a court hearing. A judge must grant an adult adoption if he finds it is in the best interests of the parties and in the public interest.

Bruce, at age 50, was not married and had no children. He received an income of $15,000 a year from a trust left to him by his grandfather. The trust gave him income for his life, and when he died, the entire trust estate would pass to his children. Bruce was fond of a 25 year old woman named Flossie -- so fond that he adopted her. Now when Bruce dies, that trust estate will pass to his child, Flossie.

SETTING ASIDE THE ADOPTION DECREE

Once a judge signs an adoption decree, it is normally considered final. But adopting parents can set aside the decree if the child shows evidence of feeble-mindedness, epilepsy or insanity, and it had these maladies before the adoption, and it was unknown to the adopting parents. They must file to nullify the adoption within five years after the decree. If there is such a petition, the child is represented by the welfare departmnt.

Other grounds for setting aside an adoption decree include gross irregularities in the proceedings or fraud.

STATE ADOPTION LAWS

	COURT WITH JURISDICTION OVER ADOPTION MATTERS	PROBATION PERIOD BEFORE ADOPTION ORDER IS FINAL	AT WHAT AGE IS CHILD'S CONSENT TO ADOPTION NECESSARY?	CAN ADOPTED CHILD INHERIT FROM NATURAL PARENTS WHO DIE WITHOUT A WILL?
ALABAMA	Probate Court	6 months	14	yes
ALASKA	Superior Court	6 months	14	no
ARIZONA	Superior Court	1 year	12	no
ARKANSAS	Probate Court	6 months	14	yes
CALIFORNIA	Superior Court	6 months	12	no
COLORADO	District Court—Juvenile Division	6 months	12	no
CONNECTICUT	District Probate Court	12-13 mos.	14	no
DELAWARE	Supreme Court	1 year	14	no
D.C.	Superior Court	6 months	14	no
FLORIDA	Circuit Court	90 days	12	yes
GEORGIA	Superior Court	6 months	14	no
HAWAII	Circuit Court	1 year	10	no
IDAHO	District Court	none	12	no
ILLINOIS	Circuit Court	6 months	14	yes
INDIANA	County Court with Probate Jurisdiction	1 year	14	yes
IOWA	District Court	1 year	14	no law
KANSAS	Probate Court	30-60 days	14	no

	COURT WITH JURISDICTION OVER ADOPTION MATTERS	PROBATION PERIOD BEFORE ADOPTION ORDER IS FINAL	AT WHAT AGE IS CHILD'S CONSENT TO ADOPTION NECESSARY?	CAN ADOPTED CHILD INHERIT FROM NATURAL PARENTS WHO DIE WITHOUT A WILL?
KENTUCKY	Circuit Court	90 days	12	no
LOUISIANA	Juvenile Court	1 year	16	yes
MAINE	Probate Court	1 year	14	yes
MARYLAND	County Circuit Court[2]	Maximum 1 year	10	no
MASSACHUSETTS	Probate Court	1 year for child under 14	12	no
MICHIGAN	Probate Court	1 year	10	yes
MINNESOTA	Juvenile Court	6 months	14	no
MISSISSIPPI	Chancery Court	6 months	14	no
MISSOURI	Circuit Court—Juvenile Division	9 months	13	no
MONTANA	District Court	6 months	12	yes
NEBRASKA	County Court	6 months	14	no
NEVADA	County District Court	6 months	14	no
NEW HAMPSHIRE	Probate Court	Maximum 1 year	14	no
NEW JERSEY	Superior Court or Juvenile & Domestic Relations Court	1 year	10	no
NEW MEXICO	District Court	6 months or until child is 1 year old	12	no
NEW YORK	Surrogate's Court or Family Court	6 months	14	no
NORTH CAROLINA	Superior Court	1 year	12	no

	COURT WITH JURISDICTION OVER ADOPTION MATTERS	PROBATION BEFORE ADOPTION ORDER IS FINAL	AT WHAT AGE IS CHILD'S CONSENT TO ADOPTION NECESSARY?	CAN ADOPTED CHILD INHERIT FROM NATURAL PARENTS WHO DIE WITHOUT A WILL?
NORTH DAKOTA	District Court	6 months	10	no
OHIO	Probate Court	6 months	12	no
OKLAHOMA	District Court	6 months	12	no law
OREGON	Court with Probate Jurisdiction	6 months	14	no
PENNSYLVANIA	Orphan's Court[3]	6 months	12	no
RHODE ISLAND	Under 18, Family Court Over 18, Probate Court	6 months	14	no
SOUTH CAROLINA	Court of Common Pleas	6 months	no law	no
SOUTH DAKOTA	District County Court	6 months	12	yes
TENNESSEE	Chancery and County Courts	1 year	14	no
TEXAS	District Court	6 months	14	yes
UTAH	District Court	1 year	12	no
VERMONT	Probate Court	6 months	14	yes
VIRGINIA	Chancery Court	6 months	14	no
WASHINGTON	Superior Court	6 months	14	no
WEST VIRGINIA	Juvenile or Circuit Court	6 months	12	yes
WISCONSIN	County Court	6 months	14	no
WYOMING	District Court	6 months	14	no law

FOOTNOTES:

[1] Juvenile Court in Denver
[2] Equity Court in Baltimore
[3] County Court in Philadelphia

CHAPTER 8

Legitimacy and Illegitimacy

The words legitimacy and illegitimacy are throwbacks to the days when people were ashamed to be born out of wedlock. But now these terms have precise legal meanings -- they should not be considered harsh terms to describe human beings who never asked to come into the world.

WHO ARE LEGITIMATES?

Children of a married couple are legitimate even if the marriage is later voided for causes such as bigamy or incest. Children produced by artificial insemination are also considered legitimate. The husband of a woman who bears such a child must support it if he has given his written consent to the insemination.

All children of a married couple who have been living together are presumed to be legitimate. In fact, children born within ten months of a couple's divorce are also presumed to be legitimate.

The question of whether a child is legitimate or illegitimate is important in the following cases:

1. *Residence:* The legal domicile or residence of a child is usually with the father, but when the child is illegitimate, the legal domicile is where the mother resides.

2. *The Right to Inherit:* Where there is no mention in a will about the difference between legitimate and proven illegitimate children, both can share equally in an estate. But if the will says that only legitimate children can inherit, the question is important.

A legitimate child can succeed to property by intestacy (no will) through his mother or his father. An illegitimate child can only take through his mother.

3. *Custody:* Either parent has the right to physical custody of legitimate children. The mother used to be the ony one to win physical custody of an illegitimate, but the U.S. Supreme Court has recently enlarged the rights of fathers in this area.

4. *Paternity Suits and Support:* Illegitimate and legitimate children have the same rights to support from their father. But if he does not acknowledge a child born out of wedlock, then the child (through a legal guardian) can file a suit in order to establish the man's paternity.

Law suits to establish legitimacy or paternity can be brought by the father, the wife, the child or the state, which may be a party if a parent fails to support his child. In many cases of illegitimate births, the state will file a criminal complaint against the alleged father for non-support and then seek to prove paternity and the ability of the man to support the child. In many of these cases the mother is on welfare, and the welfare department urges the prosecution.

Men claiming that they did not father a child may win by proving impotence or sterility. A husband can also show that the period of gestation could preclude him from being the father -- if a woman has a child four months after her marriage and had no sexual intercourse with her husband before the nuptials, the man will win his case.

Blood tests can prove that a man is *not* a father, but they cannot pin point him as the father, as the test can only put a man in a general category of those who could have fathered the child.

Before a paternity suit is tried, the woman may need support from the man, and she may ask the court to award her temporary support -- even before the child is born and before blood tests can be made. If the man later proves he was not the father, the woman does not have to repay this temporary support.

The death of an alleged father before the final outcome on a paternity suit extinguishes the claim. If a father dies after a court judgment, the child's rights survive, and he has a stake in his father's estate for support and inheritance.

LEGITIMATION BY SUBSEQUENT ACTION

The law encourages legitimation of children by the natural father -- even after the child is an adult. The most obvious way to do it is the marriage of the father and mother, and the act of legitimation is valid if the marriage itself is legally valid.

If the natural father publically acknowledges the child as his own and receives him into his family, there is a "legitimation by adoption." There are judicial decisions which allow a natural father to legitimate an unborn child by adoption. If the father goes through this process, then the child is considered legitimate from the time of its birth.

CHAPTER 9

Juveniles

JUVENILE DELINQUENCY AND DEPENDENCY

The states have the responsibility to care for their juveniles. Before the major reforms of child welfare laws, many states treated juvenile offenders in the same manner as adults. They were tried in the same courts and sent to the same prisons. But now all states have separate systems of justice for juveniles.

Acting under the premise of benevolence and the best interests of children, many states provided loose, non-uniform juvenile law procedures and poor detention facilities. Indifferent legislatures and lethargic bureaucrats failed to provide for the growing needs of society. Children could be detained without notice of the charges against them, without a fair hearing and without the representation of a lawyer. There were instances where juveniles were sentenced to long terms in reform schools -- longer than adults receive for the same crimes. The U.S. Supreme Court finally stepped into the picture in 1966 in a case called *In re Gault:*

> John Gault was 15 years old and on six months probation when he was caught making indecent phone calls. The Arizona Juvenile Court did not give adequate notice to Gault's parents of a hearing; it did not give detailed charges, and it did not provide him with a lawyer. Gault was committed to the state reformatory until he was 21 -- this amounted to a six year sentence for an offense which was punishable by a fine of $5 to $50 or not over two months imprisonment for adults. The Arizona Supreme Court affirmed this decision on the basis that the state could deny due process guarantees because of its compelling interest in the welfare of its children. The U.S. Supreme Court reversed this decision, stating that juveniles and their parents have the right to due process in juvenile court.

The U.S. Supreme Court has set national minimal standards for due process and fairness for juvenile delinquency cases:

1. A juvenile and his parents or guardian must be given written notice of all specific charges or allegations at the earliest possible time and in advance of any hearings.
2. Parent and child must be notified of the right to be represented by an attorney. If they are poor, counsel must be provided by the state.
3. A juvenile does not have to testify or incriminate himself.
4. He has the right to confront and cross-examine witnesses.
5. Guilt must be proved beyond a reasonable doubt.
6. Not all juveniles must be tried in juvenile court, but before transfer to an adult criminal court, the juvenile court must give the minor a hearing to determine if there are adequate reasons for ordering the transfer.
7. There is no right to a jury trial in juvenile court, nor does the minor have a right to bail.

PRINCIPLES OF JUVENILE JUSTICE

Juvenile delinquency and dependency laws should be based on the following principles:

(1) That the juvenile court should not intervene in the parent-child relationship unless it has a sound basis in fact for its action.
(2) That every child and his parents have a right to a fair hearing on the allegations which have brought the minor before the juvenile court, and all parties should have their legal and constitutional rights protected.
(3) That the juvenile court should protect children from unnecessary separation from their parents, whether on a temporary or on a permanent basis.
(4) That the juvenile court law should have uniform application throughout the state, upon clearly defined procedures.
(5) That no child should be taken into custody or detained without reasonable cause for believing that he has committed a delinquent offense, has exhibited tendencies, or is an abandoned or neglected child, and that such detention is necessary for his protection or that of the community.
(6) That the juvenile court should have reasonable assurance that meaningful rehabilitation services will be provided when a wardship is imposed for delinquent behavior or child neglect.
(7) That the juvenile court should exploit the clinical knowledge and skills of treatment specialists and should increase the status of probation departments.

JUVENILE COURT JURISDICTION

Juvenile courts only hear cases which involve (1) dependent children and (2) children who are delinquents or have committed crimes. In most states minors who fall in the first category are called dependents of the court, and those in the second group are wards of the court.

A juvenile court may place a minor within its control as a dependent child if it finds one of the following:

1. He needs parental care and has no parent or guardian willing or able to exercise control;
2. He is destitute or lacks such necessities as a home or food;
3. The home is unfit because of parental neglect, cruelty or depravity; or
4. The child is physically dangerous to others because of a mental or physical disorder or abnormality.

A court can make a minor a ward if it finds that:

1. He has persistently refused to obey the reasonable directions of his parents or guardian;
2. He is an habitual truant from school;
3. He is in danger of leading an idle, disreputable, lewd or immoral life; or
4. He has committed a crime or has failed to obey an order of the juvenile court.

TEMPORARY CUSTODY OF CHILDREN

A peace officer may take a minor into custody without a warrant if he believes that the child is involved in conduct which could make him a dependent or ward of the court. After the arrest the peace officer may release the child unconditionally or on a written promise to appear (like a traffic citation) or deliver him to a probation officer. The child must be immediately informed of his constitutional rights, and the parents must be immediately informed.

There is no bail for a minor but he should be released to his parents unless he is in need of good parental care, is destitute, has an unfit home, needs to be detained for the protection of others or is likely to run away.

Juvenile detention halls must segregate dependent children from wards and they should segregate the older children from the young.

If a child is detained for any of these causes, a petition should be filed to declare the child a ward or dependent of the court. There should be an immediate hearing to tell the minor and his parents of the charges and the reasons for filing the petition. There is also another advisement of the constitutional rights. (This procedure is similar to the arraignment and advice of constitutional rights which occurs in adult criminal proceedings.). If a petition is filed, a hearing before a judge or referee should be held within 30 days. If the child is in custody, the hearing should be even sooner.

THE HEARING

Hearings are usually divided into two parts. The first part deals with the grounds for the petition. That is, should the child be placed under the control of the court as a dependent or a ward?

If there are sufficient grounds to make a minor a dependent or a ward, then the hearing will go into a second phase which is called the disposition phase. If a child is declared a dependent of the court, there would be appropriate orders for the minor's care, custody and support. This includes placement with the natural parents, foster parents or an institution.

A ward of the court may be placed on probation under the supervision of a probation officer or be put in a county juvenile home, ranch, camp or other youth correctional center. The court can also certify a minor to stand trial as an adult if he is incorrigible and charged with a felony. Courts seldom do this to anyone under 16.

Parents or guardians still must support a child who has been declared a dependent or ward. They also may be liable to pay for legal services and probation supervision.

Juvenile court records should be sealed from public view and made unavailable for inspection.

CONTRIBUTING TO THE DELINQUENCY OF A MINOR

Any act by an adult which could make a minor a dependent or ward of the court is a misdemeanor commonly known as contributing to the delinquency of a minor. The crime can be committed by strangers, relatives and parents. It could include acts like serving children alcohol or engaging in sex with them.

JUVENILE RIGHTS AND LIABILITIES

The act which ostensibly requires the most thought and maturity from a citizen is voting. Now that the Constitution gives 18 year olds the right to vote, one would think that a person would reach the age of majority (legal adulthood) at 18. Not so—each state has its own ideas on the age when a person can drink alcohol, execute valid contracts, write wills, hold property, receive financial support from parents, go to school and legally consent to sexual intercourse.

A minor cannot maintain a lawsuit in his own name for personal injuries or any other types of damage. In order to sue, he must have a guardian ad litem (guardian just for the purposes of the lawsuit). The statute of limitations for bringing most lawsuits does not start to run against a minor until he has reached the age of majority.

Every state requires its resident children between certain ages to attend school, and the states are obligated to provide elementary and high schools for their children. It is the obligation of the parents to see that the child attends school regularly. Habitual truancy can make him a dependent or a ward of the juvenile court.

School officials have the right to discipline children, as long as it is reasonable and within school district and state policies. The schools may expel students for good legal cause.

Parents must support their children until they reach the age of majority or are emancipated from the home. Emancipation occurs when a child marries or permanently leaves home for work.

The states have set minimum ages and maximum daily hours for children to work, as well as the types of employment allowed. Parents are entitled to their minor child's earnings, but if a child wins a court judgment, it cannot be taken by the parents; it must be kept in a separate account which can only be tapped for good cause or when the child reaches majority.

If a minor receives property through a will, it does not belong to the parents. It must be put in safe keeping for the child until he reaches majority. Parents who lack needed funds can dip into this property to pay for the child's unusual expenses. (college tuition, braces, nose jobs, etc.) The parents usually must petition a court to do this.

All states have a "Gifts to Minors Act" to deal with gifts of valuable property to children. The essential feature of it provides for a custodian of the gift until the child reaches adulthood. The custodian can be the child's parents, guardians or the donor of the gift. The custodian manages the property for the minor's benefit without court supervision. He has discretion to disburse the property for the support, education and benefit of the child. The custodian must deal with property prudently - if he is negligent, the minor can sue him for a loss of property. The custodian is entitled to some compensation for his work.

A minor cannot be held responsible for a contract except for an item necessary for life or unless he ratifies the contract after he has reached the age of majority. A minor's parents are not responsible for his contractual debts except for necessities of life (medical bills, groceries, etc.)

The felony crime of statutory rape is committed when a male has sex with a girl under a certain age, which differs among the states. The age of legal consent is 16 on military bases. The state does not take into account parental consent or the girl's maturity. It also makes no difference if the girl was the aggressor.

The state has much more control over the lives of juveniles than it has over the lives of adults. For instance, curfew laws which forbid juveniles from being on the streets without parental control after a certain hour can be enforced anytime, but they can only be enforced in rare emergencies against adults. Juveniles often react bitterly to these types of laws because they are arbitrary — they do not take into account individual maturity. But if individual maturity and intelligence were the standard, then thousands of adults would not be allowed to vote, drink liquor, or walk the streets after 11:00 p.m.

STATE JUVENILE LAWS[1]

(m.) = MALE (f.) = FEMALE	AGE WHEN A PERSON:				JUVENILE DELINQUENCY LAWS NO LONGER APPLY AT AGE:	AGE OF CONSENT TO SEXUAL INTERCOURSE (STATUTORY RAPE)
	REACHES THE AGE OF MAJORITY	CAN ENTER INTO A CONTRACT	CAN WRITE A WILL	CAN NOMINATE A GUARDIAN		
ALABAMA	21 18, if married	21[4]	18	14	18	16
ALASKA	19[2]	19	19	14	18	19
ARIZONA	18	18	18	14	18	18
ARKANSAS	21(m.);18(f.)	21(m.);18(f.)	18	NO LAW	18	16
CALIFORNIA	18	18	18	14	18	18
COLORADO	21	21	18	14	17	18
CONNECTICUT	18	18	18	14	16	16
DELAWARE	18	18	18	14	18	7
D.C.	21	21[3]	21(m.);18(f.)	14	18	16
FLORIDA	21	21[3]	18	NO LAW	17	18
GEORGIA	18	18	14	NO LAW	17	14
HAWAII	18	18	18	16	18	16
IDAHO	18	18	18	14	18	18
ILLINOIS	18	18	18	14	17(m.);18(f.)	16
INDIANA	21	21	18	14	18	16
IOWA	19	19[7]	19	14	18	16
KANSAS	18	18	18	NO LAW	16(m.);18(f.)	16
KENTUCKY	18	18	18	14	18	18
LOUISIANA	18	18	16	NO LAW	17	17

(m.) = MALE (f.) = FEMALE	AGE WHEN A PERSON:					AGE OF CONSENT TO SEXUAL INTERCOURSE (STATUTORY RAPE)
	REACHES THE AGE OF MAJORITY	CAN ENTER INTO A CONTRACT	CAN WRITE A WILL	CAN NOMINATE A GUARDIAN	JUVENILE DELINQUENCY LAWS NO LONGER APPLY AT AGE:	
MAINE	18	18[3]	18[3]	14	17	16
MARYLAND	21	21	18	NO LAW	18[6]	16
MASSACHUSETTS	21	21	18	14	17	18
MICHIGAN	18	18	18	14	17	16
MINNESOTA	21	21	21	14	18	18
MISSISSIPPI	21	21	21	14	17	18
MISSOURI	21	21	18	14	18	16
MONTANA	18	18	18	14	18	16
NEBRASKA	19	19[3]	19[3]	14	18	16
NEVADA	21(m.);18(f.)	21(m.);18(f.)	18	14	18	16
NEW HAMPSHIRE	21	21	18[3]	14	18	16
NEW JERSEY	18	18	18	14	18	16
NEW MEXICO	18	18	18	14	18	16
NEW YORK	21	21[3]	18	14	16(m.);18(f.)	18
NORTH CAROLINA	18	18	18	NO LAW	16	16
NORTH DAKOTA	18	18	18	14	18	18
OHIO	21	21(m.);18(f.)	18	14	18	16
OKLAHOMA	18	18	18	14	16(m.);18(f.)	18
OREGON	21	21[7]	18	14	18	18
PENNSYLVANIA	18	18	18	14	18	16
RHODE ISLAND	18	18	18	14	18	18

(m.) = MALE (f.) = FEMALE	AGE WHEN A PERSON:				JUVENILE DELINQUENCY LAWS NO LONGER APPLY AT AGE:	AGE OF CONSENT TO SEXUAL INTERCOURSE (STATUTORY RAPE)
	REACHES THE AGE OF MAJORITY	CAN ENTER INTO A CONTRACT	CAN WRITE A WILL	CAN NOMINATE A GUARDIAN		
SOUTH CAROLINA	21	21	21[3]	NO LAW	17	16
SOUTH DAKOTA	21(m.);18(f.)[3]	21(m.);18(f.)	18	14	18	18
TENNESSEE	18	18	18	NO LAW	18	18
TEXAS	21	21[3]	18[3]	14	17(m.);18(f.)	18
UTAH	21(m.);18(f.)	21(m.);18(f.)	18	14	18	18
VERMONT	18	18	18	14	16	16
VIRGINIA	18	18	18	14	18	16
WASHINGTON	18[5]	18	18[3]	14	18	18
WEST VIRGINIA	18	18	18	14	18	16
WISCONSIN	18	18	18	14	18	18
WYOMING	21	21	21	14	18	18

FOOTNOTES:

[1] Since 18 year-olds can now vote, many states are changing their laws pertaining to juveniles to give them adult status at age 18.

[2] A married woman is an adult.

[3] A married person is an adult.

[4] 18; if married.

[5] A woman married to a man over 21 is considered an adult.

[6] In Baltimore; age 16.

[7] Earlier; if married.

CHAPTER 10

Abortion

PRE-1973

Prior to a Supreme Court decision in 1973, abortions were regulated entirely by the individual states. Strict anti-abortion laws had been upheld as constitutional on the grounds that the states had a compelling interest to protect and preserve society—even against the argument that the woman has a right to control the destiny of her body. Most of these strict laws were adopted when any operation was dangerous, and lawmakers wanted to protect the lives of pregnant women. This thinking proved counter productive, since abortion statutes forced women to often put their lives in the hands of quacks who sometimes killed and maimed them. Although medical science markedly increased the safety of the operation, most states did not liberalize their abortion laws.

The strictest abortion laws only allowed the operation when "it was necessary to preserve the life of the mother." By the beginning of 1973, 31 states were still enforcing such laws.

Three states allowed a woman to obtain an abortion on demand from a qualified physician without stating specific reasons (Alaska, Hawaii and Washington). Two of these states only allowed an abortion during the first trimester of pregnancy, and two allowed only their legal residents to get the abortion.

The other 15 states had liberalized the grounds for an abortion. They included rape, incest, substantial risk to the physical and mental health of the mother, and possible mutilation or birth defects. These laws also regulated the time in which an abortion could be accomplished and set residence requirements.

THE 1973 SUPREME COURT DECISION

In 1973 the Supreme Court, by a seven-to-two majority, made a momentous decision which effectively invalidated every state abortion statute. This decision allows any woman, including a minor, to obtain an abortion on demand from a qualified physician during the first two trimesters of pregnancy. The decision to abort lies strictly with the woman. The father of the fetus has no legal control whatsoever in most states.

The decision was based on the Court's belief that a woman has a constitutional right over the destiny of her body - a right which is not specifically enumerated in the Constitution, but implicitly reserved by the language of the Ninth Amendment:

> "The enumeration in the Constitution, of certain rights, shall not be construed to deny or disparage others retained by the people."

The Court recognized the right of the states to protect its inhabitants, but it felt that the zone of privacy guaranteed by the Ninth Amendment was paramount in importance to any state interest during the first two trimesters of pregnancy. The state abortion laws were constitutional when they were adopted in the 19th century because of the inherent medical dangers in abortion. But modern medicine has changed so drastically since then that the compelling state interest was no longer present.

The Supreme Court divided the right to an abortion into trimesters of pregnancy:

1. First trimester—A woman can now get an abortion upon demand from a qualified physician at any time during the first trimester of pregnancy without state interference. Safe abortions can now be accomplished during the first trimester in the doctor's office, and the Court was clear in stating that the decision on where to abort during this period is strictly between the woman and her doctor.

2. Second trimester—During the second trimester there is a little more danger to the operation. Therefore, the court allows the states to regulate the safety of the operation by demanding that it be performed in a hospital.

3. Third trimester—The Court recognized that the fetus is viable during the last trimester. Therefore, the states do have a compelling right to preserve and protect its life during this period, and laws which only allow an abortion when it is absolutely necessary to preserve the life of the mother are still valid and effective then.

During the first two trimesters the Supreme Court did not recognize the viability of the fetus or the so-called legal rights of an unborn child.

Existing state abortion laws are only invalidated as they pertain to qualified, licensed physicians. Non-physicians still cannot perform the operation.

The decision does not force a doctor to perform an abortion on a patient who makes such a demand on him. Some physicians have religious scruples against abortion and may refuse to abort as long as the patient is not in imminent danger.

CHAPTER 11

Taking Care of Others

GUARDIANSHIPS

A guardian is someone appointed to take care of the person and/or the property of another individual. One may be the guardian of a minor or an adult who is unable to care for himself.

In order to secure a guardianship, you must petition for a court order. Most states allow a child over the age of 14 to nominate or concur in the nomination of his guardian. Notice of the proceedings and notice of the date of the guardianship hearing must be sent to the minor or the incompetent and to all other interested parties including parents and other relatives. The court will entertain any objections to the petition at the time of the hearing, and after weighing the evidence, it will make an appropriate order.

At the hearing, the person seeking to become guardian must show that he is the proper individual to do this and that a guardianship is in order. In the case of a minor, the court appoints a guardian to serve in the child's best interests. If a non-parent petitions the court to appoint him a guardian of a child who already has a parent, the parents must be proved unfit.

You can make a provision in your will that certain persons be guardians of your children if they are left orphans. These directions weigh heavily in a court's determination, but they are not absolutely binding. The court will also consider the preference of the child and the qualifications of potential guardians.

> Jake and Shirley, a married couple, made out wills when their children were 14, 3 and 2. Jake wanted his parents to be guardians of the children; Shirley wanted her parents to be the guardians. Ten years later Jake and Shirley died in a plane crash. Both sets of grandparents petitioned to be appointed guardians of the two minor children; so did the oldest child who was then 24 and married. The court recognized that the wills were made 10 years earlier when circumstances were different. It awarded the guardianship to the oldest child because it was in the best interests of the minor children.

In order to impose a guardianship on an incompetent adult, the court must find that he is, by reason of old age, disease, weakness of mind, or other causes, unable to properly take care of himself or his property and is likely to be deceived or defrauded. Incompetency does not mean insanity, only an inability to take care of one's affairs. More than just poor business judgment must be shown. An alleged incompetent has a right to testify in his own behalf to show that he is capable of rationality and intelligent action. Oddly enough, an incompetent does not have a right to petition the court to impose a guardianship upon himself and his estate.

When a court appoints a guardian, it normally requires him to post a bond every year to protect the ward. The guardian is considerd a fiduciary; that is, he is liable for the preservation of estate property, and he must deal with it in a reasonable and prudent manner. A guardian has the power to sell property, but real estate can only be sold with court confirmation. A guardian is entitled to reimbursement for any expenses, and he is also entitled to compensation for his services. Within three months of the decree of guardianship, the guardian must file an inventory of the ward's estate and receive court approval of it. There must be an accounting a year later and when the guardianship terminates. The court must approve a final accounting.

A guardianship may be terminated after a minor reaches majority or when he marries. And the guardianship of an adult is discharged upon the restoration of competency. The ward or the guardian may petition the court for a hearing to make this determination.

A guardian may be removed for 1) waste, mismanagement or abuse of trust; 2) failure to file an inventory or timely accounting; 3) incapacity of the guardian; 4) gross immorality; 5) conflict of interest; 6) conviction of a felony by the guardian; 7) bankruptcy of the guardian; 8) the guardianship is no longer necessary.

CONSERVATORSHIPS

Many states have adopted a system of conservatorships which is an alternative to guardianship of incompetent adults (there is no provision for a conservatorship for minors). A conservatorship may be the preferred method of handling the estate because the court does not have to make a finding of incompetency. It protects the dignity of a person with failing faculties who does not consider himself incompetent. The terms "conservator" and "conservatee" are used instead of "guardian" and "ward". A conservatee who needs help in the management of his affairs can nominate a conservator - there is no provision for this type of nomination in guardianships.

Courts order conservatorships if they find that the proposed conservatee cannot properly care for himself or manage his property. It should be orderd if it is in the best interest of the parties. In the case where different persons are petitioning the court to be named conservators, the court should choose the individual who will act in the best interests of the conservatee.

There are substantially the same requirements in conservatorships as there are in guardianships in regard to notice of proceedings and hearings, powers of conservators, inventories, accountings, reimbursement and compensation and discharge and removal.

POWER OF ATTORNEY

A power of attorney is a document which authorizes another person to act in your behalf in personal financial matters. A *general* power of attorney authorizes a person to act in all of your personal financial transactions and affairs; a special power of attorney only authorizes him to act on specific matters such as maintaining a particular piece of property or signing checks for a limited amount of money or time. Powers of attorney must contain the following: (1) the name of the person entrusted with the power, (2) the powers and responsibilities given to that person, (3) the signature of the person giving away the power, and (4) a notarization of his signature. The signature must be the only one of the person giving the power; if he goes by another name, nicknames, or initials, these alternatives must appear on the document.

Powers of attorney are simple, inexpensive documents to prepare, and no court supervision is necessary for the person holding the power. The key element in signing a power is trust—you have got to trust the person to whom you give authority because he or she may have unbridled use of your assets. However, any misuse or embezzlement by a person holding a power of attorney can be a crime and subject to a civil action for return of the money.

JOINT TENANCY BANK ACCOUNTS

Another way of taking care of another is establishing a joint tenancy bank account. Each joint tenant (there may be more than two) has unbridled use of the bank account. There are no time limits, no need for notaries and no set responsibilities. Again the key factor is trusting the other joint tenants. Another factor to consider is that if one joint tenant dies, the other joint tenants automatically are entitled to the dead tenant's share of the account; you cannot pass this money on with a will.

Any of the tenants to this bank account can draw on it without the others' signatures. This is not true with other kinds of joint tenancy ownership.

The joint tenancy of a safe deposit box entitles all of the joint tenants to access to the box, but it does not give them equal ownership to the contents in it.

HELPING THE MENTALLY ILL

The term "insanity" has many definitions and degrees. One may be sane enough to walk the streets, but not sane enough to sign contracts or wills. Then again, one may be sane enough to enter into contracts, but so insane that he cannot be held responsible for a crime. And, too, the several categories of mental illness require different treatments — what is good for the drug addict is obviously not good for the feeble-minded.

The states regulate the care and treatment of the mentally ill. The only federal requirement is that the states deal with the mentally ill "fairly" and "reasonably" — very loose terms indeed. These state powers are awesome when you consider that it is easier to detain a mentally ill person against his will than it is to hold someone accused of a crime. There is no right to bail in a mental institution.

In every case where a family member or the state is attempting to *involuntarily* detain or commit a person for mental illness, exact procedures of state law must be followed to the letter. These state laws and the quality of treatment facilities varies considerably. Generally the states have procedures for emergency, short term hospitalization or detention. This short term detention can be a direct placement by a peace officer, or it can result by a judge's order after he has reviewed a family member's or a close friend's petition.

After the short term hospitalization, the states have procedures for extended detention. Normally, medical certificates are required, and judges must make orders for the commitment. The states allow the mentally disturbed person to appear at the hearing and representation by legal counsel. Some states even allow jury trials, and they require the unanimous verdict of the jury for any extended involuntary commitment.

The states should also have some discharge procedure, either administrative or judicial, to allow for those mental patients who no longer need treatment or detention but who are being held by state hospital authorities.

FORM FOR GENERAL POWER OF ATTORNEY

KNOW ALL MEN BY THESE PRESENTS:

THAT I,_____of the City of_____, County of_____,

State of_____ do by these presents appoint _____

of the City of _____ , County of _____ State of _____

        as my attorney in fact, for me and in my name and for my use and benefit to demand, sue for, collect, and receive all such sums of money, debts, dues, accounts, legacies, bequests, interests, dividends, annuities, and demands whatsoever, as are now or shall hereafter become due, owing, payable or belonging to me and have, use, and take all lawful ways and means in my name or otherwise for the recovery thereof by attachment, arrest, or otherwise, and to compromise and agree for the same, and to make and deliver discharges for the same for me and in my name; to contract for, purchase, receive, and take lands, tenements and hereditaments, and accept the seisin and possession of all lands, and all deeds and other assurances in the law therefor, and to lease, let, sell, release, convey, mortgage, convey by way of deed of trust, and hypothecate lands, tenements, and hereditaments upon such terms and conditions, and under such covenants as he/she shall think fit; also to bargain for, buy, sell, mortgage, hypothecate, and in any way and every way and manner deal in and with goods, wares, and merchandise, chooses in action, and other property in possession or in action, and to do every kind of business of what nature or kind soever; and also for me and in my name, and as my act and deed to make, sign, seal, execute, acknowledge, and deliver deeds, leases and assignments of lease, covenants, indentures, agreements, mortgages, deeds of trust and reconveyances thereunder, hypothecations, bottomries, charter-parties, bills of lading, bills, bonds, notes, receipts, evidences of debt, releases and satisfaction of mortgage, judgments, and other debts, and such other instruments in writing of whatever kind and nature as may be necessary, convenient, or proper in the premises including assignments of accounts receivable, notices of the expected assignments of such accounts, and cancellation of such notices; also, in case of loss ny fire, or otherwise, to adjust insurance losses.

        GIVING unto my said attorney full power to perform every act and thing which he/she may think necessary to be done in and about the premises, as fully to all intents and purposes as I might or could do if personally present with full power of substitution and revocation hereby ratifying and confirming all that my said attorney shall lawfully do or cause to be done by virtue of these presents.

        IN WITNESS WHEREOF I have hereunto set my hand the_____day of _____

one thousand nine hundred and_____ .

Signed and Delivered in the Presence of

_____

_____

                                         _____
                                                Signature Line

                       Notary Public Seal Goes Here

CHAPTER 12

You Can't Take It With You — Wills and Estate Planning

INTRODUCTION

As if death were not difficult enough to face, we also must face the problem of distribution of property after our passing. This chapter will discuss wills - their need, their requirements, contesting them and their alternatives. It will also discuss the probate of an estate including executors, attorneys and death taxes. This whole general area is commonly called "estate planning".

The public has come to fear the word "probate" because they believe it will involve them in long, arduous and expensive court procedures. In most cases, this is untrue. All states have probate courts which are specifically authorized to oversee the estates of those who are unable to care for their financial affairs - the dead, the incompetent and minors. This chapter will only deal with the deceased.

AFTER DEATH BUT BEFORE PROBATE

Death is the uninvited guest who often arrives so suddenly that the survivors do not have time to plan a funeral properly. Even when there has been a long illness, the family may be so stunned that rational planning is impossible. Clergymen, close friends or a family attorney can help the family by taking charge of the funeral plans.

The deceased may leave instructions on the placement of his body, and these instructions can be followed even if his will is invalid. He may want his body to be donated to a medical school or given to science, and this wish is legally binding on heirs, although many hospitals are loathe to accept a body if the relatives strenuously object. If the deceased leaves no instructions, then his relatives have a right to donate the body. If it lies unclaimed, the state must either bury it or give it to science.

Once the cause of death has been determined, the remains must either be cremated, buried or donated to science. If a person dies of natural causes under the treatment of a doctor, no autopsy is necessary. However, if he dies under mysterious or unexplained circumstances, an autopsy must be performed, and a medical examiner or coroner must determine the date and probable cause of death. When cause of death is determined, a death certificate will be issued. It is most important to obtain copies of this certificate for disposal of the body and later to commence a probate or distribute the deceased's property.

Once the decision has been made on burial, funeral arrangements must be made. The law only requires that a body be buried in some sort of casket; it does not require expensive embalming or preservation of the body in embellished caskets.

Choosing an honest mortician is important at this point. Check with a clergyman or friends who have been through similar experiences. Beware of funeral parlors which attempt to sell unnecessary frills through emotion and guilt. All estimates and contracts should be put in writing for the protection of the bereaved, bill-paying family.

Cremation is also available, but it is often just as expensive as burial. Beware of hidden costs and note that there are stricter laws governing cremation.

Burial expenses are the first ones paid from a deceased's estate. They may be covered by social security, veteran's or union benefits or private insurance plans.

Most probates occur after the body has been disposed. In those cases where a person has disappeared under mysterious circumstances, the family must wait for a certain period of time to officially declare their relative dead and distribute his estate. Most states make a family wait from five to seven years (Louisiana is the only one which sets the time period at 30 years).

INTESTACY–DYING WITHOUT A WILL

If a person does not leave a will or any alternate plan for the orderly passing of his property after death, then his property passes intestate—which means the property goes to his closest heirs. The order in which the heirs take the property is determined by state laws (laws of intestate succession). If there is no will and no heirs, the property passes to the state. Even if the property passes intestate, a probate court oversees its administration. Dying intestate (without a will) is inadvisable as it may cost more to administer an estate without a will, and in many cases the property will go to a person you would not have wanted to receive it.

> Mary died in an automobile accident at the age of 30. She left $10,000 and was survived by her father, two brothers, and three nephews. Although Mary loved her father, she often stated that when she died, she wanted her property to go to her brothers or to their children. However, since Mary died without leaving a will, all of her property must pass to her father, as he was her closest

living relative at the time of her death. If she had been married or had children, they would have taken her property ahead of the father. If Mary's father had predeceased her, then her brothers would have shared equally in her estate.

DEATH TAXES

Estate and inheritance taxes are of major concern to persons planning their estates. There is no federal estate tax on the first $60,000 and the exemption is $120,000 if the property passes to a spouse. The minimum federal estate tax is 3% when the "net" estate value is over $60,000. The maximum rate is 55% for $10,000,000 or more. (Net means the value of the estate less personal exemptions and deductions for burial and funeral fees, creditor's claims, attorney's fees and executor's fees.)

State inheritance taxes are payable to the state in which the deceased was a resident at the time of his death — not necessarily the state where he died. If the person had two homes, his family would be smart to choose the state where the inheritance tax was the smallest as his official residence.

Every state except Nevada has some provision for inheritance taxes. The amount depends not only on the size of the estate but also upon the relationship of the person receiving the estate to the deceased. The tax is much lower for a surviving wife or children than it is for distant relatives or friends.

The primary concern of any person planning an estate should be to insure that the persons whom he wants to share in his estate after death do just that. After this primary objective is accomplished, then the matter of the avoidance of unnecessary estate and inheritance taxes can be dealt with.

REQUIREMENTS FOR A VALID WILL

A valid will is one which has been signed in the presence of independent witnesses. (The number of witnesses varies among the states.) Independent means that the witnesses cannot share or benefit from the will. The testator must demonstrate that he knows the significance of executing his will and that he is doing so free from duress, undue influence and fraud. (A testator is a man who leaves a will at the time of his death; the female counterpart is called a testatrix; for purposes of brevity, just the masculine form will be used.)

Holographic wills—that is, wills entirely in the handwriting of the testator—are also valid in most states. However, there is a requirement that a holographic will must be completely in the handwriting of the testator; there can be no typewritten or printed material in the body of the will. The holographic will must also be signed and dated, although the signature and date can appear in the body and do not have to appear at the end in any logical order. No witnesses are necessary.

Most states allow for the validity of oral wills to distribute very small amounts of property. The amounts of property are so small that you should not even consider an oral will as a valid way to distribute property after death.

Lately there has been a do-it-yourself craze in this field of estate planning. A non-lawyer can draw his own valid will but, in many cases, this course of action is ill-advised and imprudent. Much depends on the size and nature of an estate; the relationship of the testator to his heirs and other beneficiaries; specific conditions which a testator wants in his will and any changes in the law which might prejudice the validity of the self-drawn will. Another consideration is that attorneys charge very little for the drafting of a simple will, and it is worth a modest fee to insure that the job is done correctly.

Marvin had a simple will which included bequests to his wife, two children, and two close friends. Prior to his death, one of his children and one of his friends died. When Marvin died, what happened to the bequests which were made to the predeceased friend and child? Did the property pass to Marvin's other beneficiaries or to the respective spouses, heirs or estates of the predeceased beneficiaries? If you do not know the answer to this common problem, you had better consult an attorney before executing your will.

Leroy was married and had two children, and he had a valid will dated January 27, 1950. In June of 1959, Leroy had an argument with his wife and children and left home. Soon thereafter he wrote a letter to his close friend in which he described the argument and the enmity which he had for his family. He also stated in the letter that he wanted his friend to have all of his estate after he died. The letter was dated, completely in the handwriting of Leroy, and signed by him. This letter was upheld as a valid holographic will, superceding the formal will of 1950. Therefore, Leroy's friend inherited all of his estate over the objections of Leroy's wife and children.

One may wonder why he should pay an attorney to draw a will when it is so easy to do it yourself. The answer may be found in the fact that the above case was decided by a California Court of Appeal. It probably cost Leroy's friend and beneficiary thousands of dollars for the services of an attorney to represent him and to obtain the Court's validation of this poorly drawn letter. If Leroy had paid an attorney $25 for a simple will, all of this litigation expense could have been avoided.

Once a will is properly executed and witnessed, it is valid until the date of the testator's death. A will can be destroyed, revoked, amended and altered, but it does not expire.

Nevertheless, it is a good idea to upgrade or change a will when circumstances require it. Circumstances of death or disaffection of beneficiary can change the intent of a testator.

It is also a good idea to keep a properly executed and witnessed will in a safe

FEDERAL ESTATE TAX RATES

Amount of taxable estate (1)	Tax on amount in (1) (2)	Amount of taxable estate in excess of (1) but not in excess of (3) in (3)	taxed at rate shown in (4) (4)
$ 0	$ 0	$ 5,000	3%
5,000	150	10,000	7%
10,000	500	20,000	11%
20,000	1,600	30,000	14%
30,000	3,000	40,000	18%
40,000	4,800	50,000	22%
50,000	7,000	60,000	25%
60,000	9,500	100,000	28%
100,000	20,700	250,000	30%
250,000	65,700	500,000	32%
500,000	145,700	750,000	35%
750,000	233,200	1,000,000	37%
1,000,000	325,700	1,250,000	39%
1,250,000	423,200	1,500,000	42%
1,500,000	528,200	2,000,000	45%
2,000,000	753,200	2,500,000	49%
2,500,000	998,200	3,000,000	53%
3,000,000	1,263,200	3,500,000	56%
3,500,000	1,543,200	4,000,000	59%
4,000,000	1,838,200	5,000,000	63%
5,000,000	2,468,200	6,000,000	67%
6,000,000	3,138,200	7,000,000	70%
7,000,000	3,838,200	8,000,000	73%
8,000,000	4,568,200	10,000,000	76%
10,000,000	6,088,200		77%

Column (1) shows the amount of the taxable estate; that is, the total gross estate less all deductions and an exemption of $60,000.

Column (2) shows the estate tax on the corresponding taxable estate in Column (1).

Column (4) shows the rate applicable to any amount in excess of the taxable estate shown in Column (1) but not in excess of the taxable estate shown in Column (3).

-114-

FEDERAL GIFT TAX RATES

Amount of taxable gifts (A)	Tax on amount in (A) (B)	Amounts of taxable gifts in excess of (A) but not excess of (C) is taxed at rate shown in (D) (C)	(D)
$ 0	$ 0	$ 5,000	2¼%
5,000	112.50	10,000	5¼%
10,000	375	20,000	8¼%
20,000	1,200	30,000	10½%
30,000	2,250	40,000	13½%
40,000	3,600	50,000	16½%
50,000	5,250	60,000	18¾%
60,000	7,125	100,000	21%
100,000	15,525	250,000	22½%
250,000	49,275	500,000	24%
500,000	109,275	750,000	26¼%
750,000	174,900	1,000,000	27¾%
1,000,000	244,275	1,250,000	29¼%
1,250,000	317,400	1,500,000	31½%
1,500,000	396,150	2,000,000	33¾%
2,000,000	564,900	2,500,000	36¾%
2,500,000	748,650	3,000,000	39¾%
3,000,000	947,400	3,500,000	42%
3,500,000	1,157,300	4,000,000	44¼%
4,000,000	1,378,650	5,000,000	47¼%
5,000,000	1,851,150	6,000,000	50¼%
6,000,000	2,353,650	7,000,000	52½%
7,000,000	2,878,650	8,000,000	54¾%
8,000,000	3,426,150	10,000,000	57%
10,000,000	4,566,150	————	57¾%

The amounts in Column A are net after all deductions and exemptions.

and easily accessible place. If a will is inadvertently destroyed or cannot be found, the best and most well-thought-out estate plan will go for naught, as the estate will pass intestate.

BEQUESTS

When a will directs that certain pieces of property are to go to designated persons, that gift is called a specific bequest.

In many cases, specific bequests will fail or an individual will have more property to pass at his death than he has accounted for in the specific bequests in his will. For instance, if a person directs that $10,000 go to a friend and the friend dies before the testator, that specific bequest will fail. Or, if an individual makes specific bequests totaling $30,000 in his will, and at his death there is $50,000 left in the estate to distribute, what happens to the extra $20,000?

This surplus property will pass to a residuary beneficiary or legatee if the individual also includes a residuary bequest in the will. Residuary clauses are simple and resemble the following:

"I leave the rest, residue and remainder of my estate to Aaron Burr."

If there is surplus property, and there is no residuary clause in the will, that property passes intestate as if there was no will.

If the individual wants one or more persons to share equally in his estate with no care as to who is going to receive what specific piece of property, then there is really no need for specific bequests. A simple residuary clause is sufficient. For instance, "I give the rest, residue and remainder of my estate to my children, share and share alike."

CHALLENGING A WILL

1. Courts favor the validity of a will but the probate can be successfully attacked if the will was not executed freely, voluntarily, and intelligently or there was lack of testamentary capacity of the testator. This means that the testator, at the time he executed his will, did not have the proper mental capacity to appreciate the gravity or importance of his act. There are very finite legal definitions of what constitutes legal testamentary capacity — the testator must understand the nature and extent of his property, and he must understand his relations to the persons who have claims upon his bounty (spouse, children and other close relatives). A will may also be successfully attacked if the testator suffers from an insane delusion which causes him to make or change his will.

2. Another ground for contest is undue influence. This means that the testator came under the influence of a person to such a degree that the testator's last will was executed without a free and independent mind, but was actually determined by another's undue influence. Closely akin is the ground of fraud if the testator

was purposely tricked into executing a will. A constructive fraud occurs when a testator is badly advised by a person who is very close to him and whose advice was followed in the preparation of the will. Obviously a will which is executed under force, coercion or duress is also invalid.

> Rosalind, who had eight brothers and sisters, executed a will seven days before she died, leaving $10,000 and her home to her attorney. In a second clause she left the residue of her property to the same attorney. Rosalind also stated in the will that she had no brothers or sisters. The will was prepared by a lawyer who was a good friend and former associate of the beneficiary attorney. At the time the will was drawn, Rosalind stated that she wanted $10,000 and her home to go to her attorney; the attorney preparing the will failed to advise her that she had at least $40,000 left in her estate. He asked Rosalind if she wanted to name her attorney as the residuary legatee without explaining the term to her. Rosalind assented to the suggestion, and the will was drawn and properly executed and witnessed. The brothers and sisters of Rosalind successfully attacked the will on the grounds of fraud. The attorney who drew the will should have advised Rosalind of the extra $40,000 left in her estate after she made her initial disposition to her attorney, and he should have fully advised her of the meaning of the term residuary legatee. Furthermore, the attorney who drew the will should have questioned Rosalind's motives in leaving any bequest to an attorney, as these are always suspect. Rosalind's will also could have been attacked because of a lack of testamentary capacity, since she stated she had no brothers and sisters in the will and there is evidence that she did not understand her relations to the persons who had claims on her bounty. Also, there is ample evidence to show that Rosalind did not know the nature and extent of her property.

3. There are also grounds for invalidating a will because the testator may have attempted to give away more property than he actually had the power to dispose of. Community property laws give each spouse a one-half interest in the community property. Therefore, a testator can only dispose of one-half of his community property and if he tries to give away more than this to a person other than his wife, she can contest that part of the will. Spouses who own property as tenants by the entirety have similar restrictions.

In non-community property states, husbands and wives have an interest in each other's separate property at death. These rights used to be called dower and curtesy, terms from the old English common law. These terms are not used in many states now, but the restrictions on a spouse's ability to will away separate property do remain. In community property and non-community property states, a spouse can always elect to abide by the deceased spouse's will and waive these property rights.

4. State laws protect children who are unnamed in their parents' wills. Parents do not have to leave their children any property, but they do have to show in the body of the will that they know of the existence of each of their children when the will is signed. If a child's name is left out of his parents' estate plan, he can successfully contest the will and receive a share of the estate. An illegitimate child

cannot make such claim on a father's estate; this is the law because of public policy. (If the law were to the contrary, every time a person of wealth died, scores of alleged illegitimate children would be making claims upon the estate.)

5. If two persons contract to leave their property to each other or to a mutually agreed upon third person (children), this contract will be upheld over a subsequent will which is made without the knowledge of a spouse or after a spouse has died.

6. If the beneficiary of a will has been convicted of murdering a deceased, then he cannot collect as a beneficiary under the dead person's will or insurance policy.

7. The law protects the family of a person who disinherits them in favor of a charity close to the time of his death. They are called "mortmain" statutes. All too often, as a person approaches death, he finds "religion" and attempts to give his estate to charity instead of his family. Mortmain laws do not forbid last moment charitable gifts altogether, but they do require special wording in a will. (There is no law preventing bequests to the state or to the federal government.)

EXECUTORS, ADMINISTRATORS AND ATTORNEYS

Every estate needs a person to supervise its timely and orderly liquidation. If the testator names this person in the will, he is called an executor; if there is no provision for this type of person or a deceased dies without a will, this person is known as an administrator. (If this person is a woman, then the titles are executrix and administratrix.) Since it is the duty of the executor to handle the financial aspects of an estate, he normally must engage a lawyer to file the necessary papers with the probate court to start the ball rolling.

The executor, with the lawyer's help, must discover and marshal all of the assets of the estate, pay all valid creditors' claims, pay any taxes, manage the assets of the estate while it is in probate, and finally petition the court to distribute the assets as per the estate plan or the laws of intestacy.

An executor or administrator must pay all of the valid debts of a deceased before an estate can close. A creditor must submit his claim within a time limit which is prescribed by the state where the probate is filed. This limits range from three to eighteen months. If a creditor does not present his claim within that time, the debt is extinguished.

Executors are required to post a bond to protect the beneficiaries from any possible dishonesty. However, this requirement can be waived by the testator in his will when he names the executor. The amount of bond is normally determined by the amount of cash and other liquid assets in the estate.

The executor is entitled to a fee for his services which is based on a set schedule established by state law. In many states, if the executor performs extraordinary services, he can ask the court for higher fees, and, upon a good showing to the court, he will be awarded an amount over and above the statutory fee limit. The attorney for an estate is also entitled to a fee in the same amount as the executor, and can petition the court for extra fees for extraordinary services. The executor can waive his right to a fee and this is done many times when the executor is a beneficiary and/or a close relation to the other beneficiaries. Executor fees are taxable income.

In many cases a testator will ask his attorney to act as an executor of the estate. Unfortunately, it is perfectly legal for this attorney to hire a second lawyer to "aid him" in the administration of the estate. This results in a duplication of fees and an extra charge on the estate which it should not have to bear. The first attorney should be perfectly capable of administering the estate himself. Not all lawyers engage in this practice, but there is nothing but good conscience to prevent it. If a testator wants his attorney to act as the executor of his estate, he should put a clause in the will saying that the attorney can act as the executor if he does not select another lawyer to act as his legal counsel in administering the estate.

Any adult or corporation can act as an executor. Banks and trust companies, which often advertise their services as professional executors and trustees, seldom will handle estates worth less than $50,000. In most circumstances a person will ask his spouse, an adult child or a close sibling to act as executor. It is a good idea to choose an alternative executor in case the primary choice cannot serve. The executor should also live in the same state as the testator. If the named executor dies before the testator, he should change his will to provide for a new primary and secondary choice for executor.

An executor only handles the finances of the estate; he does not have the power to become a legal guardian of orphaned children. It is important to name someone to act as the legal guardian even though this choice is not always binding on a court. The person named as executor does not necessarily have to be the same one who is named as the children's guardian.

ALTERNATIVES

There are many alternatives to a will to accomplish the purpose of passing property at or near one's death. All of these alternatives should be considered.

1. Life insurance benefits are not considered a part of a person's estate if a specific beneficiary is named. Insurance proceeds will pass into the estate if the estate is specifically named as a beneficiary or if the named beneficiaries do not survive the testator. Even though life insurance benefits may pass to a beneficiary without the necessity of probate, they are subject to federal and state inheritance tax laws. These benefits can also be the body of a trust which gives a life estate to the widow with the remainder given to the children after they reach a certain age

after the wife's death. Life insurance trusts are valuable tools in estate planning. Union death benefits are somewhat akin to life insurance in that they are not considered a part of the testator's estate when he dies, and they pass to a stated beneficiary without the necessity of probate.

2. Property held in joint tenancy will automatically pass to the surviving joint tenants. (No will is necessary.) This right of survivorship enables a surviving joint tenant to avoid probate; however, he still may have to pay some federal or state inheritance taxes on the property he has acquired. A surviving joint tenant usually must hire an attorney to change the record title of real property from the old joint tenancy to the new form.

Joint tenancy in a safe deposit box gives all of the joint tenants equal access to the contents of the box. However, it does not give them equal ownership.

Most married persons own their property in joint tenancy, but joint tenancy ownership is not reserved just for married couples. This system of estate planning can be utilized by any group of two or more persons. However, a husband cannot defeat the community or marital property rights of his wife by putting his property in joint tenancy with a third person. Also, if you transfer your property from sole ownership to joint tenancy with another person, you could be liable for a gift tax, depending on the size of the gift.

3. One can avoid probate altogether by giving property away before death. If you wish your children to receive your property after your death, there is really no reason for holding it until then. The shrewd estate planner can make timely gifts thereby avoiding the cost and delay of probate. There are also federal and state gift taxes, but these are far less onerous than inheritance taxes which would have to be paid if the same gift passed through probate. If you make a gift as part of an estate plan, the gift must be irrevocable and have no strings attached.

4. A trust consists of assets which are given over to a trustee with instructions on how they are to be administered and disbursed for the benefit of one or more beneficiaries. Depending on the provisions of each particular trust, it can save taxes, avoid probate and provide a person with some control over his assets after death. Anyone eligible to act as an executor is also an eligible trustee.

There are two types of trusts — "testamentary" and "living" or "inter vivos." Testamentary trusts take effect after death, and it will not escape probate because it has been established as part of a will.

An inter vivos trust is established by a living individual making a gift of assets to a trustee for the benefit of one or more beneficiaries. The person making the gift (called the trustor) can keep some control over the disposition of his assets — this trust is revocable or semi-revocable. The trustor can establish a trust where he has no say in the management of the assets after the agreement is drawn and the property is transferred. This is called an irrevocable trust and can escape probate and estate taxes. However, the trustor of an irrevocable trust could be liable for gift taxes.

A trust normally ties up assets for a long period of time and enables a testator to withhold the body of the estate from a child or children whom he believes to be too immature to properly handle a large sum of money at an early age. A trust agreement could provide for income to children until they reach specified ages. Some trusts give a life estate in the income from a trust to children with a gift of the entire corpus of the trust to the grandchildren after the children's death. No matter what the provisions of the trust agreement are, probate courts still have jurisdiction over these matters.

5. Another vehicle for transferring property at death without a will is known as a "totten" or "bank account" trust. All you do is name a beneficiary of your bank or savings and loan account, and whatever is in the account at your death will pass to the named beneficiary. While this method is called a trust, the owner of the account can deal with his money in any manner he chooses. There are none of the legal restrictions or obligations of the traditional trusts mentioned in the previous paragraphs. You can easily make arrangements with your local bank for this type of trustee account; a lawyer is unnecessary.

Form for a Simple Will

LAST WILL AND TESTAMENT OF

_____

I, _____ , a resident of _____ ,

_____ , _____ , make and publish this my last will and

COUNTY   STATE

testament:

I hereby declare that I am _____ . The names of my children are

(SINGLE/MARRIED/DIVORCED)

_____ (if no children, it is advisable to list the names of your

closest blood relatives).

I nominate _____ as executor/executrix of this my last will and testament.

(NAME OF PERSON)

In the event my first choice cannot serve as executor, I nominate _____ to serve as

alternate executor. (Optional: I hereby authorize either my primary or secondary choice for executor to

serve without bond.)

I leave the following specific bequests:

1. My _____ to _____ ; and

(ITEM)   (PERSON)

2. My _____ to _____ .

(ITEM)   (PERSON)

I leave the rest, residue and remainder of my estate to _____ . If he/she

predeceases me or dies within ninety (90) days of my death, then I leave the rest, residue and remainder to

_____ .

If my death leaves any of my minor children as orphans I nominate _____

to serve as the guardian of the persons and estates of my minor children.

IT WITNESS WHEREOF, I have hereunto set my hand this _____ day of _____ , 19__ ,

at _____ , _____ .

(CITY)   (STATE)

_____

– – – – – –

The foregoing instrument, entitled *Last Will and Testament* was signed today by _____

in our joint presence, and at the same time, and we therefore sign as witnesses to the execution of this will.

We declare under penalty of perjury that the foregoing is true and correct. Executed on this _____ day

of _____ , 19__ , at _____ , _____ .

(CITY)   (STATE)

1. _____

(WITNESS)

Residing at _____

2. _____

(WITNESS)

Residing at _____

3. _____

(WITNESS)

Residing at _____

STATE LAWS AFFECTING WILLS AND OTHER ESTATE MATTERS

	NUMBER OF WITNESSES REQUIRED FOR A FORMAL WILL	ARE HOLOGRAPHIC WILLS RECOGNIZED?	HOW MANY YEARS AFTER DISAPPEARANCE IS A PERSON PRESUMED DEAD?	TIME LIMIT FOR CREDITORS TO MAKE CLAIMS AGAINST ESTATE (in months) [1]
ALABAMA	2	no	7 years	6[3]
ALASKA	2	yes	5 years	6
ARIZONA	2	yes	7 years	4
ARKANSAS	2	yes	5 years	6
CALIFORNIA	2	yes	7 years	4
COLORADO	2	no	7 years	6[3]
CONNECTICUT	3	no	7 years	3-12[3,7]
DELAWARE	2	no	7 years	9
D.C.	2	no	7 years	6[3]
FLORIDA	2	no	7 years	6
GEORGIA	2	no	7 years	6[3]
HAWAII	2	no	7 years	4
IDAHO	2	yes	5 years	4
ILLINOIS	2	no	7 years	6[3]
INDIANA	2	no	5 years	6
IOWA	2	no	5 years	6
KANSAS	2	no	7 years	6
KENTUCKY	2	yes	7 years	no statutory limit
LOUISIANA	3	yes	30 years	no statutory limit
MAINE	3	no	7 years	12[3]
MARYLAND	2	no	7 years[2]	6

	NUMBER OF WITNESSES REQUIRED FOR A FORMAL WILL	ARE HOLOGRAPHIC WILLS RECOGNIZED?	HOW MANY YEARS AFTER DISAPPEARANCE IS A PERSON PRESUMED DEAD?	TIME LIMIT FOR CREDITORS TO MAKE CLAIMS AGAINST ESTATE (in months)[1]
MAINE	3	no	7 years	12[3]
MARYLAND	2	no	7 years[2]	6
MASSACHUSETTS	3	no	7 years	no statutory limit
MICHIGAN	2	no	7 years	18[4]
MINNESOTA	2	no	7 years	4[5]
MISSISSIPPI	2	yes	7 years	6
MISSOURI	2	no	7 years	6[3]
MONTANA	2	yes	7 years	4
NEBRASKA	2	no	7 years	3-18[7]
NEVADA	2	yes	7 years	3
NEW HAMPSHIRE	3	no	6 years	6[3]
NEW JERSEY	2	no	7 years	6
NEW MEXICO	2	no	7 years	4[3]
NEW YORK	2	no	5 years	7[3,6]
NORTH CAROLINA	2	yes	7 years	6
NORTH DAKOTA	2	yes	7 years	3
OHIO	2	no	7 years	4[3]
OKLAHOMA	2	yes	7 years	2
OREGON	2	no	7 years	4

	NUMBER OF WITNESSES REQUIRED FOR A FORMAL WILL	ARE HOLOGRAPHIC WILLS RECOGNIZED?	HOW MANY YEARS AFTER DISAPPEARANCE IS A PERSON PRESUMED DEAD?	TIME LIMIT FOR CREDITORS TO MAKE CLAIMS AGAINST ESTATE (in months)[1]
PENNSYLVANIA	2	yes	7 years	no statutory limit
RHODE ISLAND	2	no	7 years	6
SOUTH CAROLINA	3	no	7 years	5
SOUTH DAKOTA	2	yes	7 years	4
TENNESSEE	2	yes	7 years[2]	6[2]
TEXAS	2	yes	7 years	6[3]
UTAH	2	yes	no law	3
VERMONT	3	no	6 years	no statutory limit
VIRGINIA	2	yes	7 years	no statutory limit
WASHINGTON	2	no	7 years	4
WEST VIRGINIA	2	yes	7 years	6
WISCONSIN	2	no	7 years[2]	no statutory limit[7]
WYOMING	2	yes	7 years	3

FOOTNOTES:

(1) After first publication to creditors unless otherwise stated.
(2) The Court is not absolutely required to declare death after a 7 year absence, but it may decide that such a declaration is justified.
(3) After issuance of letters testamentary or letters of administration.
(4) After hearing for proving claims which hearing is held no later than 4 months after appointment of an executor or administrator.
(5) After court order to present claims.
(6) Date specified in public notice; if no notice, then see #3.
(7) Probate court sets the exact time limit.

COMMISSIONS FOR EXECUTORS AND ADMINISTRATORS OF ESTATES

ALABAMA	2 1/2% of monies received plus 2 1/2% of monies paid plus expenses plus 2 1/2% of value of land sold for division (not to exceed $100.00).
ALASKA	7% on first $1000 of estate value; 5% on next $1000; 4% on next $2000; 2% on remainder of estate.[1]
ARIZONA	7% on first $1000 of estate value; 5% on next $9000; 4% on remainder of estate.[1]
ARKANSAS	10% on first $1000 of personal property; 5% on next $4000; 3% on remainder of personal property in estate; additional compensation by probate court for work on real estate.
CALIFORNIA	7% on first $1000 of estate value; 4% on next $9000; 3% on next $40,000; 2% on next $100,000; 1 1/2% on next $350,000; 1% on remainder of estate.[1]
COLORADO	6% on first $25,000 of estate value; 4% on next $75,000; 3% on remainder.
CONNECTICUT	Commissions are set by the probate court on a reasonable basis.
DELAWARE	Court sets commissions on a reasonable basis, which cannot exceed 10% of estate value.
D.C.	Courts set commissions on a reasonable basis (between 1% and 10% of estate value).
FLORIDA	6% on first $1000; 4% on next $4000; 2 1/2% of remainder of estate. If there is more than one executor or administrator, probate court sets the commission.
GEORGIA	2 1/2% of monies received plus 2 1/2% of monies paid out plus the probate court may grant additional compensation for work done on real estate matters.
HAWAII	Principal of Estate: 5% on first $1000; 4% on next $9000; 3% on next $10,000; 2% on remainder of estate. Income from Estate: 7% on first $5000; 5% on remainder of income.[1]
IDAHO	Commissions are set by the probate court on a reasonable basis.
ILLINOIS	Commissions are set by the probate court on a reasonable basis.
INDIANA	Commissions are set by the probate court on a reasonable basis.

State	Commission
IOWA	6% on first $1000 of estate value; 4% on next $4000; 2% on remainder of estate.[1]
KANSAS	Commissions are set by probate court on a reasonable basis.
KENTUCKY	5% of value of personal property plus 5% of income derived therefrom plus additional compensation set by probate court for work on real estate matters.
LOUISIANA	2 1/2% on value of estate. If there is more than one executor or administrator, the probate court sets the commission.[1]
MAINE	5% of estate value plus expenses.
MARYLAND	10% on first $20,000 of value of personal property; 4% on remainder of personal property, unless the will provides for a larger commission.
MASSACHUSETTS	Commissions are set by probate court. (2 1/2%–3% on personal property up to $500,000 and 1% on remainder is considered reasonable.)
MICHIGAN	5% on first $1000 of estate value; 2 1/2% of next $4000; 2% of remainder.[1]
MINNESOTA	Commissions are set by probate court on a reasonable basis.
MISSISSIPPI	Commissions are set by probate court on a reasonable basis, but they cannot exceed 7% of value of the estate.
MISSOURI	5% of first $5000 of estate value; 4% on next $20,000; 3% on next $75,000; 2 3/4% on next $300,000; 2 1/2% on next 600,000; 2% on remainder.
MONTANA	7% on first $1000 of estate value; 5% on next $9000; 4% on next $10,000; 2% on remainder of estate.[1]
NEBRASKA	5% on first $1000 of estate value; 2½% of next $4000; 2% on remainder of estate.[1]
NEVADA	6% on first $1000 of estate value; 4% on next $4000; 2% on remainder of estate.[1]
NEW HAMPSHIRE	Commissions are set by the probate court on a reasonable basis.
NEW JERSEY	Principal of Estate: 5% on first $100,000 of estate value; court sets commissions on remainder, but in no event can commission exceed 5% of value. Income of Estate: 6% of value of income.[2]

State	Commission
NEW MEXICO	10% of first $30,000 of value of personal property; 5% on remainder of personal property; probate court sets commission on real property.[3]
NEW YORK	4% on first $25,000 paid and/or received; 3 1/2% on next $125,000; 3% of next $150,000; 2% of remainder of estate.
NORTH CAROLINA	5% of monies received and paid out. The clerk of the court can set the commission if the estate is valued at less than $2000.[1]
NORTH DAKOTA	5% on first $1000 of estate value; 3% on next $5000; 2% on next $44,000; up to 2% on remainder of estate.[1]
OHIO	6% on first $1000 of estate value; 4% on next $4000; 2% on remainder of estate.
OKLAHOMA	5% on first $1000 of estate value; 4% on next $4000; 2 1/2% on remainder of estate.[1]
OREGON	7% on first $1000 of estate value; 4% on next $9000; 3% on next $40,000; 2% on remainder of estate.[1]
PENNSYLVANIA	Commissions are set by probate court on a reasonable basis. 5% of small estates and 3% of large estates is considered reasonable.
RHODE ISLAND	Commission is set by probate court on a reasonable basis.
SOUTH CAROLINA	2 1/2% on value of personal property received plus 2 1/2% on personal property paid out plus 10% interest on money loaned to the estate.[1]
SOUTH DAKOTA	5% on first $1000 of value of personal property; 4% on next $4000; 2 1/2% of remainder plus probate court sets commission on real estate value.
TENNESSEE	Commissions are set by the probate court on a reasonable basis.
TEXAS	5% of all monies received in cash plus 5% of all monies paid out in cash with a limit that total commission cannot exceed 5% of the gross fair market value of the estate.
UTAH	5% on first $1000 of estate value; 4% on next $4000; 3% on next $5000; 2% on next $90,000; 1% on remainder of estate.
VERMONT	$4.00 per day.[1]
VIRGINIA	Commissions are set by the probate court on a reasonable basis. 5% of estate value is considered reasonable.

WASHINGTON	Commission is set by probate court on a reasonable basis.
WEST VIRGINIA	Commissions are set by the probate court on a reasonable basis. 5% of monies received is considered reasonable.
WISCONSIN	2% of value of estate.[1]
WYOMING	10% on first $1000 of estate value; 5% on next $4000; 3% on next $15,000; 2% on remainder of estate.

FOOTNOTES:

[1] The probate court can give additional compensation for extraordinary services.

[2] The probate court can allow an additional 1% for each additional executor or administrator.

[3] If the estate is all cash or life insurance benefits, the compensation rate is 5% of the first $5000 and 1% of the remainder.

[4] If there is more than one executor or administrator and the estate is worth less than $100,000, then the executors split the fee. If the estate is worth more than $100,000 and there is more than one executor or administrator, there is an elaborate plan for additional compensation depending on the number of executors or administrators of the estate.

PART IV

INJURY CLAIMS

CHAPTER 13

Negligence

INTRODUCTION

Crash! two automobiles have just collided. One of the drivers was severely injured and rushed to the intensive care ward of an emergency hospital. If the injury is severe enough, the victim can expect one of the following three visitors during his stay in the hospital: (1) a priest to administer the last rites, (2) a "friendly" insurance claims adjuster armed with a release and a check book, and/or (3) an ambulance chasing attorney or his agent armed with a contingent fee contract. Hopefully, the victim will be healthy enough to decline the services of all three.

Does this victim have a claim for money damages? If so, how much is it worth and how far can he pursue it? This chapter, in fact this entire part of the book, is designed to give you some knowledge about this area of injury claims.

Claims based on auto accident injuries are but a small part of the law of negligence, and negligence is only part of a general field of the law known as torts. "Tort" is a French word which means "wrong." The whole field of torts deals with "victims" or "claimants" who have been injured or wronged in some way by others who are known as "tortfeasors." If the tortfeasor or his insurance company cannot reach an agreement with the claimant, then the claimant must file a lawsuit in order to pursue his claim. Then the claimant becomes the plaintiff, and the tortfeasor becomes the defendant. The tortfeasor's insurance company is normally not named in a lawsuit, although the company must pay for the costs of defending the lawsuit and judgments up to the limits of the insurance policy.

There are three general categories of torts: 1) injuries caused as the result of negligence; 2) those caused by intentional acts and 3) those caused by an act which may be neither negligent nor intentional but which is so dangerous to the public that the law provides compensation without fault. This last category is known as strict or absolute liability.

NEGLIGENCE

Negligence is carelessness. All of us are under a legal obligation to use ordinary care to prevent our fellow man from being injured as a result of our conduct. If you act carelessly, expect to pay for your negligence.

There is no absolute standard or measure of human performance to judge negligence. Every act or failure to act must be judged by the circumstances surrounding it. The general rule, whether we are talking about automobile drivers, shop keepers, doctors, lawyers or homeowners—is that each of us owes everyone else that degree of care which an ordinary and prudent person would owe in the same or similar circumstances. If you breach that duty, then a negligent act has been committed; if that act causes damage, then the one responsible for the negligence must pay for all of the damages.

Children can commit acts of negligence, but they are not held to the same standard of care as an adult in most cases. Children are held to that degree of care which should be ordinarily exercised by children of the same age, mental capacity and experience. There is no specific age when a child is considered fully accountable for his actions. However, minors who have valid drivers licenses are held to the same degree of care in driving a motor vehicle that an adult would bear.

Acts of negligence can take many different forms, as the following examples should prove:

1. Jack, a warehouse manager, had no prior experience or training in operating a forklift; yet he volunteered to operate one to help his company during a warehousemen's strike. He lost control and struck and injured a pedestrian. Jack's lack of preparation and skill in the operation of a forklift is an element of negligence, and this negligence is imputable to Jack's company. Such a lack of necessary skill and experience in the operation of a machine could be applied to accidents involving inexperienced operators of automobiles, heart and lung machines, computers and other machines.

2. Robert's car ran out of gas on a small two lane road which was poorly illuminated. He went for help but left the car abandoned without flares or any other warning to passing motorists. Barney, driving at the posted speed limit, did not see Robert's car in time and crashed into its rear, causing Barney serious injury. Robert's failure to give adequate and proper warning of a dangerous condition was an act of negligence, making him liable for Barney's damages. Running out of gas may also have been a negligent act, depending upon the availability of gas stations. Leaving the car on the road without looking for a safe place to stop and park is also a negligent act. This failure to give adequate and proper warning of a dangerous condition is applied in those cases where railroads fail to provide adequate signals, where drivers fail to sound their horns or flash their lights, where construction crews do not warn of dangerous conditions, and even where golfers fail to yell "fore" to persons who are endangered by their golf shots.

3. Sally parked her car on one of those super-steep San Francisco hills, but forgot to turn the wheels toward the curb. The emergency brake failed, and her car rolled down the street into a cable car, causing injuries to some passengers. Sally's failure to take ordinary precautions was a negligent act, making her liable for all damages caused to those injured. An ordinarily prudent person in the same situation would have curbed the wheels of his car to prevent such an accident.

4. The Omnibus Department Store was greatly concerned with sales, but the management was not terribly concerned with cleaning its premises. Although they had a night janitorial crew, there was no daytime inspection for dangerous conditions. Judy, a store patron, slipped on a banana peel which, it turned out, had been on the department store floor for over four hours. Since the store had not taken reasonable steps to inspect the premises, it was negligent and liable to pay for Judy's injuries. The principle of negligence because of improper preparation or inspection can be applied to service stations which fail to inspect auto brakes, apartment house owners who fail to inspect common passageways, drivers who do not inspect their tires and utilities which fail to properly inspect and repair their equipment.

5. Rodney was late for an appointment and drove his car at 65 miles per hour in a 45 mile zone while following another car by only three car lengths. The car in front braked and Rodney could not stop in time so there was an impact which injured the other driver. Rodney was speeding and following too closely, and these violations of the vehicle code were acts of negligence. Accidents which involve the violation of statutes, ordinances, and safety regulations which were designed to prevent such accidents are deemed to be caused by negligence as a matter of law. This principle of negligence per se applies in vehicle violation cases, failure to install fire escapes or fire extinguishers, failure of mine owners and operators and construction crews to follow safety standards imposed by state law, and failure to provide warning signs or qualified life guard services for public swimming pools.

In all these examples, the negligence of a tortfeasor has caused damages to an innocent victim. In order for a victim to recover any damages, he must prove this negligence was the cause of his damages. In many cases acts of negligence may be committed, but they were not the proximate cause of the accident. For instance:

Lillie fell asleep while smoking and her bed caught fire. The blaze soon spread to five other apartments. Tom, the upstairs neighbor, did not notice the smoke and flames until the fire had already burned through his floor. He immediately called the fire department and then tried to no avail to save Lillie. The owners of the apartment house had not put fire extinguishers on the wall, so Tom sued them for fire damage to his personal property. Although the owners were clearly negligent in not providing fire extinguishers, Tom could not collect damages because the lack of extinguishers was not the proximate cause of his damage. Even if the extinguishers had been available and working, the fire had already consumed most of Tom's apartment and the extinguishers would have been useless. Tom, therefore, could only sue Lillie's estate for his damages.

SPECIAL DAMAGES

Once negligence and cause have been established, the victim is entitled to compensatory damages — special and general. (These damages are not taxable by the federal government, even though they may include repayment for lost income.) Special damages are the victim's out-of-pocket costs which resulted from an accident. They include the following:

1. Medical bills for services of physicians, chiropractors, optometrists, nurses, hospitals, convalescent homes, speech therapists, psychologists, and physiotherapists. If a doctor orders it, a victim may even recover the cost of trips to a warmer climate or to the local steambath. If at the time of trial or settlement, it can be shown that medical bills will be incurred in the future, then the tortfeasor is liable for them if they are reasonable and caused by his negligence.

2. Loss of earnings may be collected by the victim. This includes all lost wages and any anticipated loss of future wages resulting from an accident. Even an unemployed victim who was in the market for a job at the time of the accident can collect what he would have earned had he been able to work. But an unemployed victim who is not in the labor market (housewives) have no claim for a loss of wages. (Note that a housewife who must hire a maid to do her housework during the period of her injury can collect this expense as part of her damages.)

   A self-employed person would be entitled to recover his loss of income or earning capacity during the period in which he was unable to work. But this may be harder to prove than a wage loss by someone with a regular paycheck. For instance, a salesman may not be able to show an immediate loss of commissions because of his inability to work. If a self-employed person has to hire someone to replace him in his business, then this added salary expense would be the measure of damages.

   If a seriously injured victim cannot go back to his regular job or cannot earn as much as he did before the accident, his loss of earning capacity can be projected into the future through the use of actuarial tables based on his age, past earnings, new earning capacity and expected retirement age.

3. All property damage caused by an accident is repayable by the tortfeasor to the victim. This includes automobile repair or replacement, charges for substitute transportation while the car is being repaired, damage to clothing or other personal property - even the loss of a pet.

4. Loss of consortium means the intangible loss a person suffers when his spouse is injured in an accident (love, companionship, sexual relations and affection). Many states do not recognize loss of consortium. A few

states which do allow damages for this loss only give the *husband* the right to make the claim after his wife has been injured. These antiquated laws are based on the philosophy that the woman does not enjoy love, companionship, sexual relations and affection enough to allow her to sue for their loss if her husband is injured in an accident!

GENERAL DAMAGES

General damages are awarded for the physical pain and suffering which accompanies an injury. Pain and suffering include fright or shock, nervousness, hysteria, humiliation, anxiety, embarrassment and disfigurement. There is no hard and fast rule on how much general damages are awarded in each specific case of negligence. They depend upon the nature of the injury and the victim's ability to withstand pain.

What is this "pain and suffering" worth? It cannot be defined. Each case must rest on its own merits, and if it goes to trial, the judge or jury must decide. As a general rule, juries award more money damages for injuries which are objective and visible than for those which are more subjective in nature. (Objective means that the injury can be seen or felt, such as an x-ray for a broken bone; subjective means that there is no visible injury but the victim complains of pain nevertheless, such as a muscle sprain.) Therefore, scars and broken bones bring more damages than cervical or lumbar sprains - even though the latter may be more painful. This is because jurors are skeptical about what they cannot see, and it also points to the effectiveness of insurance company propaganda regarding "whiplash injuries." It can also be attributed to the mitigating testimony of the insurance company doctor. Whenever a claim is brought against an insurance company, it will attempt to diminish the seriousness of the victim's injuries. This is most easily done in "whiplash" cases where the victim's complaints are mostly subjective.

["Whiplash" is not a medical term. It loosely describes an injury caused when neck and low back muscles, ligaments and tendons are stretched beyond their normal capacity. This sudden whipping motion can also break your neck and kill you or cause serious disc and nerve problems as well as muscle sprains or strains. (The latter are known as soft tissue injuries.) Serious tearing of the muscle fiber can cause severe pain and permanent disability, but unfortunately for the victims, these injuries often do not show on an x-ray, and doctors must rely on the patient's description of pain to treat them.]

Once a lawsuit has been filed for personal injuries, the insurance company has the right to have the plaintiff examined by a doctor of its choosing. This is based on the sound legal principle that the company has a right to protect itself from frivolous and fraudulent claims. But it often abuses this right.

Insurance doctors normally set certain days aside for these defense examinations and charge $100 and up for each one. They also get $300 or more each time that they testify in court. The insurance companies are good patients - they pay high fees promptly; there is no responsibility for the treatment of the patient and no one calls an insurance doctor in the middle of the night to come to court to testify. There are thousands of these insurance cases yearly, and the profits these doctors make are enormous.

Most insurance companies pick their doctors on the basis of education and looks to impress a jury. Most of them look as if they came from central casting— they could easily stand in for Robert Young when he plays "Marcus Welby, M.D.".

The insurance doctors work for the companies and most certainly know which side of the bread contains their butter. They generally minimize the injuries of the plaintiffs in their reports and trial testimony. Although these doctors once took the Hippocratic Oath, they owe no duty to an injured plaintiff, as he is technically not a "patient". The minimization or denial of injuries is within the realm of medical opinion, especially in those cases where there is little or no objective sign of injury. Therefore, their testimony cannot be considered perjury - advocacy perhaps, but not perjury.

These doctors will often try to attribute injuries to factors other than the accident which started the whole lawsuit. They have great imaginations. Who else could blame the emotional problems accompanying back and neck injuries on non-existent venereal disease or a heart condition.

If you ever get a chance to serve as a juror in a personal injury case, pay particular attention to how many times the doctor has testified in the past and for whom. If the doctor spends more time in court than the lawyers, discount his testimony appropriately.

Insurance company doctors are not without their counterparts on the plaintiff's side. It is well known that some physicians will treat a false or frivolous injury, or they will overtreat a patient to increase his medical bills. Since many jury verdicts and insurance company settlements are in proportion to the amount of medical bills, the overtreating physician can help a claimant and his attorney receive more money. This can be accomplished by unnecessary injections, therapy, office visits, hospitalization and body casts. All of this is dangerous to an unknowing patient who may experience severe pain, discomfort and emotional distress as a result of his own doctor's greed, which rarely manifests itself unless there is some insurance to pay the physician immediately. Fortunately, the overtreating physician and the insurance company doctor are rarities in their profession.

Ken and Judy were out driving one day when Ken's car was hit from the rear by Eugene who was insured by the Deadbeat Insurance Company. Ken was a manufacturer's representative, who worked on a commission basis only; Judy was a stewardess. Ken had a severe neck and low back sprain which prevented him from working at peak efficiency for many months. He was treated conservatively by his family physician, whose bill was $300. While the initial acute neck and back pain subsided, he continually felt a dull ache in both of these areas. Ken's doctor could only prescribe pain pills and could not tell him with any certainty if the constant dull ache would be a permanent injury or would subside in a few years. Ken was not able to determine an exact loss of income because he had no definite way of showing how his physical disability affected his earnings. Judy had cut her head in the accident. The cut healed but left a scar on her face. Her total medical bill was $125, and the anticipated future medical expense for the removal of the scar was $500. She had only lost one week of work because of the accident. Since Deadbeat was unwilling to settle these claims, a lawsuit was filed, and eventually there was a jury trial. The defense produced its own Dr. Boucher, who had examined Ken for 20 minutes a few months eariler. He testified he could find no objective signs of injury and, therefore, he did not believe Ken's complaints abut a continuing injury, nor did he believe that it would be permanent. The jury returned verdicts in favor of Ken for $2000 and in favor of Judy for $7500. The verdicts included all medical damages, loss of earnings and general damages; the verdicts did not reflect the fact that Ken and Judy would have to pay a percentage of these sums to their attorney for fees.

Ivan, a 24-year-old father of two, was severely injured because of the negligence of a large public utility.He suffered permanent paralyis of the lower half of his body, causing him to be confined to a wheelchair. Ivan had to give up his $20,000 per year job. His wife had to work to make ends meet, and this necessitated the hiring of a nurse and housekeeper. His severe emotional distress and anguish required a psychiatrist. Ivan's total medical bill at the time of trial was already $11,000 with $14,000 more anticipated. The jury returned a verdict in favor of Ivan for $1,300,000.

WRONGFUL DEATH

These previous paragraphs dealing with compensatory and general damages assume that the victim is still alive. If he dies of *unrelated* causes, his estate is only entitled to his compensatory damages, not general damages. However, if a victim dies because of injuries from the accident, his family may file a wrongful death action to recover such losses as the present value of his future earnings, the value of his personal services, the last medical bills and funeral expenses.

If the deceased was a husband and a father, the chief element of the damages is the present value of the earnings he would have contributed to the family during the period of his life expectancy. To determine this amount, the average yearly income and reasonable expectancy of future income are used along with mortality and interest tables.

If the deceased was a wife and mother with no outside job, the damages will be the value of her services in the home—that is, what it would cost to obtain services which the wife would have performed had she lived. Life expectancy tables are again used.

The death of a minor child causes untold grief to his parents, but they can only recover the present value of reasonable probable future services and contributions by the child, and then they must deduct the probable cost of rearing him.

Some states limit the amount of damages which a survivor can get in a wrongful death action.

PUNITIVE DAMAGES

Punitive damages are damages which are awarded to punish a defendant. A tortfeasor cannot be punished for acts of simple negligence. Intentional, malicious acts such as assault and fraud merit punitive damages and so do acts of gross negligence which involve a willful and wanton disregard for the rights of others. The jury can consider the ability of the defendant to pay when they decide the issue.

DEFENSES

1. If an injured plaintiff was also careless, a negligent defendant can raise this defense to absolve himself from liability for damages. This is known as the doctrine of contributory negligence. Even though the degrees of negligence are not the same, the law clearly states that any contributory negligence on the part of the victim will deny him any recovery at all. Many harsh results have come from this doctrine. For instance, if a speeding drunk hits the car in front of him, there is an obvious case of negligence. But if the other car had a broken taillight or if one brake light was not working, it is possible that its driver was contributorily negligent because he failed to maintain his car properly. A jury could find that this negligence contributed to the cause of the accident and then deny the injured driver any recovery for his injury.

   Failure to wear seatbelts can be contributory negligence. It will not be considered contributory negligence automatically in most states; rather an insurance company would have to prove the failure caused injuries which would not have resulted had the seat belts been fastened securely. The insurance companies can generally prove this in cases where a victim's head hits the dashboard or goes through the windshield.

   As a practical matter, insurance companies use this defense as a bargaining point.

2. A few states follow the doctrine of comparative negligence. It allows an injured victim who was also negligent to recover damages, but the damages are reduced in proportion to the victim's own negligence. For instance, if an accident were 90 per cent the fault of the defendant and only 10 per cent the fault of the plaintiff, then the plaintiff's damages will be reduced to reflect this percentage.

3. The defense of assumption of the risk comes about when an injured victim enters into an activity even though he can foresee the risk of harm and appreciate the danger to himself. Isn't driving an automobile assuming the risk of an accident? No, not legally. The doctrine of assumption of the risk is applied in very strict circumstances, and you have the right to assume the good conduct and lack of negligence on the part of others - even when driving on the open road.

4. Some accidents are unavoidable. That is, even though all parties acted with due care, an accident still occurred causing someone damages. If there has been an unavoidable accident, the victims cannot recover damages for negligence.

Bruno was driving his truck down the Long Island Expressway when a bee flew in the cab and stung him on the nose. This caused him to momentarily lose control and crash into two cars, causing extensive property damage and personal injuries. The victims sued Bruno for damages, but the court ruled that they could not recover because the accident was unavoidable.

SPECIAL RELATIONSHIPS

The preceding paragraphs dealt with the rights and liabilities of individuals in their conduct towards one another. There may be a special relationship between them, and this may affect the rights and liabilities of the parties in the area of accident claims. Here are a few of these special relationships.

1. *Agents and Employees.* The negligence of an agent or employee who is acting within the course and scope of his employment is imputed to the principal or employer. If a driver is on the job for General Motors and negligently injures someone, then both the driver and GM are liable for the victim's damages.

2. *Owners of Automobiles.* In most states an auto owner is primarily responsible for the damages caused when he allows someone to drive his car and an accident occurs. Even if the driver is insured himself, the owner's insurance carrier is primarily liable for the damage. Many states also follow a family car doctrine which makes the head of a household responsible for the negligence of any of the members of his family when using the family cars.

3. *Husband and Wife.* In many states a husband and wife cannot sue each

other for damages as a result of negligence—such suits involve car accidents and this law is also supposed to promote harmony in the home. Some states only allow spouses to sue each other in cases where there has been an intentional or malicious act.

4. *Rescuers.* A tortfeasor is not only liable for damages to his initial victim, but he is also liable to those trying to rescue that victim. Thus, if a doctor, in attempting to reach an accident victim, falls and breaks his leg, the person who originally caused the accident would be liable for the doctor's damages too.

5. *Tavern Owners.* Some states have "dramshop acts" which make tavern owners responsible for actions of their drunk patrons—if a drunk driver hits you, you can sue him and also any tavern owner who put him in his drunken condition.

Tavern owners may also be liable under rules of simple negligence for injuries to their customers caused by the belligerent conduct of other patrons. They must protect customers from any such attacks.

6. *Transportation Carriers and Their Passengers.* Transportation carriers such as railroads, streetcars, buses, taxis, ferries and airlines owe their passengers an unusually high degree of care. This very special degree of care is not owed to drivers or pedestrians on the open road or sea.

7. *Property Owners.* Many states have traditionally defined the rights and liabilities of property owners and those using the property by classifying the status of the latter. The owners owe a very high degree of care to business invitees, a lower degree to social guests and an even lower degree of care to trespassers. A few states have eliminated these antiquated notions and now put the property owner to the same standard test of negligence—reasonableness under the circumstances.

As a general rule, property owners owe little or no duty to protect trespassers from injury—except for trespassing children. Under the law of "attractive nuisance," a landowner is liable for injury to trespassing youngsters caused by a structure or artificial condition if he knew or should have known that: (1) children are likely to trespass on his property; (2) the condition involves unreasonable risks of serious harm to children; (3) children, because of their youth and immaturity, will not appreciate the danger to them; and (4) the utility to the landowner of maintaining the condition is slight as compared to the risk to young children. The property owner must exercise ordinary due care, and there are no hard and fast rules with respect to the specific conditions and specific ages of children. Thus, objects such as tractors, swimming pools and mine shafts may be "attractive nuisances" to one age group but not to another.

8. *Parents, Children and Third Persons.* Some states do not allow children to sue their parents and vice versa under the same reasoning that husbands and

wives may not sue each other. But most states allow parents and children to sue each other for torts. (If a parent accidentally runs over his child, the child should be able to sue him through a legal guardian.)

Parents and guardians may sometimes be liable for the actions of their children on the theory of negligence. If they know about the child's dangerous propensity, they have a duty to protect innocent third persons.

Almost half of the states hold parents or legal guardians absolutely liable to the victims of their children's wanton or intentional misconduct — window breaking, reckless bike riding and fighting. There may be monetary limits on the parents' liability for each act.

> Morrie and Minnie had a precocious seven-year-old child named Harold, affectionately known to terrified neighbors as "The Hammer". While Morrie and Minnie loved their little Harold and thought that he could do no wrong, they were constantly warned by the neighbors of his assaults on other children and pets in the neighborhood and of his penchant for using his father's tools to hammer dents and holes in every available surface he could find. Morrie kept his tools away from Harold's reach, but on Harold's eighth birthday, the parents broke down and gave their apprentice carpenter a full size hammer of his own. The next day Harold proceeded to smash in the neighbor's automobile, their hot water heater, and the postman's kneecap. The parents were automatically responsible to pay for their son's intentional acts, and they were also responsible on the theory of negligence because they carelessly gave Harold the hammer to do his thing.

9. *Doctors and Patients.* A doctor owes his patient the same duty of care that any other reasonable doctor would owe in the same circumstances to his patients. The difficulty of proving a doctor's negligence is finding another doctor to testify against the one you are suing — that is, the second doctor must testify about the duty of care owed by any physician to a patient and that the doctor accused of negligence breached that duty and committed malpractice.

Since it is difficult to find one doctor to testify against another (although it is not impossible — especially in large metropolitan areas), there is a doctrine in the law known as *res ipsa loquitur,* which puts the burden on the doctor to prove that he was not negligent. *Res ipsa loquitur* translated means "that the thing speaks for itself," and it is used in those situations where an accident would not have occurred unless someone were negligent, and the injured victim was not contributorily negligent. For instance this doctrine is used for a patient who goes into the operating room for removal of her appendix and comes out with an hysterectomy or a patient who wakes up after an operation with a sponge or forceps sewn into his body.

The laws of malpractice are not limited to doctors; they apply to all professional persons. Therefore, lawyers, accountants and architects are similarly responsible to their clients.

STATE LAWS RE TORT LIABILITY AND DAMAGE CLAIMS

	COMPARATIVE NEGLIGENCE OR CONTRIBUTORY NEGLIGENCE	CAN SPOUSES SUE EACH OTHER?	MAXIMUM LIABILITY OF PARENTS FOR MALICIOUS ACTS OF MINOR CHILD	LIMIT ON WRONGFUL DEATH DAMAGES	GUEST STATUTE PREVENTING GUEST FROM SUING DRIVER FOR NEGLIGENCE	TAVERN OWNER LIABILITY FOR ACTS OF INTOXICATED PATRONS (DRAMSHOP)	LOSS OF CONSORTIUM
ALABAMA	Contributory	YES	NO LIABILITY	NONE	YES	NO	YES[10]
ALASKA	Contributory	NO	$2,000	NONE	NO	NO	YES[10]
ARIZONA	Contributory	NO	$500.00	NONE	NO	NO	YES[10]
ARKANSAS	Comparative	YES	NO LIABILITY	NONE	YES	NO	YES
CALIFORNIA	Comparative	YES	$2,000	NONE	NO	YES	YES
COLORADO	Comparative	4	$1,000	NONE[7]	YES	NO	YES[10]
CONNECTICUT	Comparative	YES	$1,500	NONE	NO	YES	NO
DELAWARE	Comparative	NO	$300.00	NONE	YES	NO	YES
D.C.	Contributory	NO	NO LIABILITY	NONE	NO	NO	YES
FLORIDA	Comparative	NO	$300.00	NONE	YES	YES	YES
GEORGIA	Comparative	NO	NO LIMIT	NONE	YES	NO	YES
HAWAII	Comparative	YES	NO LIMIT	NONE	NO	NO	YES[10]
IDAHO	Comparative	YES	$300.00	NONE	YES	NO	YES[10]
ILLINOIS	Contributory	NO	NO LIABILITY	NONE	YES	YES	YES
INDIANA	Contributory	NO	$500.00	NONE	YES	NO	YES[10]
IOWA	Contributory	NO	NO LIABILITY	NONE	YES	YES	YES
KANSAS	Contributory	YES	NO LIABILITY	$50,000 & costs	YES	NO	NO
KENTUCKY	Contributory	YES	$500.00	NONE	NO	YES	YES[10]
LOUISIANA	Contributory	NO	NO LIABILITY	NONE	NO	YES	NO
MAINE	Comparative	NO	NO LIABILITY	NONE[8]	NO	NO	YES[10]

	COMPARATIVE NEGLIGENCE OR CONTRIBUTORY NEGLIGENCE	CAN SPOUSES SUE EACH OTHER?	MAXIMUM LIABILITY OF PARENTS FOR MALICIOUS ACTS OF MINOR CHILD	LIMIT ON WRONGFUL DEATH DAMAGES	GUEST STATUTE PREVENTING GUEST FROM SUING DRIVER FOR NEGLIGENCE	TAVERN OWNER LIABILITY FOR ACTS OF INTOXICATED PATRONS (DRAMSHOP)	LOSS OF CONSORTIUM
MARYLAND	Contributory	NO	NO LIABILITY	NONE	NO	NO	YES
MASSACHUSETTS	Comparative	NO	$300.00[2]	$200,000	YES	NO	NO
MICHIGAN	Contributory	NO	$500.00	NONE[8]	YES	YES	YES
MINNESOTA	Comparative	YES	NO LIABILITY	NONE	NO	YES	YES
MISSISSIPPI	Comparative	NO	NO LIABILITY	NONE	NO	NO	YES
MISSOURI	Contributory	NO	NO LIABILITY	$50,000	NO	NO	YES[10]
MONTANA	Contributory	NO	$300	NONE	YES	NO	YES[10]
NEBRASKA	Comparative	NO	NO LIMIT	NONE	YES	NO	YES
NEVADA	Comparative	NO	$300.00	NONE	YES	NO	YES[10]
NEW HAMPSHIRE	Comparative	YES	NO LIABILITY	$120,000	NO	YES	YES[10]
NEW JERSEY	Comparative	NO	NO LIABILITY	NONE	NO	NO	YES
NEW MEXICO	Contributory	NO	$1,000[3]	NONE	YES	NO	YES[10]
NEW YORK	Contributory	YES	$500	NONE	NO	YES	YES
NORTH CAROLINA	Contributory	YES	NO LIABILITY	NONE	NO	NO	NO
NORTH DAKOTA	Comparative	YES	NO LIABILITY	NONE	YES	YES	YES[10]
OHIO	Contributory	YES	$2,000	NONE	YES	NO	YES[10]
OKLAHOMA	Comparative	YES	NO LIABILITY	NONE	NO	NO	YES[10]
OREGON	Comparative	[5]	NO LIABILITY	$25,000	YES	NO	YES
PENNSYLVANIA	Contributory	NO	$300/one person $1,000/all persons	NONE	NO	NO	YES[10]
RHODE ISLAND	Comparative	NO	NO LIABILITY	NONE	NO	NO	NO

	COMPARATIVE NEGLIGENCE OR CONTRIBUTORY NEGLIGENCE	CAN SPOUSES SUE EACH OTHER?	MAXIMUM LIABILITY OF PARENTS FOR MALICIOUS ACTS OF MINOR CHILD	LIMIT ON WRONGFUL DEATH DAMAGES	GUEST STATUTE PREVENTING GUEST FROM SUING DRIVER FOR NEGLIGENCE	TAVERN OWNER LIABILITY FOR ACTS OF INTOXICATED PATRONS (DRAMSHOP)	LOSS OF CONSORTIUM
SOUTH CAROLINA	Contributory	YES	$1,000	NONE	YES	NO	YES[10]
SOUTH DAKOTA	Comparative	YES	$300.00	NONE	YES	NO	YES
TENNESSEE	Contributory	NO	NO LIABILITY	NONE	NO	NO	YES[10]
TEXAS	Comparative	NO	NO LIABILITY	NONE	YES	NO	YES[10]
UTAH	Comparative	NO	NO LIABILITY	NONE	YES	NO	YES[10]
VERMONT	Comparative	NO	NO LIABILITY	NONE	NO	NO	YES[10]
VIRGINIA	Contributory	NO	NO LIABILITY	$75,000	YES	NO	NO
WASHINGTON	Comparative	NO	$1,000	NONE	YES	NO	NO
WEST VIRGINIA	Comparative	NO	NO LIABILITY	$10,000[10]	NO	NO	YES[10]
WISCONSIN	Comparative	*6	NO LIABILITY	NONE	NO	YES	YES[10]
WYOMING	Comparative	NO	NO LIABILITY	NONE	YES	YES	YES[10]

FOOTNOTES:

1* All torts.

2* Parents not liable for torts of child 7 years old or younger.

3* Plus attorney's fees and court costs.

4* Wife may sue husband for torts. This law is probably an unconstitutional discrimination.

5* For willful torts but not for torts caused by negligence.

6* Husband may sue wife for torts. This law is probably an unconstitutional discrimination.

7* If the decedent left no spouse, minor child or dependent parent, limit is $45,000.

8* But damages may include only pecuniary loss, plus pain and suffering prior to death.

9* Without evidence of pecuniary loss; with evidence, an additional $100,000 may be awarded.

10* Only the husband can sue.

CHAPTER 14

Liability Insurance

It is all well and good to discuss negligence, contributory negligence, causation and damages, but the most important fact to an injured victim is the ability of the responsible party to pay damages. Most of us buy auto and personal liability insurance to pay for any possible judgments.

NECESSITY FOR AUTOMOBILE INSURANCE

All states require the auto driver and owner to show that he is able to pay a certain amount for personal injury and property damages. Only a few states will not allow you to buy, lease or transfer a car without proof of ability to pay by insurance or other means (compulsory insurance). In the other states this question of ability to pay for damages does not come up until after an automobile accident occurs. Those who cannot show such proof may lose their licenses, but this is merely punitive and does nothing to help the innocent victim. The financially irresponsible driver who causes an accident can even file bankruptcy with his victim's claim listed as an unpaid debt. (Not only will the debt be eliminated, but the tortfeasor's license to drive will be reinstated.)

The preceding paragraph is not meant to encourage uninsuredness. All persons should have liability insurance—no matter how expensive it is. The thought of hounding creditors and uncompensated accident victims is most unappealing. An auto accident policy protects you and your family from uninsured motorists and hit-and-run drivers.

Automobile insurance policies provide coverage for public liability, collision, theft, vandalism, medical pay and uninsured motorists.

LIABILITY INSURANCE

PUBLIC LIABILITY

Public liability coverage protects the insured from negligence claims for bodily injury and property damage—the minimum amounts offered are set by each state. If a personal injury judgment exceeds the limits of your policy and you have very few assets, then the victim can seldom collect more than the limits of the policy. Therefore, if you own very little which a judgment can take away, the minimum coverage should suffice. If you have many assets, buy more. The premiums for additional coverage are slight compared to the expanded limits of protection.

Insurance companies are supposed to deal in good faith with accident victims so if a company refuses to settle a case within the limits of the policy after reasonable demand for settlement, then the company is liable to pay any demand in excess of its coverage. In a recent California case, an injured person demanded a settlement of $10,000 (the amount of the policy). The insurance company unreasonably refused to settle, and the victim got a judgment for $91,000. The company then had to pay the extra $81,000 as well as $25,000 to their own insured for the emotional distress it caused her in refusing to settle the original claim!

COMPREHENSIVE

Comprehensive coverage only concerns the insured. This coverage will repay him the value of his own car if it is damaged by collision, theft, vandalism or the natural elements.

MEDICAL PAY

Medical pay coverage repays the owner of a car, his family and other passengers for medical bills incurred as the result of any accident in and around the auto within one year after an accident. It also covers you and your family if the accident occurs around someone else's automobile. Minimum coverage is generally $1,000 but more can be purchased—a good idea in light of the rapidly escalating charges for medical services. Medical pay covers *all* accidents around a car, not just collisions (straining your back while reaching in the car trunk, tripping on a chuck hole while getting out of the car and slipping in auto grease).

Some insurance companies require you to repay medical pay benefits if you receive a settlement or judgment for these damages from a neligent driver. These benefits only have to be repaid if there is such a proviso in the insurance policy. Kaiser's health plan and the state health plans for the poor also have this repayment requirement.

UNINSURED MOTORIST

Uninsured motorist is one of the most important types of coverage offered in automobile insurance policies. Many states force all auto insurance companies to offer it. It insures the driver, his family and his passengers for personal injuries if hurt by a negligent uninsured motorist or a hit-and-run driver.

If he has this coverage, the injured victim makes his claim against his *own* insurance company which must pay claims with the same good faith and by the same standards it would use if the victim brought his claim against a negligent offender. The same rules of negligence, causation, damages and contributory negligence apply. The only new element is proof of uninsuredness or hit-and-run.

When you and your company cannot reach an agreement on an uninsured motorist claim, then the matter is arbitrated rather than tried in a court of law. (Most companies use the American Arbitration Association.) Medical pay benefits already paid can be deducted from any awards achieved through arbitration. The company cannot cancel a policy because of uninsured motorist claims.

If a company pays an uninsured motorist claim, it has the exclusive right to go after the uninsured motorist in court for reimbursement. As part of the right, the company can ask the state to suspend the uninsured motorist's license until the debt is satisfied.

NO-FAULT AUTO INSURANCE

There have been many "no-fault" auto insurance plans proposed to replace the present tort liability system, which is in a sad state. The Senate Commerce Committee has found that some $14.4 billion went into auto insurance premiums in 1970. Of this amount the net benefits (after legal fees and litigation costs) paid to victims came to $7 billion; the insurance companies took $6 billion for overhead and profit. There are over 200,000 auto accident lawsuits every year. They eat up 17% of the time of the nation's judicial system. While present medical pay provisions of auto insurance policies repay some part of the victim's medical bills, there is no provision for immediate reimbursement for lost wages or the cost of household services. Because of the laws of contributory negligence or other such inequities, only 45% of those seriously injured in auto accidents or the survivors of those killed are paid any benefits. One out of every ten receives nothing.

The most disturbing aspect of the present system is the long wait a person must endure if he is unable to settle with an insurance company. The average wait for a trial in most big cities is 3½ years from the date a lawsuit is filed. Add to that the time lost haggling with the insurance company before the suit is filed. Serious injustice can occur because of such a long wait—witnesses can forget important facts, die, or move from the area. If personal injury cases were heard by judges, not juries, it would not take as long to bring the case to trial. (Jury trials always last longer than court trials.) But insurance companies have made it a policy to ask for jury trials to extend the time that they will have to pay a claim. This allows them to earn millions of dollars in extra interest while the money stays in their hands.

The main opposition to no-fault plans has come from trial lawyers, which is no wonder since automobile accident cases account for 25% of the legal profession's total earnings.

Insurance companies are divided on the issue of no-fault. Although they traditionally cry the blues over the amount of damages they pay out, many companies are still happy with the status quo. Most of their opposition stems from the fact that the proposed legislation (1) forces them to reduce rates if claims decrease, (2) makes auto insurance coverage compulsory and (3) forbids an insurance company from cancelling a policy. Massachusetts had the first no-fault plan, and the state's attorneys had to go to court to force the insurance companies to reduce their rates.

There is no uniform no-fault law. It comes in a variety of proposed packages. A pure no-fault system would mean that anyone injured in an automobile accident could not sue the person who was negligently responsible for the collision. The victim could only look to his own insurance company for damages, and if there was a dispute, it would have to be decided through arbitration, not the courts. A pure no-fault plan has never been adopted.

The oldest and most famous modified no-fault plan is used in Massachusetts, which basically eliminates claims for general damages for pain and suffering for cases involving less than $500 in medical bills. Each individual's insurance pays for all of his reasonable medical, dental, nursing and funeral expenses incurred within two years of an accident, regardless of who was negligent. (This is similar to most current medical pay provisions.) The Massachusetts law requires that a victim's insurance company pay an insured his loss of salary or earnings because of an inability to work as a result of the accident. (The unemployed who can show they would have worked can also recover.) Housewives can recover the costs of ordinary, necessary household services they would have performed themselves had they not been injured. This loss has been limited to $1,000 per month.

Under the Massachusetts plan, in those cases where the medical bills are not more than $500 (or if less than $500.00, where the injury causes death, loss of all or part of a body member, permanent or serious disfigurement, or fracture or loss of sight or hearing), then there can be no lawsuit against the person who may be at fault. Each person collects from his own insurance company, no matter who was at fault. Even though accident victims who incur less than $500 in medical bills do admittedly have pain, suffering and anxiety over their injuries, this law has wiped out any chance for these people to receive any general damages.

The Senate has passed a national no-fault bill. If this bill is passed by the House of Representatives and signed into law, it will force all of the states to adopt some no-fault automobile insurance plan. The bill leaves the regulation of rates to the states, and it does not force insurers to lower premiums if their expenses decrease. Each states's no-fault plan will have to be certified by the U.S. Department of Transportation. If a state does not adopt an approved no-fault plan, then the federal government can impose one on it with the following provisions: (1) immediate reimbursement for medical bills, lost earnings, replacement services for child care, cooking and cleaning, and funeral expenses; (2) elimination of traditional tort lawsuits including the right to general damages for pain and suffering unless the injury caused permanent disfigurement, total disability or lasted for over three months. In addition, there is a $2,500 deductible from any award or settlement for general damages if the victim qualifies to sue for pain and suffering; (3) the victim can also sue for traditional tort damages if the accident involves an uninsured motorist, there is some manufacturer's or repairman's product liability, the collision was caused intentionally, or the out-of-pocket loss to the victim is in excess of the benefits paid by his own insurance company; (4) the purchase of no-fault automobile insurance will be compulsory on a non-cancellable basis, and the states will have to have a special plan for insuring the poor; (5) if no-fault benefits are not paid within 30 days by the insurance company, it must pay interest at the rate of 1½% per month (18% per year) on overdue benefit payments; (6) insurance companies cannot make lump-sum settlements for no-fault benefits for over $2,500, and any settlements for under that figure must be approved by a court, which will allow a victim to re-open his case if there is a significant change in circumstances. (If a victim uses an attorney to negotiate a lump-sum settlement, the insurance company must pay a fee on a time-expended basis, not on a contingency and this fee cannot be deducted from the final settlement); (7) most no-fault benefits will be exempt from creditors' claims; (8) if a victim is not paid on time and retains an attorney to enforce his rights, the company must pay the fee, again determined on the basis of time expended, not on a contingency; (9) if a victim does sue for regular tort damages, any no-fault benefits paid to him must be returned to the insurer if there is a settlement or judgment.

No-fault insurance plans are an unnecessary, poor substitute for traditional court procedures. The courtroom is the traditional place to settle disputes, and there is no compelling reason to completely eliminate its use. General damages for pain, suffering and anxiety should be an inviolate right of anyone who is involved in an accident.

The mere fact that your medical bills are less than $500 (or any threshold figure) should not deprive you of damages for pain which is caused by another's negligence. Anyone who has endured a traumatic injury with its concomitant long duration, discomfort, many trips to the doctor's office, cervical collars or lumbar corsets, side effects of pain medication and injections and the apprehension over the duration of disability will attest to the necessity for general damages in all accident cases.

The no-fault concept actually benefits careless drivers and imposes burdens on good drivers, for a negligent person could walk away from an accident with little or no responsibility to the good driver.

Since—under a no-fault system—insurance premiums would be based on risk of loss or loss exposure, the drivers of small economy cars would have to pay higher premiums because they have a higher risk of injury. Also, the medically infirm—drivers with weak hearts or bad backs—would have to pay higher premiums because their risk of exposure to medical bills and lost income would be higher. It would be unfair to tax these innocent people when accidents in which they are involved are not even their fault.

No-fault insurance plans do not appreciably lower insurance premiums for the general public despite arguments to the contrary.Some70%of our insurance premiums go for property damage, and this is not included in most no-fault plans. The increase in some benefits of no-fault would eat up much of the savings from the elimination of general damages.

The constitutionality of no-fault plans is also in question, as the poor would not receive equal treatment. If an indigent accident victim receives care from a clinic, there is little or no charge. But a wealthy person who has the same injury and goes to a private doctor will incur medical bills which could put him over the $500 threshold. Therefore, the poor person would be denied general damages for the same injury for which a more affluent accident victim might collect.

Before surrendering to no-fault, we should attempt reforms within the current structure. The following proposals could maintain the integrity of the present system and still allow maximum benefits to careful drivers and victims of negligent drivers:

1. Eliminate the right to a jury trial if the claim is for $10,000 or less. This would appreciably cut down the long wait in courts.

2. Insurance companies must pay interest on judgments and settlements, so that they cannot financially benefit from the long waits for courtrooms. If the injured plaintiff has made a reasonable demand, the insurance company should have to pay interest of at least 10% on the judgment or settlement which the plaintiff achieves after he has set the case for trial.

3. Attorney fees should be paid to the winner of a lawsuit. If insurance companies were forced to pay the plaintiff's attorney as well as his damages, they would settle cases a lot quicker. Fees would only be paid on the refusal to accept

a reasonable offer. Conversely the payment of attorney fees to an insurance company if the plaintiff lost his case would prevent many frivolous and fraudulent claims.

4. There should be compulsory automobile insurance in all states. No car should be allowed to leave a showroom or used car lot until the new owner can produce a certificate showing he has insurance. Also, no automobile should be transferred between private individuals until this compulsory insurance requirement is met.

5. The laws of contributory negligence should be eliminated in favor of a system of comparative negligence. There is no reason why an accident victim who may be only 1% in the wrong should be denied some financial recovery.

6. All auto insurance policies should have disability pay as well as medical pay, but there should be repayment to the insurance company for these benefits if the victim collects any settlement or judgment. (This repayment should be reduced by the attorney's fees the victim had to pay in order to collect).

Qualified plans such as this are used in Delaware, Arkansas, Texas, Maryland, Minnesota, Oregon, Virginia, and South Dakota.

CHATTEL MORTGAGE AUTOMOBILE INSURANCE

When you borrow to buy a car on time, the lender requires insurance on the car to protect his investment. If the buyer does not secure his own insurance, the lender will place a policy, usually at a much higher rate than the consumer could have found on his own. This insurance only protects the lender, since it provides for repair of the car or payment to the lender if the auto is damaged or destroyed by collision, fire, theft, or other disaster. This type of insurance does not give the consumer coverage for public liability, medical pay, or uninsured motorist.

ASSIGNED RISKS

Insurance companies are not obligated to sell everyone insurance, and they have the right to cancel policies after they go into effect if they give the policyholder a reasonable amount of time to find new insurance. No reasonable grounds are required for this refusal to supply insurance or renew existing policies.

If a motorist is unable to find a company to insure him, the states have assigned risk programs which force the local companies to provide insurance at a very high premium. The motorist has no choice of his insurer, and the company does not offer coverage for comprehensive or medical pay. This type of insurance is purely for the protection of the public, and the coverage is the minimal amount required by the state.

LIABILITY INSURANCE

A driver can remove himself from the assigned risk category by sustaining a good driving record.

PERSONAL LIABILITY INSURANCE

An individual can insure himself and his family against negligence claims. This insurance usually comes in the form of a homeowner's or tenant's package policy. This policy will protect an individual from fire and other disaster, burglary, and lawsuits based on negligence. There also may be provisions for medical pay for guests who are injured on one's property notwithstanding the issue of negligence.

This type of insurance protects the homeowner and tenant not only from claims which might come from accidents around the house (slips and falls, dog bites, etc.), but also from accidents which may occur outside of the home (errant golf shots, etc.). This coverage does not include claims arising from automobile accidents or business activities.

STATE AUTOMOBILE INSURANCE LAWS

	COMPULSORY AUTO INSURANCE FOR ALL RESIDENT MOTORISTS	MINIMUM INSURANCE COVERAGE FOR PROPERTY DAMAGE	MINIMUM INSURANCE COVERAGE FOR INJURY OR DEATH	NO-FAULT AUTO INSURANCE PLAN
ALABAMA	no	$5000	$10,000/$20,000	no
ALASKA	no	$5000	$15,000/$30,000	no
ARIZONA	no	$5000	$10,000/$20,000	no
ARKANSAS	no	$5000	$10,000/$20,000	no[2]
CALIFORNIA	no	$5000	$15,000/$30,000	no
COLORADO	yes	$5000	$15,000/$30,000	yes
CONNECTICUT	no	$5000	$20,000/$40,000	yes
DELAWARE	yes	$5000	$10,000/$20,000	no[2]
D. C.	no	$5000	$10,000/$20,000	no
FLORIDA	yes	$5000	$10,000/$20,000	yes
GEORGIA	no	$5000	$10,000/$20,000	no
HAWAII	no	$5000	$10,000/$20,000	yes
IDAHO	no	$5000	$10,000/$20,000	no
ILLINOIS	no	$5000	$10,000/$20,000	no[1]
INDIANA	no	$10,000	$15,000/$30,000	no
IOWA	no	$5000	$10,000/$20,000	no
KANSAS	no	$5000	$15,000/$30,000	yes
KENTUCKY	no	$5000	$10,000/$20,000	no
LOUISIANA	no	$1000	$ 5,000/$10,000	no

	COMPULSORY AUTO INSURANCE FOR ALL RESIDENT MOTORISTS	MINIMUM INSURANCE COVERAGE FOR PROPERTY DAMAGE	MINIMUM INSURANCE COVERAGE FOR INJURY OR DEATH	NO-FAULT AUTO INSURANCE PLAN
MAINE	no	$10,000	$20,000/$40,000	no
MARYLAND	yes	$5000	$15,000/$30,000	no[2]
MASSACHUSETTS	yes	$5000	$15,000/$30,000	yes
MICHIGAN	yes	$5000	$10,000/$20,000	yes
MINNESOTA	no	$5000	$10,000/$20,000	no[2]
MISSISSIPPI	no	$5000	$10,000/$20,000	no
MISSOURI	no	$2000	$10,000/$20,000	no
MONTANA	no	$5000	$10,000/$20,000	no
NEBRASKA	no	$5000	$10,000/$20,000	no
NEVADA	no	$5000	$15,000/$30,000	yes
NEW HAMPSHIRE	no	$5000	$20,000/$40,000	no
NEW JERSEY	yes	$5000	$10,000/$20,000	yes
NEW MEXICO	no	$5000	$10,000/$20,000	no
NEW YORK	yes	$5000	$10,000/$20,000	yes
NORTH CAROLINA	yes	$5000	$10,000/$20,000	no
NORTH DAKOTA	no	$5000	$10,000/$20,000	no
OHIO	no	$7500	$12,500/$25,000	no
OKLAHOMA	no	$5000	$ 5,000/$10,000	no
OREGON	no	$5000	$10,000/$20,000	no[2]
PENNSYLVANIA	no	$5000	$10,000/$20,000	no

	COMPULSORY AUTO INSURANCE FOR ALL RESIDENT MOTORISTS	MINIMUM INSURANCE COVERAGE FOR PROPERTY DAMAGE	MINIMUM INSURANCE COVERAGE FOR INJURY OR DEATH	NO-FAULT AUTO INSURANCE PLAN
RHODE ISLAND	no	$5000	$10,000/$20,000	no
SOUTH CAROLINA	no	$5000	$10,000/$20,000	no
SOUTH DAKOTA	no	$10,000	$15,000/$30,000	no[2]
TENNESSEE	no	$5000	$10,000/$20,000	no
TEXAS	no	$5000	$10,000/$20,000	no[2]
UTAH	no	$5000	$10,000/$20,000	yes
VERMONT	no	$5000	$10,000/$20,000	no
VIRGINIA	no	$5000	$20,000/$40,000	no[2]
WASHINGTON	no	$5000	$15,000/$30,000	no
WEST VIRGINIA	no	$5000	$10,000/$20,000	no
WISCONSIN	no	$5000	$15,000/$30,000	no
WYOMING	no	$5000	$10,000/$20,000	no

FOOTNOTE:
(1) Illinois had a no-fault insurance plan, but its state supreme court nullified the law because it unconstitutionally discriminated against the poor.

(2) There is a qualified plan, but it does not restrict tort suits.

CHAPTER 15

Intentional Torts

Negligence means an accidental mistake. Intentional torts are wrongs which are caused by the intentional act of a tortfeasor. The person who causes the injury may not have expected the resulting damage, but, nevertheless, his actions are intentional.

Claims for medical expenses, loss of earnings, and pain and suffering can be collected by the victim of an intentional tort. The big difference between unintentional and intentional torts is the matter of punitive damages. Where a party has committed an intentional tort, the victim can also collect punitive damages to punish the wrong doer for his malicious act. Punitive damages can also be collected for acts which are not intentional, but amount to willful and wanton disregard for the rights of others; for instance, firing a gun into a crowd of people. Punitive damages are based on the severity of the act committed and the ability of the defendant to pay. Contributory neligence and assumption of the risk are not defenses to intentional torts.

Some intentional torts are also crimes. It is possible for one to incur both civil and criminal penalties for the same act. Thus, one who commits a murder not only will go to jail, but he also will be liable to the family of the deceased in a wrongful death action. Some states have taken the position that the victim of a crime has been wronged by society, and these states give some compensation to victims of crimes.

ASSAULT AND BATTERY

The most well-known of the intentional torts are assaults and batteries. Although most people use the terms synonymously, they actually have different meanings. An assault is an unlawful attempt coupled with the present ability to commit an injury; battery is any willful and unlawful use of force or violence. The assault is the attempt, and the battery is the actual touching.

Consent can be a defense to an assault or battery. The traditional defense to an assault and battery suit is the privilege of self defense. Any necessary force may be used to protect yourself from injury to your person, your property or to a member of your family. However, only that amount of force which is reasonably necessary to *repel* a battery can be used. Excessive force is not a defense.

> Malcolm and Norman were competing for the amorous interest of Darlene. One night Malcolm caught Norman and Darlene together as they were leaving a theatre. Malcolm and Norman confronted each other with abusive language and tempers flared. Malcolm, being a gentleman and a staunch believer in non-violence, did not strike Norman with his fists or a weapon; he spat at him. Norman successfully dodged the moisture, which landed on Darlene's face. While the spitting incident did not cause Norman or Darlene any medical expenses, they were extremely upset over it, and they both sued Malcolm for punitive damages. Darlene's suit was on the basis of a battery, because Malcolm's action was an offensive touching. Malcolm argued that his actions were not intended for Darlene, but the court ruled that the act of spitting was intentional, and the intent to hit Norman was transferred to Darlene. Norman's lawsuit was based on assault.

The trouble with most assault and battery cases, and for that matter, most intentional torts, is that the wrongdoer rarely has enough money to pay for special, general, or punitive damages. Insurance companies do not write policies to cover intentional torts. The run-of-the-mill bully who vents his aggression by beating up innocent people rarely has enough money to pay his own bar tabs, let alone another's medical bills. If you are fortunate enough to obtain a judgment against an intentional tortfeasor, he can usually go bankrupt and relieve himself of any obligation to pay the victim for his damages except punitive damages. Since it is extremely hard to collect on judgments against these people, it should be no surprise that it is hard to find an attorney who will represent an injured party where the tortfeasor is "judgment-proof". But every once in a while a scrappy, persistent attorney will represent an injured party, obtain a judgment, and see to it that the judgment is paid.

FALSE IMPRISONMENT

False imprisonment is an intentional tort which occurs when one person directly restrains another for some appreciable length of time, compelling him to stay or go somewhere against his will. Defenses include the privilege of a lawful arrest and reasonable detention without arrest. It applies to storekeepers who have the privilege of detaining a person when they reasonably believe a theft has been committed. What is a reasonable time detention depends on the circumstances. One who maliciously instigates or participates in an unlawful arrest or imprisonment is also liable for damages for this tort.

INTENTIONAL INFLICTION OF EMOTIONAL DISTRESS

Most physical injuries will cause a victim some emotional distress, but there is a separate category of torts to cover those who intentionally cause another emotional distress. For instance, threats of violence, humiliation by bus drivers or landlords and high pressure collection tactics fall into this tort category. Other examples are the aggressive use of authority, practical jokes, shocking false stories and unwarranted interference with a dead body.

> The Nogoodnik Disability Insurance Company sold its insurance through ads in the local newspaper. Rafael purchased one of its policies and made regular payments on it. At age 28, two years after he had purchased the policy, Rafael contracted a rare disease which left him unable to work and eligible for monthly payments of $100 from the insurance company until Rafael was 70. The insurance company made prompt payments for two years. After a change in claims managers, Nogoodnik abruptly cut off Rafael's payments and accused him of dishonest conduct in his original insurance application. Rafael was terribly upset over this loss of income and was forced to go through the humiliating acceptance of welfare. He hired a lawyer who obtained a judgment against Nogoodnik for reinstatement of the policy and payment of any back disability payments which were due, $25,000 for general damages for the shock, humiliation and anxiety which Rafael experienced and $100,000 punitive damages for the unjustifiably oppressive conduct of Nogoodnik. The actions of the insurance company amounted to an intentional infliction of emotional distress, not just a simple breach of contract. A disability insurance policy is considered a vested property right, and any unwarranted interference by an insurance company with this property is also considered a tort known as unlawful invasion of a property interest.

Closely akin to this tort is another one called alienation of affection. It happens when someone maliciously interferes with a marriage and causes a loss of companionship to the husband or wife. But mere adultery is not enough without showing that there was a malicious intent to break up a marriage. This means that a parent who wants to see a child's marriage break up is a more likely candidate to be sued for this tort than a fun seeking lecher. Alienation of affection is a common law tort, and many states have abolished it by legislation or judicial decision.

INVASION OF PROPERTY INTERESTS

Trespass to property is the unlawful interference with its possession. Trespass may be to real or personal property. There are many privileges that one may set up as a defense to this tort, and these privileges usually apply to someone who has some rights to be on the property.

Conversion involves the wrongful exercise of dominion over someone else's personal property. It can include destruction or damage to the personal property.

Trademarks, tradenames and literary property are all considered personal property. Their wrongful imitation, use or copying is a tort.

MALICIOUS PROSECUTION

Malicious prosecution occurs when one person starts unjustifiable litigation, civil, criminal or administrative, against another, causing him damage to reputation and the expense of defending himself. The person who institutes the unjustified litigation must have malicious motives, and he must be acting without probable cause. Before a plaintiff can start his own lawsuit for malicious prosecution, he must show a termination of the legal proceedings against him and a favorable outcome. In criminal cases, this would mean an acquittal or dismissal of the charges. In a civil or administrative action, it would be a dismissal of the lawsuit or a finding in his favor.

That a criminally accused defendant obtains an acquittal or dismissal of his case does not mean that he automatically has a case for malicious prosecution. In the first place, the prosecution must prove that the accused is guilty beyond a reasonable doubt, and that this quantum of proof cannot be met does not mean that the accused is not guilty of the crime. Second, the motive for the lawsuit must be malicious.

Judges, prosecutors and other law enforcement officers are often protected from malicious prosecution suits by immunity statutes.

There is also a tort known as abuse of process which covers the misuse of such legal processes as attachment, execution and injunctions. Malice is a necessary element of this tort.

NUISANCE

Everyone has a right to a tranquil life and peaceful enjoyment of his property. If a neighbor upsets that tranquility by some activity, then the neighbor has created a nuisance. If the neighbor will not voluntarily stop, then the victims may go to court to abate the nuisance and collect any damages which have been caused by it.

Nuisance is actually a hybrid between an intentional tort and a negligent tort. The activity may be done intentionally, or it may result from carelessness. In either event, the result is the same: the peaceful enjoyment of life has been upset.

Nuisance lawsuits normally involve typical neighborly disputes over barking dogs, loud music, latenight partying, family fights which carry over into the neighbors' lives, and undue garbage accumulation. Nuisance lawsuits can also be instigated against neighboring businesses and industries for pollution or some other activity which upsets the peaceful enjoyment of the land.

The only remedy available to a victim for all of the other torts mentioned in this Part IV has been money damages to compensate the victim after the tort has been committed. Only in the case of nuisance can a victim get an injunction to stop the nuisance in addition to money damages for any past pecuniary loss.

A court will not automatically grant an injunction to abate a nuisance. The plaintiff must make a very clear and convincing showing that a court should act. A court will balance the equities—that is, it will look to the gravity of the harm created by the nuisance and weigh that against the need for carrying on the activity.

Also, if a plaintiff has lived with a nuisance for a long period of time, his slowness in initiating action may prevent him from getting any court relief. And too, if the plaintiff is conducting the same type of activity on his property or engaged in some other nefarious schemes, the court will not act. Lastly, if the plaintiff's complaint is petty and trivial, a court will not dignify it by granting an injunction.

Once a plaintiff has an injunction which orders a neighbor to abate a nuisance, any violation of that order could put the defendant in contempt of court. If the contempt were severe enough, the defendant could pay a large fine and face jail in addition to being responsible for paying further damages to the plaintiff.

CHAPTER 16

Absolute Liability

There is a category of torts which gives a victim damages even though his injury was caused neither by negligence nor by an intentional act. The courts have come to recognize that some activities are so dangerous to human life or property that their very performance makes the owners or operators strictly liable for any damage which might result to an innocent person.

Anyone who keeps a dangerous animal, whether wild or domestic, is absolutely liable for damage inflicted by it. Dog owners used to be liable only if they knew the animal was dangerous. (In other words, the dog was allowed one bite.) Now many states make dog owners strictly liable for damages suffered by any person who was bitten by the dog while in a public place or lawfully in a private place - including the property of the owner of the dog. (This law only covers dog bites, not other accidents which might be caused by dogs.)

Other activities which have been classified as ultra-hazardous are: (1) blasting with explosives, (2) fumigating with deadly poisons and (3) testing of rocket motors. Although there have been no cases yet, I am sure nuclear accidents would qualify too.

Activities which are not considered ultra-hazardous are: (1) fire-fighting, (2) impounding of water, (3) escape of weeds, (4) excavation of earth and other earthmoving activities, (5) ordinary building construction and (6) the discharge of firearms. Aviation was once considered an ultra-hazardous activity, but now an airplane is not considered an inherently dangerous instrument. Even though these activities are not considered ultra-hazardous, a victim can still collect damages by proving negligence.

Contributory negligence is not considered a defense to actions based on absolute or strict liability, but assumption of the risk is.

CHAPTER 17

Products Liability

Every year thousands of Americans are injured by defectively manufactured or processed products. Private and government agencies have been created to regulate and prevent this, but many defective products are still circulating and causing injury.

One of the best consumer remedies is the lawsuit for personal injuries. Nothing makes a businessman more responsive than the possible loss of his profits. Personal injury lawsuits based on product liability—along with the attendant publicity—can mean large judgments and large business losses.

Consumers who were injured by defective products formerly recovered damages on only two theories of the law—negligence and breach of warranty. Both have serious drawbacks which prevented many from collecting damages although the courts stretched and tortured them for the consumers' benefit. Some states have augmented these two basic theories of recovery with a new theory based on strict liability of any business which manufactures, distributes or otherwise circulates a defective product.

BREACH OF WARRANTY

All products sold carry with them certain warranties of fitness which run from the seller to the buyer. An injured buyer can sue the seller for a breach of warranty under this theory.

In most product-liability situations there are many middlemen who will handle a product from the time it leaves the manufacturer until the time it reaches the consumer. The manufacturer and other middlemen will disclaim any liability for breach of warranty because there is no "privity of contract" between them and the consumer. In other words, the consumer can only sue the person from whom he directly purchased the defective goods.

But this has severe drawbacks - suppose, for instance, that a bystander, such as a child or a social guest, were injured without having been the purchaser. This person could not maintain an action based on breach of warranty because he never entered into any kind of a contract with the seller of the goods. There are also other technical defenses such as a failure to give notice and disclaims by the manufacturers. The Uniform Commercial Code (in force in 49 of the 50 states and the District of Columbia) has been amended to provide that warranties run to a consumer's family and household guests in products liability cases - but these victims can only sue the business which directly sold the defective product to the consumer because of the privity requirement.

Some states have abolished the privity requirement in food and drug cases only and others have abolished it altogether where the defective product has caused a personal injury. If the requirement has been abolished, all persons who touch the defective product while it is in the stream of commerce are strictly liable to consumers.

> Benjamin bought a ladder from the Shakey Hardware Store in Reno, Nevada which had been manufactured by the Clumsy Ladder Company of Nevada. One of the rungs collapsed, and Benjamin fell to the ground, breaking his leg. He could not show negligence against the manufacturer, but could show that the ladder was defective. Benjamin could not sue the manufacturer for breach of warranty because Nevada is one of those states which requires some privity of contract between a consumer and a seller. He did sue the Shakey Hardware Company for personal injury damages, but the company went bankrupt during the lawsuit, and he recovered nothing.

NEGLIGENCE

Consumers who are injured by manufactured products can also sue for damages based upon the theory of negligence. The law states that a manufacturer who fails to exercise reasonable care in its production process is liable for physical harm caused by its negligence. The negligence may occur in the manufacturing, design, failure to warn, failure to test or failure to instruct in proper use. The responsible parties are not limited to just manufacturers and sellers; liability can also run to assemblers, wholesalers, lessors and other middlemen. There are even cases where the bank which took an active role in the manufacture of a product was held for negligence.

There is no privity requirement when you sue on the theory of negligence, as a careless manufacturer is liable to all those persons reasonably expected to be harmed by the normal use of his product. This means that a motorist who is injured by another person's defective automobile can sue its manufacturer or seller because he is clearly one of the persons who might reasonably be injured by a badly made car.

The problem with suing on the theory of negligence is that the injured person has to prove his case by showing the conduct of the business and proving the standard of care which it should have followed. The manufacturer can allege that his conduct was beyond reproach and that any negligence was caused by some mishandling by a middleman. Manufacturers and sellers can also make a defense of contributory negligence. The burden of proof on the consumer is onerous and expensive especially in those cases where the manufacturer is a long distance from his home and the place of the trial.

STRICT LIABILITY

The strict liability theory was founded on the principle that businesses must bear the responsibility and burden for placing defective products in the flow of commerce. The injured consumer should not have to be put to the burden of establishing privity of contract or lack of due care. If businessmen wish to reap the profits of commerce, then they must pay the penalty for defective products. Therefore, the laws of many states declare that anyone who sells a product in a defective condition (unreasonably dangerous to the consumer) is subject to liability for physical harm caused to the ultimate user of his goods. This rule applies even when the seller has exercised all possible care in the preparation and sale of the product. All purchasers, users and even mere bystanders are covered by the rule. However, there is no coverage for those who discover a defective condition and continue to use the product (and persons who misuse products). Consumers with rare and unique allergies are not covered either.

Since all products are covered under this theory, one would immediately wonder about the liability of cigarette and liquor manufacturers. Lung cancer victims have sued the cigarette companies, but the courts have consistently held that the present state of the law does not subject the manufacturer to strict liability if the cigarettes are reasonably safe for the purpose intended—that is, they are free from foreign substances. Similarly, alcoholic beverages (which do not contain any foreign or deleterious matter) cannot be the subject of a strict liability suit because the ingestion of alcohol has undesirable consequences.

Under the strict liability theory of recovery, manufacturers and sellers are primarily liable for damages, but middlemen, lessors, and licensors may also be held responsible. In a recent California case, the courts extended this doctrine to include the builders of mass produced and tract housing.

The biggest problem of the attorney in a strict liability case is proving the defectiveness of the product in question. "Defective" means that it is harmful to normal individuals during normal use. Some products (although they are faultlessly made) may be intrinsicly dangerous. If this is the case, the manufacturer must warn of known dangers, and failure to warn would make the product legally defective. A defect can also be shown by improper design, failure to properly test or inspect, misrepresentation on the quality or use of the product and improper instructions on its use.

It is important to note that this strict liability theory applies only to products, not personal services. Any person who is injured as a result of another's personal services (i.e., attorneys, accountants, doctors, and repairmen) can only seek recovery on the basis of negligence or breach of warranty.

In 1968 the Tacky Construction Company bought a bulldozer from the Thomas Tractor Company. In 1972, Stanley, an equipment operator for Tacky, was standing on the deckplate of his bulldozer when the hinge of the plate snapped. This caused him to fall into the engine department, and he lost his left leg. Stanley could not maintain an action for breach of warranty against the Thomas Tractor Company because he was not the one who purchased the machine. If Stanley's attorney can prove that the design of the bulldozer was negligent and that this negligence caused Stanley's accident, then an action for negligence could be maintained against Thomas. Notwithstanding negligence, if Stanley's attorney can show that the part which broke on the bulldozer and caused the accident was defective, then Thomas is strictly liable for Stanley's damages.

HAS THE DEFENSE OF PRIVITY OF CONTRACT BEEN EFFECTIVELY ABOLISHED IN PRODUCTS LIABILITY CASES INVOLVING BODILY INJURIES?

ALABAMA	YES	KENTUCKY	YES
ALASKA	NO	LOUISIANA	YES[1]
ARIZONA	NO	MAINE	NO
ARKANSAS	YES	MARYLAND	NO
CALIFORNIA	YES	MASSACHUSETTS	YES
COLORADO	NO, Except in Food and Drug Cases	MICHIGAN	NO
		MINNESOTA	YES
		MISSISSIPPI	NO
CONNECTICUT	YES	MISSOURI	YES
DELAWARE	YES	MONTANA	NO
D.C.	NO	NEBRASKA	NO
FLORIDA	NO, Except in Food and Drug Cases	NEVADA	NO
		NEW HAMPSHIRE	NO
GEORGIA	YES	NEW JERSEY	YES
HAWAII	YES	NEW MEXICO	NO
IDAHO	NO	NEW YORK	NO, Except in Food and Drug Cases
ILLINOIS	YES		
INDIANA	YES	NORTH CAROLINA	NO
IOWA	YES		
KANSAS	NO		

NORTH DAKOTA	NO
OHIO	YES
OKLAHOMA	NO
OREGON	YES
PENNSYLVANIA	NO, Except in Food and Drug Cases
RHODE ISLAND	NO, Except in Food and Drug Cases
SOUTH CAROLINA	YES
SOUTH DAKOTA	YES
TENNESSEE	YES
TEXAS	YES
UTAH	NO
VERMONT	YES
VIRGINIA	NO
WASHINGTON	YES
WEST VIRGINIA	NO
WISCONSIN	YES
WYOMING	NO

FOOTNOTE:

[1] No privity required in limited circumstances where defective product was advertised and promoted to public and where the seller knew the product was defective.

CHAPTER 18

Attorneys in Personal Injury Cases

Now that you have some knowledge of your rights to money damages in an accident case, do you still need an attorney to represent you? Most certainly, for it takes one who is sophisticated and experienced in matters of injury settlements to represent you to make sure that you receive the maximum amount for your injuries. Bargaining with an insurance company without the counsel of an attorney could be disastrous. Remember that insurance is a profit making business, and the companies do not take an altruistic outlook on the payment of claims —they pay no more than they have to. There is no definite amount a company must pay for damages, and adjusters are going to settle claims for as little as possible.

Many times an adjuster will approach a victim while he lies in a sick bed and offer a check if he releases the company from any further liability. Even assuming that the victim is in the proper mental condition to sign such a release, no settlement should be made unless you know the exact nature and extent of your injuries. Often the seriousness of an injury is not known until many months later. If you settle prematurely, there is no later recourse against the insurance company for unexpected misery.

Some people feel that they should bargain with the insurance adjuster until they are ready to settle, and then take the case to an attorney to seek his advice. This is a bad idea because valuable evidence and time may be lost. A good attorney who is hired immediately after an accident will send out investigators to start gathering proof of fault including statements of witnesses and photographs of the cars involved as well as the scene of the accident. Too often the victim assumes that he is completely in the right and then goes to trial only to see that the facts are so misconstrued that he is made to appear the villain.

FEES

Attorneys contract to take on personal injury cases on a contingency basis with a fixed fee which is usually one-third of the net settlement or judgment after all the costs of suit and investigation are deducted. Attorneys argue that the contingent fee arrangement is an inducement for them to work harder—the more that is won, the more they get. Many contingent fee contracts call for increasing percentages as the case progresses toward trial. For instance, an attorney will take one-third of the settlement before trial, and 40% of the settlement after trial has commenced. If the case goes up on appeal, then the percentage may get higher.

Under this arrangement, the lawyer advances all the costs necessary for litigation including the expenses of private investigators, expert witnesses, jury fees and deposition costs.

Some attorneys will attempt to impress a gullible client with their prowess in the personal injury field and charge a much higher percentage for their services—sometimes 50% or more. Such percentages are only justified when the liability for an accident is extremely questionable. It is wise to shop around and get a better rate. Good attorneys will often accept a low but fair percentage—25% is not unusual. Lawyers are professionals but not above competition for a lucrative injury case.

If a minor is the plaintiff, the court must approve the attorney's fee—usually 25% but more in difficult cases.

SPECIALISTS AND REFERRALS

Although many lawyers specialize in bodily injury work, you cannot get a list of them from a telephone book or from the bar association. Legal ethics forbid this. However, it is not really necessary to go to a specialist since many general practitioners can do an excellent job in obtaining satisfactory personal injury settlements.

Sometimes a general practitioner will refer an injury case to another attorney who does specialize in the field. For making the referral, the first lawyer will receive a fee—usually a percentage of the new attorney's fee. This practice is entirely ethical as long as the specialist does not attempt to alter the original contingent fee contract to the detriment of the client. The general practitioner may aid the specialist in the preparation of the case, or he may just hand over the file with no further contact. The client whose attorney refers his case to a specialist really has nothing to lose and everything to gain.

AMBULANCE-CHASING

Beware the ambulance-chasing attorney! The rules of professional conduct for attorneys strictly prohibit solicitation of clients, and ambulance-chasing is the most blatant form of solicitation. Ambulance-chasing is rampant in most states, and many state bars (the organization responsible to police the profession) have dismal records in the investigation or discipline of this practice.

Ambulance-chasers pay illegal kickbacks to those who refer them injury cases —people like insurance agents, hospital workers, doctors, nurses, policemen and ambulance drivers.

The ambulance-chase always starts with an accident and an injured victim. The contact man will attempt to gain an invitation for the attorney to visit and sign up the victim on a contingent fee contract. Sometimes the tipster will even sign up the victim himself without the client ever having met the lawyer.

Some attorneys engage in an even more flagrant form of ambulance-chasing by using salaried private investigators who have two-way police radios installed in their offices and automobiles. An accident call brings them to the scene like vultures and, on learning who the victim is, they go to his hospital room and engage in some heavy-handed practices to get the victim's signature on a contingent fee contract.

I once represented a girl who was injured in an accident in San Francisco. She reported the accident to her insurance agent, who worked for a major insurance company. It so happened that the tortfeasor was insured by the same company. The agent came to her home and told her about a terrific lawyer in San Jose (some 60 miles from her home); and he talked her into signing a contingent fee contract. She never met the lawyer, and after a few months of silence, she fired him. She then received a phone call from the same insurance agent who tried to talk her out of it. When I was retained, I asked her former lawyer for the file. He wanted an exorbitant fee and also wanted repayment for expenses he said he had already paid. This included a $100 charge for a private investigator's report which did not exist!

There is no reason why a victim should reward an unethical attorney with a contract when there are so many competent, ethical attorneys who would handle the case and obtain good results. It stands to reason that an attorney who is unethical in one aspect of his practice may engage in other types of unethical conduct to the detriment of his client.

The proper way to retain a lawyer in a personal injury is to invite him to visit you to discuss the case or make an appointment at his office if you are healthy enough. For the name of an attorney, ask the advice and help of a family member or close friend. If a lawyer is recommended by a stranger, find out why he is recommending this attorney. You can always phone your local bar association for the name of a competent attorney.

CHAPTER 19

Defamation

DEFINITIONS

Defamation is a verbal or written false publication which causes an injury to reputation. Defamatory matter can generally be divided into two categories —libel and slander. Libel is a printing or "something affixed to the eye" (such as a television broadcast) and is a more permanent form of defamation. Slander is an oral statement or gesture.

All living persons, businesses, and classes of persons (police departments and labor unions) can sue for defamation, but municipalities or governmental bodies cannot.

Everyone, at some time in his life, has been legally defamed by another, but relatively few lawsuits arise over defamatory statements. They are extremely expensive to pursue. The usual case involves a very small amount of actual monetary damages but a large amount of punitive damages for malice, and most defendants who make the defamatory statement cannot afford to pay the amounts the plaintiff may want.

Defamation suits often prove to be counter-productive, as the entire matter and the injury to reputation will stay alive during the course of a lawsuit. Most defamed persons would rather bury the statement than have it live for the many months that it takes to prosecute a lawsuit.

PUBLICATION

In order for a statement to be legally defamatory, it must be published— that is, communicated to a third person who understands its ugly meaning and applies it to a particular person. The communication may be to one person or to one million. If one repeats a statement which he heard from another, then he too is liable for damages to the defamed party. Therefore, all persons who communicate, publish, or otherwise pass along defamatory statements are liable, no matter where the matter originated.

Cecil Dirkson was the sole owner of the local tavern. An unknown person wrote the name and telephone number of Susan Toulouse in rather large letters on the wall of the men's room. He also scribbled out a brief statement describing Susan's desire for relations with the entire population, male and female, of Bakersfield, California. When Susan received a telephone call from a prospective suitor, she learned about the defamatory statement on the wall and she immediately phoned Cecil and demanded that he erase the writing on his bathroom wall. One week later Cecil had not bothered to do this. Susan sued Cecil for defamation on the grounds that he was responsible for the republication of defamatory material about her and won compensatory damages.

DEFENSES

Another big reason for the rarity of defamation suits is that many defenses can be successfully asserted against this charge. The most obvious defense is the truth of the statement asserted since truth is an absolute defense.

There are other defenses of privilege. A privileged defense means that, even though a statement is defamatory, the law allows it to be published with impunity because of an overriding social policy.

Some statements (even malicious ones) are absolutely privileged such as ones made in legislative, judicial or other official proceedings authorized by law. In the case of judicial proceedings, the privilege covers any publication which relates to the proceeding, not just statements made in court. Therefore, one can allege all sorts of misdeeds in a court pleading, and these statements would be absolutely privileged.

The nation as a whole suffered through the gross abuse of this absolute privilege when the late Senator Joseph McCarthy made outlandish defamatory statements and called all sorts of innocent people Communists while on the floor of the Senate where all such statements are absolutely privileged. But had he uttered such lies outside this protected bastion, his estate would have been left penniless from the claims from those whom he had unjustifiably defamed.

An absolute privilege also exists if the defamed victim has consented to the publication of such remarks.

There also exists a qualified privilege to communicate or publish defamatory matter. The qualification is that the statement cannot be made with malice, and must be made to protect some interest. A newspaper or other form of media can publish defamatory matter about a public official as long as it is done in good faith and without malice.

Other examples of the defense of qualified privilege are the following: 1) police reports (parties who report criminals to the police are protected under this defense as long as they make their report without malice); 2) fair comment by newspapers or other forms of media (this includes honest expressions of opinion

DEFAMATION

by movie critics, political cartoonists and the editorial staff); 3) employment or credit investigations (when a prospective employer inquires into the credentials of a job-seeker from an ex-boss); 4) answers to defamatory charges; 5) fair and true reports of a public proceeding (Newspapers may report on defamatory statements made in official proceedings. A legislator has an absolute privilege to defame a party on the floor of Congress, so a newspaper has a qualified privilege to accurately report on the defamatory statement.)

In most states newspapers and other reporters of the news have an opportunity to escape liability for making unprivileged defamatory statements by printing a retraction. The person who is defamed must make a demand for a retraction in writing soon after the defamatory article appears, and the newspaper must print the retraction in the same conspicuous manner as the original defamatory statement.

That a party who makes an unprivileged defamatory statement has acted with innocence or good faith is no defense. The law clearly states that the originator of the statement and all others who circulate and perpetuate it are liable. But if one has acted with innocence and good faith, his lack of malice will go toward the mitigation of damages which might be assessed.

While defamatory statements made with innocence or good faith are not a defense, defamatory matter made in jest (where a reasonable audience can determine that the statement was not to appear as truth) are not considered defamation.

DAMAGES

A defamation victim can collect all of his losses which result from the defamation, including medical bills, lost income, etc. If malice or wanton disregard of the facts are involved, then the victim can possibly collect punitive damages. However, a recent Supreme Court ruling has thrown into question the whole area of punitive damages in defamation.

OTHER KINDS OF DEFAMATION

This section has dealt with injuries to one's personal reputation. There is also a tort action for the victims whose property rights have been damaged by the publication of defamatory statements. Slander of title - a false, unprivileged disparagement of the title to real or personal property - results in actual monetary damage. Trade libel is a false statement of fact or opinion which intentionally disparages the quality of property and which results in monetary damage. The defenses of truth, absolute privilege and qualified privilege apply in these types of actions also.

INVASION OF PRIVACY

Closely akin to defamation is the tort of invasion of privacy. The right of privacy is guaranteed by the Fourth Amendment, but this only protects us from governmental intrusions. The law also recognizes the right of an individual to live a private life, free from unwarranted publicity or other public display. If your right to privacy is unjustifiably invaded, you may sue under this theory of infringement of privacy. This tort is different from defamation because malice and truth are not elements to be considered.

Infringements on the right to privacy include unwarranted disclosure of private affairs, commercial exploitation of one's picture or name and unauthorized non-commercial use of photographs.

The defenses to this action involve consent and the public interest. If one expressly consents to publicity or the use of his name or photograph, then he cannot attack an act he has consented to. Public figures such as politicians and movie stars have put themselves in the public limelight, and they have little right to a private life.

Private persons who do not seek any type of publicity may inadvertently become involved in incidents of public interest and thereby lose their right of privacy. The public has a right to know the news. There is a dividing line between an individual's right to privacy and the public's right to know, but it is hard to pin down and must be measured by the facts of each case.

The right to privacy is violated only by publicity or disclosure to a large body of the public, not when disclosure is made to an individual or a very small group of persons.

The greatest threat to personal privacy comes from our own government. The federal government operates approximately 850 computers which store and regurgitate over a billion items of information on American citizens. This information is supposed to be for departmental use only and not available for unofficial use, but experience tells us that nothing can be kept confidential in Washington, D.C. (Twenty-eight of these computers keep nothing but derogatory information about American citizens.)

As yet there is no federal law which protects its citizens from governmental invasion of privacy by computer — whether negligent or malicious. What is needed is a law which restricts the use of Social Security numbers or any number which permanently classifies an individual, the destruction of obsolete data, the restriction of use of data by governmental agencies, heavy penalties for misuse of government information, and the ability of the citizen to change any incorrect data which is being kept on him.

CHAPTER 20

Workmen's Compensation

INTRODUCTION

Workmen's compensation laws provide payment and medical care to working men and women for injuries which they receive on the job. None of the tort factors of fault, negligence, or contributory negligence are considered. All 50 states have their own workmen's compensation laws, and these laws vary widely from state to state. These laws do have one thing in common: they all inadequately compensate the worker for on-the-job injuries and illnesses. The awards for temporary and permanent disability are low. Medical treatment is often substandard and some states put a dollar limit on the amount of medical treatment an employee may receive. Many farm workers and other laborers are not covered and in a few states the workmen's compensation laws are not even compulsory.

It is a basic legal presumption that workmen's compensation laws should be liberally interpreted in favor of the employee. If a dispute over compensation benefits arises, the dispute is settled by a referee in an administrative hearing, not a court of law. The employer and employee both have the right to have the representation of an attorney and they have the right to appeal their case to a higher administrative board and to the appellate courts of the state. The hearing rules and procedures must be fair to all parties.

WHO IS COVERED?

In most states the workmen's compensation laws apply to all employers including the counties, the state, the cities, public agencies, and corporations. The state laws do not apply to employees of the federal government (which has its own plan). Nor do they apply to transportation carriers involved in interstate commerce. The latter employees are covered under the Federal Employer's Liability Act (FELA).

Workmen's compensation laws also provide for an injured employee who may have multiple employers. If an employee is stricken with a progressive illness (ulcers, for instance), it could well be that many employers will be liable to pay him.

Most states exclude persons who are working at casual odd jobs, domestics and farm laborers from coverage. An independent contractor is not considered an employee; therefore, he would not be covered. Many states allow small employers to avoid giving their workers compensation.

WHAT INJURIES ARE COMPENSABLE?

All injuries incurred while the employee is on the job are covered. This normally does not include going to and coming from work but there are exceptions as in the case where an injury occurs on the employer's parking lot, or the employer provides transportation and lodging as part of the job (traveling salesman), or where an employee is on a special errand when he is injured. Injuries which occur during personal activities of the employee and are unrelated to the job are not compensable. But again, there are many exceptions, especially where the personal acts are expectable by the employer, as coffee breaks or recreational activity.

Heart attacks, ulcers, black lung disease and other diseases from "special exposures" at work can be compensable injuries under the law. Also, industrial injuries aggravating pre-existing diseases are compensable, but there is an apportionment of any award to reflect the percentage of the industrial cause of the injury. An employee's injuries are not covered if they result from horse play or a fight in which the injured worker is the aggressor.

AWARDS

Injured workers are given awards for medical treatment, temporary disability, permanent disability and death benefits (for survivors of a deceased worker). The purpose of a workmen's compensation award is to provide medical care and to prevent the employee and his dependents from becoming public charges during the period of disability.

(1) Medical Treatment: Less than half of the states allow an injured employee to choose his own physician. Most states let the insurance company choose him. Only where the employer refuses to provide an injured employee with a doctor, can the employee choose his own treating physician. If the worker is unhappy with the employer's choice, in most cases, the worker can request and receive a new doctor.

Many states limit the amount of medical care which an injured worker can receive. Their limitation is either based on the dollar amount of medical bills and/ or the period of time in which the employer must give medical care.

(2) Temporary Disability: While the worker is temporarily off the job because of his work-related injury, he is paid temporary disability benefits. The amount of the payment depends on the salary of the employee, the injury and the maximum coverage imposed by state law. For instance, the lowest maximum temporary disability payment in Arkansas and Texas is only $49 per week. The highest maximum weekly benefit is paid in Alaska — $175 per week. The states may have limitations on the length of temporary benefits and on their total dollar amounts.

It must be remembered that temporary disability is paid by the employer or his insurance company; it is not paid by the state. The state may have its own plan for disability coverage for its citizens.

(3) Permanent Disability: After an employee has been off work for a while, his injury or illness usually stabilizes and becomes "stationary." If the employee is permanently disabled from his job, either totally or partially, he is entitled to some weekly benefits for permanent disability. Each state has its own formula for determining permanent disability benefits. This formula is based on a complex set of factors which may include the nature and extent of the injury, the age, the occupation and family status of the employee, and his past earnings. For instance, a 60-year-old executive would receive less in permanent disability for the loss of an arm than would a 30-year-old truck driver with the same injury.

Permanent disability awards are payable on a weekly basis. Some states provide for payment in a lump sum if the employer's insurance company is given credit for interest. The employee can also receive lump sum payment by compromising his claim with the insurance company—this normally means that the worker must give up his rights to future medical benefits.

(4) Death Benefits: If an employee dies because of a work-related injury or illness, the employer will be obligated to pay a lump sum for funeral expenses and a weekly or lump sum amount of cash to the employee's survivors. The state laws decide the maximum amount payable as death benefits. Some states limit death benefits to dependents who are in the immediate family of the deceased worker.

(5) Penalty Payments: Some states will penalize the employer or the insurance carrier for mistreatment of an employee, unsafe working conditions and late payment of benefits.

> Winston was married and the father of two minor children. He earned $18,000 per year as a heavy equipment operator for an oil refinery in Norwalk, California. At age 48, Winston was injured in an industrial accident which damaged his heart necessitating hospitalization and surgery. After nine months off work, it was determined that Winston's damage was permanent and he could not return to his old job. Two years after the accident Winston died because of his work-related heart ailment. Since Winston was injured in California, the California Workmen's Compensation Act applied. Therefore, the employer's insurance company paid the complete medical bill of $18,500, tem-

porary disability of $119 per week for nine months, permanent disability of $70 per week for one year and three months, a $1000 cash payment for funeral expenses and $105 per week for a maximum of $28,000 to Winston's widow and surviving children. If Winston had been a domestic or casual worker, he would not have been covered by the California law.

If Winston had suffered the same injury while working for an employer in a state which did not make the workmen's compensation laws compulsory and if the employer or Winston did not elect to be covered, then Winston and his family would not have received any benefits. If the same set of circmstances had occurred in Iowa, a compulsory state, then the employer would have paid only $7500 toward the medical bills. (The rest would have been payable by Winston and his family.) Winston would have received temporary disability for nine months at the rate of $68 per week. He would have received permanent disability for one year and three months at the rate of $60 per week, the funeral allowance would have been the same and the death benefit payable to Winston's wife and children would have been $63 per week for 300 weeks or a total of $18,900.

THE DISTINCTION BETWEEN TORT DAMAGES AND WORKMEN'S COMPENSATION

In most of the states the exclusive remedy for compensation for an employee who is injured on the job is through workmen's compensation laws. This means that the employee cannot sue the employer for tort damages if the employer is negligent or has acted intentionally. The prior discussions in other chapters in this Part IV on injury claims have dealt with traditional tort damages where a victim can collect medical bills, lost income, property damages and damages for pain and suffering. You must remember that the workmen's compensation laws do not contemplate these types of damages. The laws only provide for awards, which are discussed in the paragraphs immediately preceding this one.

If an employee is injured at work because of the negligence of a third person (not his employer) then the worker can sue that third person for regular tort damages. The worker can also make a workmen's compensation claim, but he must pay back the employer's insurance company if and when he settles his claim against the third party.

Dean, an employee at the Wolf Warehouse, was injured while operating a fork lift which was loading a truck owned and operated by Mitchell. Mitchell had negligently driven the truck away from the dock without waiting for Dean to remove his fork lift, and this caused Dean to tip over and crush his right arm. All of Dean's medical bills were paid by his employer who also paid him temporary disability for many months thereafter. Dean sued Mitchell for his negligence, and the case was settled for $75,000. Since Wolf Warehouse had spent $10,500 in medical treatment and disability payments, they had a lien for this amount from Dean's settlement.

STATE WORKMEN'S COMPENSATION AWARDS

	TEMPORARY TOTAL DISABILITY Benefit Limitations			PERMANENT TOTAL DISABILITY Benefit Limitations			DEATH BENEFITS Benefit Limitations			
	MAXIMUM WEEKLY BENEFIT	DURATION (IN WEEKS)	AMOUNT	MAXIMUM WEEKLY BENEFIT	DURATION (IN WEEKS)	AMOUNT	FUNERAL ALLOWANCE	MAXIMUM WEEKLY BENEFIT	DURATION (IN WEEKS)	AMOUNT
ALABAMA	$ 60	400	$24,000	$ 60	550	$24,000	$ 800	$ 60	400	$24,000
ALASKA	175		30,000	114	Duration of disability		1000	175	W, C-19	20,000
ARIZONA	150+2.30 per dependent	433		150	Duration of disability		800	80.77-153.85	W, C-18	No limit
ARKANSAS	49	450	19,500	49	Duration of disability		750	49	W, C-18	No limit
CALIFORNIA	119	240		119	varies according to degree of disability		1000	119		45,000
COLORADO	65	No Limitations		65	Duration of disability		500	64.25-78.25	312	20,266.75 24,492.25
CONNECTICUT	95 - 143	No Limitations		95+5 per child	Duration of disability		1000	95 - 143	W, C-18	No limit
DELAWARE	75	No Limitations		75	Duration of disability		700	56 - 90	400	No limit
D.C.	167	No Limitations		167	Duration of disability		1000	167	W, C-23	No limit
FLORIDA	66	350		66	Duration of disability		500	66	350	15,000
GEORGIA	50	400	18,000	50	400	18,000	750	42.50	400	17,000
HAWAII	113	No Limitations		112	Duration of disability		1500	84 - 112	W, C-22	35,100
IDAHO	71 - 106	52	Thereafter 60% of State Wage	71 - 106	52	Reduced Benefit for life	750	71	500	
ILLINOIS	89 - 109 71 - 85	64 after 64	21,600 31,250	71 - 85	After $21,600-$30,250 paid, reduced benefit for life		1250	71 - 85	W, C-19	21,600 30,250
INDIANA	60 - 75	500	30,000	60 - 75	500	30,000	1500	60	500	30,000
IOWA	68	300	34,000	63	500		1000	63	300	30,000
KANSAS	56	415	23,240	56	415	23,240	750	56 - 76	W, C-21	18,500 25,000
KENTUCKY	81	No Limitations		81	Duration of disability		1500	81	W, C-21	No limit
LOUISIANA	49	300		49	500		1000	49	500	No limit
MAINE	81	No Limitations		81	Duration of disability		1000	81	W, C-18	No limit
MARYLAND	91	No Limitations		91		45,000	750	91	500	27,500

| | TEMPORARY TOTAL DISABILITY | | | PERMANENT TOTAL DISABILITY | | | | DEATH BENEFITS | | |
| | Benefit Limitations | | | Benefit Limitations | | | | Benefit Limitations | | |
	MAXIMUM WEEKLY BENEFIT	DURATION (IN WEEKS)	AMOUNT	MAXIMUM WEEKLY BENEFIT	DURATION (IN WEEKS)	AMOUNT	FUNERAL ALLOWANCE	MAXIMUM WEEKLY BENEFIT	DURATION (IN WEEKS)	AMOUNT
MASSACHUSETTS	80 + 6 per dependent		$20,000	80+6 per dependent	Duration of disability		$1000	45+6 per child	W, C-18	No limit unless W self support
MICHIGAN	84-113	No limitations		84-113	Duration of disability		1500	84-107	500	
MINNESOTA	80	350		80	Duration of disability		1000	80	W, C-19	$35,000
MISSISSIPPI	56	450	21,000	56	450	21,000	500	56	450	21,000
MISSOURI	70	400		60	300	$50 weekly for life	800	70	W, C-21	22,500
MONTANA	60-80	300		37-60	500	Board may extend	500	37-60		
NEBRASKA	62	300	Thereafter $47 weekly	62	300	$47 weekly for life	1000	62	W-life C-325	No limit for W
NEVADA	75-103	433		62-86	Duration of disability		650	38+11 per child	W, C-18	No limit
NEW HAMPSHIRE	92	No limitations		92	Duration of disability		1000	92	341	31,372
NEW JERSEY	108	300		108	450	Board may extend	750	108	W, C-18	(2)
NEW MEXICO	57	500	28,000	57	500	28,500	750	57	500	28,500
NEW YORK	95	No limitations		80	Duration of disability		750	48-80	W, C-18	No limit
NORTH CAROLINA	56	400	20,000	56	500	Board may waive limit in some cases	500	25-64	W, C-18	No limit
NORTH DAKOTA	68 + 5 per child	No limitations		68+5 per child	Duration of disability		500	25-64	W, C-18	No limit
OHIO	84	After 12 weeks	77-10	77	Duration of disability		750	77		21,000 24,000
OKLAHOMA	60	300		50	500		NONE	Lump sum payment		14,000 25,000
OREGON	85	No limitations		50-63	Duration of disability		600	25-95	W, C-18	No limit
PENNSYLVANIA	94	No limitations		94	Duration of disability		750	94	W, C-18	No limit
RHODE ISLAND	79 + 6 per dependent	No limitations		79+6 per dependent	Duration of disability		750	79+6 per child	500	

| | TEMPORARY TOTAL DISABILITY | | | PERMANENT TOTAL DISABILITY | | | DEATH BENEFITS | | | |
| | Benefit Limitations | | | Benefit Limitations | | | | Benefit Limitations | | |
	MAXIMUM WEEKLY BENEFIT	DURATION (IN WEEKS)	AMOUNT	MAXIMUM WEEKLY BENEFIT	DURATION (IN WEEKS)	AMOUNT	FUNERAL ALLOWANCE	MAXIMUM WEEKLY BENEFIT	DURATION (IN WEEKS)	AMOUNT
SOUTH CAROLINA	63	500	$25,000	63		$25,000	$400	$63	350	$25,000
SOUTH DAKOTA	60	312		60	30 yrs.		1000	(3)	W, C-18	22,000
TENNESSEE	55		22,000	55	400	Thereafter $15 weekly to $22,000	500	55	W, C-18	22,000
TEXAS	49	401		49	401		500	49	360	
UTAH	54-79	312	16,848 24,648	57-79	312	After $24,648 $54 weekly for life	1000	54-79	312	16,848 24,648
VERMONT	68 + 5 per child	No Limitations		68	350		500	68	W, C-18	No limit
VIRGINIA	70	450	31,500	70	Duration of disability		800	70	450	31,500
WASHINGTON	117	No Limitations		117	Duration of disability		800	117	W, C-19	No limit
WEST VIRGINIA	83	208		83	Duration of disability		1200	37+12 per child	W, C-22	No limit
WISCONSIN	90	No Limitations		90	Duration of disability		750	64	400	25,714
WYOMING	55 - 79	No Limitations		43-62		17,500- 27,500	600	43-62	W, C-18	13,000 23,000

FOOTNOTES:

(1) W = Wife; C = Child
(2) After 450 weeks any earnings by W are deducted.
(3) 5 years' wages 10,000 – 25,000 to W plus 25 per month for each child under 18.

STATE WORKMEN'S COMPENSATION LAWS

	COMPULSORY COMPENSATION LAWS	EXEMPTIONS FIRMS EMPLOYING LESS THAN	EXEMPTIONS GROUPS OF WORKERS	MEDICAL BENEFITS MAXIMUM MEDICAL CARE	MEDICAL BENEFITS WHO CHOOSES TREATING DOCTOR?
ALABAMA	No	4	Farm, Domestic, Casual	3 yrs. — $17,500	Employer
ALASKA	Yes	0	Harvest or Transient Help	Full	Worker
ARIZONA	Yes	3	Farm (unless using machines), Domestic, Casual	Full	Worker
ARKANSAS	Yes	5	Farm, Domestic	Full	Employer
CALIFORNIA	Yes	0	Domestic, Casual, Nonprofit, Athletes	Full	Employer
COLORADO	Yes, Farm Only	4	Domestic, Casual	$7,500	Employer
CONNECTICUT	Yes	0	Outworkers, Casual	Full	Employer
DELAWARE	Yes	3	Farm, Domestic, Casual	Full	Worker
D.C.	Yes	0	Farm, Domestic, Casual	Full	Worker
FLORIDA	Yes	3	Farm, Domestic	Full	Employer
GEORGIA	Yes	10	Farm, Domestic, Casual	$5,000	Employer
HAWAII	Yes	0	Domestic	Full	Worker
IDAHO	Yes	0	Farm, Domestic, Casual	Full	Employer
ILLINOIS	Yes		Covers only specified extra hazardous work, others may elect.	Full	Employer
INDIANA	Yes Mining Only	0	Farm, Domestic, Casual	Full	Employer
IOWA	Yes	0	Farm, Domestic, Casual	$7,500	Employer
KANSAS	No	3	Farm, Casual	$10,500	Employer
KENTUCKY	Yes	0	Farm, Domestic	Full	Employer

- 183 -

	COMPULSORY COMPENSATION LAWS	EXEMPTIONS		MEDICAL BENEFITS	
		FIRM EMPLOYING LESS THAN	GROUPS OF WORKERS	MAXIMUM MEDICAL CARE	WHO CHOOSES TREATING DOCTOR?
LOUISIANA	No	0	Covers only specified hazardous work	$12,500	Employer
MAINE	No	0	Farm, Domestic, Casual	Full	Worker
MARYLAND	Yes	0	Farm, Domestic	Full	Worker
MASSACHUSETTS	Yes	4	Domestic, Casual, Athletes	Full	Worker
MICHIGAN	Yes	3	Farm, Domestic	Full	Employer
MINNESOTA	Yes	0	Farm, Domestic, Casual, Athletes	Full	Worker
MISSISSIPPI	Yes	5	Farm, Domestic, Public	Full	Employer
MISSOURI	No	7	Farm, Domestic, Public	180 Days	Employer
MONTANA	Yes	0	Farm, Domestic, Casual	3 years	Worker
NEBRASKA	Yes	0	Farm, Domestic, Casual	Full	Employer
NEVADA	Yes	2	Farm, Domestic. Casual	6 months	Worker
NEW HAMPSHIRE	Yes	0	Domestic, Casual	Full	Worker
NEW JERSEY	No	0	Casual	Full	Employer
NEW MEXICO	No	4	Farm, Domestic, Casual	$25,000	Employer
NEW YORK	Yes	0	Farm	Full	Worker
NORTH CAROLINA	No	5	Farm, Domestic, Casual, some saw mills & loggers	10 wks.	Employer
NORTH DAKOTA	Yes	0	Farm, Domestic, Casual	Full	Worker
OHIO	Yes	3	Farm (unless using machines), Domestic, Casual	Full	Worker
OKLAHOMA	Yes	2	Clerical, Farm	60 days	Employer
OREGON	Yes	0	Domestic, Casual	Full	Worker

	EXEMPTIONS			MEDICAL BENEFITS	
	COMPULSORY COMPENSATION LAWS	FIRM EMPLOYING LESS THAN	GROUPS OF WORKERS	MAXIMUM MEDICAL CARE	WHO CHOOSES TREATING DOCTOR?
PENNSYLVANIA	No	0	Casual	Full	Employer
RHODE ISLAND	Yes	4	Farm, Domestic, Casual	Full	Worker
SOUTH CAROLINA	No	6	Farm, Domestic, Casual, saw mills, loggers	10 wks.	Employer
SOUTH DAKOTA	Yes	0	Farm (unless using machines), Domestic,	$175,000	Employer
TENNESSEE	No	5	Farm, Domestic, Casual, Public	2 years	Worker
TEXAS	No	3	Farm, Domestic, Casual	Full	Employer
UTAH	Yes	0	Farm, Domestic, Casual	Full	Employer
VERMONT	No	3	Casual	Full	Employer
VIRGINIA	Yes	5	Farm, Domestic, Casual	3 yrs.	Employer
WASHINGTON	Yes	0	Domestic, Casual	Full	Worker
WEST VIRGINIA	No	0	Farm, Domestic	$3,000	Worker
WISCONSIN	Yes	0	Domestic, Casual	Full	Worker
WYOMING	Yes	0	Clerical, Farm, Domestic, Casual	$880	Worker

PART V

CONSUMER PROTECTION

CHAPTER 21

Personal Consumer Agreements

INTRODUCTION

Caveat emptor is one of the few Latin phrases which is still used in the law. It means "Let the buyer beware." *Caveat emptor* has been the philosophy of the courts and the legislatures for many years until the wrath of consumers forced the states and Congress to act. Now there are many laws and agencies which protect the consumer from fraudulent or unfair business practices. But, unfortunately, the consumers still have little say about the price and quality of the goods and services which they purchase every day.

CONTRACTS

Contracts are legally enforceable agreements between parties. Consumer contracts involve agreements between a business and an individual in which the business provides goods or services in return for money. Purchases from the corner grocer, installation and use of the telephone and newspaper subscriptions all involve consumer contracts.

Contracts are formed when there is a meeting of the minds. When a business offers to give certain goods or services for a price and the consumer agrees to accept them for that agreed price, there is a meeting of the minds and the contract is formed. It is not necessary for most contracts to be in writing to be enforceable. Some of the contracts which must be in writing are contracts for the sale or use of land, agreements which cannot be fulfilled within one year, guarantees to pay the debt of another and the sale of goods for over $500.00.

If any of the terms of a contract are not met, there is a breach. If you feel you have been wronged by the breach, it is up to you to go to court and prove your financial loss. These are called out-of-pocket costs or compensatory damages. General and punitive damages cannot be obtained in breach of contract suits.

DEFENSES TO BREACH OF CONTRACT SUITS

Just because a person has breached a contract does not mean that he is necessarily liable for the other party's out-of-pocket costs. There are defenses to breach of contract suits, some of which are the following: (1) fraud, (2) mutual mistake, (3) duress, (4) undue influence and (5) failure of performance or consideration, that is the party who is suing for damages did not adequately perform his part of the bargain.

Some contracts are unenforceable as a matter of public policy — contracts for the commission of a crime, gambling contracts (except in Nevada) and contracts which allow usurious interest rates.

Contracts cannot be enforced against a minor who is considered legally incompetent to enter into a binding contract (except for the necessities of life). Even though a minor may have accepted goods, used them or even destroyed them, the person who contracted with the juvenile cannot enforce the contract. However, if a minor makes a contract and then reaches the age of majority (adulthood), he can ratify the contract by using the goods and his subsequent ratification makes the contract enforceable.

When the subject matter of a contract is destroyed before it changes hands through no fault of any of the parties involved, the breach is legally excusable. For instance, if a consumer contracted to purchase a home and the home was destroyed by a fire before he moved in, the contract could not be enforced.

The victim of a broken contract must make a good-faith effort to reduce his loss. This means that if a business fails to deliver goods to you, you have to make an effort to find substitute goods at comparable prices. This is called "mitigation of damages".

Out-of-pocket damages do not include reimbursement for attorneys' fees to enforce a contract. The only time that a business or consumer can recover attorneys' fees is when there is a clause providing for it in the contract.

The past discussion on contracts involves rights which were available to consumers and businesses for many years. Recently, some state courts have come to recognize the disparity in bargaining power between the consumer and a large business. When such a disparity occurs, the courts call the contracts which have resulted "adhesion contracts". These adhesion contracts are interpreted liberally in favor of consumers.

Special problems have occurred in some areas of consumer purchases, and many state legislatures and the Federal Trade Commission (FTC) have made rules to deal with contracts in these fields, which include swimming pool installation, dance lesson sales, health studio memberships, raw land sales, door-to-door sales and home repair contracts. Members of these industries have abused consumers so badly that many states and the FTC allow a consumer to withdraw from these contracts even after he has put his name on the dotted line.

Since contracts involve a meeting of the minds, the placing of goods in a household or the performance of service without a consumer's asking for it would not be a contract. A few mail-order houses used to mail out goods with a cover letter stating that the consumer had to return the goods to the business if he did not want to pay for them. This type of merchandising has been curtailed in most states by a law which allows anyone who receives goods or services which are unsolicited to keep them as a gift without any liability for payment.

WORDS OF WISDOM

The subject of contracts is a vast and complicated field far beyond the scope of this book. The best advice for a consumer is still *caveat emptor,* despite all of the legislation which is intended to aid him. Before entering into any contract, the consumer should carefully weigh the need for the goods and services he is buying. Put major agreements in writing for your own protection. And when it is in writing, make sure you understand each and every word in the document. If there are blank spaces in a written agreement, they should be x'd out so that nothing can be added later. If there are any deletions to the contract, they must be initialed by all parties. If the consumer is planning to buy a major item, it is a good idea to read *Consumer Reports* to check out its quality.

WARRANTIES

There are two types of warranties which may run in favor of the purchaser. Express warranties are written statements from the manufacturer or retailer specifically guaranteeing the performance of the goods. Implied warranties are warranties which attach to all consumer goods.

There are implied warranties of merchantability. (The goods must be fit for the ordinary purposes for which they are sold and free from defects.) Goods must be adequately contained, packaged and labeled and they must conform to the promises or affirmations of fact made on their container or label. There are also implied warranties of fitness which pass with the sale of all consumer goods. This means that when the seller knows the purpose for which the goods are required and that the consumer is relying on his skill and judgment to furnish suitable goods, then the goods must be fit for this purpose. All goods sold automatically carry these implied warranties of merchantability and fitness unless the seller provides a visible warning that the sale is "as is" or "with all faults".

The Uniform Commercial Code (which has been adopted in all of the states except Louisiana) covers this area of express and implied warranties. The consumer must give proper, timely notice to the seller of defective goods. If, after the proper notice, the business does not abide by the warranty and satisfactorily rectify the defect, then the consumer can either rescind the sale or recover damages for a breach of warranty.

FRAUD AND DECEIT

Fraud is both a civil and criminal wrong. Fraud actions are among the better remedies for consumers because, if you prove a case of fraud, you can collect not only out-of-pocket expenses, but also punitive damages to punish the wrongdoer. Fraud consists of: (1) a misrepresentation; (2) knowledge of the falsity; (3) intent to defraud; (4) justifiable reliance on the misrepresentation; and (5) resulting damages.

The first element of fraud is the misrepresentation of fact. This type of lie takes many forms but it does not include opinions which can be considered sales puffing. In other words, when a salesman states that his product is the best, this is normally an opinion and not a misrepresentation of fact. However, the misrepresentation of opinions are illegal if the opinion-giver holds himself out as an expert or asserts it as if it were an existing fact (statements concerning the value of property by real estate appraisers). Also, opinions made by one who is placed in a position of trust such as an attorney, an accountant, a real estate broker, etc., can be considered misrepresentations of fact.

Normally nondisclosure or concealment of facts are not misrepresentations of facts unless the person who holds the position of trust (stockbrokers, attorneys, etc.) fails to make an important disclosure.

The second element of fraud is knowledge of falsity. That is, the swindler must either know that the statement which he has made is false or, in the alternative, he must have no belief in its truth. If you actually believe the representations you have made to be true, then you cannot be guilty of fraud; however, you may be responsible for a negligent misrepresentation.

The third element of fraud is the intent to defraud. The lie must be made to a person with the intent to induce a particular act. If others who were not intended to hear it become aware of the statement by hearsay, there is no liability for fraud. But in the case where a lie is told to an entire class of people or the general public, then one who practices this deceit is liable to all members of that general class.

A person claiming he was cheated or defrauded must show that he actually relied on the misrepresentation made. In other words, if the victim would have purchased a product even without the lies, then he cannot claim fraud. Fraudulent statements must have substantially influenced his choice. If the victim makes an independent investigation which should have revealed true facts, then there is no fraud. The victim is not responsible for making such investigations, but if he does it, he is then charged with the knowledge it produces.

The reliance on a fraudulent statement must be justifiable. What is justifiable depends on the circumstances of the victim and the swindler. Sophisticated businessmen and investors are charged with much more diligence in ferreting out fraud than are ordinary consumers.

The victim of fraud is entitled to his out-of-pocket expenses (compensatory damages) and also punitive damages.

There is also a tort known as negligent misrepresentation to cover those situations where misrepresentations were made innocently. Since the basis of the action is negligence, there can be no punitive damages.

UNFAIR BUSINESS PRACTICES

Many states, during the great consumer revolt of the late 1960's and early 1970's, passed legislation to prevent business practices which were deceitful or unfair. Some states adopted the Uniform Deceptive Trade Practices Act; others enacted their own pervasive legislation which closely paralleled the Uniform Act. These laws designate what practices are considered unfair to the consumer (who cannot waive any of his rights under these laws when he contracts with a business). This legislation applies only to consumers. It is not designed for industrial or commercial sales. These laws are liberally construed by the courts for the benefit of consumers. The following are some of the deceptive business practices which they prohibit:

(1) Passing off goods or services as those of another;

(2) Misrepresenting the source, sponsorship, approval, or certification of goods and services;

(3) Misrepresenting the affiliation, connection or association with, or certification by another;

(4) Using deceptive representations or designations of geographic origin in connection with goods or services;

(5) Representing that goods or services have sponsorship, approval, characteristics, ingredients, uses, benefits, or quantities which they do not have or that a person has a sponsorship, approval, status, affiliation, or connection which he does not have;

(6) Representing that goods are original or new if they have deteriorated unreasonably or are altered, reconditioned, reclaimed, used, or secondhand;

(7) Representing that goods or services are of a particular standard, quality, or grade, or that goods are of a particular style or model if they are of another;

(8) Disparaging the goods, services or business of another by false or misleading representations of fact;

(9) Advertising goods or services with intent not to sell them as advertised;

(10) Advertising goods or services with intent not to supply reasonably expectable demand, unless the advertisement discloses limitation of quantity;

(11) Making false or misleading statements of fact concerning reasons for, existence of, or amounts of price reductions;

(12) Representing that a transaction confers or involves rights, remedies, or obligations which it does not have or involve, or which are prohibited by law;

(13) Representing that a part, replacement or repair service is needed when it is not;

(14) Representing that the subject of a transaction has been supplied in accordance with a previous representation when it has not;

(15) Representing that the consumer will receive a rebate, discount, or other economic benefit, if the earnings of the benefit is contingent on an event to occur subsequent to the consummation of the transaction (this covers the situation where a customer is promised some sort of rebate if he brings more customers into the store) and

(16) Misrepresenting the authority of a salesman, representative or agent to negotiate the final terms of a transaction with a consumer.

If a business has committed any of these deceptive practices, most states allow their attorney general, a district attorney or the victimized consumer to sue the business for damages and to obtain an injunction to stop these unfair practices. The individual consumer can sue the business on behalf of the entire class of consumers which has been victimized by this unfair business practice (class actions).

Businesses which use deceptive trade practices are also liable to pay punitive damages and in most states there is no limit on the amount. While businesses which engage in unfair deceptive practices may not be intimidated by the individual consumer, they are certainly intimidated by consumer class actions where the amount of compensatory and punitive damages could run into the millions.

CLASS ACTIONS

The traditional lawsuit has one plaintiff and one defendant. Where there are many people who have a common legal interest and seek judicial relief, one person can represent all of them if he can show (1) that he represents a class of people too numerous to make it practical to join them all in a lawsuit; (2) that there are common questions of law or fact among the people in the class; and (3) that he will fairly and adequately protect the interest of the class. These lawsuits are called *representative* or *class* suits or actions.

Each state has its own rules on when a private attorney or a public attorney (attorney general, district attorney or city attorney) can legally bring a class action. There is also a provision for class suits in federal courts, although recent decisions of the U.S. Supreme Court have severely limited their application. (The plaintiff has to send letters to everyone he knows to be within the class to advise them of the suit and their rights. This put a damper on class action suits for money damages because it required the plaintiff to pay for all the mailing and administrative expenses to send these letters. If there are 10,000 people in the class, the cost of postage alone will nip many class actions in the bud.) The use of class actions in federal courts is also limited because a plaintiff must show that every person in the class has suffered at least $10,000 worth of damages.

Typical examples of where class action suits are used are taxpayer suits to attack the unlawful expenditure of public funds; creditor suits to stop the dissipation of the assets in a common fund; actions by a tract home owner on behalf of himself and all the other owners to prevent discontinuing water service; environmental lawsuits to stop pollution; and consumer class actions to prevent and punish deceptive business practices and compensate its victims.

The last is a good example of why class actions are necessary. If a business is illegally receiving money from the public on the sale of its goods or services, each individual consumer can sue the business on his own behalf. If the consumer is cheated out of a few cents or dollars, then it is unlikely that he will pursue his rights or be able to find an attorney to represent him when the amount of the damages is so low. Finding an attorney is very easy when one consumer can represent an entire class, and the amount of damages runs into the thousands or millions. In this case if the attorney is successful, the court can set the attorney's fee on the basis of the result achieved, which makes the class action lucrative to attorneys and beneficial to consumers as a whole. In fact, class action lawsuits, as a consumer remedy, have rectified many unfair business practices.

If a plaintiff wins or settles a class action lawsuit for damages, he must make a good-faith attempt to locate all of the other persons in the class and pay them their proportionate share of the damages. The court oversees this distribution for the protection of the class.

OTHER CONSUMER REMEDIES

The states control and regulate many occupations and professions and can deny, suspend, revoke or limit the use of a license in these areas. If a consumer has been wronged, he must make a complaint to the agency which regulates the particular occupation or profession. It is then up to the agency to investigate the complaint, hold hearings and take the appropriate action.

The states license and control members of the healing arts, (including M.D.'s, nurses, osteopaths, chiropractors, podiatrists, dentists, laboratory technicians, physical therapists, optometrists, psychologists, psychiatric technicians, and veterinarians), accountants, advertisers, architects, attorneys, barbers, engineers, collection agencies, contractors, guide dogs for the blind, cosmetologists, private detectives, funeral directors and embalmers, court reporters, pest control operators, land surveyors, yacht and ship brokers, social workers, cleaning and pressing operations, cemeteries, real estate salesmen and brokers, bars and liquor store operations and boxing promoters (among others).

There are state public utility commissions to regulate businesses which enjoy monopolistic control in fields like transportation, electrical power and telephone and telegraph communications. The state can only control monopolistic practices within its own borders. Any control beyond state boundaries would come under the jurisdiction of some federal regulatory agency.

The federal government also has agencies to protect consumers. The two most powerful are the Federal Trade Commission (FTC) and the Food and Drug Administration (FDA).

The FTC is a separate federal agency responsible for regulating trade. It investigates and regulates anti-trust activities and unfair or deceptive business practices toward consumers and is charged with the responsibility of maintaining truth in lending, truth in labelling and truth in advertising.

The FDA is a law enforcement agency within the Department of Health, Education and Welfare. It tests and inspects foods and drugs and is generally responsible for maintaining and regulating food and drug protection laws. It can remove unsafe products from the marketplace.

"LOST OUR LEASE! GOING OUT OF BUSINESS! PRICES SLASHED BY ONE-HALF! OUR LOSS IS YOUR GAIN! ONLY 30 DAYS LEFT TO SAVE, SAVE, SAVE!"

These signs were posted over the windows of Schmata's Clothing Store. The owners still had five years left on their lease. Their prices were the same as before they had advertised the sale. As part of the illusion of a "sale," the owners took the goods off the shelves and racks and put them on sale tables.

Hilda, believing the window signs, purchased $150.00 worth of clothing. Two months later she again passed by Schmata's and noticed the same window advertising and the replenished stock of goods in the store. Hilda immediately consulted her husband, Harvey, who just happened to be the Attorney General of the state. He advised Hilda that she could employ any of the following remedies:

(1) The Attorney General could obtain an injunction to enjoin Schmata's from unfair business practices;

(2) She could rescind the sale by returning the goods and obtaining a cash refund;

(3) She could sue for fraud;

(4) She could go through the procedures of the Unfair Business Practices Act and sue in her own name for compensatory damages, punitive damages, and a permanent injunction;

(5) She could sue on behalf of an entire class of persons who were the victims of Schmata's deception and obtain the same relief as listed in No. 4 for herself and the class.

CHAPTER 22

Real Property

GENERAL PROPERTY LAWS

TYPES OF PROPERTY

Property is any object which can be controlled or possessed. Property can be owned, leased, bought, sold, given away, bequeathed in a will and used as collateral for a loan among other things. It cannot be taken by the government without just compensation and due process of law.

Generally, the law recognizes the sanctity of private property, but it also imposes social obligations on the use of private property. Thus, the law may impose criminal sanctions for its misappropriation (robbery, embezzlement and receipt of stolen property), destruction (arson), illegal possession (narcotics) and illegal use (criminal anti-trust laws); the law can impose civil liability for using your property to create a nuisance and for interfering with the right of someone else to use his property; the law can regulate the use of private property (zoning and liquor license control laws); and the law allows the government to tax your property (and take it from you involuntarily if you refuse to pay taxes) to pay for the cost of "doing the people's business."

Property is generally divided into two types. Real property is land and anything permanently attached to it. Any interest in land is considered real property. This includes outright ownership (fee simple), life estates (where you have the right to use and control property only during your lifetime), leases and easements. Real property also includes objects which are attached to land. This means that crops, minerals and trees are real property. If these items are removed, severed or cut, they are no longer attached to the land — they become personal property. Therefore, if a piece of real estate is sold or leased while these items are attached to the land, the new owner should have all of the rights to them. If the old owner removes them before leasing, he is responsible to pay their value to the new owners.

Some objects may become so permanently attached to the land that they are considered part of the real property. This would include built-in fireplaces, stoves, refrigerators and bookcases. If removal of these attached objects would cause heavy damage to the property, then they are considered fixtures and part of the real estate.

As you can see, the character of property can change as it passes through the stream of commerce. For instance, a tree in its natural state is real property. When it is chopped to the ground, it becomes personal property. As it is processed into lumber, it is still personal property. But, once it is used to build a home, then it becomes real property again.

TYPES OF OWNERSHIP

Property can be owned and used by individuals, corporations, partnerships, estates and trusts. You can own property, real and personal, as an individual or in joint ownership with another person or entity.

Joint tenancy means ownership of property by two or more persons. The key element of joint tenancy is that if one of the owners dies, the other surviving owners will automatically inherit the dead owner's interest. This is called the *right of survivorship*. This right of survivorship is upheld even if the deceased joint tenant directed some other distribution of the property in his will.

Tenancy in common is a method of joint ownership without any right of survivorship. It is available to two or more persons who want to own property jointly. The percentage of each owner's interest should be spelled out to prevent future disputes. If an owner dies, his interest will pass to his heirs.

Community property is joint ownership by a husband and wife by those eight states which have community property laws. (See Chapter 6.) There is no automatic right of survivorship as a husband and wife can will away his or her half of the community property.

Tenancy by the entirety is joint ownership of property by a husband and wife in the majority of states which do not have community property laws. There is an automatic right of survivorship.

DEEDS

Any interest in land must be in writing to be effective. Ownership of property is normally transferred through a written document called a deed, which must list the following: (1) The name of the seller (grantor), (2) the name of the buyer (grantee), (3) the legal description of the property, (4) words in the deed showing that there is a transfer ("I give . . . ", "I grant . . . ", "I quitclaim . . . " or "I assign . . . "), (5) the proper signature of all grantors along with a notary public's seal that the signatures are authentic, (6) delivery of the deed from the old owner to the new owner.

There are three basic types of deeds: (1) warranty deeds, (2) grant deeds and

(3) quitclaim deeds.

Warranty deeds contain a guarantee of title and possession from the seller to the buyer. The seller agrees to defend the title against any claims of third persons.

The grant deed warrants to the buyer that the seller has not conveyed the same estate, right, title or interest to anyone else.

The quitclaim deed passes whatever right, title or interest the seller has in the property to the buyer. The buyer must take the property subject to all encumbrances and claims which could have been asserted against the seller.

RECORDING

At Old English Common Law, the transfer of an interest in real estate was done in public. The boundaries of the land transferred were announced before members of the countryside who could act as witnesses if there was a later dispute. There was also a symbolic transfer by passing a twig or a handful of dirt from the old owner to the new owner. Although the modern transfer of land is a little more sophisticated, there is still a great deal of importance in making ownership of real estate public.

To make the transfer of the land public, the new owner must record the deed with the county recorder or clerk. He (she) keeps a record of all sales transactions, creditors' abstracts of judgment, liens against the property, homesteads, notices of pending lawsuits which could affect the title of the property, restrictions on the use of property, and any other claims or clouds on the ownership or possession of real estate. (The records are kept according to lot and block number, not the ordinary street address.) The county recorder does not go out and look for real estate transactions, nor is it absolutely necessary for a person to record his interest in property.

To protect himself a prospective buyer should always check the record title of the real estate he wants to purchase. This title search can be done by the buyer himself (with the help of a friendly civil servant), a lawyer, or in most cases, a title company. The latter will issue an abstract title, which is a summary of deeds and other documents which have been recorded against the property. If a lawyer or title company makes a mistake in searching the title, they can be sued for the damages caused by their negligence. Title companies also issue title insurance which guarantees against losses caused by defects in the title search.

Once the deed is delivered, it is up to the new owner to record the deed to protect himself from the old owner selling the property to someone else. In that case, the owner who did not record his deed might lose his land to a bona fide purchaser of the property who had no notice of the sale, and the owner's only recourse would be to sue the original seller for breach of contract and/or fraud.

Richard owned a valuable piece of property called Utopia. Contemplating retirement in a few years, Charles bought Utopia from Richard for $75,000, but he allowed Richard to live there for the next four years. Although the deed was transferred, Charles failed to record it with the county recorder because he was also contemplating skipping out on his wife and creditors, and he did not want any public record of this real estate transaction. After three years, Utopia doubled in value, and Richard, having lost his moral compass, sold Utopia to Mortimer, who had no knowledge of the prior sale to Charles. When Charles discovered Mortimer living on Utopia, he showed Mortimer his deed and demanded that he leave the premises, but these demands fell upon the sympathetic but unmoved ears of Mortimer, his attorney and the judge who ruled that Mortimer was entitled to stay on the property because Charles had not recorded his deed. Charles' only legal recourse was to sue Richard, who had long since deposited himself and his money in a foreign country.

EASEMENTS

An easement is the limited right to use or pass over land. You don't actually own the property, you just have a right to make some personal use of it.

Most easements are either sold or given away by a property owner. They appear in a deed which prescribes the specific use. For instance, the right to use 50 feet of land for telephone lines, utility poles, sewer lines, a drainage ditch, cable television or a driveway.

If an owner of land does not voluntarily grant an easement, the person who needs it can go to court to get it if he can show that the easement is a necessity of living. For instance, if you live on a piece of land which has no access road to a main highway, a court would certainly recognize that an access road is a necessity of modern life and grant you an easement to use your neighbor's property if that easement would not unnecessarily upset the neighbor's business. You will still have to pay for the easement, and you will have to pay for some or all of the costs of maintaining it.

You can also get an *easement by prescription*, if you meet the four requirements of the law: (1) Your use of your neighbor's property must be "hostile", that is, your technical trespass must be without his permission; (2) The use of the neighbor's property must be open for your neighbor and all the world to see, not a covert operation; (3) The use must be exclusive to you, for if the public uses your neighbor's property in the same way, it could be called a public easement; and (4) The open, hostile and exclusive use must occur on a fairly continuous basis for a number of years. (The time limit is set by the states, and it varies from 5 to 25 years.)

REAL PROPERTY

HOMESTEADS

Homesteads were originally grants of 160-acre parcels of land to settlers in the western territories of the United States. After these parcels of land were given away, the states soon recognized that a man's home should be protected against unsecured creditors. (Secured creditors hold mortgages or deeds of trust to protect them in case a debtor does not pay his loan.)

The homestead only protects the homeowner from the claims of judgment creditors and lien holders which are filed after the homestead is filed.

A person can only have one homestead at a time. If you sell your property, then your homestead is automatically abandoned. If you buy a second piece of property and want to protect it against any creditors, then you must abandon your first homestead and file a new homestead on the second piece of property.

The amount of money and the limit on the size of land which you can protect through a homestead varies among the states. Most states allow both single and married persons to file homesteads. This declaration must be in writing, notarized and filed with the county recorder or clerk's office to be effective.

Some states now allow homesteads for condominiums, cooperative apartments and mobile homes. A few states have no allowance for homesteads.

LIENS AGAINST THE LAND

Anyone who puts out labor or material for the construction or repair of a building has a special legal remedy to collect for his services. It is known as a mechanic's lien, and it can be used by the following persons: (1) a general contractor, architect, engineer or surveyor; (2) sub-contractors, who only deal with the general contractor to do a specialized part of the work; (3) persons who furnish material for the job such as lumber and cement; (4) laborers who have not been paid by their contractor-employers.

Most real estate building contracts call for the owner to pay the contractor directly, and they leave the payment of the various sub-contractors, materialmen and employees to the general contractor. To protect yourself from a dishonest contractor and mechanic's liens on your property by his subordinates, you should demand a bond.

The mechanic's lien laws allow a person to file a written lien with the county recorder within a certain time period after the construction job is complete. Then he must file a lawsuit to foreclose on the property on account of the lien, and he must prove his claim in court. If he wins a judgment, then the property can be sold if the owner cannot pay the money judgment. All states have certain time limits when these mechanic's liens must be filed, when the lawsuits must be filed, and when the suit must be tried in court. If these time limits are not met, then the contractor can lose his right to sue for a lien and foreclose on

DECLARATION OF HOMESTEAD
(Joint Declaration by Husband & Wife)

_____ and _____ , as husband and wife, hereby declare:

1. _____ is the head of a family that includes his wife, _____ ,
and _____ (children) _____ .

2. _____ and _____ and said family now reside on that land
and premises in the City of_____ , County of_____ , State of
_____ , known and described as follows:

Legal description of property _____

_____

_____

_____

3. We, _____ and _____ , as husband and wife, hereby
jointly claim and declare said premises as a homestead for our joint benefit.

4. We estimate the actual cash value of said premises to be $ _____ .

Dated: _____ , 19 ____ .

_____
(husband)

_____
(wife)

— — — — — —

DECLARATION OF HOMESTEAD
(By person not head of family)

I, _____ now reside on and hereby claim as a homestead all that real property
in the City of_____ , County of_____ , State of _____ ,
known and described as_____ , including the dwelling house and outbuildings there-
on. I estimate the actual cash value of said premises to be $ _____ .

Dated: _____ , 19 ____ .

_____

the property, but he can still sue for a money judgment in the status of a regular creditor.

Most states have laws which require a contractor — general or sub — to have a license. If he doesn't have a license, then he has no right to use the mechanic's lien laws. Materialmen and laborers do not need licenses.

The Government has an even better shot at your land for payment of back taxes than mechanics and judgment creditors. If you don't pay a tax (federal, state, income, estate, inheritance, sales, . . . it goes on forever), the government puts a lien on your property and eventually forces the sale of it at an auction. A homestead has no effect on tax liens, and a tax lien for property taxes is superior to any private liens. This means that if property is sold for the nonpayment of property taxes, the new owner takes it without having to pay for any prior mortgages, mechanic's liens or judgments recorded against the property. Real estate sold to pay for other types of taxes still has the burden of prior liens attached to it.

GOVERNMENT REGULATION

Government regulation of land use can be seen in environmental laws, zoning ordinances and building codes. The environmental crisis has created many inter-county, inter-state and federal agencies, whose power to control and restrict the use of land is awesome. This power over the free use of land has been upheld because of the gravity of the ecological crisis. Most regulation over land use comes from local communities in the form of zoning, sanitary and building laws.

Unrestrained growth and lack of foresight has created ugly urban sprawl. To rectify this and prevent future abuses, most cities and counties have created planning agencies to develop master plans or proposed goals to deal with population density, water and sewage, light and air, and traffic congestion.

To stem the abuses which have followed unlimited growth, some communities have adopted no-growth policies which absolutely or severely restrict new construction. They can do this by outright refusal to grant building permits or by indirect methods such as refusing to build roads, establish sewer lines or provide water. The purpose behind this policy is to protect the present community's standard of living and way of life, but the constitutionality of this use of power is in question and it has not been tested by the U.S. Supreme Court.

Even before master plans were created, the legislative body of the local communities created zones to strictly regulate the use of land. The constitutional power to zone and take away some of the property owner's freedom to use his land has consistently been upheld by the U.S. Supreme Court if this zoning is rational and not done in an arbitrary or capricious manner. (In the last such case, the Court held that a local community could prevent a commune from existing in an area which is zoned for a single family residence.)

Typical zones are agricultural (farms, golf courses and single family residences with a minimum lot size of an acre); residential with varying lot sizes and population densities; commercial (retail stores, professional offices and apartments); and industrial (heavy industry, light industry and shopping centers). In addition, zoning laws can control the height of buildings, the size of the yard and the type of animals which can live on the property.

Just as the legislative body creates zones, it can also alter them, but this is a timely, expensive process. In order to change a zone, the normal procedure involves public hearings before planning departments after notices to all neighboring land owners is sent. The staff of the planning agency must make a report and recommendation to the planning department which either approves or disapproves the plan. Their decision is passed to the city council or county board of supervisors, which must make a decision based on the public necessity and convenience. This decision to rezone must be based on rational grounds; if it is arbitrary and capricious, then the action of the council or board can be reversed by the courts.

Rezoning involves changing the classification of an entire area. If one property owner within a zone wants a variance, he can apply to an administrative board which is set up by the county or city. In order to obtain a zoning variance, you must show some hardship. If you are unhappy with the decision of the planning agency, you are entitled to a court review of the decision to see if it is based on irrational or illegal grounds.

Building codes regulate the quality and safety of construction of new housing and remodeling. Most building codes provide for building permits before construction begins. These permits are granted after the plans and specifications for a job pass inspection for code compliance. The codes are enforced by building inspectors, who inspect the job site to see that the actual construction conforms with the approved plans. Building inspectors also make inspections of existing structures to see that they conform with local health and safety codes. Building codes can also be altered for specific jobs through an administrative or legislative act by showing hardship.

Although building codes and zoning laws are noble in purpose, they have all too often been used and abused by political corruption, cronyism, conflicts of interest, bureaucratic lethargy, lack of budgeting for enforcement and public apathy. However, the trend toward post-Watergate morality and the no-growth /limited growth philosophy may put an end to these shortcomings.

Government regulation of land use may also come in the form of nuisance laws. If a person uses his land to upset the tranquility of a large segment of the population, he may have created a public nuisance which can be abated by a law enforcement agency (see chapter on Environmental Protection). If your neighbor creates a nuisance on his land so as to upset your normal tranquil life, you may be able to personally abate the nuisance (see chapter on Intentional Torts).

CAN THE GOVERNMENT TAKE YOUR PROPERTY?

Yes, the Constitution only guarantees that the government cannot take property without due process of law and just compensation. This power of the government—federal, state and local—is called the power of *condemnation* or *eminent domain.* The government is allowed to take property if it uses it for the welfare or benefit of society — public schools, courthouses, military bases, and highways. This awesome power of eminent domain even allows the government to assign its power of taking to a corporation for such public purposes as the installation of power plants, telephone lines, and railroad tracks.

Sometimes, a government activity on its own land will destroy or diminish the use of private property. For instance, if the commander of an army base alters the direction or flow of a stream on government property, but that alteration ruins the crops of adjoining land owners, then the government must pay for the losses it has caused. This is called *inverse condemnation,* and when it occurs, the government must pay just compensation for its indirect taking of private property.

> The Armed Forces used to hang "off limits" signs on businesses after too many GIs came back to the base with venereal disease and missing wallets and jewelry. (The "off limits" sign meant that military personnel could not go into the premises, and if they were caught there, they could be arrested and court martialed.) Even though this sign diminished the income of a business, the decision to post or unpost the "off limits" sign rested with the service without any right to appeal for the merchant. However, the government stopped hanging these signs when one proprietor successfully sued the government for condemnation damages, claiming that the "off limits" sign was a taking of private property, for which he was entitled to just compensation.

The government starts condemnation by sending a notice to the property owner. The only way to stop the condemnation is to go to court to dispute the authority of the government or to prove that the taking of your property is invalid because it will not be used for the public welfare.

If you do not fight the condemnation or you lose in your efforts to stop it, then it comes time for the government to pay you just compensation, which is the fair market value of the property taken. The fair market value is not just the value of the land — it also includes the fair market value of a business which depends on the unique character of the land (restaurants and movie theaters). The government has its appraiser for this determination, and you can hire your own private appraiser (at your own cost). If no settlement can be reached, then the value can be determined by an arbitrator, commissioner, jury or judge.

This right of just compensation not only belongs to property owners, it also is a right of tenants with leases.

SQUATTER'S RIGHTS

The normal method of acquiring a piece of real estate is by buying it or receiving it through a gift or legacy from an estate. But the law also provides for a squatter or trespasser to gain title to real estate. The formal name for this process is called *adverse possession*.

There are strict requirements to get title by adverse possession: (1) the squatter's possession must be hostile — he must be there without the permission of the owner of the land; (2) the squatter must openly defy the true owner's right to possession; (3) he must use the land exclusively, not share it with a large segment of the public; and (4) this hostile, open and exclusive use must occur on a continuous basis for a number of years (the number of years varies greatly among the states from five to twenty-five years).

Adverse possession may become an important issue in boundary disputes between neighbors. For instance, if you and your neighbor dispute the boundaries of your property, which is presently divided by a fence, and nothing is done for the period of time in which you can get title by adverse possession in your state, then the status quo (the line established by the fence), becomes the legal boundary. Remember that adverse possession does not depend on good faith or honesty; all that matters is the open, hostile, exclusive and continuous use of the property.

BUYING AND SELLING REAL ESTATE

PRELIMINARY NEGOTIATIONS AND CONSIDERATIONS

For most Americans the purchase of a home is the largest single purchase they will make in their lifetimes. This chapter will deal in generalities about real estate and attempt to explain some of its basic terms and concepts.

Most real estate purchases are negotiated through a broker who is the representative of the *seller* and who receives his commission only after negotiating a sale. The buyer should be well aware of this fact in dealing with a broker. Real estate brokers and sales persons are licensed by the state; if they conduct themselves dishonestly, they are liable to lose their license.

One can also use the services of an attorney to make a real estate deal. When property is sold through a real estate broker and financed through a traditional lending institution, a lawyer is usually unnecessary. However, a sale between two independent parties without a professional intermediary should be passed upon by an attorney to protect the interest of the seller or the buyer.

Be careful when you buy real estate. Know what you want. Besides your personal needs (number of bedrooms, garage, etc.) the prospective buyer should know the tax rates, zoning laws and quality of governmental services in the area.

During the real estate negotiations the seller or his broker may make representations about the property. The buyer's best protection against misrepresentation or misconception is to put all important statements in his contract of sale. This will preserve for posterity the representations, and this type of demand may force the truth or resolve any ambiguity before the property changes hands.

If you want to build your own home, the problems are a little different. Your best protection comes through hiring an architect who is licensed by the state. He will design a home that conforms to all the zoning laws and building codes applicable in the area. The architect will also put the plans out to bid to a contractor and supervise the contractor's work. The building contract should provide that the job will not be complete until an architect issues his certificate of completion. (The only trouble with architects is their fees which tend to run between

10 to 15 per cent of the total price of the construction.)

You can build your home without an architect by going straight to a general contractor with building plans or by asking the contractor to use his best judgment after listening to your desires. If this cheaper method is used, the only problem is finding an honest, prompt general contractor.

Remember that if you do not pay your contractor, he will have a lien against your real property, and the contractor can eventually sell it to satisfy the debt. Unfortunately, the buyer has no such recourse against the contractor. The buyer's best protection is the written building contract, and for this he should consult an attorney. Here are some of the things to look for in a building contract:

(1) The method of payment should be at intervals as the construction proceeds - it is naive to pay the complete contract price prior to construction or in its early phases.

(2) Insist that the contract include a completion date, a statement that time is of the essence and a clause requiring the builder to pay specific damages for each day he takes the project past the agreed upon completion date.

(3) The buyer should make sure that all of the work which he desires is specified in the contract. All too often a buyer will change specifications in the middle of the job, and this can be expensive.

(4) Most contracts call for satisfactory performance. This is a vague clause which builders often circumvent, but it is still better to have it in than leave it out.

(5) The buyer should require completion or performance bonds for which he will have to pay a low premium, considering the high cost of building a home.

In some real estate transactions, the seller will offer a specified price, but the buyer wants a little time to think it over without worrying that someone else will purchase the property. The buyer may, in this case, obtain an option to purchase later. The buyer must pay for the option to make it valid. The seller cannot sell to anyone else during the option period.

The buyer and seller must put their final agreement in writing. Oral contracts for the sale of land are not enforceable.

Real estate contracts must give the names of all of the buyers and all of the sellers, a description of the property, the price to be paid, the name of the escrow holder, the conditions of escrow, a list of the furniture, fixtures and claims against the property, insurance and the time and place of the closing. The total sales price is always contingent upon the buyer obtaining the necessary mortgage financing.

FINANCING

Most real estate buyers must get loans to finance the purchase. They are normally obtained from a bank, savings and loan association, insurance company, or other lending institution. Sometimes the sellers will finance the deal themselves (there are tax benefits, and it may be the only way he can sell).

The loan is secured by the property which is purchased through an instrument known as a mortgage or deed of trust and this will specify the principal amount of the loan, the interest rate, the duration of the loan and the times when payments are due. The mortgagee (the lender) usually protects himself by requiring the mortgagor (the buyer) to carry casualty insurance. The buyer also must agree that the entire amount of the loan will become due if he defaults on his payments, but there is usually a grace period. The mortgage may also call for the payment to include taxes and insurance.

With a conventional mortgage, the lender has a lien on the property of the buyer. A deed of trust which is used in most states is similar to a mortgage but it places the title in trust with a third party, rather than with the lender, until the loan is paid in full - at which point there is a reconveyance deed to the buyer of the property.

In many cases the buyer may have to get financing from more than one lender. This will involve a second mortgage or second deed of trust, which commands a higher rate of interest because this lender's rights to enforce payment of the loan are subordinate to the rights of the person who has the first mortgage.

With conventional mortgages, the lender takes all the risk that a buyer will pay his loan, although the risk is softened by the security of the property. Buyers can also use FHA (Federal Housing Administration) mortgages obtained from private lending institutions and guaranteed by the federal government. Interest rates and other lending terms are regulated by federal law. The buyer must pay a small premium for the use of an FHA loan, but it is more than compensated for by a lower rate of interest for a longer term. (Lending institutions do not have to offer FHA financing.)

Veterans Administration (VA) mortgages are similar to FHA insured mortgages but are only available to armed services' veterans.

If a buyer is purchasing property that has an existing mortgage, he may be able to assume it without new financing, but this depends on the disposition of the lender, going interest rates, appraised value of the property, amount of equity already in the property and the credit rating of the buyer.

Getting realty financing is crucial. Mortgage terms will depend on the type and age of real estate, going interest rates, the neighborhood and the state of the money market. During tight money periods, lenders are not competitive in their interest rates and other terms, and it is difficult to get good loans. The lending institutions can hardly be considered competitive; when one rasies or reduces its rates, the others mechanically follow. When money is loose, the lenders are a little more competitive but the small consumer is still at their mercy. Getting a good real estate loan is such a hard, time-consuming process that few consumers have the time to shop around for more favorable interest rates and terms.

As if the lending institutions do not earn enough money from interest, they also charge for their administrative expenses ("points"), which is one of the most unfair practices perpetrated on the consumer. Each "point" equals one per cent of the amount of the loan. (There is legislation pending before Congress to forbid this type of premium.)

Another obnoxious condition a lender might impose is "a pre-payment penalty," which calls for payment of a penalty if the buyer refinances or sells and pays off his entire loan prior to its maturity. Again, it's legal, but a shrewd buyer should try to negotiate these obnoxious items out of his loan contract.

Sometimes the seller will finance all or part of the sale himself by taking back a first or second mortgage. The seller may be forced to do this because he cannot find a buyer who can obtain other financing. The seller may also be more interested in the interest he can receive from his mortgage than obtaining cash in one lump sum, and self-financing can present income tax advantages to a seller. When a seller does finance real estate himself it usually results in more advantageous terms to the buyer (lower interest rates, no prepayment penalties and no points).

ESCROW AND CLOSING

Even though the buyer and seller may have a valid contract and the buyer has secured financing, it still takes some time to complete all the conditions of the contract. In order to protect both parties during this closing period an escrow is usually established to act as a middleman and see to it that important details are handled properly for both sides.

The seller deposits the deed to the property, and the buyer deposits the money for the real estate. Both parties sign written escrow instructions, which is a written contract. The person or company keeping the escrow should order a title search and require the seller to clear any defects in the title such as judgments recorded against the property and delinquent taxes.

Anyone over the age of majority can act as an escrow, but the job is usually handled professionally by a title company or an attorney. Since the escrow must remain neutral and represent both parties, it would be improper for the attorney or the real estate broker for either the buyer or the seller to act as the escrow agent.

FORECLOSURE

All mortgages or deeds of trust provide for some foreclosure procedure by the lender if the borrower does not make regular payments or he defaults on his loan. Most mortgages provide for the lender to start a lawsuit for foreclosure. A judgment for foreclosure will order the property sold and the proceeds applied to the loan. If the proceeds of this sale plus the legal fees and other costs are not enough to pay the loan, the borrower will owe a deficiency judgment. If the proceeds of the sale provide a surplus then the net surplus must be given to the borrower.

Deeds of trust give lenders the alternative of a power of sale so that the lender can auction the property without a court order. Deeds of trust and purchase money mortgages do not provide for deficiency judgments.

Lending institutions are not happy about foreclosing and will normally bend over backwards to keep the property in the borrower's hands. This backward arch may take the form of patience beyond the law, acceptance of only interest during the borrower's financial crisis or refinancing at a smaller monthly payment.

A judgment creditor (other than the holder of a mortgage or deed of trust) can enforce payment of a debt by foreclosing on the debtor's home. This creditor must first record an abstract of his judgment and then proceed according to the laws of the state where the property is located. The debtor's only protection is a homestead.

While foreclosure is not a tax sale, it would be a good idea at this point to note that taxing agencies of the government can enforce payment of delinquent taxes by selling your home.

Less than half of our states give the dispossessed homeowner a chance to redeem his property after it has been sold in a foreclosure sale. These states allow him to reclaim his property (1) if he can pay the complete amount of his loan plus the cost of administering the foreclosure sale or (2) if he can come up with this money in a certain period of time after the foreclosure sale is complete.

RECREATIONAL REAL ESTATE INVESTMENTS

The suede-shoe boys in the aluminum siding industry of the 1950's have been replaced by the sellers of raw "recreational land." The suede-shoe operations were but small potatoes compared to the well-financed high pressure and irresponsible invasion by some major corporations and some individual land sellers into the pocketbooks of American consumers. The unscrupulous tactics of dishonest developers and subdividers make it difficult for an honest developer to compete.

The modus operandi of the con artists is to buy a large block of land near a body of water or other facility which could theoretically be used as a recreational resource. All too often the place is swamp-infested and only provides a decent home for a mosquito. The land is subdivided and sold in small lots to consumers on easy credit terms. The price depends on its proximity to roads and water with terms like "beach front property" tortured to mean five miles to the nearest pond.

The sales pitch used is "buy now when the price is cheap." The developer promises to put in sewers, roads and other facilities but often fails to deliver these items (and probably never intended to).

The buyer is also told that if he is unhappy, there is a ready resale market for the land. This is the biggest lie of all. You generally are stuck with the land and all of the easy payments that go along with it.

Some purchasers buy without even seeing the land. Some of the big companies fly prospective buyers to the land site and put on the hard sell during the airplane trip back when the consumer cannot escape (a few drinks often help).

These scandalous practices do not go on unabated. The consumer can sue for a breach of contract and fraud. But who wants to buy a lawsuit? It's more effective to pass laws which allow the state attorney general or a county district attorney to sue on behalf of the entire class of citizens who are being harmed by unfair business practices. This allows public officials to obtain an injunction against the dishonest companies and their representatives, and it allows the officials to receive compensatory and punitive damages for the entire class of persons whom he represents. Private attorneys can also start this kind of class action.

There is a new federal law covering interstate land sales. (About 99% of undeveloped land sales are across state lines.) It requires full disclosure and truth from developers. It provides for the following:

1) The property report must warn consumers in bold red type that they read the document before signing it.

2) The purchaser can revoke a sales contract within 48 hours of signing it. The loophole to this law is that the buyer can waive this right.

3) The developer must make a certified disclosure of his financial position to the buyer and the government.

4) Developers must make honest disclosures of promised improvements and a timetable for them.

5) The developers have a higher standard for truth in advertising and promotion.

CONDOMINIUMS AND COOPERATIVE APARTMENTS

Inflation, the demand for living space in both urban and vacation areas and the tax advantages of property ownership have created a relatively new real estate animal called condominiums. They are usually apartment houses where the dweller of each apartment owns the space in which he lives, but he must share the burdens and benefits of the common areas of the apartment building with the other occupants. This group ownership usually takes the form of a non-profit corporation, which is financed by the condominium owners who pay a monthly assessment for maintenance and use of the hallways, swimming pool, game rooms, driveways, and garbage chutes. Most condominiums have rules for the mutual benefit of all of the occupants, and if an owner breaks the rules, he can be fined by the board of directors. If the rules permit, the monthly assessment and any fines can be enforced as a lien against the condominium ownership.

If a condominium owner goes broke, the other owners do not have to pay for his mortgage or real estate taxes, but they will have to make up for his share of the maintenance of the common areas.

A stock cooperative is an apartment house which is owned by a small non-profit corporation, and each person who owns shares of stock in this corporation is entitled to live in an apartment in the building. The actual ownership of the entire building is by the corporation, which is primarily responsible for the mortgage financing and real estate taxes. The stockholders pay rent which is their share of the mortgage, taxes, insurance and upkeep. The individual owners usually finance their stock ownership with pledges of the stock, but banks are less inclined to lend on cooperative apartments because their security is only stock, not outright ownership of a piece of real estate. If a shareholder of a cooperative apartment cannot make his payments, the corporation — all of the other shareholders — will have to bear the burden. Cooperative apartment arrangements can also be made on leased land where the shareholders buy long-term leases to their property.

Condominiums and cooperative apartments are regulated by governmental agencies in most states, but this does not stop many shabby, unfair practices by developers. Besides the traditional complaint of faulty construction, many condominium owners are pushed into developments which force rental of swimming pools and other recreational areas in the apartment complex at exhorbitant rates, and some developers impose themselves as property managers for excessive periods at high rates.

MORTGAGES, TRUST DEEDS AND FORECLOSURES

	Time Allowed for Redemption of Real Property After a Foreclosure Sale	Laws Allowing Trust Deeds in Lieu of Mortgages		Time Allowed for Redemption of Real Property After a Foreclosure Sale	Laws Allowing Trust Deeds in Lieu of Mortgages
ALABAMA	2 Years	Yes	NEBRASKA	Date of Court Confirmation of Sale	No
ALASKA	1 Year	Yes	NEVADA	1 Year	Yes
ARIZONA	6 Months	Yes	NEW HAMPSHIRE	1 Year	Yes
ARKANSAS	1 Year	Yes	NEW JERSEY	Date of Sale	Yes[2]
CALIFORNIA	1 Year	Yes	NEW MEXICO	9 Months	Yes
COLORADO	6 Months	Yes	NEW YORK	Date of Sale	Yes[7]
CONNECTICUT	Date of Sale	Yes	NORTH CAROLINA	Date of Sale	Yes
DELAWARE	Date of Sale	Yes	NORTH DAKOTA	1 Year	Yes[7]
D.C.	Date of Sale	Yes[1]	OHIO	Date of Court Confirmation of Sale	No
FLORIDA	Date of Sale	Yes	OKLAHOMA	Date of Sale	Yes
GEORGIA	Date of Sale	Yes	OREGON	Date of Sale	Yes[5]
HAWAII	Date of Sale	Yes[2]	PENNSYLVANIA	Date of Sale	No
IDAHO	1 Year	Yes[3]	RHODE ISLAND	Date of Sale	No
ILLINOIS	6 Months	Yes	SOUTH CAROLINA	Date of Sale	Yes
INDIANA	1 Year	Yes[4]	SOUTH DAKOTA	1 Year	Yes[2]
IOWA	1 Year	Yes	TENNESSEE	2 Years	Yes
KANSAS	18 Months	Yes[4]	TEXAS	Date of Sale	Yes
KENTUCKY	1 Year[6]	Yes	UTAH	6 Months	Yes
LOUISIANA	Date of Sale	No	VERMONT	6 Months	Yes
MAINE	1 Year	Yes[2]	VIRGINIA	Date of Sale[8]	Yes
MARYLAND	Date of Sale	Yes	WASHINGTON	1 Year	Yes
MASSACHUSETTS	Date of Sale	Yes[2]	WEST VIRGINIA	Date of Sale	Yes
MICHIGAN	6 Months	Yes[2]	WISCONSIN	Date of Sale	Yes
MINNESOTA	6 Months	Yes[2]	WYOMING	6 Months	Yes
MISSISSIPPI	No Redemption Allowed	Yes			
MISSOURI	Date of Sale	Yes			
MONTANA	Date of Sale	Yes[5]			

FOOTNOTES:

[1] Mortgages are not even used in D.C.

[2] Trust deeds are very seldom used.

[3] Trust deeds only good in incorporated cities and then only for real property less than 20 acres.

[4] No power of sale unless there is a court judgment.

[5] Trust deeds not good for real property over 3 acres.

[6] Redemption is allowed if property is sold for less than two-thirds of appraised value.

[7] They may be called trust deeds, but they are deemed mortgages; and the same laws which apply to mortgages also apply to trust deeds.

[8] The court can grant 6 additional months for the debtor to redeem his property.

-215-

CHAPTER 23

Personal Property

Personal property is a movable object which is not a part of the land. Personal property is divided into tangible property — physical objects which have value in and of themselves such as gold, automobiles and food; and intangible property which is an object with no intrinsic value but which gives you the right to own other tangible property. Examples of intangibles are paper money, promissory notes, stock certificates and bonds. (A stock certificate has no intrinsic value except for the negligible value of the paper, but it does represent a certain number of shares of stock in a corporation.)

LOANED PROPERTY

When one person loans personal property to another (transfer of possession, not ownership), it is called a *bailment.* The person who loans the property is called the *bailor,* and the person who receives it is called the *bailee.* A bailment may be for the benefit of just the bailor (loaning a radio to a friend to repair it for you for free); for the benefit of just the bailee (loaning a hot water bottle to a sick friend); or for the mutual benefit of both (a straight business deal where you give your furniture to a transit company which will move it according to your specifications for a price).

Remember there must be actual delivery or transfer of possession of the personal property from one person to another to be a bailment. If you park your car in a parking lot without giving it and the keys to the parking lot attendant, there is no bailment. Likewise, if you hang your coat on the wall hook in a restaurant, the restaurant has not taken possession of your property.

Once there is a bailment, there is an implied contract to properly care for the goods. This means that the bailee can only use the goods with the permission of the owner. (A parking attendant can move your car around the lot, but he cannot use it to run errands unless he has your express permission.) The bailee is generally responsible to take care of the property and keep it in good condition, and the bailee is usually responsible for any loss or damage which is caused by his own negligence.

The bailee must return the personal property at the time specified. If he fails to return it or uses it without the proper authorization, there is a breach of contract and also there is a conversion, which is a tort for the wrongful use or taking of personal property.

> The very first court case that I ever won involved a claim over a bailment which occurred while I was still in law school: One rainy October evening I entered a San Francisco bar, whose owner took my wet raincoat and placed it on a wall hook. When I left (sober), my raincoat was missing. The proprietor told me it was a case of mistaken identity and to come back in a week when it would probably reappear. After many weeks it failed to show and the proprietor refused to pay me for it. Knowing my rights after having completed a course in personal property, I sued the bar owner in Small Claims Court. The judge properly pointed out that since the proprietor had personally taken my raincoat, he was responsible for its loss even though he knew nothing about the theft. (If I had placed my raincoat on the wall, the bar would have been off the hook—no pun intended.) I won a judgment for $20.00. Justice prevailed. (I suppose I should have saved the $20.00 check for posterity, but I needed the money for the coming rainy season.)

As consumers we are constantly delivering our property to businesses such as laundries, shoe repair shops, watchmakers, television repairmen and automobile mechanics. If the business does not do a proper job on time, you still must pay for the service in order to get your property back because most of these businesses have a workmen's lien on the property until payment is made. Your only remedy is to sue the business for breach of contract, whether they keep your property or not. If the business does keep your property and you do not pay for it within a time limit set by your own state's law, then the business can sell the property to pay for its bill, storage charges, interest and any costs of sale. If there is a surplus after all these costs are deducted, then it goes to you.

Many establishments which are in the business of bailments try to limit their responsibility for taking care of your property by posting signs on their walls or putting these warnings on the back of claim tickets. Some states will allow a business to limit the extent of the liability, but the trend is to look at the adequacy of the warning to the consumer — fine print contracts, which are one-sided in favor of the business and which can only be read with a magnifying glass are not upheld. Even though a contract may limit a bailee's liability for fire, theft and other damage, he cannot escape liability if your property is destroyed because of his negligence.

Regular transit carriers (railroads, trucking companies and airlines) are governed by rules of the Interstate Commerce Commission. They are responsible for all loss or damage to your property including damages from the unreasonable delay in delivering it except when the loss is caused by (1) acts of God — tornadoes, snow storms, floods, etc., (2) riots, strikes or government seizures and (3) your own negligence or fraud. These carriers have a right to set reasonable limits on the amount of money they will pay for a loss or damaged goods, although you can insure your property for more by paying an extra premium.

Most states make hotels fully responsible for the loss or damage to a guest's property unless the loss was caused by the guest's own negligence or an act of God. But, many of these states allow the hotel to limit its liability by posting a fair notice to you at the hotel register or in the room, if they provide you with a safe to store your valuables. (Even with a safe the hotel can still limit its liability if you fail to declare the value of the property.) Most states also allow a hotel to have a lien on your property if you don't pay for the hotel's services. In fact, running away from a hotel without paying the bill is a crime called defrauding an innkeeper.

The big problem with lost or destroyed property is not establishing the bailment relationship, but is the valuation of the personal property. A bailee — no matter how negligent—does not have to pay for the sentimental loss of a wedding ring, family pictures or a pet. Bailees (or their insurance companies) only have to pay you for the depreciated value of the property at the time of the loss, not what it cost you new or what it would cost you to replace it. If your car is destroyed, the value of your loss is usually a compromise between the high and low blue book, although being put in the position of having to buy a used car to replace your old car is no great deal. If there is no ready market for used property, then you have a much bigger problem. For instance, if the cleaner ruins your clothes, then it only has to pay for their depreciated value, which is usually less than 50% of their purchase price; but where are you going to find used clothing which compares to your lost articles? (Even if you could find used clothing, would you really want to buy it?)

LOST, FOUND AND ABANDONED

"Finders keepers, losers weepers" is not a law, although it may be an unfortunate fact of life. If you lose personal property, the ordinary citizen has no duty to look for it; but if he does find and take it into his possession, he has a reasonable duty to take care of it and return it to you. If someone finds your property with a reasonable knowledge that it is lost and keeps it for his own use, then he is guilty of theft.

On the other hand, if you abandon property, then anyone who finds it can keep it for his own. The line between lost and abandoned is determined by intent and reasonableness. For instance, if you find a wallet with cash in it on a bus, it is reasonable to assume that the owner of the wallet lost it — he did not abandon it for any finder to keep. If you find a piece of used furniture in a garbage dump, it is reasonable to assume that the owner has abandoned it.

Firms which are in the business of bailments (cleaners, checkrooms, pet kennels, transit and storage companies) can sell your property if you don't claim it within a reasonable time, but the proceeds of the sale after the costs of the storage must be returned to you. If there is no reasonable way to find your address, then the business can treat the property or the proceeds of its sale as abandoned property. Again, the responsibility of the business depends on reasonableness.

Some abandoned property cannot be claimed by an individual. The states have laws that if certain types of property are not claimed by their rightful owner after a number of years (seven years in most states), then the ownership of that property will pass to the state. This property includes bank deposits, travelers checks, money orders, contents of a safe deposit box, life insurance or union death benefits, dividends, interest, unclaimed wages and unclaimed estate and trust fund benefits.

Finding buried treasure, especially in light of today's gold prices, is an exciting thought, but most states and foreign countries regard this treasure trove as their property.

GIFTS

A gift is a voluntary transfer of personal property without any expectation or duty of return gratification. A person who gives a gift is called the *donor,* and the person who receives the gift is called a *donee.*

In order to be valid, a donor must deliver the gift while he is still alive, not in contemplation of impending death. A gift must be irrevocable with no strings attached. If a gift is made in contemplation of death *(causa mortis)* and the donor dies, his estate can force the return of the property. If the donor lives and he wants his property back, he can get it back. A donor can also force the return of a gift if he can show that it was made because of fraud, mistake or undue influence.

Most states allow a donor who has made a gift in contemplation of a future marriage to get his property back if the marriage does not take place. This is true no matter who the donor is, what the gift is, the reasons for the broken engagement and who caused the broken engagement. Therefore, gifts of engagement rings, furniture and money can be revoked by the donor. Once the wedding ceremony takes place, it's too late.

PROPERTY USED AS COLLATERAL

Your property can be used as collateral to reassure a creditor that he has some security to fall back on if you don't pay your debt. You can use your property as security when you buy it on time, or you can use your fully owned property as a *pledge* to secure a new debt. Most of these security situations allow you to possess the property unless and until you default on the debt.

Most states do not allow you to move secured property out of the state unless you have the consent of the creditor. It is also against the law to sell property used as collateral unless you pay the secured creditor or get his consent to the sale.

If you pledge the same property as collateral for more than one loan without the knowledge of all of the creditors, then it is fraud. The secured creditor on the first loan would have priority, and the others could sue you for fraud or they could prevent you from going bankrupt on their unpaid debts.

Most secured creditors want you to carry insurance to protect their collateral if it is damaged or destroyed. If you can't find your own insurance, the creditor can usually furnish some—but at a very high price. Remember that this type of insurance may only protect the creditor to the extent of his interest in your property and not protect you to the full extent you would expect from an insurance policy.

The one situation where you do not get to keep the property which you put up as security for a loan is a pawn. The pawn contract allows the pawnbroker to keep your property for the period of the contract and return it only if you pay principal and interest — but he can only keep it, not use it, unless you allow him to. The pawnbroker has to take reasonable care of it, and he is liable for any damage caused by his own negligence. If you don't pay your debt and redeem your property on time, the pawnbroker can sell it, but he must notify you of the pending public sale. The laws governing pawnbrokers vary among the states, and the more consumer-oriented states put limits on the interest charges of pawnbrokers, force them to hold unclaimed property for one year, and pay back the debtor any surplus from the debtor's pledged property after the unpaid balance of the loan, interest and the costs of sale are deducted.

CHECKING ACCOUNTS

A checking account is an agreement you have with your bank. You give your money to the bank, and it puts it in a special account for checking. Although the bank can use your money for its own investment purposes, its agreement to hold your money in the checking account means that it must honor all of your properly signed and written checks as long as you have enough funds in your account to cover them. The agreement also includes your obligation to pay for the checks and a service charge unless you have a minimum balance in your account.

If you innocently write a check for more than is in your account, the bank may still honor the check and charge you with an overdraft. This depends on the bank's policy, how good a customer you are and the amount of the overdraft. Many banks have instant credit plans for their checking account customers.

If you intentionally write a check for more money than you have in your account, and the bank does not honor the check, then you have committed a crime. Also, if you write a check with the intent to stop payment on it immediately after you write it, it is also a crime. If you write a check in good faith and later discover that you have been cheated or not received the true benefit of a bargain, then it is proper to order the bank to stop payment. If a stop payment notice reaches a bank before your check has cleared your own bank, then your bank must honor the notice. Once the check has cleared your own bank, there is nothing you can do to prevent payment, but you still may have legal recourse against the person who received your check.

With computers it takes less than 24 hours for a check to clear if the entire transaction is done in the same geographical locality. Even in a long distance deal, it only takes a few days for a check to clear. Therefore, you must send a stop payment notice as quickly as possible. You run a considerable risk of writing a check with insufficient funds but with the expectation of covering the check. A more prudent method is postdating a check, since a bank will not honor it until the date on its face.

The person who owns a checking account and writes checks is called a maker or drawer. The bank is called the payor. The person to whom you write the check is called the payee. In order to qualify as a check the paper must include the following: (1) a date, (2) your authentic signature, (3) a specific sum to be paid and (4) directions to the bank "to pay to the order of" a named payee or "to bearer." If there is a difference in the numerical sum specified to be paid and the written sum, then the written sum prevails. If you want to make a change in a check after it is written, the bank should only honor it if the change is initialed by the maker.

A check is called a negotiable instrument. It is negotiable because it circulates freely. This means that once the check has passed from the maker to the payee, the payee can sign it over to another payee, who can in turn do the same. If a person is a *holder in due course* (holds the check without notice of any legal defects in any of the prior transactions before the check came to him), then he holds the check free from any defenses or disputes between the original parties to the check, such as fraud or mistake. If the check is dishonored by the bank, then the holder in due course can sue the maker of the check and the person who passed it along to the holder.

If a check is made out to the order of someone, then the written signature of the payee must appear on the back of the check in order to get it cashed. The endorsement is actually a transfer of title to the check to a new payee and a conditional promise to pay the value of the check if the bank does not honor it. A person who endorses a check guarantees that he has proper title to the check, all signatures and prior endorsements are genuine, the check has not been altered and that he has no knowledge of any defect in the check. This means that the person who endorses a forged check, even though he had no knowledge of the forgery, is responsible to pay the value of the check to any persons to whom he passes it. An endorsement may be blank, special, restrictive or conditional.

1. A blank endorsement is a mere signature. If a check is endorsed in blank, it becomes bearer paper, which means that it can be transferred from holder to holder without any further signature. Be warned that once you endorse a check in blank and that check is stolen or lost, you stand to lose the entire amount of the check. Therefore, it is always a good idea to endorse checks with some restrictions or to endorse them in blank only when you get to the cashier's window at your bank.

2. A special endorsement names the person to whom the check is payable, and his endorsement is necessary to cash or further negotiate the check. A special endorsement is accomplished by putting the following words on the back of the check: "Pay to the order of . . . ".

3. A restrictive endorsement stops any further negotiation of the check and restricts its cashing to one particular purpose. The most common example of this is cashing a check with the words "For deposit only." This means that the bank can only cash the check if it deposits the funds in the endorser's own account.

4. A qualified endorsement means that it is made without accepting any liability if the check is not honored. You should be aware that a check can be passed to you this way, but only if it contains the specific words of qualification, "Without recourse."

Sometimes a person or business will not accept your personal check because the amount is too high, there is a prior history of bad checks, or other reasons— valid and invalid. So that you do not have to pay in cash and take the danger of a robbery, you can use a *cashier's* check or a *certified* check. The former is a check by the bank to the person you want paid. The bank issues cashier's checks only when you have enough money to pay for them, and once they are written by the bank, the amount of the check is frozen in your account.

A certified check is a check written by you but with a certification written on it by the bank stating that you have enough funds in your account to cover the check. Once the check is certified and passed, even if you don't have enough funds in your account, the bank must honor its certification. Obviously the bank will not put a certification on your check unless it knows you have the funds to back it, and the bank will freeze those funds from your account.

It is a crime to forge a signature on a check, alter the figures on a properly written check, and attempt to negotiate a forged check. If your signature has been forged on a check and the bank honors this check, you are not responsible to pay no matter how perfect or sloppy the forgery. Since the bank reaps commercial benefits from checking accounts, it must bear the burdens of forgeries — an unfortunate side effect of modern commerce.

A joint bank account means that any of the persons listed as owners of the account can write checks on that account. Obviously, you have to have a great deal of trust in anyone with whom you share a joint bank account for even though you may have contributed all of the funds, the other joint tenants can wipe out the account at anytime with one check.

CREATIVE PROPERTY

The United States Constitution, Article I, Section 8:

"The Congress shall have power: ... To promote the progress of science and useful arts, by securing the limited times to authors and inventors the exclusive right to their respective writings and discoveries."

1. **Patents.** A patent is a grant by the federal government to an inventor for the exclusive right to manufacture, use, or sell or otherwise exploit his invention for 17 years. The invention must be new, novel, useful and relate to machines, manufactured articles, methods of producing industrial results (computer programs), compositions of matter (chemical patents) or plants.

If an invention is already used by the public or is identical or indistinguishable from another invention which has already been patented, then no patent can be granted. If there are two or more patent applications pending for the same type of invention, the U.S. Patent Office has a hearing to determine who was the first inventor and entitled to the patent.

An idea, in and of itself, cannot be patented. Only when the idea is actually reduced to a physical invention can it receive protection. Inventions, no matter how new and novel, cannot be patented unless they have some actual useful purpose. For instance, a Rube Goldberg contraption, which is a complicated mechanism for accomplishing nothing (technology's answer to bureaucracy) cannot be patented. (However a Rube Goldberg cartoon can be copyrighted because of its literary value.)

Patents can also be obtained for substantial improvements, changes and additions to existing patented inventions.

There are also design patents for inventions which have no actual useful function but which are still new and novel. These would include new designs for furniture, jewelry and automobiles. After the initial filing fee of $20.00, design patents can be secured for three and a half years (a $10.00 fee), seven years (a $20.00 fee), or fourteen years (a $30.00 fee).

Congress has delegated its power to control patents to the U.S. Patent Office in Washington D.C., which is headed by a Commissioner of Patents. This office has over three million domestic patents on file as well as the patents from other foreign countries. If your application for a patent is turned down, you can ask the commissioner to re-evaluate it. If it's turned down a second time, you can appeal to a Board of Appeals in the Patent Office. If the Board rejects your application, then you can bring an action in the federal courts—a very costly process.

Patent law is a technical legal specialty, which means that patent attorneys should be highly skilled in processing patent applications, and which also means that patent attorneys can charge higher rates than their counterparts in the general practice of law. The first step for a patent application is a frank discussion with a patent lawyer about your invention — its patentability, commercial ability and costs. If the lawyer feels that there is merit in your invention, he (she) will help you with a drawing or model of the invention, which must be prepared to conform with the Patent Office requirements. Then a preliminary patent search is made at the search room and scientific library at the Patent Office. This search will turn up other filed patents or claims of the same or similar inventions. A conservative estimate of the cost of this patent search is $250, in complex cases it could be much higher.

Once a patent application is made, it takes months, even years, before a final determination is made. During that time you will be assigned a number and a stamp stating that there is a "patent pending" on your invention. Once a patent is issued, it is good for 17 years after the date of issuance, not the date of the original application. The filing fee for a petition is $65.00 and if the application is granted, there is a final fee of $100.00.

Unfortunately, very few individual inventors have the money to commercially exploit their inventions to full advantage. If you are in that position, you can either sell your patent outright, go into some sort of partnership with a firm which can develop and sell your invention or license someone to use all or part of it for a royalty.

Even with the protection of the U.S. patent laws, many inventors are loathe to show their inventions around because of their paranoia (often justified) over infringement. The U.S. patent laws allow a protected inventor to sue for patent infringement — the remedies are either an injunction to stop the unlawful use of your protected ideas and/or money damages for your losses. However, money may talk much louder than patent rights in these infringement cases because it is extremely expensive for lawyers' fees, expert witness fees and the accumulation of necessary technical data to prove your case — not to mention the length of time it may take to get a trial.

2. **Copyrights.** A copyright is an exclusive right to own, publish or exploit a work of art or literature. The Copyright Act protects books, newspapers and magazines, lectures and sermons, plays, musical compositions, maps, works of art including models and reproductions, drawings or models of scientific or technical works, photographs, prints and illustrations, scripts for motion pictures and motion pictures.

Ideas, without being reduced to some form of writing or graphic display, cannot be copyrighted. Neither can works designed for recording information (electrocardiograms and presidential tapes); writings containing public information (calendars and airplane schedules); sound recordings; government publications; titles; slogans or familiar symbols or designs; and libelous, obscene or fraudulent works.

It is much easier to get a copyright than a patent. The requirements are easily met. For complete information write to the Register of Copyrights, Copyright Office, Washington, D.C. The fee for registration is $6.00 for published works and $4.00 for other works.

The copyright symbol © gives the author protection in the fifty countries which are part of the Universal Copyright Convention, which is an international treaty signed by the United States in 1955.

A copyright gives the author exclusive rights for 28 years, and it is renewable for another 28 years. During the period of protection, an author can sue anyone who unlawfully prints, copies, sells or distributes part or all of his protected work. Infringement even includes translating a work into a foreign language. It does not include fair use, which means a teacher copying portions of a text book for use in lectures or a reviewer's right to quote from the work he is criticizing. Any other quotation must be done with permission and a note showing the source of the quote.

If there is an infringement, the author can sue for an injunction to stop any future publication and for damages for lost royalties or profits. In lieu of lost profits or royalties the law allows the court to assess damages at $10 for every infringing copy of a painting, statue or sculpture; $1.00 for every copy of other works (books and periodicals); $50 for every unauthorized lecture; $100 for the first dramatic or musical performances and $50 for each subsequent performance; and $10 for each performance of all other musical works. The law also allows for impounding infringing materials during the lawsuit, destruction of the infringing materials, attorneys fees and even criminal penalties for willful infringement or fraudulent copyright notices. These lawsuits must be filed within three years of the infringement.

Even if there is no copyright on file, there is common law protection for authors, if someone steals your manuscript. Also, if you deal with a publisher exclusively and he plagiarizes your idea, you can sue. But, if you publish your work without the proper copyright notice, it is dedicated to public use for anyone to exploit.

3. Trademarks. A trademark is a distinctive mark or symbol used to identify a particular brand or line of goods. It can be a name (Coke) or a symbol (SAS). Since trademarks indicate manufacturers and the origin of a product, it serves to tell the consumer something about its quality and, therefore, it has a distinct value. It can be registered with the Commissioner of Patents in Washington, D.C. and in most states.

In order to register a trademark, you must submit your written application with five specimens of the mark and a filing fee. If the application is rejected, you can ask for a reconsideration. If it is rejected a second time, you can appeal to the Trademark Trial and Appeal Board. If there is a conflict between pending trademark applications, the Commissioner of Patents will have a hearing to determine who has a right to trademark registration. The initial filing fee is $35.00 and the trademark registration lasts for 20 years. It can be renewed for a fee of $25.00 for additional 20 year periods for an unlimited time. A registered trademark must be identified by putting either "reg. U.S. Pat. Off." or the symbol after the trademark.

Even if a trademark is not registered with the state or federal government, it is still entitled to legal protection if it has been in continuous use and has acquired a separate distinct meaning. However, a federally registered trademark gives you better legal leverage. As with other creative property, infringement of a trademark entitles you to an injunction and damages. (If there is infringement of a federally registered trademark, you are entitled to triple damages.)

4. Trade names. Trade names are names used in commerce to designate a partnership, individual proprietorship or corporation. After they are used for a long period of time, they acquire an identity, and it would be unfair to the business or to the public to allow someone else to use that name. However, trade names are not registered by the government, but the courts will protect against their unauthorized use in suits for unfair competition.

5. Trade Secrets. Most firms have a unique way of manufacturing, processing, selling and generally conducting their business. Although this unique aspect of commerce is not protected by registration laws, the courts generally recognize the right to protect a trade secret. Even an invention which has not been patented could come under this type of protection. Infringements of trade secrets usually occur when an employee leaves one company and delivers its trade secrets to his new employer.

CHAPTER 24

Credit

INTRODUCTION

Whatever happened to cash? There used to be a day when the consumer with cash in his hand could command a decent bargaining position with a retailer. Now the consumer who offers to make a cash deal is an anomaly in a plastic, paper world of credit cards and installment contracts.

There was a time in our economic history when easy credit was looked upon as a sin. Unfortunately those innocent individuals who abstained were dragged down with the rest of the population in those many panics, recessions and depressions which have marred America's illustrious economic history. The great bankers and merchandisers have now joined hands and embraced the "permissive society" to create such household words as revolving credit, easy terms, and buy now-pay later!

The Congress was slow to react to the abuses of consumer credit, but it finally reacted in 1969 with the Consumer Credit Protection Act (more commonly as the Truth in Lending) and the Fair Credit Reporting Act. There are also many state statutes which control the cost of credit, the method of charging the consumer, shady, unfair credit practices, credit reporting abuses and the procedures for collection of debts.

THE COST OF CREDIT

The substance of the Consumer Credit Protection Act is most succinctly stated in its nickname, "Truth in Lending." It demands that creditors inform consumers of the exact charges for credit, and these charges must be translated into an annual percentage rate of interest. The cost of credit must be printed in bold type for easy identification, and it must appear on all monthly statements. The lender cannot conceal finance charges.

A creditor must tell the consumer what savings he can earn if the purchase is made by cash or if the remainder of an installment contract is paid in one lump

-227-

sum. This provision is most important in those states which allow lenders to continue to make a complete finance charge even though a purchase is paid off before the installment period has run. In the consumer-oriented states a creditor must give a purchaser credit for these finance charges when he pays an installment debt before maturity.

A lender must inform the consumer of his method of billing. He can charge interest on the consumer's previous balance or an adjusted balance. The "previous balance" method of billing does not allow the consumer any credit for payments which he may have made during the month, nor does it allow him credit for any returns of merchandise during that month. The "adjusted balance" method of billing accounts for these items. Hopefully, the consumer will be aware of these two different methods of billing and choose to do business with the creditor who uses the adjusted balance method.

The lender cannot conceal extra charges so that items such as insurance and interest on insurance loans must be made known to the consumer.

One of the major abuses of loan contracts has been the hidden "balloon payment"—a final payment which is far larger than the regular equal payments that the debtor has been paying. For instance, a loan contract may call for a regular monthly payment of $35.00, and then at the end of 23 months, the final payment will be $175.00. Many consumers were caught unaware by the large balloon payment and forced to give back goods, or they were forced to refinance the balloon payment at a very high interest rate. Truth in Lending provides that if there is a balloon payment, it must appear in large bold type in any loan contract, and there must be a clause which states the methods available to refinance it. Truth in Lending also requires a lender to inform the buyer of the rules and charges for late payments.

Truth in Lending is a classic example of "you can lead a horse to water, but you can't make him drink it" philosophy. No doubt it does stop many of the abuses of the fine-print or no-print consumer credit frauds, but Truth in Lending only requires creditors to offer consumers the bare minimum, the truth. It does not limit the amount of interest a creditor can charge; it does not stimulate competition among lenders—which would decrease the cost of credit; it does not eliminate unfair deficiency judgments against defaulting consumers; it does not adequately provide for consumers who wish to pay cash for their purchases and it does not provide for minimum down payments of cash. Some consumers are fortunate enough to reside in states which have such protection.

RETAIL INSTALLMENT SALES

Thirty-seven states have some laws controlling retail installment sales or retail sales on credit. Some states have adopted the Uniform Consumer Credit Act;

other states have their own pervasive plans in this field. These laws only apply to retail installment sales for goods and services to consumers.

State consumer credit laws make many of the same demands on lenders as Truth in Lending: all costs and terms of credit must be revealed to the consumer. There can be no blank spots in a contract, and the print on the contract must be large with the finance charges in even bolder print than the rest of the contract. The buyer must be given a copy of the installment sales agreement.

Consumer laws limit the amount of interest or finance charges for credit and provide for a reduction of finance charges if a debt is paid before maturity.

Many laws provide for a minimum balloon payment, and they give the consumer the ability to refinance the balloon payment at the same finance charges as the original purchase.

One of the most perplexing problems in this area of consumer credit is the "holder in due course." Many times a retailer will negotiate an installment sales contract and then sell the contract to a bank or other financial institution. What happens if the goods purchased were defective or there was some fraud in the negotiation of the contract? These circumstances would prevent the retailer from collecting on the contract. But what is the status of the financial institution which has purchased the installment sales contract without any knowledge of these circumstances? (These bona fide purchasers are known as "holders in due course.") In many states the consumer's defenses are only good against the retailer. A holder in due course does not lose his right to collect from the consumer; the consumer must pay the bank and pursue his rights against the retailer, even though in many cases the retailer has gone broke or moved.

The more consumer-oriented states say that the third party financial institution must bear the risk of a consumer's valid defenses - consumer defenses must be borne as a cost of doing business, and it is far easier for financial institutions to investigate the business practices of its retailer clients.

A consumer cannot waive his rights under these consumer credit acts. If a dispute arises over a retail installment sales contract, the winning party usually must pay the losing party's attorney fees and court costs.

In those cases where the consumer goods are security for his payment (conditional sales contracts), the retailer or a holder in due course has a right to repossess them if the buyer does not pay off. If the retailer chooses to repossess, he must give the consumer reasonable notice of his intention. The consumer then has the option of paying his contract in full or losing the goods. Even after the goods are repossessed, the consumer has a right to get them back if he pays the balance of the installment sales contract and any costs for repossession, storage and repair of the goods.

Most states still allow a retailer to get a deficiency judgment against a consumer after repossession and these deficiency judgments have resulted in unjust hardships. In the more consumer-oriented states, a retailer or a holder in due course must make an election if the consumer has defaulted in his contract. He must either sue the consumer for the remainder due on the contract, or he can repossess the goods for use and resale. If the retailer elects to repossess, he cannot get a deficiency judgment at a later date if the resale price of the goods does not match the amount which is still due on the contract.

The retail credit sales of automobiles and other motor vehicles are the subject of separate consumer legislation. These laws are generally the same as the ones on retail installment goods, except that most states allow deficiency judgments against a consumer when a motor vehicle is involved.

> Raoul purchased a used Oldsmobile for $1,750 from Straight Arrow Used Cars, Inc. Raoul did not pay cash; he had an installment sales contract which called for nothing down and easy monthly payments for three years. Raoul made timely payments for two and one-half years until he contracted tuberculosis, lost his job, and his wife left him with nothing except the bills and the Oldsmobile. Straight Arrow sold Raoul's contract to the Exorbitant Finance Company, which repossessed the car and sold it for $150. At the time of repossession Raoul still owed $350. Exorbitant won a deficiency judgment against him for the $200 difference between the auction price and the amount owed by Raoul plus a $20 towing and storage charge, a $78 repair bill, a $20 auctioneer's charge and a $150 charge for attorney's fees. If the item involved had been a refrigerator or any appliance other than an automobile, there might have been no deficiency judgment. If the Oldsmobile were defective when Raoul bought it or if the original contract were induced by fraud, then Raoul would have had a defense to the legal action brought by Exorbitant. If Raoul had won the lawsuit, then Exorbitant would have had to pay Raoul's attorney fees.

CREDIT REPORTING

Computers and the vast communication networks have been anathema to the fraud and the deadbeat applying for credit. Unfortunately modern technology has also made life miserable for many innocent people who have been victimized by erroneous, undocumented and irrelevant information supplied by a credit bureau.

Since credit is a privilege, not a right, you must often fill out an application which asks many questions about your personal life. The application is normally stored with a credit bureau which also may send a representative into the field to make a private investigation. The source of the investigation is often unreliable hearsay, and little or nothing is said in the credit report about the veracity of the investigator or his informants. Also included in the credit report may be medical information, employment records and police records. Much of this information is confidential and may be illegally obtained.

The Retail Credit Company, the country's largest credit investigator, was indicted along with seven other credit investigative firms on charges of bribing members of the New York Police Department to obtain arrest records, which are confidential in New York. The indicted firms pleaded guilty to a misdemeanor charge of giving an unlawful gratuity to a public official, and after this plea the bribery charge was dropped.

There are approximately 2500 credit bureaus across the United States and Canada, and most of these credit bureaus belong to the Associated Credit Bureaus, Inc., a trade association. Financial and personal data are stored in computer banks, and this data passes freely among the credit bureaus. They are free to disclose their information to any person or organization with a legitimate business interest in the information, and they are virtually immune to libel and invasion of privacy suits. An unfavorable credit report can mean more than just the denial of a BankAmericard - it could result in the loss of a home mortgage, necessary business loan, insurance policy or job. The thought of someone losing a job because of misleading, erroneous or undocumented evidence is unconscionable.

In order to rectify many of the abuses of credit reporting, Congress passed the Fair Credit Reporting Act of 1971. (Many of the states also have legislation which is similar to this Act.) It allows an individual to be advised by a prospective lender, insurer or employer when the individual has been turned down because of an unfavorable credit report. (First, the individual must learn that he has been denied credit or employment because of the credit report.) If you ever learn that you have been denied credit or employment because of an unfavorable credit report, you can force the person who used the information to give you the name of the credit bureau which supplied it. Then you can force the credit bureau to tell you the "nature and substance" of its report. You do not have a right to inspect the entire credit report, nor are you entitled to see the substance of any medical data the bureau may have on you.

You can check on your credit before some other person makes inquiries. However, in a large city where there are many credit bureaus, you may have a long expensive search to find the bureau which has a file on you.

If you find that a report contains false, incomplete or obsolete data, you have a right to challenge its accuracy, and the credit bureau must recheck its information, which must occur in a reasonable period of time (10 days). If the bureau finds that its information was indeed false, it must change its report to reflect the truth. Any information over seven years old must be deleted as obsolete, but there are many exceptions to this rule.

If you are unable to prove that negative information is false, you may enter your version of the story in a brief statement (100 words or less) and the credit bureau must include this statement in all future reports. The credit bureau also must send copies of this statement to anyone who has had access to its information during the previous six months if you so request. If the material was used for prospective employment, it must be sent to anyone who has had access to it during the previous two years.

The Fair Credit Reporting Act does not require credit bureaus to give you the source of its information on your character and reputation. This means that it can contact your former business associate or neighbor, who could tell a vicious lie about you, and this lie would become a permanent part of the credit bureau's report. The magnitude of the lie is compounded when this information is passed from bureau to bureau. You may discover the substance of the lie, but be unable to discover its source unless you go to the time and expense of filing a lawsuit for libel against the credit bureau. And one may never know of the existence of false information about him until the damage is done.

The Act has been less than a smashing success. It was intended to insure the relevancy, confidentiality and accuracy of consumer credit dossiers. The ability of an agency to keep its records confidential is always questionable. The credit bureaus themselves determine standards for relevancy, and common sense tells you that any question of relevancy would be decided in favor of inclusion in a credit report. Accuracy is always a problem in the performance of human endeavors, despite computers and social security numbers. Perhaps the word "fair" is a misnomer in the title of the Act—to be fair, credit applicants should be given a copy of all files which are kept on them, the names of all persons who have given information and the names of any persons who are making inquiries about them.

CREDITORS' REMEDIES AND DEBTORS' RIGHTS

Creditors used to have it all their way until the rising tide of consumerism brought legislation and court decisions favorable to debtors. The emergence of neighborhood legal aid offices for the poor has helped the poor and the middle classes in preventing creditors and collection agencies from abusing their financial power.

Creditors normally start the collection of delinquent debts by sending letters advising you of your debt and asking for prompt payment (due letter). If the creditor doesn't get paid, he may send more letters, give the matter to a collection agency or file a lawsuit.

A new federal law encourages settlement of disputed bills before they are assigned to a collection agency or to court action. If a consumer complains about a billing error in writing, the business must acknowledge the letter within 30 days and either correct the mistake or explain to you why it is correct within 90 days, and the creditor cannot dun you or turn the debt over to a collection agency until it checks out your side of the dispute. Also if you buy defective merchandise with a bank credit card, your claim against the merchant is good against the bank which services the credit card. (This same law prohibits discrimination on the basis of sex or marital status in the granting or denying of credit.)

Collection agencies operate on a contingent basis, receiving from 33%to50% of anything they collect from a debtor. Collection agencies are now under the scrutiny of the Federal Trade Commission which prohibits them from threatening or harrassing debtors in ways which might jeopardize their reputations or their jobs. Since collection agents make extensive use of the telephone, these activities are also controlled by the Federal Communications Commission which forbids persons to use the telephone to frighten, torment, or harrass someone. (This should eliminate phone calls in the middle of the night or phone calls to a debtor's friends, family and employer.) The states also control the activities of collection agencies. Over-zealous tactics of collection agencies may make them liable in tort damages to you for an invasion of privacy, defamation or intentional infliction of emotional distress. Creditors can never legally use physical force to collect a debt, and imprisonment for a debt is unconstitutional.

Creditors recently lost one of their most effective legal weapons for debt collection as the result of a U.S. Supreme Court decision. The attachment was a process creditors used to freeze the assets of a debtor (usually wages or bank accounts) until a lawsuit between the debtor and creditor was decided. When the creditor filed his lawsuit, he could also file for a writ of attachment. The sheriff would then attach the debtor's wages, bank account or other asset and keep it frozen until the creditor agreed to release it or the lawsuit was finally settled. The attachment was levied without any prior notice to the debtor.

The attachment was a most effective weapon since the creditor was assured of receiving some money once a judgment had been attained, and often the debtor made arrangements for complete payment of the debt to avoid any further embarrassment. The Supreme Court ruled that attachments were an unconstitutional taking of property without due process of law because the debtor was never given fair notice of the attachment. Even though the assets were frozen, not given to the creditor, the Court felt that an attachment was a taking from the debtor.

The sheriff can still take a debtor's assets, but only after a creditor has filed and served the debtor with his lawsuit and obtained a judgment (judgment creditor). The sheriff can garnish wages, bank accounts, homes and other assets. In the case of self-employed debtors, the creditor can put a sheriff at the debtor's place of business to collect his daily receipts.

Most states allow a judgment creditor to record an abstract of his judgment with the county recorder. This does not allow the creditor to sell the real estate, but it does put any new buyer on notice that this judgment must be paid before the property is transferred. In addition, most states also allow judgment creditors to force the sale of real estate to pay a debt but only after a long involved procedure is followed and only if the debtor does not have a homestead recorded prior to the recording of the judgment. Most states allow a debtor to redeem his land within one year by paying the amount of the judgment plus legal costs.

Once a creditor has an unpaid judgment, he can subpoena the debtor back to court for an order of examination to ask him the whereabouts of his assets. The debtor must answer these questions about his financial worth under oath, making him liable for perjury for any lies he may utter. If a debtor does not appear at the examination, he can be found in contempt of court. In fact, failure to appear with due notice usually results in a warrant for the debtor's arrest.

EXEMPTIONS

Although the creditor has a right to get the sheriff to take a debtor's assets, some of these assets are exempt from execution because of state law. Each state has its own laws on the nature and extent of exempt property. The purpose behind exemptions is to keep the debtor's head above water and prevent him from becoming a public ward.

The most important exemption is the homestead. It allows you to retain some equity in your home. Homestead rights only apply after a debtor has filed a declaration of homestead with his county recorder. The homestead protects the debtor from all creditors except mortgagees of the real estate and creditors who have recorded an abstract of their judgment before the debtor has had a chance to record his homestead.

The limit of the value of the homestead varies from state to state. Some states limit the area of real property which can be protected. Eight states do not give their residents homestead protection. A few states allow homesteads for condominiums, cooperative apartments and mobile homes.

A debtor can only have one homestead at a particular time; if you sell a homesteaded piece of property and move to another home, you must file a new declaration of homestead to protect yourself. If a debtor owns two pieces of real estate, he must make his choice—only one can be protected.

Truth in Lending, a federal law, puts a limit on the amount of a debtor's wages which can be garnisheed by a creditor: 25% of a paycheck per pay period. It also prohibits an employer from firing an employee because his wages have been garnisheed. The states also have wage protection laws, but most of these laws (enacted before the federal law) do not give as much protection as Truth in Lending. A few states give more protection to the debtor—for instance, Connecticut does not allow any taking of a debtor's wages.

In addition to homestead and wage exemptions, most states grant exemptions for wearing apparel, household furniture, tools of a trade, family provisions and other property in varying amounts. They put the burden on the debtor to stop the creditor from taking exempt property.

CREDIT AND THE CONSUMER'S POCKETBOOK

When the competitors of the Bank of America entered the lucrative charge card business, they sent unsolicited Master Charge cards to thousands of persons. This invitation to virtual unbridled use of credit caused considerable confusion and injustice. Many crooks, knowing of the anticipated mailing of the cards, stole them from mail boxes and made fraudulent charges which were eventually billed to innocent consumers.

It is a crime to use a credit card fraudulently, but this law did little to relieve the disgruntled consumer. Truth in Lending now forbids the direct mailing or giving away of unsolicited credit cards. It also limits the consumer's liability for charges from a lost, misused or stolen credit card to $50. Some states relieve the consumer from any liability whatsoever if he tells the credit card company of the loss or theft within a reasonable time.

Credit card companies make their money by charging consumers interest on time payments and charges for late payments, and they make money by charging the retailers from 2% to 8% on all purchases with their cards. As if that were not enough, some companies charge the consumer a yearly fee for the privilege of carrying their card. (Oh yes, this fee also entitles you to a one year subscription to the company's monthly magazine.)

The fee charged to the retailer is passed on to the consumer in higher prices. Credit card companies have done such a fantastic job in merchandising that few retailers can afford to do business without offering their customers the option of using a credit card. However, customers have not been given a choice of paying cash at a 2%-8% discount or charging their purchase on a credit card. The credit card companies have been forcing the retailers to sign an agreement that they will not offer a cash discount to customers. The Consumers Union challenged American Express on this issue in a lawsuit, and American Express yielded—it now allows its member retailers to offer cash discounts (although this is not publicized to the customers). Now that American Express has fallen, it is just a matter of time before BankAmericard, Master Charge, Diners Club and the others succumb. No doubt credit cards, with all of their drawbacks and abuses are a tremendous convenience to consumers, but the extra charge for the use of a credit card is a hidden cost which must be exposed to the consumer and he should be given an opportunity for a cash discount.

Zachariah and Zelda, married with no children, are both employed. He is a carpenter, and she is a photographer; they both earn $2,000.00 per month. They live in Beverly Hills, California, in a home that cost $50,000, and their equity is $19,000. The home is homesteaded. Zach has $950 in a local savings and loan; she has $1,475 in her credit union. They own, free and clear, $10,000 worth of furniture including a piano. Both are driving new cars which they are buying on time; both have equities of less than $350 in these cars. Zach has over $750 worth of carpenter's tools which he uses in his occupation. Zelda has over $2,000 worth of photography equipment which she uses in her occupation.

Zach and Zelda have been living far beyond their means. They owe over $100,000 in unsecured debts. The creditors who have judgments have been trying to execute on Zach and Zelda's property, but California's exemption laws do not allow them to touch any of the property listed in the previous paragraph. The only recourse for the judgment creditors is to garnish both salaries, but even then the creditors can only take 25% per pay period. If Zach and Zelda are forced into bankruptcy, the trustee cannot take any of this property because the bankruptcy court respects the exemption laws of the state in which a bankrupt debtor lives. If they had all of this property but resided in Pennsylvania, none of it would have been exempt except for their clothing and $300 worth of personal property.

STATE CONSUMER PROTECTION LAWS

	PERVASIVE CONSUMER CREDIT LAWS	PROTECTION FOR CONSUMERS AGAINST HOLDERS IN DUE COURSE	MAXIMUM INTEREST RATES FOR RETAIL CREDIT SALES	DEFICIENCY JUDGMENTS ALLOWED IN RETAIL CREDIT SALES	PERVASIVE LAWS AGAINST DECEPTIVE BUSINESS PRACTICES
ALABAMA	YES	YES	YES	NO	NO
ALASKA	YES	NO	YES	YES	NO
ARIZONA	YES	NO	YES	YES	NO
ARKANSAS	NO	NO	NO	YES	YES
CALIFORNIA	YES	YES	YES	NO	YES
COLORADO	YES	YES	YES	NO	YES
CONNECTICUT	YES	YES	YES	NO	YES
DELAWARE	YES	YES	YES	NO	YES
D. C.	YES	YES	YES	NO	NO
FLORIDA	YES	NO	YES	YES	NO
GEORGIA	YES	YES	YES	YES	NO
HAWAII	YES	YES	YES	NO	YES
IDAHO	YES	YES	YES	NO	YES
ILLINOIS	YES	YES	YES	YES	YES
INDIANA	YES	YES	YES	NO	YES
IOWA	NO	NO	NO	YES	NO
KANSAS	YES	NO	NO	YES	NO
KENTUCKY	YES	NO	NO	YES	NO
LOUISIANA	YES	YES	YES	YES	YES
MAINE	NO	NO	NO	NO	YES

	PERVASIVE CONSUMER CREDIT LAWS	PROTECTION FOR CONSUMERS AGAINST HOLDERS IN DUE COURSE	MAXIMUM INTEREST RATES FOR RETAIL CREDIT SALES	DEFICIENCY JUDGMENTS ALLOWED IN RETAIL CREDIT SALES	PERVASIVE LAWS AGAINST DECEPTIVE BUSINESS PRACTICES
MARYLAND	YES	YES	YES	NO	YES
MASSACHUSETTS	YES	YES	YES	NO	YES
MICHIGAN	YES	YES	YES	NO	NO
MINNESOTA	YES	YES	NO	YES	NO
MISSISSIPPI	NO	NO	NO	YES	NO
MISSOURI	YES	NO	YES	YES	NO
MONTANA	YES	NO	YES	YES	YES
NEBRASKA	NO	NO	YES	YES	NO
NEVADA	NO	NO	YES	YES	NO
NEW HAMPSHIRE	NO	NO	NO	YES	NO
NEW JERSEY	YES	YES	YES	NO	NO
NEW MEXICO	YES	YES	YES	NO	YES
NEW YORK	YES	YES	YES	YES	YES
NORTH CAROLINA	YES	YES[1]	YES	YES	YES
NORTH DAKOTA	YES	YES	YES	YES	NO
OHIO	YES	YES	YES	YES	YES
OKLAHOMA	YES	YES	YES	NO	YES
OREGON	YES	YES	YES	NO	YES
PENNSYLVANIA	YES	YES	YES	YES	YES
RHODE ISLAND	YES	YES	YES	YES[c]	YES

	PERVASIVE CONSUMER CREDIT LAWS	PROTECTION FOR CONSUMERS AGAINST HOLDERS IN DUE COURSE	MAXIMUM INTEREST RATES FOR RETAIL CREDIT SALES	DEFICIENCY JUDGMENTS ALLOWED IN RETAIL CREDIT SALES	PERVASIVE LAWS AGAINST DECEPTIVE BUSINESS PRACTICES
SOUTH CAROLINA	NO	NO	NO	YES	NO
SOUTH DAKOTA	NO	NO	NO	YES	YES
TENNESSEE	YES	NO	YES	YES	NO
TEXAS	YES	YES	YES	YES	YES
UTAH	YES	YES	YES	NO	NO
VERMONT	YES	NO	YES	YES	NO
VIRGINIA	NO	NO	NO	YES	YES
WASHINGTON	YES	NO	YES	YES	NO
WEST VIRGINIA	NO	NO	YES	YES	NO
WISCONSIN	NO	NO	NO	YES	NO
WYOMING	YES	YES	YES	NO	NO

FOOTNOTES:

1. Only where real estate is held as collateral.

STATE EXEMPTION LAWS

	HOMESTEAD VALUE LIMITS	WAGES[16]	CLOTHING	HOUSEHOLD FURNITURE	AUTO	TOOLS OF THE TRADE	LIFE INSURANCE	SAVINGS & LOAN ACCOUNTS	CROPS & LIVE-STOCK	FAMILY PRO-VISIONS
ALABAMA	$2000[1]	75%	$1000 of personal property						YES	
ALASKA	$12,000	75%								
ARIZONA	$15,000	75%					$10,000			
ARKANSAS	$2500[3]	75%	$500 limit on any personal property; $200 if single person							
CALIFORNIA	$20,000	75%	All[17]	All	$350	All	All	$100[18]		
COLORADO	$5000	75%			Yes, if used for work		$5000			
CONNECTICUT	NO LAW	100%	All	All						
DELAWARE	NO LAW	90%[19]	$2000 maximum on personal property[19]			$75				
D.C.	NO LAW	75%	$300			$200				
FLORIDA	NO $ LIMIT[4]	100%								
GEORGIA	$500[5] in city or town; $200 elsewhere	75%	$1000 limit on personal property							
HAWAII	$20,000[6]	75%								
IDAHO	$10,000	75%								
ILLINOIS	$5000	85%	$100 limit on other personal property $300 if debtor is head of household							
INDIANA	$ 700	75%	$600 limit on any personal property							

	HOMESTEAD VALUE LIMITS	WAGES[16]	CLOTHING	HOUSEHOLD FURNITURE	AUTO	TOOLS OF THE TRADE	LIFE INSURANCE	SAVINGS & LOAN ACCOUNTS	CROPS & LIVE-STOCK	FAMILY PRO-VISIONS
IOWA	$ 500[7]	75%	YES	$200	Yes, if for work	YES				YES
KANSAS	NO LIMIT	90%	$5000 limit on personal property $2000 if single person							YES
KENTUCKY	$1000	75%		$1500	Yes, if for work	$300	$300		$1500	
LOUISIANA	$4000[1]	80%	$4000 limit on livestock and other moveable property on homestead farm						YES	
MAINE	$1000	75%	YES[20]	YES						
MARYLAND	NO LAW	75%	$500 limit on personal property including $100 cash							
MASSACHUSETTS	$10,000	75%								
MICHIGAN	$3500[8]	75%	YES	$1000		$1000		$1000		YES
MINNESOTA	NO LIMIT	75%	$3000 on personal property				$5000		YES	YES
MISSISSIPPI	$15,000[1]	75%	$1200	$250 limit on other personal property for head of house-hold			$50,000			
MISSOURI	$1500[9]	90%	All	$200[21]		All				YES
MONTANA	$7500[10]	75%	YES			All				YES
NEBRASKA	$2000[11]	90%[24]	$500 limit for head of household in lieu of homestead							
NEVADA	$10,000	75%					All			
NEW HAMPSHIRE	$1500	75%		$500		$300				YES

-241-

	HOMESTEAD VALUE LIMITS	WAGES[16]	CLOTHING	HOUSEHOLD FURNITURE	AUTO	TOOLS OF THE TRADE	LIFE INSURANCE	SAVINGS & LOAN ACCOUNTS	CROPS & LIVESTOCK	FAMILY PROVISIONS
NEW JERSEY	NO LAW	90%	$500 limit on personal property							
NEW MEXICO	$10,000	75%	YES	$275		$150			YES	
NEW YORK	$1000	90%						$600		
NORTH CAROLINA	$1000	75%	$500 limit on personal property							
NORTH DAKOTA	$40,000 in town; no limit in country[12]	75%	$1500 limit on personal property in lieu of crops on 160 acres [22]			22				
OHIO	$1000	75%								
OKLAHOMA	$5000 in city, no limit elsewhere[3]	75%	All	All		All			YES	YES
OREGON	$7500[13]	75%	YES	YES		YES				
PENNSYLVANIA	NO LAW	75%	All	$300 limit on personal property						
RHODE ISLAND	NO LAW	75%	YES	$1000		$500				YES
SOUTH CAROLINA	$1000	75%	$500 limit on personal property $300 limit of single person							
SOUTH DAKOTA	$15,000[3]	100%	$1500 limit on personal property $600 if single person				$10,000			YES
TENNESSEE	$1000	75%	$1500 limit on personal property $900 if single person							
TEXAS	$10,000[14]	100%	All	All	Yes	All			YES	YES
UTAH	$4000 plus $600 per child	75%					Amt. covered by $500 yearly premium			

	HOMESTEAD VALUE LIMITS	WAGES[16]	CLOTHING	HOUSEHOLD FURNITURE	AUTO	TOOLS OF THE TRADE	LIFE INSURANCE	SAVINGS & LOAN ACCOUNTS	CROPS & LIVE-STOCK	FAMILY PRO-VISIONS
VERMONT	$5000	75%	YES	YES						
VIRGINIA	$2000	75%	YES	YES			$10,000			
WASHINGTON	$10,000	75%	$500	$1000		All			YES[23]	YES
WEST VIRGINIA	$1000	80%	YES	$200		$50				
WISCONSIN	$10,000[15]	75%	YES	YES		YES	$5000	YES		
WYOMING	$4000	75%	$150	$500		$300				

FOOTNOTES:

1 Limited to 160 acres.
2 Limited to 1/4 acre in city and 160 acres elsewhere.
3 Limited to 1 acre in city and 160 acres elsewhere.
4 Limited to 1/2 acre in city and 160 acres elsewhere.
5 Limited to 50 acres in country plus 5 acres per child under 16 years of age.
6 Limited to 1 acre.
7 Limited to 1/2 acre in city and 40 acres elsewhere.
8 Limited to 1 lot in city and 40 acres elsewhere.
9 Limited to 5 acres maximum in city and 160 acres in country; $3000 maximum in cities.
10 Limited to 1/4 acre in city and 320 acres in country.
11 Limited to 2 lots in city and 160 acres in country.
12 Limited to 2 acres in city and 160 acres in country.
13 Limited to 1 block in city and 160 acres in country.
14 Limited to 200 acres in country; 1 or more lots in city.
15 No less than 1/4 acre nor more than 40 acres.
16 Truth in Lending, a federal law, only allows a creditor to take 25% of a debtor's wages. The debtor's home state may have even stricter limitations on a creditor's right to garnish wages.
17 This includes orthopedic appliances, one shotgun, and one rifle.
18 Also $1500 in a credit union.
19 Maximum limit of exemption differs from county to county.
20 Limits vary widely on types of personal property.
21 Unavailable to single persons.
22 If debtor is not a head of household, exemption is $150.
23 $1500 in farm equipment.
24 If debtor is not a head of household, exemption is 75%.

CHAPTER 25

Bankruptcy

INTRODUCTION

Bankruptcy is a method for debtors to eliminate their debts without payment. Since the Constitution gives Congress the power to regulate bankruptcy, the proceedings are always in the federal courts. A referee oversees these matters for the protection of the debtors and the creditors.

Bankruptcy is not a matter which should be taken lightly and a debtor should only file bankruptcy as a last resort. You can only declare bankruptcy once every six years.

Most people file for bankruptcy because they have mismanaged their money and their credit. Many debtors have been unable to meet their obligations because an illness has kept them from earning a living. Still others are strapped for funds because of a family problem. No matter what the reason for the debtor's bankruptcy, there should be no stigma attached to this declaration. The bankruptcy laws are a legal right for all citizens. They are intended to give the individual a fresh start from which he can rebuild his economic life and a debtor should feel no disgrace in exercising his right to start anew.

A bankrupt debtor cannot be punished for declaring bankruptcy. He cannot, for instance, be fired from his job. However, he can be denied credit in the future. It used to be that debtors were afraid to file bankruptcy because it would impair their future credit. Creditors used to stick together like a fraternity and deny credit to those who had stung their fraternity brothers. But this is no longer the case and debtors can re-establish credit after they have filed bankruptcy - indeed, a bankrupt is a better credit risk than most as he cannot go bankrupt again for at least another six years.

PROCEDURE

How do you start a bankruptcy? First, you file a petition in the U.S. District Court. This is usually on a voluntary basis, although creditors can force a debtor into bankruptcy. The filing fee is $50.

The petition contains a statement listing all of your debts and assets. You also must file a Statement of Affairs which describes your personal background. It is not necessary for both husband and wife to petition for bankruptcy, but it is a prudent move when the property which they own is in both of their names and both are liable for the debts.

The petition must be signed under oath and if a debtor lies or fails to make an important disclosure, he is liable for perjury and the bankruptcy may be negated. If the debtor makes a mistake in his petition, he can file an amended one to reflect the necessary change. A debtor is considered officially bankrupt as of the date he files his petition.

Soon after the petition is filed, there is a first meeting of creditors who are informed by the clerk of the court about the bankruptcy. At this first meeting the creditors may question the bankrupt about his financial affairs, and they may nominate their own trustee. If they do not make a nomination, the referee will appoint a trustee.

The trustee acts on behalf of all the creditors. It is his job to marshal the bankrupt's assets, reduce them to cash, and pay the creditors on a pro rata basis. Before the creditors are paid, all administrative costs (including the trustee's fee) must be paid. Also, some debts (like wages, taxes and rents) have priority over other creditors' claims.

EXCLUDABLE DEBTS

Taxes, alimony, child support and claims for punitive damages for malicious or wanton acts are not dischargeable in bankruptcy. If the trustee cannot pay off these obligations, then the debtors will still owe them.

If a bankrupt does not list a debt when he files, then it cannot be discharged. If he forgets to list a debt, he can later amend his petition to effectively discharge it.

Although they are not excludable debts, mention should be made at this point of certain debts which the debtor may not want to discharge. He will probably find that many of his debts are secured by property and if he discharges the debt, then he will automatically lose the property which secures it. If a debtor is buying a home, it is likely that the home secures a mortgage or deed of trust. In most cases he wants to remain in the house so he will not list the bank holding the mortgage as a creditor he wants to be rid of. The same may also be true of conditional sales contracts or chattel mortgages on automobiles and furniture.

EXEMPTIONS

As mentioned in the previous chapter on credit, there are certain assets which are exempt from execution by creditors and are also exempt from execution or confiscation by a trustee in bankruptcy. Although bankruptcy is a federal matter, the assets which are exempt are determined by state law.

ALTERNATIVES

Bankruptcy should be employed by an insolvent debtor as a last resort. There are alternatives which can be used to discharge debts in an orderly, reasonable manner.

Many times creditors will compromise their claim for a cash payment. A pragmatic creditor knows it is far better to accept less than the total owed than the paltry sum he would receive if the debtor went bankrupt. In these situations cash has a loud, strong appeal.

In those cases where the debtor has many creditors, he may call them together and ask them to submit to a voluntary plan for the timely payments of their debts. Creditors know very well the debtor's ability to declare bankruptcy, and they will often submit to a voluntary plan.

Chapter 13 of the Bankruptcy Act provides for a plan for wage earners to pay their debts. It is similar to a regular bankruptcy except that the debtor is not completely discharged from his debts. The Bankruptcy Court along with the debtor, his attorney and a trustee work out a plan for the wage earner to pay his debts. This plan is most advisable to wage earners who face uncooperative creditors but who want to pay their debts in full.

CHAPTER 26

Landlord
and Tenant

INTRODUCTION

Unfortunately, many states in our country still have archaic laws which find their roots and traditions in English feudalism. The more advanced states look upon the renting of a dwelling unit as more than an ordinary business activity dealing with an ordinary commodity. Their laws recognize and respect the rights of a landlord and his real estate investment, but they also recognize and respect the rights of a tenant to a secure, decent place to live—the right to shelter involves more than just a leaky roof over your head.

The problem for tenants has been obtaining a right to a decent place to live and equating this right with the obligation to pay rent. All of the states have come around to recognize a right to shelter, but few of them have made the tenant's obligation to pay rent contingent on the landlord's keeping the premises fit. Municipal housing, building and health codes have been enacted by local communities to insure the safety and quality of housing, but, unfortunately in many cases, the noble intent of these ordinances has been prostituted to serve the interests of some featherbedding construction unions and unethical contractors and landlords.

This chapter will discuss the general rights and liabilities of landlords and tenants—with and without leases. Remember the laws of the states may vary markedly.

TENANCIES

A tenancy is that period of time in which a tenant may use a landlord's property. If there are no leases or rental agreements between the landlord and tenant, the tenant has possession on a month-to-month basis. If either the landlord or the tenant wants to terminate a month-to-month tenancy, he must give the other party a 30-day notice. If the landlord wants to start eviction proceedings, his notice must be in writing. However, there is no need for a written notice from the landlord if the tenant is the one who has given notice of leaving.

LANDLORD AND TENANT

Month-to-month tenancies involve legal duties and obligations without written leases or rental agreements. The tenant has a duty to pay his rent on time. He cannot commit waste upon the premises; that is, he cannot tear gaping holes in the floor or the walls or commit other acts which would waste the property. Also, the tenant cannot carry on any activities on the premises which would create a public or private nuisance.

The landlord must keep the dwelling habitable. This means that he must provide repairs and services to keep the place in a decent, livable condition. In some states and cities, the landlord must give a "warranty of habitability" which guarantees that his property is suitable for living. If the landlord breaches this warranty, it affects the tenant's duty to pay rent.

Generally, the landlord has no right to enter the rented apartment or home without the tenant's consent, but there are many exceptions and the parties can make an agreement to the contrary.

LEASES AND RENTAL AGREEMENTS

An agreement between a landlord and tenant is known as a lease if it provides for a specific rental period. It is known as a rental agreement if it is on a month-to-month basis without a specified term of tenancy. A lease for a year or more must be in writing to be legally effective. A landlord and a tenant can agree to just about anything in negotiating the terms of a lease, but some states give the tenant rights which cannot be waived because of public policy.

There is a tremendous disparity in the bargaining power between a landlord and a tenant. Where there is a shortage of good housing, the landlord can usually name his terms, and the prospective tenant must agree to them in order to get a house or apartment. Many written leases are form leases given to landlords by real estate and title insurance companies, and they are designed to be most favorable to the landlord. Rarely will a landlord alter the lease form for the benefit of his tenants. A few courts recognize this disparity in bargaining power and often, when a dispute occurs between the two over a written lease, the courts will strictly construe the lease against the landlord and liberally interpret it in favor of the tenant.

In those cases where the term of a lease has expired and the tenant stays with the consent of the landlord, the tenant is called a "hold-over tenant." He is bound by the terms of the lease except for the period of tenancy. The hold-over tenant now rents the property on a month-to-month basis, and the tenancy can be terminated by a 30-day notice by either party.

Although a lease may impose strict conditions on rentals, the landlord and tenant may waive some of these conditions. The waiver may be express, or it may be implied by the action of a party. For instance, a lease may stipulate that the tenant cannot have any pets. If he has a dog, and the landlord knows about it and makes no objection, then that particular part of the lease has been *impliedly* waived by the landlord. However, most leases have a provision that a waiver at one period of time will not mean a waiver for the entire term of the tenancy.

WHO IS RESPONSIBLE FOR REPAIRS AND UPKEEP?

As a general rule the landlord must keep his rental property fit for human occupation, and he must repair any problems which make the apartment unlivable unless they have been caused by the tenant's intentional or negligent actions. However, the landlord and tenant can agree that the tenant must repair and maintain the apartment.

When a tenant's beneficial enjoyment of his home is disturbed by the landlord or when the place is unfit for occupancy through no fault of the tenant, then a "constructive eviction" has resulted. If there is a constructive eviction, the tenant may move and relieve himself of any further duty to pay rent. The tenant must move immediately; he cannot stay and use the apartment and then refuse to pay rent. An example of constructive eviction occurs when a landlord shuts off a tenant's heat or electricity.

The rising tide of consumerism and environmental quality has manifest itself in a drastic change in a few states' laws regarding landlord-tenant relations. Formerly a tenant had no right to withhold rent for necessary repairs or remodeling, but now 17 states allow some form of withholding of rent, and the number of states which are leaning in this direction seems to be growing. These laws generally allow a tenant to set off rental expenses against his rent and/or they allow him to deposit his rent in a special trust account to be applied to necessary repairs after a court or arbitration hearing. (For instance, in California if a landlord does not make necessary repairs, the tenant can pay for the repairs and deduct these expenses from the rent up to an amount which cannot exceed one month's rent. The tenant can use the repair expenses as a set off only once a year.)

A small but growing number of states also prevent "retaliatory evictions." If the landlord's dominant purpose in seeking an eviction or unreasonably raising rent is retaliation against the tenant for using part of his rent to repair and maintain his home, this law will protect the tenant for a reasonable amount of time after he has acted. It also protects the tenant who has complained to municipal housing or health authorities because of indecent living conditions and code violations.

As a general rule the landlord is not responsible to the tenant if he is injured because the rented property is not adequately kept. But this general rule is being dented because of new housing codes which shift the burden to the landlord and builder.

CAN THE LANDLORD KEEP YOUR PERSONAL PROPERTY?

The right of a landlord to withhold a tenant's personal property for payment of back rent has been abolished by statute and court decision in most states although it is still prevalent in the East and South. The landlord should not have a lien on this property without a court hearing entitling him to it. Even if the landlord puts a clause in the lease for a lien on personal property for non-payment of rent, the legality of this type of clause is questionable because most household furniture and personal belongings are exempt from a creditor's grasp.

Most states do allow a landlord to keep abandoned property.

PREPAID RENT—SECURITY DEPOSITS—CLEANING DEPOSITS

In many rental situations, the landlord will demand payment of the last month's rent in advance. This prepaid rent vests with the landlord immediately upon receipt, and he does not have to return it unless he has ended the tenancy by his own wrongful act. In order to treat money paid in advance as prepaid rent, there must be an express statement in the lease. Without any special language, the money could be considered a "security deposit" payable to the tenant after the lease has run out.

A security deposit is a payment to the landlord to insure funds for reasonable and necessary repairs after the tenant has left. Any unused part of the security deposit must be returned to the tenant after he leaves. A security deposit should not be used for ordinary wear and tear or a major renovation which is not caused by the tenant's negligence.

Cleaning deposits are kept by the landlord to pay for reasonable and necessary clean-up jobs after a tenant has left. If the tenant cleans the place himself, then the landlord must return this deposit.

If the landlord sells the property during the term of the lease, he must either give the prepaid rent, security deposit or cleaning deposit to the new owner or return it to the tenant.

For your own protection you should always establish immediately how much of your initial "deposit" is for prepaid rent, security, and cleaning. Disputes between landlords and tenants are common in this area, and both would be smart to take pictures of the dwelling and gather witnesses if a dispute over cleanliness or damage goes as far as the courtroom. The landlord usually has the upper hand because he has the money and the tenant has already left the place when the fight starts. But the local small claims court can give the tenant a quick and satisfactory remedy.

EVICTION

Some states still allow a landlord to physically evict a tenant without a court hearing and without using the sheriff or other peace officer. If the landlord resorts to "self-help," he can only use reasonable force at reasonable times, and he cannot commit a breach of the peace. If the landlord acts unreasonably, he can be liable for a minor misdemeanor and for damages (including punitive damages if there is malice) to the tenant. (For instance, if a landlord shoots his tenant or throws him out of the apartment in the middle of the night, the tenant can sue for damages.) In the majority of states which do not allow any self-help by the landlord, any kind of forcible entry and eviction by the landlord is illegal even if the lease allows the landlord the automatic right of re-entry. Neither violence nor physical damage is necessary for a tenant to win such a lawsuit.

Instead of using forcible entry many landlords will attempt to coerce the tenant to move by turning off his power or water. This type of action may be in violation of state and local laws, and the landlord will leave himself open for tort liability in case of any accidents.

The states provide for a very quick *legal* procedure for landlords to evict tenants who have not paid their rent or who are in some other breach of a rental agreement. This procedure is called "unlawful detainer" or "summary dispossess." In order to employ it a landlord must give the proper notice to the tenant, stating the grounds for which he seeks eviction. If the tenant does not move or abide by the instructions in the notice, the landlord must file a lawsuit. (Many states allow the landlord to use the small claims court so he can avoid the cost of a lawyer.) If, after the trial, there is a judgment in favor of the landlord and the tenant still refuses to move, the landlord must use the sheriff to physically evict him. The grounds and procedure for unlawful detainer vary among the states, and the following is a brief description of the law in one state, California:

1. Grounds for Eviction

The following are the ground which a landlord can use to lawfully evict a tenant: (1) failure to pay rent, (2) failure to perform a condition or promise in a lease or rental agreement, (3) wasting or destroying the premises, (4) committing a public or a private nuisance and (5) refusal to move after a tenant has received a 30-day notice to leave and the period has run.

If the tenant has not paid his rent on time, failed to meet a condition of his lease, committed waste or a nuisance on the property, then the landlord must give the tenant three days' written notice to move. The three-day notice must specifically state the grounds upon which the landlord seeks to end the tenancy.

If a three-day notice is given for non-payment of rent, it must be in the alternative—the tenant has a choice of paying the back due rent or losing his right to live there besides being liable for all past due rent. If the tenant pays the past due rent within the three days, then he will not lose his occupancy rights. However, once the three-day period has passed, the tenant cannot stop the eviction by paying unless the landlord consents. If the landlord accepts not only back rent but also future rent, this acceptance is considered an implied consent to allow the tenant to stay.

In the other situations where the landlord must give a three-day notice, the notice does not have to be stated in the alternative. But if it is and the tenant cures the problem within three days, then the tenant can remain.

If a three-day notice is given to a tenant because of a breach of a promise or condition of the lease, the breach must be significant. The law hates forfeitures, and a court would not uphold an eviction and forfeiture of a lease because of a trivial breach.

The three-day notice must be personally delivered to the tenant. If he cannot be found, the notice can be left with an adult who is at the tenant's residence or usual place of business and a copy must be sent by mail to the tenant. If there is no responsible adult to accept the three-day notice, then the landlord can serve it by putting it in a conspicuous place on the property and sending a copy through the mail to the tenant. This is known as the "mail and nail" method of service.

Even if a tenant has an exemplary record, the landlord can evict him when the tenant's lease has run out or after serving the tenant with a 30-day notice if there is no lease. The written notice must describe the premises and clearly demand their possession with no alternatives. It does not have to be personally served on the tenant; it can be sent by certified or registered mail.

2. Lawsuit

Once a proper notice has been served and the tenant has not moved or otherwise responded to it, a landlord must file a lawsuit in the county where the rental unit is located.

A copy of the complaint and summons for unlawful detainer must be personally served on the tenant; if no personal service can be accomplished, a proper form of substituted service must be used. The defendant-tenant has five days to respond, and if he fails to, the landlord can take a default judgment.

If the tenant answers the complaint, there is an immediate trial. There is no long waiting period for a trial because unlawful detainer actions are given priority on the trial calendar.

Any eviction which is based on the race, religion, national origin or sex of the tenant is unlawful. The landlord cannot use legal grounds for eviction as a subterfuge to mask his unlawful prejudice.

If the landlord wins an unlawful detainer suit, he re-obtains possession of the premises, and he is also entitled to damages. If the tenant has not paid his rent, the damages are all the past due rent up until the time of the judgment. If the place has been wasted by the tenant, then the damages include the cost of repairs or remodeling.

3. Eviction by Sheriff

If a landlord wins an unlawful detainer suit and the tenant does not move, the landlord must use the sheriff to physically evict the tenant. He must pay for the cost of the sheriff's services in advance, and give the sheriff a "Writ of Execution for Possession."

The sheriff personally serves this writ on the tenant, but if no personal service is possible, the sheriff can post the writ on the property and mail a copy of it to him.

If the tenant does not move within five days after the sheriff's service of the writ, the sheriff must physically remove him. At the time of the eviction, the sheriff makes a written inventory of the tenant's personal property remaining on the premises. The landlord must pay for its safe storage for 30 days. The tenant may redeem it at any time if he pays the storage costs. If the tenant does not redeem the property within 30 days, it is abandoned and may be sold at a public sale whose proceeds are applied to the cost of storage and sale.

The landlord cannot keep personal property left on the premises by the tenant to satisfy his award for money damages. unless he obtains another writ. This property may be exempt if the tenant files a "claim of exemption" to protect it from the grasp of the landlord.

A judge can stay the execution of an unlawful detainer judgment by the sheriff to give the tenant even more time to find another place to live.

Ingrid, who was a freelance writer, owned a six-unit apartment house in Carmel, California. All of the tenants signed two-year leases when Ingrid left Carmel to live on the island of Ibiza to write a book. There was a resident manager, but he was an alcoholic and terribly mismanaged the property. Nine months later when Ingrid returned, she found the following:

The tenant in apartment No. 1 had moved out because the faulty, unrepaired plumbing caused the toilets to overflow and made the place uninhabitable. Even though there was a lease, the tenant paid no rent after she moved out. The tenant in apartment No. 2 had sublet the apartment even though there was a clause in the lease which prevented him from assigning or subletting his apartment.

The tenant in apartment No. 3 had not paid rent for two months.

The tenant in apartment No. 4 had turned her apartment into a kennel for every stray animal in town. The animals caused a nuisance to the other tenants, and they caused major destruction to the apartment.

The tenants in apartment Nos. 5 and 6 were current in their rent, had caused no apparent damage and were abiding by their leases.

Ingrid decided to make a clean sweep and serve all tenants with the proper notice for eviction and damages.

LANDLORD AND TENANT

1. The tenant in apartment No. 1 had already vacated. She was not liable for any rent even though there was a lease because she had been constructively evicted by the faulty plumbing.

2. All the tenants in apartment No. 2 were evicted after the three day notice because Ingrid did not allow the original tenant to sublet the apartment. But was there a waiver by the manager?

3. The tenant in apartment No. 3 was evicted because he did not pay the rent after receiving a three day notice. The tenant was liable for all the back rent until the time of the court judgment.

4. The tenant in apartment No. 4 was evicted for causing waste and for maintaining a nuisance. The tenant was also liable for the actual damages caused by the kennel operation.

5. The tenants in apartments No. 5 and No. 6 could not be evicted with a 30-day notice because they had leases which still had 15 months to run. Their leases provided for attorneys' fees in case any legal action had to be taken. Since the tenants won the lawsuit, the landlord had to pay these fees.

STATE TENANT PROTECTION LAWS

WHICH STATES GIVE A TENANT A WARRANTY OF HABITABILITY	WHICH STATES GIVE A TENANT A RIGHT TO WITH-HOLD RENT FOR REPAIRS	WHICH STATES PREVENT RETALIATORY EVICTIONS	WHICH STATES ALLOW SELF-HELP EVICTIONS BY REASONABLE FORCE
CALIFORNIA	ARKANSAS	CALIFORNIA	DISTRICT OF COLUMBIA
CONNECTICUT (The city of Hartford only)	CALIFORNIA	DISTRICT OF COLUMBIA	MAINE
DISTRICT OF COLUMBIA	CONNECTICUT	ILLINOIS	MARYLAND
HAWAII	INDIANA	MASSACHUSETTS	MASSACHUSETTS
LOUISIANA	MASSACHUSETTS	MICHIGAN	MONTANA
MAINE	MARYLAND	NEW JERSEY	NEW HAMPSHIRE
MONTANA	MICHIGAN	RHODE ISLAND	NEW JERSEY
NEW YORK	MISSOURI		NEW YORK
NORTH DAKOTA	NEW JERSEY		PENNSYLVANIA
OKLAHOMA	NEW YORK		RHODE ISLAND
SOUTH DAKOTA	NORTH DAKOTA		SOUTH CAROLINA
	OHIO		VIRGINIA
	OKLAHOMA		WYOMING
	PENNSYLVANIA		
	RHODE ISLAND		
	SOUTH DAKOTA		

CHAPTER 27

Business Organizations

PARTNERSHIPS

INTRODUCTION

There are generally three forms of business ownership and enterprise: (1) The *sole proprietorship* means a one-owner operation. He or she is solely responsible for all of the debts of the business, and the sole owner gets to reap all of the profits (after taxes). (2) The *corporation* will be discussed in the next section. (3) A *partnership* is an association of two or more persons to conduct a business for profit. The laws concerning the formation, operation and break-up of a partnership are handled by the states, most of which have adopted the Uniform Partnership Act.

The major drawback of a partnership is that the general partners have unlimited liability for the debts of the partnership. This means that if a partnership does not have enough money to pay a creditor, he (the creditor) can go after any of the partners he chooses to collect his debt. Needless to say, you should not take this aspect of unlimited liability lightly, and you should always enter into a general partnership with complete confidence in the ability and integrity of your partners and adequate safeguards to protect you from a partner's negligence or dishonesty.

There is a way for a person, who wants to invest in a business but not take an active role in its management to limit his liability in the partnership to the amount of his investment and nothing more. This is called a limited partnership, and it is composed of one or more general partners and one or more limited partners. This special partner's share of the profits is not limited by his limited partner status. Limited partnerships are allowed in all but nine states (Alabama, Connecticut, Kansas, Kentucky, Louisiana, Maine, Mississippi, Oregon and Wyoming).

We often hear the term silent or secret partner. These terms have no special legal meanings—they merely describe the relationship between the partners. If the state law requires public disclosure of all partners and there is some sort of secret relationship, then the partners have obviously violated the law. If a business goes broke and the true secret partner is discovered, then he is as responsible for the debts of the business as the partners who are more well known to the creditors. Most partnerships and, in fact, sole proprietorships do business under a fictitious or an assumed name. For instance, if Messrs. Wrench, Pipe and Plunger want to do business as plumbing contractors, they can operate under the name of the Rusty Plumbing Company. (Partnerships of lawyers, doctors and other professionals cannot use fictitious names.) Doing business under a fictitious name is perfectly legitimate as long as the name is registered with the county clerk and otherwise conforms with state and local laws, and it does not deceive the public. Most states do not allow businesses using fictitious names to use the courts unless they have complied with fictitious name laws.

A partnership has to file income tax returns to show its profits or losses, but it does not pay income tax as a business entity. Instead, each of the partners pays income taxes (or takes tax losses) according to his percentage of ownership in the partnership.

FORMATION OF PARTNERSHIPS

Since a partnership is an agreement between two or more persons, it is a contract. The agreement can be oral, written or even implied by the actions of the parties. Obviously the best way to establish a partnership and the rights, duties and obligations of the partners is by a written contract.

The partnership agreement should include (1) the amount of money or other valuable consideration to be contributed by each partner, (2) the percentage ownership of each partner, (3) the function of each partner in the business (truck driver, manager, bookkeeper, etc.), (4) the name of the partnership, (5) the ability of partners to contract and incur liabilities, (6) who can sign the checks, (7) key-man life insurance, (8) what happens if a partner dies, divorces, goes bankrupt, becomes insane or becomes disabled, (9) what happens if a partner wants to leave the business, (10) how profits are to be distributed, (11) rules for settling disputes among the partners and (12) rules for settlement of the affairs of the business if the partnership breaks up.

If these matters are not specifically dealt with in writing, there is a large body of partnership law which does apply. Limited partnerships must be in writing and comply with state law in order to limit a partner's liability to his investment.

Although general partners are equally responsible for the debts of the business, this does not necessarily mean that each partner has to put in an equal share of cash when the business is formed. It may be that one person has a considerable amount of expertise or talent and he wants to combine his efforts with someone with a lot of cash. It may be that a person is given a large partnership share with no contribution of cash or talent because his name is valuable as a tool for raising more money or getting business. Anything is possible because of the free ability of adults to contract with each other — as long as there is no fraud involved.

It should be pointed out that some business associations are not partnerships even though there may be an agreement for the sharing of profits. For instance, landlords with percentage leases, commissioned salesmen and Uncle Sam. These people are not legally considered partners because they have no liability for losses if the business loses money. Also, associations of persons for political, social, educational or religious purposes are not legal partnerships because they are not formed for commercial purposes.

MANAGEMENT OF THE BUSINESS

Each general partner is a manager of the business. If there is a dispute about a management decision, each partner has one vote no matter how much each partner has contributed to the business. This one man-one vote rule can be changed by a partnership agreement, and this usually happens when one partner contributes a disproportionate share of time and money to the business.

If there are an even number of partners with equal votes and there is a tie vote about a management decision, you have a problem. If there is no agreement, the only solution is go to court to break up the partnership and wind up the business. To deal with this predicament, it is best to have a written agreement for binding arbitration to solve these disputes to save the business.

Each partner owes an undivided loyalty to the partnership business and the other partners. This means that a partner cannot make secret profits from business assets and, too, a partner cannot conduct business when it amounts to a secret conflict of interest. Each partner must account for all of the money handled by him and if there are any secret profits, they must be returned to the business.

Unless there is an agrement, partners are not entitled to a salary; they are only entitled to a draw on the profits. If there is a loss, the partners will have to return that draw to pay for their share of the losses.

Each partner is an agent of the business. This means that if one partner signs a contract or a check, it binds all of the others. For this reason, it is a good idea to have a written agreement to provide for more than one signature for the cashing of large checks and limited authority to contract. Also, if a partner commits a tort while he is working for the business—for example, getting in an automobile accident on a sales trip—all of the other partners are responsible to pay for tort damages. Most partnership agreements provide for profits to be divided in proportion to the amount of money or services contributed to the business. If there is no agreement, partners divide their share of the profits equally, no matter who made what contribution in money or services.

BREAKING UP THE PARTNERSHIP

Nothing good ever lasts including congenial business associations like partnerships. Even though the law has rules for terminating a partnership, it is always a good idea to have a written agreement to provide for the contingencies of death, bankruptcy, insanity, incompetence, personal hostilities and the multitude of other problems which can disrupt a business association.

If one partner, for any reason leaves the business, the partnership is technically dissolved. If there is no written agreement to keep the business entity going under a different structure, the partnership must be dissolved. This means selling all of the assets, paying the debts and dividing the net proceeds among the partners. If there is any question about the honesty of the dissolution, a court can supervise it and require an accounting from all of the partners. If there is a net deficit, each partner must contribute to pay off the debt.

If a person dies or retires and the former business partnership continues to do business, the retired partner or his estate is entitled to his financial interest in the dissolved partnership plus legal interest (7%) from the date he left the partnership. If a partner leaves the business and a new partnership or other business entity carries on, the old partner should protect himself from any liability for future debts. He can do this by sending notice to creditors and advising the public through advertising in the classified section of a newspaper for a period of time. Although this protects him from any future liability, he is still responsible to pay for any old debts before he left the business.

Winding up a business after a partnership breaks up is a rather harsh result and foolish to undertake when a partnership agreement can prevent this from happening after a partner's withdrawal. The business can be saved by putting in a clause that the remaining partners can pay off the withdrawing partner (or his estate). The buy-out arrangement can have a specified price or a formula for determining the sales price. Many partnerships have life insurance on the partners to make sure that the business has enough cash to buy out the estate of a partner who dies (key-man life insurance).

CORPORATIONS

INTRODUCTION

The corporation is the most popular form of doing business in the United States. It is usually associated with large multimillion dollar companies, but it is also used by small businessmen who want to take advantage of the corporate form of doing business.

Corporation cannot be defined in one sentence. It is neither animal, vegetable nor mineral. It is a form of business organization which is created by the state solely through legislation. These laws allow anyone to incorporate an existing business (partnerships or sole proprietorships) or start a new business in a corporate form. Professionals (doctors, lawyers, dentists, etc.) can now incorporate themselves in many states, although non-professionals cannot hold stock in these corporations. The ownership of a corporation is represented by shares of stock, and the persons who own these shares of stock are called stockholders.

The principal feature of a corporation is *limited liability* — the shareholders are not liable for corporate debts. The only thing that the stockholders risk is the amount of their investment to buy ownership into the corporation. Therefore, a corporation can go bankrupt, but its stockholders can remain in a sweet financial position even though they have lost the value of their stock.

Whereas partnerships are rigid and lose their status when one of the partners leaves, a corporation is permanent and flexible. Stockholders can come and go by buying and selling shares of stock without any major change in the management of the corporation.

Stockholders have no direct say in the management of a corporation. This responsibility rests with a board of directors which is elected by the stockholders. (Each share of stock is entitled to one vote.) The board of directors in turn delegate much of their authority for the day-to-day operations of the company to corporate officers (president, vice-president, secretary, treasurer, etc.). Therefore, the top dog of a corporation is the chairman of the board, not the president. In small, closely held corporations the stockholders, members of the board and corporate officers are usually, but not necessarily, the same people. The reason they have to assume the formality of all of these different positions is that they must follow the corporate form of doing business in order to take advantage of its benefits.

The corporate form may make it easier to raise money for the management to finance their existence or new projects. If corporate stock is offered to the general public, then the corporation must comply with the complex rules of the Securities and Exchange Commission, which was created during the depression to protect the public from the many fraudulent schemes which were perpetrated during the 1920s and before. Small issues of stock offered by closely held corporations may be regulated by the individual states in what has come to be known as *Blue Sky Laws*. Unfortunately, federal and state laws regulating corporate financing have not eliminated fraud, but they have created a mountainous bureaucracy which makes it more expensive and dangerous to defraud the public.

Investments in stock offer the public a chance to own shares of large corporations whose stocks are listed on major stock exchanges. This makes the investment liquid, as it can be bought and sold on a moment's notice. This instant liquidity is not available for small closely held corporations, and it is often difficult for stockholders in these ventures to sell shares to an outsider.

Profitable corporations reward their investors by paying dividends, which are declared by the board of directors after business expenses and corporate taxes are accounted for. The board does not have to give the entire amount of after-tax-profit, as it can retain some or all of these earnings for future working capital for daily operations or for anticipated expenses for the expansion of the business.

Corporations are considered persons, separate and distinct from the persons who manage them and the persons who hold stock in them. Although a corporation cannot vote, it must pay taxes, can be sued in its own name, can inherit property, and is held responsible for crimes and torts (along with its managers).

TAX ASPECTS OF CORPORATIONS

The net income of corporations is taxed by the federal and state government. (If a corporation does business in more than one state, those states compute the corporation's taxes by a complex allocation formula.) The federal income tax rate is 20% of the first $25,000 of net profit, 22% of the next $25,000 and 48% of anything thereafter. The dividends declared by a corporation are taxable income to the stockholders. This double taxation could present a disadvantage to a small businessman who conducts his business through a corporation.

The major tax advantage of a corporation to a small businessman is the ability to deduct many expenses, which he could not take as a sole proprietor, from his gross income. For instance, the cost of pension and profit-sharing plans and health insurance can be deducted as legitimate business expenses if offered to *all* corporate employees, not just the major stockholders.

The major tax disadvantage to a corporation is that if the corporation loses money, the stockholders cannot write off the loss from their personal income tax. (The income tax laws do allow small corporations with ten or less stockholders to write off corporate losses as their own personal losses for tax purposes, but these laws also make the shareholders responsible to pay for corporate profits as if they were their own personal profits. These are called Subchapter S corporations, and the corporation must apply for this status through the Internal Revenue Service.)

Shares of stock are considered capital assets for income tax purposes. This means, if you own stock for more than six months and sell it, any profits you get from the sale are taxed at a special rate—you can pay 25% of the net capital gain or divide the capital gain in half and add it to your ordinary income. Likewise, if you lose money on stock held for more than six months, then you can only deduct one-half of your net long term loss from your income with a limit of $1,000 per year. If you sell capital stock after holding it for less than six months, then it is considered a short term capital gain or loss. These losses are added to or deducted from ordinary income without any special tax preference except that you still can only deduct a maximum of $1,000 per year.

If you own stock in a small corporation which has gone bankrupt, your stock loss can be deducted from your ordinary income if the corporation has processed the proper papers for this special tax status. (Section 1244 Corporations.)

FORMATION OF CORPORATIONS

Since corporations are considered persons, they must have a place of residence. Although a corporation resides in one state, it can still do business in the other states and foreign countries, although it may have to qualify as a foreign corporation authorized to do business in another state. Each state has its own laws on the activities of its resident corporations, and naturally, the states with the loosest controls on corporate activities are the favorites (Delaware and Nevada). However, it is always a good idea for a small corporation to gain its corporate existence from the state where it conducts most of its business.

Corporations are formed by filing articles of incorporation at the state capitol with the secretary of state (or other state official). The articles should list the following: (1) the purpose of the corporation, (2) the principal place of doing business in the state, (3) the total number of shares authorized by the incorporators, (4) the value of each share, (5) the voting rights or preferences of each class of stock if more than one class is issued, (6) the amount of capital with which the corporation will start business, (7) the names and addresses of the first directors and the incorporators, and (8) the name of the corporation.

The incorporators can use any name as long as someone else has not already reserved the name for its use and the name does not deceive the public. (Even if you want to use your own personal name as the name of the corporation, it cannot be used if someone with the same name is already using it or if it might deceive the public.) The corporate name also must include the words "Inc.", "Corp." or "Ltd." to advise the general public that it may be doing business with a corporation. The world "Co." or "Company" in the corporate name is not enough in most states.

The general rule is that it takes at least three persons to start a corporation, although all three do not necessarily have to own stock to become incorporators. Once the proposed articles are approved by the secretary of state, the corporation has an official existence. If the articles are not approved or they are later found to be fraudulent or fatally defective, then the incorporators are treated as partners, and they lose the limited liability advantage of incorporation. After the articles are certified, the board of directors must meet to adopt bylaws to run the corporation and to elect corporate officers. A copy of the articles of incorporation should also be filed in the county where the principal place of doing business for the corporation is. A permanent written record of all meetings of the board of directors must be kept, and all board members must be given fair notice of board meetings.

MANAGEMENT OF CORPORATIONS

Stockholders. Although they are owners, the stockholders have the least say in the management of their corporation. The stockholders meet once a year (or more often if a special meeting is properly called) to receive a report from the directors on the status of the corporation and to vote for the board members for the next year. The stockholders do not have to attend this meeting, as they will be sent a printed report of the company's financial status and a proxy to authorize someone else to vote for them.

A small stockholder in a large corporation is about as significant as a drop of snow in the Arctic. He can ask questions of the board and officers at the annual meetings (and he may get answers). The large corporations will also give a free cup of coffee. It is only when large groups of stockholders are unhappy that major shake-ups in management occur.

In small corporations stockholders have much more clout, as they can place themselves or persons loyal to them on the board of directors. Major disputes among stockholders in both large and small corporations are extremely expensive and usually counterproductive to the primary objective of a corporation —profits.

Stockholders have the right to inspect corporate books at reasonable times.

If there are accumulated net profits, they may receive dividends.

Board of Directors. Stockholders elect the directors to serve on its board for a one-year term. If one of the directors resigns, dies or is removed from office, his position is filled by a vote of the other members of the board.

The board sets the tone and policy for a corporation. It has the fundamental responsibility for its management even though a board member does not have to be a stockholder in the corporation. The board receives its authority to act through the corporate bylaws, and it must abide by these bylaws and the laws of the state of corporate residence. This means that the board cannot issue a directive unless there is a majority consent of the directors, and there must be a quorum of directors for a valid vote. The directors are concerned with major policy decisions, not the day-to-day running of the corporation. They are not considered agents of the corporation because they have no authority to sign contracts or enter into major business deals.

Directors cannot take individual action; they must act as a whole. All directors must be given fair notice of regular and special meetings.

Directors are not normally paid a salary, although they are given a small fee or per diem allowance for the meetings which they attend. Although they are not salaried employees, directors owe a high duty of fidelity and good faith in exercising their responsibility. They must act with diligence, care, reasonableness and skill. If a director does not live up to these standards, he can be removed, and he can be sued if his double dealing or incompetence causes the corporation to lose money. In fact, any secret profits that a director enjoys because of inside information must be returned to the corporation.

The directors cannot vote for a merger, consolidation, dissolution or sale of the major assets of a corporation; this requires stockholder approval.

Officers. The officers of a corporation are agents and employees who run the daily operations of the business. They, too, owe the corporation a high degree of care to act reasonably and honestly. If they are involved in a conflict of interest or double dealing, they have to return any secret profits, and they can be liable for punitive damages. Although an officer of the corporation can sign contracts, he is not personally responsible for the contract if he executes it as the agent of the corporation. The proper way to accomplish this is by the following: "XYZ Corporation by A.B. See, President." If an officer signs a contract without signifying that he is acting for the corporation and the people he is contracting with don't know about the corporate status, then the officer will be liable if his corporation doesn't come through. Officers of a corporation are also personally responsible if they commit a tort while working on behalf of the corporation. This means that if a corporate president defrauds someone, he and his corporation will be liable for damages.

CORPORATE STOCK

There are several different types of corporate stock:

1. Common stock is the ordinary shares of ownership of a corporation.

2. Treasury stock is stock which has been sold to stockholders and then repurshased by the corporation and held by it.

3. Unissued stock is stock which is authorized to be sold by the corporation but is as yet unsold.

4. Preferred stock is stock ownership in a corporation with the added element of preference over common stockholders in dividends or dissolution of the corporation. This means that if there are profits to pay dividends, the preferred stockholders get their dividend first, and if anything is left over, the common stockholders can divide the rest. Preferred stock may be *cumulative* which means that if a dividend is not paid in a particular year, any unpaid dividends must be paid in later years before the common stockholders can receive anything. Preferred stock can be *convertible,* which means that its owners have the option of exchanging it for shares of common stock at a predetermined price. Preferred stock can also be *redeemable,* which means that the corporation has the option of repurchasing it at a certain price.

Even though articles of incorporation may have been approved by a secretary of state, the corporation is not allowed to issue shares of stock until it has complied with the state law and with the SEC if a large public offering is made. Even after these organizations have approved the issuing of stock, sometimes they cannot be resold unless certain other legal requirements are met. The more money and stockholders involved, the more government red tape must be cut. The government regulatory agencies are there to make sure that the stock offering is fair and equitable and that potential stockholders are supplied with the truth before they make their investment decision.

Generally, corporate stock can be issued for money, property, personal services and to cancel a debt. A corporation cannot give shares of stock away without getting something of value in return.

MYTHS ABOUT THE CORPORATE STATUS

The key feature to a corporation for a small businessman is limited liability. Conducting business and carrying debts without becoming personally responsible is very appealing, but the small businessman who is contemplating the costly process of incorporation should be aware of two things: many businesses will not accept a corporate signature without a personal guarantee by one or more of the stockholders, and many times the corporate veil of security can be pierced by a creditor.

BUSINESS ORGANIZATIONS

The limited liability aspect of corporations is no secret. Many large creditors, especially banks, will never take the risk of making a loan to a corporation without a personal guarantee. The persons who seem to get burned the most by a corporation's limited liability are trade creditors who are anxious to extend credit to increase sales.

It is not enough to call your company a corporation in order to take advantage of the benefits of incorporation. Even if the articles of incorporation and the issuance of stock is approved by the state, a corporation still may be run in such a way that it is the *alter ego* of its owner, not really run as a corporation. If a business is run by just one or two individuals and the corporate status would actually promote fraud or injustice on the public, the courts will disregard the corporate existence. Also, if a corporation is not capitalized properly (not enough money is put into the corporate treasury by the stockholders to pay for the anticipated operation of the business), the courts will not recognize the corporation. This is called piercing the corporate veil, and if it happens, then the stockholders are held liable as if they were equal partners.

DISSOLVING THE CORPORATION

Since corporations are creatures of the state and most of them have a perpetual existence, the state also oversees their break-up. Merely going out of business or selling all of the assets is not enough to terminate a corporate existence. When a corporation is dissolved, all of its creditors are paid first. Then the stockholders divide what is left in proportion to their stock holdings.

A voluntary dissolution is one which is brought about by a vote of the stockholders. The percentage of stockholders needed for a voluntary dissolution varies in each state, but generally it ranges from 66% to 75%. When the required number of stockholders vote to dissolve the corporation, a certificate of dissolution is issued by a state official after all state taxes have been paid. Then the corporation goes about selling the assets to satisfy the creditors and eventually pay the stockholders. Most states require voluntary dissolution to be approved by a court for the protection of the public.

There are also involuntary dissolutions of corporations. They can be brought about by (1) creditors who can force an insolvent corporation into bankruptcy; (2) the state because of fraud or the non-payment of taxes; and (3) by a petition of minority stockholders who must prove fraud, mismanagement or stockholder dissension which is so bad that it is impossible to continue the business of the corporation.

GOVERNMENT CORPORATIONS

The state and federal government can create government corporations through legislation. The power of these corporations is derived and limited by the charters granted by the legislature or Congress. These corporations are run by a board of directors, but there are no stockholders or dividends. They are generally funded by taxpayers, and they can finance themselves with public bond issues. They are more efficient than government bureaus because there is a centralized management which makes the divisions on wages and prices without going through the arduous efforts of legislation. Examples of federal corporations are the Tennessee Valley Authority (TVA) and the U.S. Postal Service. Examples of state corporations are government owned utilities, irrigation districts and airports. Cities and towns also incorporate themselves to take advantage of sales taxes which might otherwise be disbursed throughout the county.

NON-PROFIT, TAX-EXEMPT CORPORATIONS AND FOUNDATIONS

The states allow for non-profit, tax-exempt corporations for charitable, educational or religious purposes—the purpose cannot be political or commercial. They include fraternal societies, labor unions and chambers of commerce. Specific examples are the Salvation Army, Harvard University and the Ford Foundation.

The major difference from private corporations is that no stock is issued and no dividends can be paid, as any profits from operations must go to some charity.

In order to officially qualify as a tax-exempt corporation there must be approval by the state and the Internal Revenue Service, which scrutinizes the operations of the charity to make sure that profits are not channeled to private persons through subterfuges such as unreasonably high salaries, free rent, or low interest loans without security. If a charity gets too political and attempts to influence legislation, it loses its tax-exempt status.

If a corporation qualifies as tax-exempt, it pays no federal or state income tax, no property tax on buildings used for charitable purposes and no federal excise tax on items such as telephone bills or airplane tickets. Some tax-exempt corporations get a lower postal rate. A person who makes a gift to a tax-exempt corporation can take it as a deduction on his income tax return with no liability for gift taxes.

CHAPTER 28

Consumers and Their Environment

INTRODUCTION

No field of the law is more dynamic than the legal protection of our environment. The problems of pollution—air, water, thermal, radiation, and pesticide hazards, solid waste disposal, conservation of resources and population management—are the subjects of a vast number of federal and state laws and court decisions. There are many new bills pending before the Congress and state legislatures concerning the environment, and there are many environmental lawsuits pending trial and appellate review. New laws and new court decisions could make this chapter obsolete in a matter of months so our purpose here is to explain the problems of protecting the future, to explain in very basic terms the laws which are presently available to the environmentalist and to show the trend for future laws on the subject.

"Conservation" and the "protection of the environment" are now terms as sacred as mom and apple pie. Politicians, captains of industry and consumers all give lip service to conservation but when many individuals are economically affected by conservationist measures, they scream foul. Big business is not the only offender; consumers are sometimes guilty of apathy and selfishness: In California the legislature adopted a law which demanded the installation of smog control devices on all automobiles on the road. The cost of the crankcase device would have been approximately $25. The consumers screamed so loud that the implementation of the law had to be postponed, leaving millions of cars spreading noxious pollutants in the air.

The fight to preserve the environment must be waged on three fronts:

1. Public information campaigns to reveal which industries or businesses are polluting.

2. In the political arena through tough new laws for the regulation and control of pollution.

3. In the courts to enforce environment laws and gain interpretation of the laws favorable to the ecological movement.

The problems of the environment will not be solved by laws and lawsuits alone. We must elect officials who will strictly enforce existing laws for the environment's protection. This requires not only direct supervision, but also the appointment of honest, conscientious administrators and substantial appropriations to properly carry on the fight. (The Environmental Protection Agency [EPA] is subtly controlled by the Office of Management and Budget, which directly· controls the appropriations which the EPA can use to enforce and administer the federal laws to protect the environment.)

The problem of preserving the environment is basically an economic problem. Big business has had the unbridled use of natural resources for many years, and it has obviously used them badly. These businesses will not voluntarily install pollution control devices and seriously alter their production methods unless it is profitable to do so.

Private lawsuits to abate industrial pollution were relatively unsuccessful in the past because the country and the courts were pro-business. Individuals sometimes won suits, but it was cheaper for businesses to pay the damages than go through re-tooling and installation of expensive pollution control devices. The damages were simply absorbed into the cost of production and passed along to the consumer.

It was also very disappointing to environmentalists to discover that the government is one of the biggest offenders. Officials on all levels have failed to enforce existing laws because of apathy, corruption, or a lack of funds. And it is extremely difficult, impossible in some cases, to force officials to act affirmatively in enforcement. Also, governments are heavy polluters themselves—city sewage plants and garbage dumps.

As in the case of personal freedom and civil rights, the courts seem to be the last resort for those who seek to protect the environment. This is not a desirable solution because of the long delays in trial and appellate procedures, but still the ultimate decisions will probably rest with the states' highest courts and the United States Supreme Court.

WHO CAN SUE AND BE SUED?

The government is primarily obligated to bring lawsuits to eradicate pollution and control the environment. Governmental lawsuits may seek criminal sanctions or civil remedies. Unfortunately, the official agencies cannot be depended upon to stop pollution. Corporate pressure has inhibited vigorous government prosecution. Since the government is a party to much of the pollution which goes on, one agency will rarely seek to enjoin another because it could be politically embarrassing. Thus, individuals and groups of environmentalists have been forced to take the initiative in the courts.

One lone individual can bring a lawsuit for monetary damages and get an injunction against the polluter if he can show the pollution directly affects him. This seldom happens since most polluters affect a very large segment of the population indirectly. When pollution hurts a great many of us, it is classified as a public nuisance rather than a private nuisance. Public nuisances can only be abated, in most jurisdictions, by a governmental authority. (Some states allow any citizen to bring a private environmental action in court even though he is not directly affected by the polluter.)

It's hard to find just the right individual with the proper standing to sue, and this has slowed down the filing of many anti-pollution lawsuits.

The petitioner or plaintiff must have some special economic interest in the lawsuit. Since environmental lawsuits rarely involve economic interests but rather conservation of natural resources or the maintenance of natural beauty, environmental groups had problems accomplishing the proper standing in order to sue. The lower federal courts finally recognized the need of the private lawsuit to preserve and maintain the environmental balance, and they liberalized the standing rule to recognize the rights of groups especially concerned with the preservation of natural resources and aesthetics.

(This liberalized rule on standing was initiated by a United States District Court and upheld by a United States Circuit Court of Appeals, but it was later rejected by the United States Supreme Court in a case brought by the Sierra Club against Walt Disney, Inc. to prevent the construction of a resort in the Sierra Nevada Mountains in California.)

An individual litigant or an individual attorney with little or no experience in handling environmental lawsuits will have a very slim chance of defeating a large business or governmental entity in the courts. Even if the individual gets over the standing hurdle, the trial of the matter on its merits could present a tremendous financial and time drain on the plaintiff. Since he has the burden of proof in any lawsuit, he must amass an impressive array of documentary evidence including scientific displays and reports which can end up costing him a fortune.

Ecology organizations are still our best environmental watchdogs. They have large and experienced legal staffs, who can offer free, voluntary help, and they also have a dedicated staff of experts who can document claims with competent, impressive evidence. These groups have such a good record that they have proven to be embarrassing to government, for they have shown that our politicians are lax in environmental enforcement and that sometimes the government is in complicity with industry in the pollution of the planet. These groups include the Sierra Club, National Audubon Society, Wilderness Society, Environmental

Defense Fund, National Resources Defense Counsel, Friends of the Earth, Izaak Walton League, National Parks and Recreation Association and The Center for Law and Social Policy.

Once you decide to institute a lawsuit and the problem of standing is resolved, you must decide whom to sue. There should be no problem when there is just one private polluter, but pollution suits are rarely that simple. Pollution normally involves multiple parties, all of whom must be enjoined in the lawsuit in order to effectively stop it. It will not do any good to just sue General Motors for the installation of smog control devices; the lawsuit would have to include all automobile manufacturers, foreign and domestic, to effectively stop air pollution.

Suing the government to abate pollution is a far more difficult process than suing a private party because of the antiquated doctrine of sovereign immunity. Private citizens are allowed to sue the government as long as the proper procedures are followed but prior to any lawsuit, the actions of a governmental body must normally be attacked on an administrative level. (Most decisions which involve governmental pollution emanate from administrative bodies like the Atomic Energy Commission or the Federal Power Commission.)

The traditional legal remedy for individual victims of pollution has been to sue for the type of tort damages discussed in Part IV of this book (trespass, negligence, strict liability and nuisance). These traditional common law remedies have done little to effectively stop pollution because of the difficulty in gathering the proper amount of proof. Even if the victim could get a judgment, the damages are rarely enough to make it worthwhile to a polluter to re-tool his plant to diminish or eliminate the environmental problem. In nuisance cases where the victim is asking a court to stop the polluting activity, the court can "balance the equities" and find in favor of the polluter even though what the victim says is absolutely true. Because of this lack of effectiveness of judicial remedies the environmentalists had to look to the legislative branch of government for new laws.

FEDERAL LAWS FOR THE PROTECTION OF THE ENVIRONMENT

The National Environmental Protection Act of 1970

The National Environmental Protection Act, which took effect on January 1, 1970, has been hailed as an environmental Bill of Rights and a modern day Magna Carta for ecology. Prior to its enactment, the agencies of the Federal Government had absolutely no obligation to consider the effects upon the environment when they adopted regulations, granted permits and entered into activities. The Atomic Energy Commission conducted tests and gave permits for the construction of nuclear power plants without considering the effects of their actions on thermal and water pollution. The Department of Agriculture authorized the use of DDT and other pesticides without considering their effects on the total environment. The Army Corps of Engineers approved construction of dams, canals and waterways without consideration of ecological dangers. The Department of Transportation funded freeways without thinking about the aesthetics or air pollution which could be caused by more cars. Given the vast power and reach of the federal government, this list could go on forever.

The NEPA was enacted by Congress in 1969 because of national shock over deterioration of the environment. The Act establishes environmental protection as a priority of the first order and also recognizes that the government and its administrative agencies do not always act in the best public interest. So it establishes legal standing and recognition to those broad groups of people who are passionately interested in the protection of the future of our natural resources.

NEPA requires all government agencies to minimize the environmental harm of their actions, and each agency must list in detail the environmental impact of its proposals, and it must detail the alternatives and the effects of its alternatives. This detailed statement must accompany all proposals which are submitted for agency review, and the statement must play an important role in the decision-making process.

NEPA applies not only to projects which are undertaken exclusively by the government (building of power plants or the construction of dams) but also to the licensing and funding of private and semi-private projects (FHA loans and HUD grants).

NEPA has created the Environmental Protection Agency to administer and enforce the law. This federal agency is directly answerable to the President. Within the agency are various departments, which were formerly small parts of other government departments such as the Federal Water Quality Administration (formerly in the Department of Interior).

NEPA also guarantees the public judicial protection. Individuals can bring lawsuits against federal agencies to force them to follow the provisions of NEPA and file reports on the environmental impacts of their decisions. Individuals can also attack the adequacy of a report to force the agency to file a more complete and revealing one.

It is too early to determine if the EPA is a success. Given the fact that the appointments to the EPA are political and the funding for the EPA is politically controlled, it seems apparent that public interest conservation groups still must act as watchdogs.

Other Laws

In addition to NEPA there are many other laws and regulations designed to protect the environment. Some of them are:

(1) The Water Quality Improvement Act of 1970 which deals with pollution due to oil spills, sewage and mine waste and makes polluters absolutely liable for the cost of cleaning up spills and increase the penalties for them.

(2) The Clean Air Act of 1967 and 1970.

(3) The Solid Waste Disposal Act of 1965.

(4) The Water Pollution Control Act of 1948 and additions in 1964, 1965, 1966.

(5) The Rivers and Harbors Act of 1899 which provides very light criminal sanctions and fines for dumping refuse in navigable waters. (Union Oil was fined $2,500 under this Act for the oil spill in the Santa Barbara Channel in 1969.)

(6) The Wilderness Act of 1964 setting some federally owned areas as wilderness areas.

(7) The Federal Insecticide, Fungicide, and Rodentcide Act.

STATE AND LOCAL LAWS FOR THE PROTECTION OF THE ENVIRONMENT

There is an obvious need for federal standards to control pollution and the use of resources. If there were not uniform rules across the United States, strict measures taken in one state might be offset by uninhibited actions in another. The federal standards are minimal standards and it is up to the states and the local governments to augment them with stricter pollution controls in proportion to the severity of their ecological problems.

All of the states except New Hampshire and North Dakota have some pervasive legislation dealing with environmental protection and control. Illinois and Montana have gone so far as to adopt constitutional amendments guaranteeing the right to a healthy environment and giving all citizens the right to sue to protect their constitutional environmental interests.

The states have been most concerned with the areas of air and water pollution. They have set up supervising agencies which have the power to investigate, hold hearings and subpoena witnesses to the hearings, issue regulations, restrictions and permits, grant exemptions, pursue injunctions and prosecute violators of environmental laws. The duties, functions and powers of these administrative agencies vary markedly among the states. For more information, write your own state's agency listed in the chart at the end of this chapter.

Violators of state pollution laws are liable to pay a penalty. Some states only provide for monetary penalties; others provide for monetary penalties and imprisonment; some provide for no penalty except that an injunction can be obtained against a polluter, if he continues to violate the order, then the agency can seek a contempt of court finding which could subject a violator to a fine and imprisonment. In many of these states where there are pollution law penalties, each day that the law is broken constitutes a separate violation. In addition to penalties, polluters are also civilly liable for any actual damages they cause.

Very few of the states have laws against noise pollution; even fewer states have laws for the management of land. Those which guard against pesticide and rodentcide hazards usually handle the problems through a state department of agriculture. Disposal of solid waste can be handled by a separate department or, in many states, through the agencies controlling air and water pollution.

The individual states have entered into agreements with their neighbors to protect common areas of interest. For instance, California and Nevada have an agreement to protect Lake Tahoe. Similar agreements protect the Ohio River and the Mississippi River and the rivers and streams of New England.

California and Montana have environmental quality acts which are patterned after the Federal Act. These laws require all state agencies to prepare environmental impact reports for projects which would have a significant effect. The acts require local governments to adopt conservation and open space plans and any new projects must be in accordance with these policies.

The states have also provided for local communities and districts to adopt pollution control measures to deal with problems which are indigenous to their respective areas.

As with the federal government, the success of the states in combating pollution depends on the determination of official pollution fighters, budget allotments and the strength of environmental laws. If a state's legislature and bureaucrats have let them down in this area, the people may have to take matters in their own hands through the initiative process. For instance, in California the legislature failed to adopt any laws to protect the coastlines, so the people adopted a state constitutional amendment.

The ultimate solution of the environmental problem lies in population control. With the tremendous increase in people came more demand for services such as energy, transportation, freeways, housing, and sewage treatment. The tax structure and budget priorities did not allow for technological funding to meet the environmental needs of a burgeoning population. Once population growth is controlled, hopefully technology can help alleviate the pollution, ameliorate the competing interest of industry, government and the people, and improve the quality of life.

STATE POLLUTION LAWS

	WATER POLLUTION			AIR POLLUTION			NOISE
	PERVASIVE PLAN	SUPERVISING BODY	MAXIMUM PENALTIES	PERVASIVE PLAN	SUPERVISING BODY	MAXIMUM PENALTIES	NOISE POLLUTION LAWS
ALABAMA	YES	Dept. of Health; Water Improvement Commission	Cease & Desist Orders	YES	Dept. of Health; Air Pollution Control Comm.	$10,000/violation/day; 1 yr. jail	NO
ALASKA	YES	Dept. of Environmental Conservation	$25,000/violation; 1 yr. in jail	YES	Dept. of Environmental Conservation	$25,000/violation; 1 yr. in jail	NO
ARIZONA	YES	Dept. of Health; Water Quality Control Council	Injunction; 1 yr. jail	YES	Dept. of Health; Div. of Air Pollution Control	$5,000/day	NO
ARKANSAS	YES	State Pollution Control Commission	$1,000/day+30 days jail	YES	State Pollution Control Commission	$1,000/day; 30 days jail	NO
CALIFORNIA	YES	State Water Quality Control Board; Local Water Quality Control Boards	6 mos. jail & injunction	YES	State Air Resources Board; Local Air Pollution Control Districts	$6,000/day	YES
COLORADO	YES	Dept. of Health; Water Pollution Control Comm.	Injunctions	YES	Dept. of Health; Air Pollution Control Comm.	None stated except injunctions	YES
CONNECTICUT	YES	Dept. of Environmental Protection	$1,000/day	YES	Dept. of Environmental Protection	$5,000/week	YES
DELAWARE	YES	Dept. of Natural Resources & Environmental Control	$500/violation	YES	Dept. of Natural Resources & Environmental Control	$500/violation	NO
D.C.	YES	Federal Statues and Agencies Apply	$1,000; 3 yrs. jail	YES	Dept. of Environmental Services	$300/day; 90 days jail	NO
FLORIDA	YES	Air & Water Pollution Control Board	$5,000/violation	YES	Air & Water Pollution Control Board	$5,000/violation	NO
GEORGIA	YES	Dept. of Natural Resources Div. of Environmental Protection	$1,000/violation & 500/day	YES	Dept. of Natural Resources Div. of Environmental Protection	$1,000/violation & $500/day	NO
HAWAII	YES	Dept. of Health	$2,500/violation/day	YES	Dept. of Health	$2,500/violation/day	YES
IDAHO	YES	State Board of Health	None stated	YES	State Board of Health	None stated	NO
ILLINOIS	YES²	Illinois Inst. for Environmental Quality Control Bd., Environmental Protection Agency	$10,000 + $1,000/day	YES²	Illinois Inst. for Environmental Quality Control Bd., Environmental Protection Agency	$10,000 + $1,000/day	YES

	WATER POLLUTION			AIR POLLUTION			NOISE
	PERVASIVE PLAN	SUPERVISING BODY	MAXIMUM PENALTIES	PERVASIVE PLAN	SUPERVISING BODY	MAXIMUM PENALTIES	NOISE POLLUTION LAWS
INDIANA	YES	Indiana Environmental Mgt. Bd., Stream Pollution Control Board	$10,000/violation & $1000/day	YES	Indiana Environmental Mgt. Bd., Air Pollution Control Board	$10,000/violation & $1000/day	NO
IOWA	YES	Dept. of Environmental Quality; Water Quality Commission	$500/day	YES	Dept. of Environmental Quality; Air Quality Commission	$500/day	NO
KANSAS	YES	State Board of Health	$1000/violation/day	YES	State Board of Health	$1000/violation/day	NO
KENTUCKY	YES	Dept. of Environmental Protection	$1000/violation/day; 1 yr. jail	YES	Dept. of Environmental Protection	$1000/violation/day; 1 yr. jail	YES
LOUISIANA	YES	La. Stream Control Comm.	$10,000/violation/day	YES	La. Air Control Comm.	$2000/violation/day	NO
MAINE	YES	Board of Environmental Protection	Fine & jail[8] sentence	YES	Board of Environmental Protection	Fine & jail[8] sentence	NO
MARYLAND	YES	Dept. of Water Resources	$10,000/violation/day	YES	Dept. of Health; Div. of Air Quality Control	$10,000/violation/day	NO
MASSACHUSETTS	YES	Water Resources Comm. Div. of Water Pollution	$1000/violation/day	YES	Commission of Public Health	$500/violation/day[1]	YES
MICHIGAN	YES	Dept. of Natural Resources Water Resources Comm	$500/violation/day	YES	State Dept. of Health Air Pollution Control Commission	$500/violation & $100/day	NO
MINNESOTA	YES	Pollution Control Agency	Fine & jail[8] sentence	YES	Pollution Control Agency	Fine & jail[8] sentence	YES
MISSISSIPPI	YES	State Air & Water Pollution Control Comm.	$3000/violation/day	YES	State Air & Water Pollution Control Comm.	$3000/violation/day	NO
MISSOURI	YES	Water Pollution Board	$500/violation/day; 90 days jail	YES	Air Conservation Board	$200/violation/day	NO
MONTANA	YES[2 & 3]	Dept. of Health & Environmental Sciences	$1000/violation/day	YES[2 & 3]	Dept. of Health & Environmental Sciences	$1000/Violation/day	NO
NEBRASKA	YES	Dept. of Environmental Control	$500/violation & $10/day	YES	Dept. of Environmental Control	$500/violation & $10/day	NO
NEVADA	YES	State Water Pollution Control Agency	$2500/violation/day	YES	State Air Pollution Control Agency	$5000/violation/day	NO

	WATER POLLUTION				AIR POLLUTION		NOISE
	PERVASIVE PLAN	SUPERVISING BODY	MAXIMUM PENALTIES	PERVASIVE PLAN	SUPERVISING BODY	MAXIMUM PENALTIES	NOISE POLLUTION LAWS
NEW HAMPSHIRE	NO	NONE	NONE	NO	NONE	NONE	NO
NEW JERSEY	YES	Dept. of Environmental Protection	$3000/violation /day	YES	Dept. of Environmental Protection	$2500/violation /day	NO
NEW MEXICO	YES	Environmental Improvement Agency	NONE	YES	Environmental Improvement Agency	$1000/violation /day	NO
NEW YORK	YES	Dept. of Environmental Conservation	NONE	YES (weak)	Dept. of Environmental Conservation	Fine or jail after abatement order	
NORTH CAROLINA	YES	Dept. of Conservation & Development[4]	NONE	YES	Dept. of Conservation & Development[4]	NONE	NO
NORTH DAKOTA	NO	NONE	NONE	NO	NONE	NONE	YES
OHIO	YES	State Dept. of Health; Water Pollution Control Board	$500/violation /day	YES	Air Pollution Control Board	$10,000/violation /day	NO
OKLAHOMA	YES	Oklahoma Water Resources Board; State Dept. of Pollution Control	$500/violation	YES	State Dept. of Health; State Dept. of Pollution Control	Misd. fine & jail[8] sentence	NO
OREGON	YES	Dept. of Environmental Quality	Misd. fine & jail[8] sentence	YES	Dept. of Environmental Quality	Misd. fine & jail[8] sentence	NO
PENNSYLVANIA	YES	Dept. of Environmental Resources	Misd. fine & jail[6] sentence	YES	Dept. of Environmental Resources	Misd. fine & jail[5] sentence	NO
RHODE ISLAND	YES	Dept. of Natural Resources	$500 and/or 30 days/violation	YES	Director of Dept. of Health	$500 and/or 30 days/violation	NO
SOUTH CAROLINA	YES	Pollution Control Authority	$5000 and/or 2 yrs./violation/day	YES	Pollution Control Authority	$5000/and/or 2 yrs. /violation/day	NO
SOUTH DAKOTA	YES	Committee on Water Pollution	$100 and/or 1 yr. /violation/day	YES	Air Pollution Commission	$500/violation /day	NO
TENNESSEE	YES	Tenn. Water Quality Control Board	$10,000 and/or 2 yrs./violation/ day	YES	Air Pollution Control Bd.	$1000/violation/ day	NO
TEXAS	YES	Water Quality Board	$1000/violation/ day	YES	Air Control Board	$1000/violation/ day	NO
UTAH	YES	Div. of Health; Committee on Water Pollution	Misd. fine & jail[8] sentence	YES	Div. of Health, Committee on Air Conservation	$1000/violation/ day	NO
VERMONT	YES	Agency of Environmental Conservation; Dept. of Water Resources	Misd. fine & jail[8] sentence	YES	Agency of Environmental Conservation & Board of Health	Misd. fine & jail[8] sentence	NO

	WATER POLLUTION			AIR POLLUTION			NOISE
	PERVASIVE PLAN	SUPERVISING BODY	MAXIMUM PENALTIES	PERVASIVE PLAN	SUPERVISING BODY	MAXIMUM PENALTIES	NOISE POLLUTION LAWS
VIRGINIA	YES	State Water Control Board	$5000 and/or 1 yr./violation /day	YES	State Air Pollution Board Board	$1000/violation/day	NO
WASHINGTON	YES	Dept. of Ecology; Water Pollution Control Comm.	$100/violation /day	YES	Dept. of Ecology; Air Pollution Control Authority	$1000/violation; 1 yr. in jail; $250/day	NO
WEST VIRGINIA	YES	State Water Resources Bd.	Fine and/or jail sentence[8]	YES	Air Pollution Control Comm.	$1000/violation/day	NO
WISCONSIN	YES	Dept. of Natural Resources	$5000/violation /day	YES	Dept. of Natural Resources	$5000/violation/day	NO
WYOMING	YES	Dept. of Health & Social Services; Div. of Health & Medical Services	$200 and/or 6 mos./violation/ day	YES	Dept. of Health & Social Services; Air Resources Council	$750/violation/week	NO

FOOTNOTES:

[1] For the second conviction; the maximum penalty for the first offense is $100/violation/day.

[2] State Constitutional Amendment gives all citizens the right to a healthful environment and gives all citizens the right to sue to protect environment.

[3] Environmental Quality Council provides for interdepartmental planning.

[4] Advisory only.

[5] Misdemeanor after third offense.

[6] Misdemeanor after second offense.

[7] For dumping oil in state waters the fine is $20,000.00.

[8] The source material for this chart, Martindale-Hubbell Digest of American Laws, Volume 5, 1973, did not list the exact amount of maximum fines and penalties; it only listed violations of pollution laws as punishable by fine and/or jail sentence.

PART VI

CONSTITUTIONAL FREEDOMS

CHAPTER 29

Freedom of Speech

First Amendment to the United States Constitution

"Congress shall make no law ... abridging the freedom of speech ... or the right of the people peaceably to assemble, and to petition the government for a redress of grievances."

EXPRESSION, ASSEMBLY AND PROTEST

INTRODUCTION

If any "good" was produced by the Vietnam War and the social injustice in our country, it would only be that a large mass of Americans have rediscovered the United States Constitution (more specifically, the First Amendment).

After the turbulent years during the depression when labor struggled for recognition, there was a 20-year period in which relatively few demonstrations were held to protest the actions of any governmental body. It was a period of apathy and fear. It grew out of World War II patriotism, the Cold War and the red-baiting witch hunts of Senator McCarthy.

The young people of the '50s became known as the "silent generation". But, by the end of the decade the voices of dissent and protest became louder and stronger. In the '60s demonstrations against injustice became a way of life. A new element of civil disobedience on a mass scale was added to the traditional forms for redressing grievances. This generation shook the First Amendment from its doldroms, and it brought many old issues and some new issues concerning free speech and the right to protest before the Supreme Court.

The escalation of the war in Indochina brought larger and more vigorous protests, which brought more stringent security measures by government agencies, which were unprepared to cope with the demonstrations of this size. Irresponsible politicians denounced and violently repressed the legal protest movements. This conflict polarized Americans into warring camps.

The purpose of this chapter is not to take sides or act as a mediator in the conflict. Its object is to explain the purpose and spirit of the First Amendment right to protest and the legal limitations on it.

THE PRINCIPLE

The philosophy of free expression underlies all Supreme Court decisions which have interpreted the First Amendment. In a free democratic society, freedom of expression is absolutely necessary to allow the citizen intelligent choices and decisions. Free expression allows us to hear all relevant facts and interests —it opens up a "marketplace for new ideas."

Freedom of expression also is a means of keeping the peace, as it allows angry citizens to express their grievances publicly in the hope they might obtain peaceful reform and redress.

Lastly, freedom of speech and expression gives an individual dignity. It is vitally important to know that one can speak his mind and express himself on any issue in a free country.

The progress of the U.S. Supreme Court in rendering First Amendment decisions has been slow. While this Amendment has always applied to the federal government, the Court did not officially declare that the states were also bound by it through the Fourteenth Amendment until 1925.

The Supreme Court has established standards, however vague, in deciding how far one can go to exercise his right to protest - it is not an absolute right. The government *does* have the right to protect itself from undemocratic, violent overthrow and other breaches of the law. There has to be some balancing of the two positions, but the right of the public to a free market place of ideas is of paramount importance.

Justice Oliver Wendell Holmes said it best:

> ". . . the ultimate good desired is better reached by free trade in ideas . . . the best test of truth is the power of thought to get itself accepted in the competition of the market . . . We should be eternally vigilant against attempts to check the expression of opinions that we loathe and believe to be wrought with death, unless they so imminently threaten immediate interference with the lawful and pressing purposes of the law that an immediate check is required to save the country."

VERBAL AND SYMBOLIC SPEECH

The general rule is that all forms of speech, expression, public assembly, and protest are presumed lawful and should be free from interference. Only where there is a compelling government or public interest and that interest can be shown by clear and convincing proof, will a court interfere with the right to protest. Even then, a court will only interfere to the point where the government interest is assuaged. Courts should bend over backwards to ensure that protests can still be held.

The Supreme Court has never made a precise list of what conduct is legal and what conduct is illegal. All one can do is state what activity has been allowed, what disallowed and make reasonable estimates on conduct that may fall in the no-man's-land in the middle. For instance, most forms of verbal communication, distribution of written materials, and display of signs and symbols are protected by the First Amendment. Physical violence, seizure of property, false advertising, and obstruction of government operations (like selective service offices) are not protected activities. Profane words which are used to incite a fight or riot are not protected, but the mere use of profanity in public without any specific unlawful purpose is protected - it has nothing to do with good or bad taste.

Freedom of speech is not limited to just verbal utterances. Constitutional lawyers have advanced the theory that action should be considered symbolic speech, and members of the Supreme Court have upheld this position. Thus, the waving of Viet-Cong flags is a protected activity. The Supreme Court now distinguishes between speech (protected), other kinds of expression called speech plus (?), and non-speech (unprotected). Again, there is no hard and fast rule by which one can judge an activity. For instance, the wearing of black arm bands by high school students as a war protest was deemed a perfectly legal form of protest. But the burning of draft cards and of the American flag has been deemed illegal and unprotected, as the Court held there was an overriding governmental interest in preserving these objects. The courts have generally held that sit-ins and other obstructions of property are not protected by the First Amendment.

TIME, PLACE AND MANNER

The time, place and manner in which you exercise freedom of speech is most important. A protest means little if it is done in a place where you cannot be heard by others. Freedom of speech is not limited to the confines of the home or to singing in the shower. The denial of an audience is tantamount to the denial of the freedom itself.

In 1939, the Supreme Court decided that all persons have the right to use streets, parks and other open areas for public assembly and protest (there are a few exceptions - such as prisons.) The Court has not spoken on closed public places, and it will probably not make a decision including them all. Decisions will depend on the use and nature of the facility.

Privately-owned property which has the same function as public property or has been dedicated to public use falls within this public access rule. The fact that the property owner objects to the use to which it is being put has no bearing on the case since this location was dedicated to public use. Therefore, the streets of a company town or of a large shopping center can be legally used for public protests and demonstrations. However, the Court recently retreated from this position in a case involving distribution of handbills in a privately owned store which was within a shopping center.

Just as freedom of speech is not absolute, so the freedom to use public places is not either. The government does have a right to regulate the time, place and manner of the protest. These regulations can only be imposed for sound, logical reasons; they cannot be used as a subterfuge to subvert the First Amendment right of the protesters. Time, place and manner regulations of speech and expression usually occur on the local municipal level in the form of permits to use public parks, streets and other facilities.

Any set of standards which a governmental body wishes to impose must be definite and must be applied uniformly; there cannot be one set of standards for establishment groups and another set of standards for non-conformists. Many governmental efforts to regulate speech, expression, public assemblies, and protests have been struck down because of vague, indefinite and overbroad rules. All permit denials must allow for immediate court review, either in the state or federal courts. (Unfortunately, this is a time-consuming form of relief, but it does provide judicial review of local officials.)

FORMS OF INTERFERENCE

The most repugnant form of interference with speech and protest is prior restraint. This occurs when free speech or expression is forbidden by court injunction or denial of a permit to use public places. Prior restraint is valid only on an extremely convincing showing that the activity will later incite violence. The fact that extra police or other security measures will have to be taken for the public safety is not a compelling ground. The First Amendment right to protest is paramount.

Prior restraint should not be granted because of a fear of violence from a hostile audience. Thus, the fear that civil rights demonstrators would be attacked by Klansmen or that hardhats might assault anti-war marchers is not enough to prevent a demonstration. If this were the case, it would be too easy to stop unpopular protests. There can be no prior restraint where the speech involved might incite non-violent criminal action (as in the case when a legislator advocated refusing the draft).

Another form of interference with First Amendment rights is the criminal prosecution of those accused of breaking the law during protests. The government may seek punishment by accusing protesters of incitement to riot, crossing state lines to incite a riot and conspiracy to commit other crimes. (For instance, Dr.

Benjamin Spock, the Chicago Seven and the Vietnam Veterans Against the War.) Most of these costly trials have ended in acquittals.

Another form of government interference can come by way of a display of force by the local police force; an undisciplined, club-wielding police force is an obnoxious form of repression, and it has the most direct, chilling effect on the First Amendment.

TESTS

It seems that every time the Supreme Court decides a case involving First Amendment rights, the majority formulates a test which is used to decide the legality of protest and the legality of government interference. This lack of consistency by the courts makes it very difficult for local officials to make prudent decisions regarding First Amendment rights. There are two basic tests which have been used by the Court:

(1) A clear and present danger test was advanced by Justice Oliver Wendell Holmes and improved upon by Justice Louis Brandeis and Chief Justice Fred Vinson. If the form of expression constitutes a clear and present danger so grave as to place it outside the protection of the First Amendment, then government interference is valid. This test was used by the Court to uphold many of the sedition convictions which occurred during World War I, and it was used to uphold the conviction of many Communist Party leaders.

Another test which sounds as if it is just a different way of describing the clear and present danger test, asks the following question: "Does the communication in question constitute a direct incitement to unlawful action?"

(2) The second test balances the interest of freedom versus the interest of the government. The court must balance the value of free speech against the competing values which the government contends justify the control of speech. This test is by far the most conservative, and it was proposed by Justice Felix Frankfurter. (It was used in the draft card burning cases.)

The new Supreme Court has a more conservative look than its predecessor of a few years ago. Their position will probably manifest itself in that no-man's-land where speech and non-speech expressions are concerned and in the use of the "balancing" test. But, however conservative, the new Court is still dedicated to the continuity of law, the Constitution and precedents established by earlier Courts. Therefore, one cannot expect a wholesale reversal of earlier Court decisions.

Some of our readers may strongly dislike the so-called liberal Supreme Court decisions on the right to protest. They may feel that many of the acts described should be punished by jail sentences or enjoined altogether. But before any rash statements are made or angry positions taken, remember the historical context in which the First Amendment right to protest and to redress grievances was founded. The Constitution does not distinguish between good taste and bad taste; it merely grants us all the freedom to express ourselves.

FREEDOM OF ASSOCIATION

INTRODUCTION

The freedom to join and to belong to groups with impunity is a basic right protected by the Constitution. Many people feel that they are attacked by the government just because they belong to an organization — whether it's the Communist Party, the Nazi Party, the AFL-CIO or the Republican Party. Also, the whole business of loyalty oaths, employment black-listing and registration of groups with the government is a question of the First Amendment right to freely associate.

Some critics attack courts which have upheld the freedom to associate by invalidating or limiting state and federal laws and reversing some criminal convictions. These critics are generally uninformed about constitutional law. The law says that it is just as lawful to belong to the Communist Party as the John Birch Society. The First Amendment protects one's right to belong to the Boy Scouts and the Ku Klux Klan. The Constitution does not protect members of groups who actively participate in violent or other illegal activity. Guilt by association is not legal; guilt can only be attributed to actual participation in violent or other illegal activity.

The courts didn't try many cases involving the freedom to associate until the 1920's. A surge of patriotism after World War I, fear of new immigrants and fear of anarchists, syndicalists and Bolsheviks brought many state laws making it a crime to belong to organizations which might preach or advocate the violent overthrow of the government. In the 1920's the constitutionality of these state statutes was tested, and the Supreme Court began formulating rules which attempted to ameliorate the First Amendment right to freely associate with governmental intrusions.

In 1940 the federal government got into the picture with the Smith Act which provided, in part, that it was a crime for anyone to organize or be a member of any society, group or assembly of persons who teach, advocate or encourage the duty, necessity, desirability or propriety of overthrowing or destroying any government in the United States by force or violence, providing that the person knows of the illegal purposes of the organization. The first big court test of the constitutionality of the Smith Act came after the conviction of 11 leaders of the American Communist Party in 1948.

THE GOVERNMENT TEST

The Supreme Court in *Dennis vs. United States* sustained the conviction of all 11 defendants and rejected their defense of the First Amendment freedom to associate. The majority opinion used a clear and present danger test to justify this. The test was put in the form of a question: "Does the gravity of the evil, discounted by its improbability, justify such invasion of free speech as is necessary to avoid the danger?" Chief Justice Vinson added that the world conditions at the time (the Cold War) and the ideological and philosophical similarities between the defendants and Communists abroad justified the convictions.

However, the court has been steadily retreating from the Dennis case standards. Now, mere membership alone in the Communist Party or any other organization which advocates the violent overthrow of the government is not enough to sustain a conviction. There is the added constitutional requirement that there be "teaching and advocacy of action for the accomplishment of overthrowing organized government by language reasonably and ordinarily calculated to incite persons to such action."

It is not enough to believe in violent overthrow of the government or to belong to a group which so believes; it is necessary to prove open advocacy of unlawful action. No matter what the organization is and no matter what the avowed intent of the organization as a whole is, an individual cannot be convicted for belonging to an organization unless it is shown that he had specific individual intent to overthrow the government by unlawful means. Anything less would violate not only the First Amendment right to freely associate, but also the Fifth Amendment right which protects the individual from guilt by association and sympathy. Even the abstract teaching of the moral propriety or necessity for a violent or forceful overthrow of the government is protected by reason of the First Amendment.

REGISTRATION STATUTES

Criminal prosecution for membership in groups or associations is only one method of infringement of the First Amendment right to freely associate. Another comes about through registration and identification statutes. The most famous of these is the Subversive Activities Control Act of 1950, legislation which was the brainchild of the House Un-American Activities Committee.

This Act provided for: (1) identification and registration of Communist action, Communist front, and Communist affiliated organizations; (2) the identification and registration of their members and (3) the attachment of various disabilities to these members. The Subversive Activities Control Board decided just what a Communist-oriented group was and held public hearings in order to aid them in its determinations.

The first constitutional challenge to this act came in 1961 when the Supreme Court found, in a five-to-four decision, in favor of the government. Justice Frankfurter, writing for the majority, found that compulsory disclosure of association membership was justified in light of the First Amendment because of the very nature of the threat of the world Communist movement and the right the government had to preserve itself in light of this challenge. The minority felt that compulsory disclosure of associations violated a Fifth Amendment right against self-incrimination when the associations or membership in them were illegal according to the Smith Act.

A few years later the minority opinion became the majority when the Court ruled that the Subversive Activities Control Board could not coerce an individual into admitting membership to the Communist Party because of the Fifth Amendment and, further, the board could not place a person on its subversive list because he had invoked his Fifth Amendment rights. The Court later held that the Communist Party itself did not have to divulge its membership list, as it could plead the privilege of self-incrimination.

The entire discussion concerning the freedom to associate has dealt with the extreme example of the Communist Party or other organizations which openly advocate the violent overthrow of the government. One must remember that the government must always make a very strong showing in order to infringe upon the right to associate. These cases involving groups with clearly subversive policies are extreme cases, and the government would not be justified in infringing upon the freedom to associate in anything other than an extreme case. Therefore, in cases where a state has tried to obtain membership lists of civil rights organizations under the authority of some "foreign corporation" registration statute, the Supreme Court found no logical relationship between the required disclosures of members and the objectives of the state.

LOYALTY OATHS

Freedom to associate has also been infringed upon by the requirement of loyalty oaths to obtain employment. This oath found popularity in the federal government and in many state governments in 1948 around the time when Senator McCarthy was accusing members of the government of disloyalty. A person generally had to swear under oath that he did not knowingly belong to any of a number of organizations. The list was prepared by the U.S. Attorney General. There were no criminal penalties attached to membership, but such admissions often led to loss of a job and other economic sanctions. The only criminal penalty was perjury for those who lied about membership.

One of the organizations on the list was the Abraham Lincoln Brigade whose history is interesting and points to the inequity and unfairness of the loyalty oath. The

Loyalist Government of Spain was the democratically elected government. The revolutionary opposition to it was headed by General Franco. The Loyalists were given outside support by world Socialist and Communist parties. Franco was given support by Hitler, Mussolini and other Fascist organizations. The Abraham Lincoln Brigade was formed in the United States to help the Loyalists. Members of the Brigade did not swear allegiance to another country or another form of government; they merely fought for or contributed to the Loyalists. After Franco won the Civil War, the Brigade was effectively disbanded. Yet that organization remained on the list of subversives, and former members of the Brigade in the 1930s were barred from jobs two decades later.

The constitutionality of the loyalty oath was upheld by the Supreme Court in 1950 and the Court also upheld the necessity for the filing of an affidavit of non-Communist affiliation by an officer of a labor union (not even a government employee) on the grounds that Congress has the right to protect the free flow of commerce, and Congress has the right to protect the nation from harmful conduct which is allegedly carried on by persons who may be identified by their political affiliations. The federal loyalty oath was soon followed by state loyalty oaths and some of the states provided their own list of subversive organizations.

Later decisions by the Supreme Court (the decisions that prevail today) have retreated from the position of the '50s. Now a loyalty oath can only demand that a person swear to the fact that he does not have the specific intent to seek the violent overthrow of the government. The Supreme Court has gone so far in its protection of the constitutional right to freely associate that it has declared that mere membership alone in the Communist Party is not reason enough to bar members of Communist organizations from employment. Any future cases involving government loyalty oaths will largely depend on the language of the loyalty oath and the particular type of government employment involved. (The government, for instance, can require much more in the way of loyalty from an employee of the Defense Department than it can from an employee in the Social Security Administration.)

LEGISLATIVE INVESTIGATIONS

The most indirect but perhaps the most devastating form of infringement upon the right to freely associate is the legislative investigating committee. The House Un-American Activities Committee (now called the Committee on Internal Security) can subpoena witnesses to appear before it, and its members can question them about alleged subversive activities or organizational membership. The witnesses do not have to answer all questions because of their Fifth Amendment rights, but the refusal to answer could subject them to irreparable damage—blacklisting, firing and the loss of so-called friends. This was the case with many

Hollywood artists who refused to answer HUAC questions during an investigation of communism in the film industry.

The constitutional right of congressional committees to hold hearings, subpoena witnesses, and ask questions about subversive activities has been upheld by the Supreme Court. This decision has never been reversed, nor is there any trend in that direction. The Court held that Congress' investigatory power, especially in the field of subversion and self-preservation of the government, was superior to the freedom of association.

The individual states also formed legislative investigatory committees, but their power is not so far reaching as that of Congress. In a case where the president of the Miami Branch of the NAACP refused to allow a Florida legislative committee to see his membership records, the Supreme Court upheld his right of refusal. In this case, the Court felt that freedom of association was superior to the state legislature's investigatory power.

CHAPTER 30

Freedom of the Press

First Amendment to the United States Constitution
"Congress shall make no law . . . abridging the freedom of . . . the press; . . ."

OBSCENITY AND THE LAW

At one time obscenity or obscene material was not considered within the area of that type of speech which was protected by the First Amendment. In fact, the Supreme Court did not make a decision on an obscenity case until 1957, although there were many state court and lower federal court decisions in the area before that time, including the famous *Ulysses* case. The Supreme Court, in deciding some 25 obscenity matters, has ventured into an area where it is impossible to take a definite stand. It is impossible to set moral standards for an entire nation. The Supreme Court is not in the business of pleasing people; it is used to criticism, but it has been condemned from all quarters for its obscenity decisions. The conservative judges have been called Philistines. The liberal justices have been described as "engineers of permissiveness" and "architects of moral decay."

The prosecution of an obscenity case receives undue newspaper publicity, but little space is devoted to the constitutionally imposed restrictions on a law which attempts to prohibit freedom of speech and freedom of the press. The purpose behind the state's prosecution of pornography is to prevent citizens from viewing the material, but often this purpose is thwarted and the prosecution is counter productive because of the profitable effect of the publicity. For instance, one New York City judge did more to increase the box office receipts of the pornographic film "Deep Throat" than a million dollars worth of advertising could have accomplished.

The obscenity laws only involve the commercial exploitation of matter involving sex. The possession of pornographic material by an individual for his own personal, non-commercial use is legal. It seems inconsistent that a person can enjoy obscene materials in his home, but he cannot let others enjoy the same material for profit.

While the publication or distribution of obscene material has been ruled an exception to freedom of the press, no court has ever prevented or punished a display or presentation of violence.

In the obscenity field most restrictions take the form of criminal sanctions against a party who utters the speech or distributes the matter. Such sanctions are usually leveled after or during the allegedly obscene act. Therefore, even if one announces he is going to stage an act which could be obscene, the government will not normally try to stop it before the act has even begun—outright censorship is unconstitutional.

One must remember that there are more subtle forms of censorship. The government may put strict permit regulations into effect in order to control a facility, but such regulations must be reasonable and uniformly applied to be legally effective. Unreasonable permit regulations—used as a subterfuge to circumvent the First Amendment—are unconstitutional.

There are private organizations which can censor and limit distribution of material, and these organizations are not controlled by the Constitution. For instance, the old Hays Office controlled motion picture distribution and could order illicit scenes deleted from a film or prevent the distribution of a film entirely. The Hays Office is gone, but its modern counterpart is the Motion Picture Association of America, which has the power to label a movie (G, PG, R or X) and thereby restrict its audience.

THE TEST FOR OBSCENITY

The first case in which the Supreme Court struck down a state obscenity statute on the grounds that it was repugnant to the First Amendment occurred in 1957 in the case of *Butler vs. Michigan.* In that case the State of Michigan had a statute which made it a crime for anyone to publish matter which would corrupt the morals of youth. The Supreme Court declared this law unconstitutional because it applied the same standards to youth as it did to adults and said it was too vague and uncertain. The Court declared that adults could not be prevented from reading or observing material just because it might be objectionable to the parents of children of more tender and innocent years. To enforce such a law would only allow the adult population of the state of Michigan to read no more than children's books.

In this decision and in all subsequent decisions on obscenity cases, the Supreme Court has maintained that the state *does* have a right to protect its youth from obscene matter - this right has never been questioned. In all the obscenity cases, the court has essentially limited itself to obscene matter which has been distributed to an audience of *adults*.

Also in 1957, the Supreme Court, by virtue of the decision in *Roth vs. U.S.*, established a national test for lower courts to use in determining the validity of obscenity laws. In the Roth case the Court stated that obscenity is matter that appeals to the prurient interest of the average person applying contemporary standards. A few years later the Court added the requirements that the matter had to be patently offensive, and that it had to be utterly without redeeming social importance. Until June, 1973, the test was as follows: "obscene" means that to the average person, applying contemporary standards, the dominant appeal of the matter, taken as a whole, is to prurient interest, i.e., a shameful or morbid interest in nudity, sex or excretion, which goes substantially beyond customary limits of candor in description or representation of such matters and which is utterly without redeeming social importance. Some states adopted this exact language as their own statutory law on the subject.

In June of 1973 the more conservative Burger Court redefined the constitutional test for obscenity by a 5-to-4 vote (*Miller vs. Calif.*). Most of the old test was retained, but the requirement that the matter had to be utterly without redeeming social importance was dropped. The decision stated that the states can prescribe punishment for the printing or sale of works "which appeal to the prurient interest in sex, which portray sexual conduct in a patently offensive way and which, taken as a whole, do not have serious literary, artistic, political or scientific value."

A major change in the interpretation of the test for obscenity involves the community standards by which a jury must judge whether a work arouses the prurient interest. The old test used national community standards. The prosecution had to prove the community standards with reference to the allegedly obscene material beyond a reasonable doubt. The prosecution used police officers, clergymen, film critics and physicians to testify to community standards. The defendants would counter with their own witnesses from similar professions.

The new test allows a jury to use local community standards. But the new test does not define "local". Does "local" mean the community standards of the state, the county, the city, or even the neighborhood? Perhaps the states will establish obscenity control districts as they have created pollution control districts!

In establishing the new test, the Burger Majority reasoned that the community standards of a city in Maine or Mississippi may vary markedly from the community standards of New York City, and that the legal limits of censorship can vary similarly among the states. The substitution of local standards makes it impossible for the distributors of films, books, or other forms of public information to know if they are breaking state law before they disseminate their material. The Court's reasoning could lead to ridiculous situations: An adult from a small town in Utah could travel a few hundred miles to Las Vegas and legally see a lavish nightclub act featuring nude bodies; yet that same act performed live, on film, or depicted in a book could be prosecuted as obscene in his home town.

The Court "clarified" its definition of local in June of 1974. The X-rated movie "Carnal Knowledge" had played in theaters across the United States without incident except in Albany, Georgia where the theater owner was arrested for showing it. A local jury convicted him for violating the Georgia obscenity law, and it based its verdict on the local standards of the Albany community, despite the film's national distribution and critical acclaim. The conviction was appealed to the U.S. Supreme Court, which said that jurors can judge the meaning of obscenity based upon the standards of the small locality in which they live. This would lead you to logically infer that the conviction of "Carnal Knowledge" was upheld. Wrong—the Court went on to say that the Albany jury had gone beyond its constitutional limit without elaboration on the new obscenity test. To be consistent with this decision and fair to national media distributors, the Court will have to review every single book, movie or live show which has led to an obscenity conviction.

In establishing a new test for obscenity, the Court again had to come to grips with the important constitutional question of whether the state can prevent an adult citizen from enjoying and commercially exploiting material involving sex. The Report of the President's Commission on Pornography—the most comprehensive and scientific analysis of the subject—found that there was no causal connection between pornography and anti-social behavior. The only real victims of the obscenity laws are the persons arrested and the taxpayers who have to foot the bill for all this costly enforcement. Nevertheless, Chief Justice Burger stated that there is "ample basis for legislatures to conclude that a sensitive key relationship of human existence, central to family life, community welfare and the development of human personality, can be debased and distorted by crass commercial exploitation of sex."

Under both tests the matter is not obscene when its dominant theme is educational or scientific. Thus, movies with graphic displays of all forms of sexual intercourse are protected if their dominant theme is to educate the public. Courts will look to the advertising and promotion of the matter to determine its dominant purpose.

FREEDOM OF THE PRESS AND
THE LAWS OF DEFAMATION

Slander and libel were traditionally considered forms of speech not protected by the First Amendment. They were considered actions in tort where the victim of defamation could sue his detractor for damages. The very first libel case decided by the Supreme Court (1964) was *New York Times vs. Sullivan.*

The New York Times had published an article attacking an Alabama police department. The police filed suit in Alabama against the Times and obtained a large punitive judgment. Alabama's highest court upheld the decision, and the Times appealed to the U.S. Supreme Court on the basis that the libel laws of Alabama infringed on the constitutional freedom of the press. The Court agreed and ruled that any public official who is defamed by the press must prove that the allegations are not only untrue but are also published with malice or a willful and wanton disregard for the truth.

In any defamation case, the truth is always an absolute defense. The Times had alleged that its article did state the truth but the trial court jury decided against it on this issue and this ruling was upheld in the Supreme Court. However, there was no mention of malice or wanton disregard of the true facts at the trial, as this was not a requirement of the Alabama law. The reasoning of the Supreme Court was that it was most important for the press to carry on an uninhibited, robust debate of public issues. The Court felt that public figures should have tough hides, and it realized that members of the press do sometimes make mistakes in their reporting.

The *New York Times vs. Sullivan* case limited the scope of First Amendment protection to public officials. Later the Court extended this ruling to cover public figures such as movie stars.

> In October of 1969, Look Magazine published an article about San Francisco's Mayor, Joseph L. Alioto, linking him with the Mafia. Mayor Alioto sued Look, its editors, and the writers of the article for millions of dollars in punitive damages. The jurors were unanimous in finding that the article was untrue and defamatory, but they were unable to decide on the issue of malice.

FREEDOM OF THE PRESS AND
NATIONAL SECURITY

In matters of national security, the government must resort to the traditional clear and present danger test in order to stop the publication of matter which it deems contrary to the national interest. The case of the *United States vs. the New York Times and the Washington Post* to prevent publication of the Pentagon Papers marks the very first time the government has sought to restrict the publication of a newspaper.

In cases of obscenity and libel, infringement on the First Amendment usually comes in the form of a criminal penalty or civil judgment *after* the matter has been published. In the Pentagon Papers case, the government sought to stop publication altogether. A Federal District Court did grant a temporary five-day injunction which restrained the New York Times and Washington Post from further printing of the Pentagon Papers. This five-day period was granted in order to allow the Justice Department and the attorneys for the newspapers to prepare and argue their cases; however, it marks the very first time in American history that the government has successfuly restrained a newspaper from printing legitimate news.

The Federal District Court found that the Justice Department could not make a clear and convincing showing that the publication of the Pentagon Papers was a clear and present danger to the national security of the United States. While publication of the Pentagon Papers may have been damaging to our prestige and embarrassing to many government officials, the revelation of the truth and the constitutionally protected freedom of the press to print the truth could not be violated.

The Supreme Court decided to hear the case immediately because of the gravity of the issues involved. The Supreme Court upheld the decision of the Federal District Court by a six to three vote. The three dissenting justices did not find overriding justification in the government's position; rather they felt that the matter had been decided too quickly and that it should be sent back to the District Court for further review and consideration.

FREEDOM OF THE PRESS AND
TELEVISION AND RADIO BROADCASTING

The television and radio broadcasting industry enjoys many of the First Amendment privileges accorded to the press. However, some of their operations, unlike other forms of media, are controlled by Congress. It was decided long ago that the airwaves are public and a part of interstate commerce and therefore subject to the control of the people through their government. An independent agency, the Federal Communications Commission, was established, and the constitutionality of that commission and its powers over broadcasters has been tested and upheld.

Broadcasters are much more careful to avoid "obscenity" than are other forms of the media. The nude bodies and rough language that one might see and hear in an X-rated movie could hardly be shown on commercial television, even if the audience were forewarned. Where movies deal with a captive paying audience, television is in no such position. By the time any objectionable material might pass over the screen, it is too late to change channels. The degree to which the FCC controls obscenity or profanity usually depends on the type of program involved. Adult subjects and spicy language are more likely on a late night talk show than on an earlier program which children watch. Many broadcasters are afraid to present more adult subjects because they fear FCC censorship and do not wish to establish precedents which could bring on even more governmental control.

Radio and television stations have an affirmative obligation to take editorial stands on public issues, and the broadcasters must give equal time to spokesmen for the other side. Newspapers do not have to give equal time.

A broadcaster cannot favor one political candidate over another. If he gives one free time, the broadcaster must offer all of the opponents equal free time.

The FCC has the power to grant and renew broadcast licenses and can take away the license of a broadcaster who does not fulfill his obligation to present public issues or does not give equal time. Hearings to renew or grant a license are public, and citizens may present evidence against the broadcaster.

FREEDOM OF THE PRESS AND
GRAND JURY INVESTIGATIONS

New York Times reporter, Earl Caldwell, wrote articles on the Black Panther Party after a number of private interviews with its members. Caldwell was later called as a witness before the Federal Grand Jury in San Francisco, which was investigating the Panthers. He refused to answer questions regarding his sources of information on the basis that the First Amendment right of freedom of the press protected this private information. Caldwell was held in contempt for his refusal to appear, and the case was appealed all the way to the Supreme Court.

The government argued that the right of a federal grand jury to investigate was supreme to any First Amendment rights to freedom of the press. Lawyers for Caldwell and the New York Times argued that if reporters were forced to divulge the names of their contacts, their information would soon dry up and this would diminish the public's right to be informed on important issues. In a 5-4 decision the Court found in favor of the government position and upheld Caldwell's contempt conviction.

Fifteen states give newspapermen a privilege which they can invoke during grand jury investigations and trials to protect private sources of information.

FREEDOM OF THE PRESS
VS.
THE RIGHT TO A FAIR TRIAL

What happens when there is a conflict between provisions of the Constitution? One such conflict exists when a pending criminal trial can attract so much publicity that it becomes impossible for the defendant to receive a fair trial, which is guaranteed to him by the due process of law clause in the Fifth Amendment.

Can the freedom of the press and the attendant right of the public to know be completely emasculated in order to protect the defendant's right to a fair trial? Does the public have an immediate right to know, or can this right be postponed until after the trial is over? These constitutional questions have been debated, but they have never really been answered. The definitive law on the subject comes from a Supreme Court decision in the Sheppard case (described in Chapter 5) which states that too much adverse publicity can prevent a defendant from getting a fair trial. If a criminal conviction is tainted with too much pre-trial and mid-trial publicity, it can be reversed.

The burden of protecting these rights rests with the trial judge, who has control over the courtroom, the court attaches, and the attorneys involved in the criminal case. This has resulted in gag rules prohibiting anyone associated with the case from divulging aspects of the case to the press. Anyone who violates the gag rule can be held in contempt of court.

In issuing such an order the judge must respect freedom of the press. But if undue publicity might prejudice a fair trial, the defendant's rights are paramount. The public can learn all of the facts after the trial is over. To do otherwise would unfairly put the defendant in danger of a long jail sentence, and it would subject the taxpayers to the costly expense of another trial.

The extent of a judge's gag power is in question. Some judges have gone beyond necessary and constitutional limits. An Oakland, California judge recently ordered jurors to abstain from any comments to the press about the trial *after* they had rendered a not guilty verdict. I seriously doubt the constitutionality of this order, as a juror should be free to speak to anyone after a trial - especially since the defendant was acquitted and could not possibly be retried.

If a judge's gag order is violated and a story is leaked to the press, the newsman who writes the story can be called to court to testify about the source of his information. Newsmen have consistently refused to testify on the basis that the source of their stories is confidential information. Most states do not give newsmen the privilege to withhold this information, and the journalist can be jailed for contempt of court if he refuses to answer these questions.

Freedom of the press does not give reporters any rights to exclusive stories. We often forget the competitive nature of the news industry and fail to realize the value of "exclusives." The Sheppard case, for instance, is full of examples of how newspapers can print false and misleading stories in order to maintain a competitive edge.

If the gag rule accomplishes nothing else, it at least prevents ambitious district attorneys from using the trial to gain free publicity for the advancement of their political ambitions and it prevents defense attorneys from gaining undue press coverage at the expense of their clients.

STATES WHICH GIVE JOURNALISTS THE PRIVILEGE OF REFUSING TO DISCLOSE THE NAMES OF THEIR CONFIDENTIAL NEWS SOURCES

ALABAMA	YES	KENTUCKY	YES	NORTH DAKOTA	NO
ALASKA	NO	LOUISIANA	NO	OHIO	NO
ARIZONA	YES	MAINE	NO	OKLAHOMA	NO
ARKANSAS	YES	MARYLAND	YES	OREGON	YES
CALIFORNIA	YES	MASSACHUSETTS	NO	PENNSYLVANIA	YES
COLORADO	NO	MICHIGAN	YES	RHODE ISLAND	NO
CONNECTICUT	NO	MINNESOTA	NO	SOUTH CAROLINA	NO
DELAWARE	NO	MISSISSIPPI	NO	SOUTH DAKOTA	NO
D.C.	NO	MISSOURI	NO	TENNESSEE	NO
FLORIDA	NO	MONTANA	YES	TEXAS	NO
GEORGIA	YES	NEBRASKA	NO	UTAH	NO
HAWAII	NO	NEVADA	NO	VERMONT	NO
IDAHO	NO	NEW HAMPSHIRE	NO	VIRGINIA	NO
ILLINOIS	NO	NEW JERSEY	YES	WASHINGTON	NO
INDIANA	YES	NEW MEXICO	NO	WEST VIRGINIA	NO
IOWA	NO	NEW YORK	YES	WISCONSIN	NO
KANSAS	NO	NORTH CAROLINA	NO	WYOMING	NO

I wish to thank the office of Senator Alan Cranston (Dem.-California), who provided this information.

CHAPTER 31

Freedom of Religion

First Amendment to the United States Constitution:

"Congress shall make no law respecting an establishment of religion, or prohibiting the free exercise thereof; . . ."

The First Amendment of the Constitution was designed to create a wall between church and state. Its purpose is two fold: (1) to prevent governmental interference in the practice of religion, and, for that matter, non-religion or atheism; and (2) to prevent the establishment of a state or government religion and stopping the state from favoring one religion over another. This section of the First Amendment has been incorporated into the Fourteenth Amendment, and it applies to the states as well as to the federal government. Freedom of religion is not absolute; it can be limited by other compelling reasons.

FREE EXERCISE OF RELIGION

FREE EXERCISE OF RELIGION AND THE CRIMINAL LAW

On some occasions the free practice of one's religion comes into conflict with a state criminal law. Obviously, a religion which practiced human sacrifice could not be tolerated. In every case where there is a conflict between the free exercise of religion and a state law, a court must weigh the interest of the state in promulgating the law against the individual's right to freely practice his religion. If a particular state law is rational and there is a compelling reason for its uniform application, then the law will be upheld as a proper infringement on individual freedom. The following are interesting examples of how the courts sometimes reach completely opposite conclusions.

George Reynolds, a Mormon, was tried for the crime of bigamy in 1870. Reynolds proved at his trial that polygamy was an obligation of the male members of the Mormon Church. In fact, the Mormon who did not practice polygamy would suffer damnation. The trial judge instructed the jury that if Reynolds had married a second time without the benefit of a divorce, he was guilty of bigamy, whatever his religious belief. Reynolds appealed to the Supreme Court on the basis that any law prohibiting polygamy was not applicable to him as it violated his free exercise of religion. The government contended that religious belief could not be superior to law and the Supreme Cout found against Reynolds. The Court found that the bigamy laws were a restraint on the free exercise of the Mormon religion, but this restraint was valid and not repugnant to the First Amendment because bigamy laws were not directed against one religion but were enacted to maintain the integrity of the family unit, and the state had a compelling interest to promote that purpose.

The Navajo Indians of California had been using the drug peyote in their religious rites and sacraments years before California became a state. Peyote contains mescaline, an hallucinatory drug, which has been classified as a narcotic in California. The hallucinatory property is believed by the Native American Church, the religious organization of the Califonia Navajo Indians, to allow participants in the religious ceremony to experience the Diety. In fact, the church feels that non-religious use of peyote is sacrilegious. In 1962, a group of Navajo Indians taking part in a religious ceremony in a sparsely populated area in the desert near Needles, California, were arrested for the possession of peyote. They were convicted, and they appealed to the California Supreme Court on the basis that their convictions were unconstitutional infringments on their right to freely exercise their religion. The court held that the police interference with the religious ceremonial use of peyote violated the free exercise of religion of the First Amendment as incorporated in the Fourteenth Amendment. It also held that the state could only abridge religious practices on a showing of compelling state interest. In this case the religious use of peyote presented only a minimal danger to the state and the enforcemet of its narcotics laws. Justice Matthew O. Tobriner stated "in a mass society, which presses at every point toward conformity, the protection of the self-expression, however unique, of the individual and the group becomes ever more important. The varying current of sub-cultures that flow into the mainstream of our national life give it depth and beauty. We preserve a greater value than ancient tradition when we protect the rights of Indians who honestly practice an old religion using peyote one night in a meeting in a desert hogan near Needles, California."

Since this case was decided, many defendants have alleged that they use drugs as expressions of their own private transcendental worship, but to no avail. The courts have given this Navajo Indian case very limited and narrow interpretation and have not applied the Navajo rule to any other form of religion, organized or otherwise.

THE PLEDGE OF ALLEGIANCE

In 1940 the Supreme Court upheld the expulsion of a young Jehovah's Witness from a small school in Pennsylvania. He was expelled because he refused to stand and pledge allegiance to the American flag on account of his religious teachings. However the Supreme Court soon reversed itself in 1943 in a similar case involving a Jehovah's Witness in West Virginia.

On one side the Court felt that requiring all of the students of a classroom to stand at a particular time involved a very minor state interest and that the right of a child to exercise his religion freely was overwhelming. In fact, in this circumstance, there is a unique opportunity for a teacher to explain constitutional rights to the children - the child's refusal demonstrates the Constitution in action better than any perfunctory reading of the Pledge of Allegiance.

PUBLIC EMPLOYEES

At one time many of the states demanded that public officials and even public employees declare they believed in God. No specific religion was mentioned but these affirmations were struck down by the Supreme Court because they violated the right of a non-believer or aetheist to freely exercise his opinion, and religious affirmation has no practical value in determining the ability of an employee.

THE DRAFT

The drafting of young men to serve in the Vietnam war brought renewed interest in the free exercise of religion clause of the First Amendment. The Supreme Court has never ruled that the Constitution protects an individual from serving in a war because he has religious scruples. But Congress, in enacting selective service laws, has allowed for the conscientious objector and the question of whether the Supreme Court would allow draft avoidance without the benefit of specific legislation is academic. Certainly, anyone attempting to invoke his right to freely exercise his religion could make a strong showing on the basis of the First Amendment.

The Selective Service Law was enacted in 1917. It gave exemption to conscientious objectors who were members of a recognized religious sect whose teachings forbid participation in combat (the Quakers, for instance.) The draft law enacted at the beginning of World War II did not require membership in a recognized religious sect but based conscientious exemption on individual training and belief. The draft law enacted during the Cold War required belief in a supreme being for exemption. But this requirement was severely limited when the Supreme Court interpreted the law to mean that belief could be in a sincere, deeply held objection to war; the particular belief had to be parallel to that filled by the orthodox belief in God by one who would qualify for an exemption from the draft. After this decision, Congress amended the Selective Service Law eliminating the requirement of belief in a supreme being, but retaining the requirement that the objection to war must be based upon religious training and belief. Since that time, the Court has liberalized the meaning of "teaching" and "belief." The conscientious objector must oppose all wars in all forms you cannot selectively object to one war, such as Vietnam.

THE ESTABLISHMENT CLAUSE

SCHOOL PRAYERS

The wall between church and state not only protects the free exercise of religion, but also prevents the government from favoring one religion over another religion, or favoring religion over non-religion. The most famous establishment clause cases involve prayers and Bible-reading in public schools. The first such matter decided by the Supreme Court involved a nondenominational prayer which was prescribed by the New York State Board of Regents, the agency which supervised that state's public schools.

The prayer read, "Almighty God, we acknowledge our dependence upon Thee, and we beg Thy blessings upon us, our parents, our teachers, and our country." It was ordered to be read aloud daily in each class in the presence of a teacher. Children who objected to reciting the prayer were allowed to remain silent or were excused from the room.

The Supreme Court held that the prayer was a religious activity and that it was a part of a governmental program to further religious belief. The Court felt that it was immaterial that any objecting pupil could remain silent or be excused from the room, because the establishment clause forbade governmental prayers. Nor did it matter that the prayer was non-denominational, as the Court felt that the slightest encroachment in the public schools would be unconstitutional. The Court said that it did not wish to seem hostile toward religion or prayer, nor did it feel it was sacrilegious or anti-religious, but it said that the Constitution set up a wall between church and state for good reasons. It felt that prayer and religion was an activity for the individual or for the family, not an act to be directed or sponsored by a governmental agency.

A second case involved state statutes requiring Bible verses to be read without comment at the opening of school exercises every day. The Supreme Court held that such laws were unconstitutional as an abridgment of the establishment clause of the First Amendment. Even though pupils who did not desire to attend the prayer readings were excused from class, the Court felt that the coerced reading of prayers was a governmental activity in the field of religion. The Court said that the government should remain neutral in the field of religion and that coerced Bible reading in school was hardly a neutral act.

A few years later the Court struck down a statute requiring anti-evolution teachings in Arkansas public schools. The statute promoted a religious sectarian viewpoint on the evolution of man and was thus religious in nature and had no place in the public school system.

GOVERNMENT AID TO CHURCH-RELATED SCHOOLS

There are approximately six million students in church-related schools in the United States, and over five million of them are enrolled in Catholic schools, some 15 per cent of the nation's total school population. Church-related schools, just like public schools, are in need of financial aid, but their eligibility for public funds is a perplexing constitutional question.

The basis for federal grants to education is found in the Elementary and Secondary Education Act of 1965, which states that ". . . nothing contained in this Act shall be construed to authorize the making of any payment under this Act . . . for religious worship or instruction." However federal grants are made to church-related schools for non-church functions (libraries, text books and buses), and help is given to schools in poverty areas.

OTHER INSTITUTIONS

While prayer and Bible-reading in public schools have been banned, there are many other public displays of religion or religious beliefs which have withstood the Court test. Such activities as prayer-reading in Congress, the "In God We Trust" motto on our legal currency and publicly financed nativity scenes have all been okayed by the Court as traditional, innocuous activities which do not encroach or infringe upon the establishment clause of the First Amendment.

The Court has held that government financing of sectarian hospitals is proper since the financing enhances the hospital function and does not aid in the establishment of a religion or favoring one religion over another. Even though the hospital is run by a religious sect, it still serves sick people from all backgrounds.

The Court has also upheld blue laws which force businesses to close down on Sunday. Although these laws were originally enacted for religious purposes, the forced closings are legal because they benefit the public since they insure that all citizens have a day of rest.

CHAPTER 32

The Right of Privacy

The Fourth Amendment to the United States Constitution:

"The right of the people to be secure in their persons, houses, papers, and effects, against unreasonable searches and seizures, shall not be violated, and no warrants shall issue, but upon probable cause, supported by oath or affirmation, and particularly describing the place to be searched, and the persons or things to be seized."

INTRODUCTION

In order for the term "freedom" to have any meaning we must feel that our right of privacy is intact and safe from intrusion. The Constitution not only protects the sanctity of the individual, but it also protects the sanctity of his home and other areas where he conducts his affairs and expects privacy. Whenever the police attempt to violate the sanctity of privacy, they must do so: (1) pursuant to a valid search warrant; (2) as an incident to a valid arrest; (3) upon probable cause if a search warrant is unfeasible in the situation; or (4) upon consent of the individual.

THE FOURTH AMENDMENT, THE FOURTEENTH AMENDMENT, AND THE EXCLUSIONARY RULE

The Fourth Amendment, as originally construed, only applied to the federal government. The local police departments had no minimum standard which they had to follow. Citizens had no minimum standards of protection of privacy from local police. The U.S. Supreme Court - as it has done with most of the provisions of the Bill of Rights - has ruled that the Fourth Amendment applies to the states through the Fourteenth Amendment. Therefore, the minimum federal standards are now the minimum national standards.

In those cases where a police search has failed to meet constitutional requirements, any evidence produced by the search (including evidence discovered at a later time which is the fruit of the invalid search) is excluded from any trial or hearing against the person whose privacy was invaded. This exclusionary rule has applied to federal cases since 1914. The Supreme Court applied this rule to all of the states in 1961 in *Mapp vs. Ohio.*

In many cases in which a court invalidates a search because it went beyond the limits of the Constitution, the individual charged was guilty of a crime. The exclusion of evidence produced by the illegal search usually, but not necessarily, results in acquittal and release. Critics of these rulings which have limited the actions of the police argue that the courts are coddling criminals and are more concerned with the rights of lawbreakers than with the rights of the law-abiding community. What these critics fail to realize is that the Constitution is supreme and if the police act in a way which is repugnant to the Constitution, then this illegal action cannot be given validity by a court of law no matter what the consequences are.

The courts are not happy about freeing bookmakers, drug addicts, or other criminals; but there is no choice when an unconstitutional act by the police or other governmental authority is involved. The damage to the entire society by the validation of an unconstitutional act is far worse than the release of one criminal. The courts have established certain constitutional standards for the police to follow in conducting searches and seizures of property, and they are capable of following them.

Civil rights legislation now gives the victim of unconstitutionl police actions - whether he is guilty or innocent - a chance to file suits for monetary damages in a civil court. But, so far, this kind of lawsuit has been unsuccessful.

AREAS OF PRIVACY PROTECTED
BY THE FOURTH AMENDMENT

One normally associates the right of privacy with a home, but the Supreme Court has extended the area of privacy protection to offices, hotel rooms, telephone booths and automobiles.

It used to be that only physical intrusion into the privacy of an individual was a violation of the Fourth Amendment. The Court had to find some sort of physical trespass by the government in order to invalidate a search. But in 1967 the Court disregarded this old test and formulated a new one which protects that area which the individual seeks to preserve as private, even in an area accessible to the public. (This particular case involved a public telephone booth which was bugged by an electronic listening device placed on the outside. The Court recognized that the law had to keep up with modern technology.)

SEARCH WARRANTS

It is obvious from the wording of the Fourth Amendment that the Founding

Fathers felt that the proper way for the police to conduct a search was by obtaining a validly issued search warrant from a magistrate. The theory behind the warrant requirement is that, before a search can be conducted, a neutral magistrate must order it after examination of an affidavit detailing facts which must justify the search. In other words, the warrant will not issue unless the affidavit shows there is probable cause for an invasion of privacy and the affidavit must state with particularity what is inside of the enclosure which the police wish to search and must state the reasons for search. Furthermore, the warrant must state with particularity the area which can be searched.

If the affidavit is defective in any respect, the warrant and the search are also defective, and the evidence produced by the defective search is inadmissible in a court of law. If the scope of the search goes beyond the limits of the warrant, any evidence produced by the illegally enlarged search is also inadmissible. For instance, if a search warrant authorizes the search of a particular room in a house, the police cannot search the garage—any evidence they find in the garage will be inadmissible.

The key to a search warrant is the magistrate or independent party who must pass over the facts justifying the warrant. The application for a warrant is not a contested matter. The police or a district attorney approach the magistrate, who is usually, but not necessarily, a judge. Appellate courts have recognized the tendency of a magistrate to rubber stamp search warrants and, accordingly, they have required a great deal of specificity in the affidavit.

PROBABLE CAUSE

While a search conducted through the auspices of a warrant is preferred, the Supreme Court has recognized that a search may be constitutionally conducted without a warrant when probable cause exists for the police to believe that certain important evidence lies in a private place and there is no time to obtain the warrant. In order to substantiate such a search, the government must prove that probable cause.

For instance, a policeman cannot just break into a house full of long-haired men just because he feels that long-hairs use drugs. This is just guessing, conjecture or mere possibility. However, if the police had received information from a reliable informant that there were narcotics in the living room of the residence and that the dope users knew the police were coming and were about to destroy or remove the narcotics, the police would have probable cause to search the premises. That important evidence was about to be destroyed eliminates the need for a search warrant.

The term "probable cause" is unfortunately vague. The facts justifying each and every warrantless search by a policeman must be reviewed by a court to determine if the police did, in fact, have probable cause. Sometimes police use inane circumstances to justify large exploratory searches. The courts have come to recognize many of these circumstances were used as subterfuges. (For instance, stopping a driver for a minor traffic violation in order to thoroughly search his car is now considered unconstitutional. Also a detailed search of an auto which has been towed to a garage is no longer permissible.)

SEARCH AFTER AN ARREST

A warrantless search can also be made when it is incident to a valid arrest. The same standards of probable cause apply to a search made incident to an arrest as to a search made prior to it. In the past, after police made an arrest, they made a search of the arrestee's home, automobile, garbage cans, boat, and summer cottage at Lake Tahoe. But now the court has imposed a standard of reasonableness in the extent of this kind of search.

Only the immediate area in which the suspect is found can be searched, and police can no longer make a pervasive exploratory search of his dwelling and other areas indirectly within his control. Only the areas directly or immediately within his control can be searched.

In all of the above instances, police must give notice of their authority and the purpose of their visit to the person who will be subject to the search. But there are exceptions to this rule where there is a danger to the officers or there is a danger of destruction of the evidence when they announce their intention to search. There is also a general prohibition of searches in the night time—but there are also exceptions to this rule where the circumstances merit.

CONSENT

Police may also conduct searches without a warrant where a person with authority over the subject area consents to the search. A landlord cannot give police permission to search the room of a tenant. The police do not have to advise a person of his constitutional right to refuse the police entry to search, but the consent cannot be coerced.

SURVEILLANCE AND SEIZURE WITHOUT SEARCH

That secret agents or informers gain entry into a person's home under false pretenses is not a violation of the Constitution. The informer cannot search the premises once he is in the door, but he can observe what he sees around him and report it to the police. His observations may be used to obtain a search warrant or make an arrest.

THE RIGHT OF PRIVACY

There is no constitutional infringement when a policeman finds evidence of a crime by looking into an open window or at an open area. For instance, if a policeman sees a machine gun in the back seat of a car or sees marijuana lying on a table, he can make a valid arrest and seize that evidence. The contraband is in plain and open sight for all the world, including the police, to see. Evidence which is in plain and open sight is not considered the product of a search of a private area.

The Fourth Amendment only protects the citizen from unreasonable searches and seizures by government agents. If a private individual (for instance, an airlines baggage handler), not acting within the scope of any governmental authority, searches private property and turns over evidence to the police, this evidence is admissible in court despite the unreasonableness of the search which produced it.

ELECTRONIC SURVEILLANCE AND
WIRE TAPPING

The Founding Fathers, in drafting the Fourth Amendment, obviously made no provision for electronic surveillance or wire tapping. Police surveillance has always been a part of the law, but it used to only involve the observer being in the physical presence of the suspect. The use of electronic bugging and wire tapping devices monitored by police agents long distances from the suspects is clearly an invasion of privacy, but the Supreme Court has been very slow to apply the Fourth Amendment to the new technology.

The courts originally felt that only electronic surveillance which involved the physical intrusion into a protected area was unconstitutional. If a spike was driven through a wall and a microphone was attached to it, then there was a physical intrusion. However, the Court felt a wire tap on telephone wires far away from a protected area was legal. While the Supreme Court has discarded the strict limitations of physical intrusions, these problems of governmental electronic surveillance are still undecided.

There is no constitutional limitation on a policeman tape recording his own conversations with another person even though the suspect never consented or knew about the taping. Nor is there such a limitation on a person tape recording his own telephone conversations even though the other party does not know of the taping (the latter activity is only against the tariff regulations of the telephone company, and both activities may be against state laws).

The original Federal Communications Act of 1934 forbids divulgence of intercepted communications (interception means listening to two other persons' telephone conversation without their knowledge or consent). The key word here is divulgence because divulgence does not prevent wire tapping altogether; it just prevents relating what is heard later in court. This statute only covered telephone and telegraph communications; it did not include bugging devices.

The Crime Control and Safe Streets Act of 1968 prohibits interception of oral communications of any kind by mechanical or electronic device - such evidence is inadmissible in federal and state courts. However, the Act does make exceptions for law enforcement officers in certain felony cases most of which involve narcotics and organized crime. For a federal law enforcement agency to obtain permission for electronic surveillance, the U.S. Attorney General must obtain a warrant from a judge, and the warrant must make a strong showing that the eavesdropping is necessary. The warrant must state with particularity the persons and places which can be bugged, and it is only good for 30 days, but there is provision for time extensions. State attorneys general may also go to state courts to get eavesdropping warrants if the state authorizes this procedure.

Anyone who has been the subject of this kind of surveillance must be served with an inventory of the dates it occurred. If he is called as a witness before a grand jury, he must be advised before the questioning that he has been the subject of electronic surveillance.

The Crime Control and Safe Streets Act of 1968 does not require court-approved warrants for electronic eavesdropping in cases involving the national security. There is no question that the executive branch of the government has the constitutional power to use bugging and wire tapping devices in cases involving foreign powers only. (The bugging of foreign embassies has always been accepted as part of the game.) The Nixon Administration took the position that certain domestic groups were a threat to national security and that it could bug members of these groups without prior court approval. However, the Supreme Court ruled this kind of surveillance without a warrant was illegal.

CHAPTER 33

Equal Rights,
Equal Protection
and Equal Opportunity

The Constitution demands that the states treat each citizen equally, and the due process of law clause in the Fifth Amendment has been interpreted to mean that the federal government must treat all of its citizens equally. Equality may sound like an absolute term, but it had been interpreted rather loosely.

In 1953, the Supreme Court started taking a very strict view on the meaning of "equal protection." Court decisions, which were later augmented by federal and state legislation and constitutional amendments, wiped out thousands of laws which overtly legalized and invited discrimination on the basis of race, national origin and sex. This chapter will deal with how the law provides equality in the areas of voting, education, employment and housing.

THE RIGHT TO VOTE

The right to vote is the most basic and paramount right in a democracy, and the Constitution deals with it extensively. The Fourteenth Amendment demands that the states give their citizens equal protection of the laws including the voting laws. The Fifteenth Amendment prohibits any state from denying a person the right to vote on account of race, color, or his previous condition of servitude. The Nineteenth Amendment forbids any state from denying voting rights to any person on account of sex. The Twenty-Fourth Amendment forbids a state from imposing poll taxes on votes in federal elections. Sections 4 and 8 of Article I give Congress the power to regulate times, places and manners of holding elections for senators and representatives and to make laws to enforce this. The Twenty-sixth Amendment lets 18-year-olds vote. Congress has also enacted many voting laws, including the Civil Rights Acts of 1957 and 1960 and the Voting Rights Act of 1965.

THE HISTORY OF THE VOTE IN THE UNITED STATES

The right to vote has had a rather sordid history in this country which prides itself on democratic principles. During our first half century, only male property owners could vote. Property ownership as a voting qualification was finally abandoned by all states in 1856—but then they instituted a tax paying requirement, which is still a qualification in some local bond elections. Vast economic and social changes brought suffrage to most whites, but state control of election laws and a timid, unresponsive Congress and Supreme Court denied blacks and other minorities the vote for many more years.

The disenfranchisement of the black voter is an especially ugly stain on American history. After the Civil War and the Fifteenth Amendment, Congress passed the Enforcement Act of 1870 which brought federal supervision to elections to insure the voting rights of all citizens, but this Act was curtailed in 1884. In 1885, the Southern states started establishing poll taxes, strict residence requirements and literacy tests—all directed against blacks. The literacy test, while valid and rational on its face, was administered unfairly and whites took different tests than black voters. Citizens had to interpret lengthy sections of the state constitution, a task few lawyers could accomplish, and registrars had unlimited discretion to pass or fail voters. Other discriminatory ploys included (1) a system in which a new registrant needed a voucher from a registered voter as to his good character; (2) rejection because of insignificant errors on registration forms; (3) delaying tactics; and (4) refusal to give assistance to young applicants.

Blacks were excluded from membership and voting in the Democratic Party in many Southern states until 1928 when the Supreme Court forbade this practice. At that time the Democratic Primary was the only meaningful political contest in these states, and the Court ruled that political parties were valid functions of the state, not private clubs.

Federal civil rights laws passed from 1957 to 1965 prohibited many pratices which effectively disenfranchised the minorities. These acts authorized the Attorney General to eliminate voting discrimination.

VALID STATE RESTRICTIONS
ON THE RIGHT TO VOTE

The states can make valid restrictions on the right to vote because of age, residence and citizenship—but only if they can show a compelling interest.

Each state used to establish its own residence requirements for voters, and they varied widely until the Supreme Court struck down residence requirements which it felt were unreasonably long. The test case involved a Tennessee law which demanded one year of residence, and the Court decided that it should be no more than 30 days. Although the justices did not declare that this period should be uniform among the states. Their reasoning seems to invalidate any requirement in excess of 30 days.

Most states require their prospective voters to register before they can vote because registration prevents fraudulent voting and stuffing of the ballot box.

The states may also bar the mentally incompetent, non-citizens, the insane, prisoners and convicted felons from the right to vote.

THE VALUE OF ONE VOTE

State legislatures have always had the right to reapportion themselves as well as the congressional districts within their state. However, they were reluctant to do so since such changes might cost many lawmakers their comfortable seats. Prior to 1962 there was no constitutional duty on the part of the state legislatures to reapportion since the courts felt that it was a legislative rather than a judicial matter.

Most states established their voting districts during an agrarian era, and as America changed to an urban industrial society, legislatures failed to reapportion voting districts in proportion to the shifts in population. It was not uncommon for a legislator representing 3,000 rural voters to have a vote equal to a legislator speaking for 300,00 votes. Rural districts generally controlled the legislatures.

In 1962 the Supreme Court said in *Baker vs. Carr* that the Fourteenth Amendment demands that membership in Congress must be based on equal representation of the people with each citizen's vote having equal weight. The principal was extended to the state legislatures, even the bicameral ones patterned after the federal principle of one house representing the population and the other representing geographical units. The Court demanded that both houses be based on population only—not economics, geography or traditional political subdivisions.

The courts were then authorized to oversee apportionment on a *one man one vote* basis if the state legislatures could not reapportion themselves. Rather than let this happen, the legislatures started responding.

"One man-one vote" by the way, does not demand that the state legislative districts be divided exactly on the basis of population—geographic problems are still considered but the districts must have substantially equal populations. (They cannot vary more than 16 per cent.)

Baker vs. Carr and other subsequent decisions did not alter the Electoral College, which declares the winner of a presidential election. It is still possible for a presidential candidate to receive a majority of the popular vote but still lose the election because his opponent gets the majority of the electoral votes. This is obviously against the "one man-one vote" concept, but the Electoral College is written into the Constitution, and it can only be changed by an amendment.

EQUAL OPPORTUNITY IN EDUCATION

Education used to be a privilege for the very rich. The growth of democracy and the right to vote demanded that all of the people be properly educated. Establishment of the free public school for all children became a nationwide institution. It is now recognized that public education is the primary function of the individual states.

Education has gone from the point of mere privilege to where it is a necessity of economic life in a modern industrial society. The minds of our youth are this nation's greatest natural resource. It is the function of the courts under the Fourteenth Amendment to the Constitution to see that educational opportunity is applied equally to all citizens.

One of the burning domestic issues of the 1950's was integration of public school systems and the dismantling of de jure segregation. Opposition was so intransigent that President Eisenhower had to call the U.S. Army to enforce an integration order at Central High School in Little Rock, Arkansas. After many hard years, the public has generally accepted integration of public school systems and other public facilities and the right of all children to a good education. The big issue of the 1960's and 70's has been the method of achieving integration, as parents have rebelled, sometimes violently, against busing children from neighborhood schools in order to achieve racial balance.

DE JURE SEGREGATION

De jure segregation means segregation which is imposed or sanctified by law. After Reconstruction, all of the Southern states and some border states established segregated public facilities for whites and blacks, notwithstanding the Fourteenth Amendment. The legal imposition of separate public facilities was upheld by the Supreme Court in 1896 in *Plessy vs. Ferguson.* The high court held that as long as a state provided equal facilities to all the members of its population—even if these facilities were separate or segregated between the races by state statute—that they were not repugnant to the Fourteenth Amendment.

This "separate but equal" doctrine dignified segregated public school systems from 1896 until 1954, although the Court did chip away at it with decisions that insisted on substantial equality for blacks.

In 1954, 20 states and the District of Columbia had segregated school systems. The Truman Administration had encouraged litigation to challenge the separate but equal doctrine, and finally, in 1954, the Supreme Court decided in a case called *Brown vs. The Board of Education of Topeka, Kansas* that separate public education was inherently unequal and unconstitutional. As long as public schools were segregated, blacks or any other minority groups who were forced to attend separate schools would receive substandard, unequal treatment. A good example of this type of unequal treatment is found in the per pupil expenditure for black and white school children for the years 1949 to 1950 in some of the states which had segregated schools:

STATE	EXPENDITURES FOR WHITES	EXPENDITURES FOR BLACKS
	(On a per-pupil basis)	
Alabama	$130.09	$ 92.69
Arkansas	123.60	73.03
Florida	196.42	136.71
Georgia	145.15	79.73
Maryland	217.41	198.76
Mississippi	122.93	32.55
North Carolina	148.21	122.90
South Carolina	154.62	79.82
District of Columbia	289.68	220.70

The Brown decision was a unanimous decision and Chief Justice Earl Warren wrote:

"Today, education is perhaps the most important function of state and local governments. Compulsory school attendance laws and expenditures for education both demonstrate our recognition of the importance of education to our democratic society. It is required in the performance of our most basic public responsibilities, even service in the armed forces. It is the very foundation of good citizenship. Today it is a principal instrument in awakening the child to cultural values, preparing him for later professional training, and in helping him to adjust to his environment. In these days, it is doubtful that anyone can reasonably be expected to succeed in life if he is denied the opportunity of an education. Such an opportunity, where the state has undertaken to provide it, is a right that must be made available to all on equal terms.

"We come then to the question presented: does segregation of children in public schools, solely on the basis of race, even though the physical facilities and other tangible factors may be equal, deprive the children of a minority group of equal education opportunities? We believe that it does."

The Brown decision provided the basis for the invalidation of all laws which provided for segregation of public facilities including buses, parks, swimming pools, restrooms, police and fire protection and public housing.

In 1955 the Supreme Court ruled that all public school desegregation should be accomplished with "all deliberate speed." Immediate steps were taken in the District of Columbia and some border states, but the South proved recalcitrant. Massive resistance took the form of outright refusal to obey court orders as well as legal subterfuges and circumventions including making public schools private and gerrymandering local school districts. The NAACP, which has been the primary moving force in many school desegregation suits, was officially harrassed by many state officials. Those brave individuals who dared to cross the color line for the first time were assaulted and intimidated by public officials as well as private individuals. The governors of Arkansas, Alabama and Mississippi publicly defied the courts and the President and brought on the most dangerous threat to the national unity since the Civil War.

Courts only interpret the laws. The executive branch must enforce court orders and eliminate de jure segregation. Recent civil rights acts have made it easier for the federal government to gather evidence in school desegregation cases, and the advent of federal aid to education—and the refusal to give such aid to segregated school districts—has precipitated some changes.

Many of these districts which had employed de jure segregation pleaded for more time to integrate, and the courts were lenient because, in the early years, their pleas seemed reasonable. But when it became apparent that many of these boards were only stalling, the courts began to implement reasonable integration plans immediately. The courts now refuse to grant a stay of execution of integration orders even if the board appeals to a higher court.

DE FACTO SEGREGATION

School systems segregated by law are disappearing, but residential housing patterns have created ghettos which have in turn created segregated schools as a matter of fact, not a matter of law. This has been especially true in the major cities of the North and West. New York, Los Angeles, Chicago and Philadelphia have schools with 95 per cent black or Latin enrollments.

The courts must face this dilemma of "de facto segregation". The Brown decision only prohibits segregation by law. Racial separation which does not result from any deliberate or conscious action by school authorities is not inconsistent with the Constitution's Fourteenth Amendment, and there is no constitutional compulsion to eliminate de facto segregation.

Yet, the Brown decision states that public school segregation in any form has a detrimental effect on minority children, as the sense of inferiority affects the motivation to learn. So, even if segregation results from neighborhood residential patterns, many courts have held that the state still has a constitutional obligation to eliminate it. A few state supreme courts (namely New York, New Jersey, and California) have taken the position that elimination of de facto segregation in public schools must be achieved in a manner consistent with sound educational practice. Federal courts have upheld this view and decided that if school authorities try to eliminate de facto segregation, their action will be upheld - if it is not arbitrary and capricious.

But parents often strongly object to the busing of their children from neighborhood schools to more remote classrooms to achieve integration. (It's ironic to note that the heaviest use of buses occurred in areas where they were utilized extensively to help white children avoid going to integrated schools.) The foes of busing have many legitimate arguments, and there is no easy compromise on the issue in sight—political demagoguery on the subject has done little but fan already inflamed passions.

Many court orders for busing have been based on the 1970 Supreme Court decision called *Swann vs. Charlotte*. Chief Justice Burger stated that mass transportation of children to obtain integration was a legitimate means of rectifying an illegimate public school system. This decision demanded immediate steps by school boards since they had been on notice to integrate since 1954. The *Swann* case involved a *de jure* segregation.

Denver was one of the first Northern cities forced into massive busing by a federal court order. Segregation there resulted from an unofficial policy of the board. The Federal District Court in Denver ordered the entire school system integrated by massive cross-city busing, not just the all black or Latin schools. The Supreme Court upheld the order, and found that segregation which resulted from policy was tantamount to de jure segregation. The Court did not state that de facto segregation resulting from neighborhood racial patters is automatically unconstitutional.

Since the problems of segregation transcend individual school districts, integrationists want busing to go beyond city or school board limits. Federal courts made such orders in Richmond, Virginia and Detroit, Michigan, but the U.S. Supreme Court recently reversed these court imposed plans because segregated school systems were not shown in *both* of the districts included in the courts' busing for integration plan.

QUOTAS

To correct and make amends for past racial injustices of our society many colleges and universities have quota systems as part of their admission standards. That is, Black, Latin, Oriental, female and Native American students are admitted to these schools on the basis of their race or sex, not just their academic achievement. This is constitutionally questionable in overcrowded school systems where white male students with the demonstrated academic capability and desire to learn are denied admission to make room for the quota students.

The decision in *Brown vs Board of Education* takes a very strict view of the Fourteenth Amendment. Equal means equal, and that decision leaves no room for discrimination against any race. Nevertheless, a large number of state schools have instituted quota systems called "minority recruitment programs" or "minority advancement programs." The Supreme Court had a chance to rule on the constitutionality of racial quotas, but it conveniently ducked the issue.

Marco deFunis was an honor student at the University of Washington. He applied for admission to that university's law school in 1970 but was denied because of the school's minority recruitment program. (DeFunis had better grades than 35 of the quota students.) DeFunis filed suit alleging that the quota system was reverse discrimination and an unconstitutional violation of his Fourteenth Amendment rights. The trial court in Seattle agreed and ordered the University to admit him to its law school. The University appealed and won in the State Supreme Court of Washington, but deFunis was allowed to stay in school pending his appeal to the United States Supreme Court. This case got there two years later, but the Court refused to make a decision in deFunis' case because he had graduated from law school by that time, and the Court said that the issue was moot. The Court will only make decisions in actual cases or controversies, and a bare five-man majority felt that a decision on the actual merits of the quota system would not directly affect Mr. deFunis. This means that any future case on quota systems will have to be litigated by a person who is actually denied acceptance into a school for the long period of time which it takes to get a case before the U.S. Supreme Court.

EQUAL OPPORTUNITY IN EMPLOYMENT

The Fourteenth Amendment prohibits the states from discriminating on the basis of race, sex, religion or national origin in the performance of functions for the state including public employment. There is no constitutional prohibition against discrimination by private persons or business, but there are federal and state laws prohibiting it. Recent lawsuits brought under these various civil rights statutes have forced many large corporate employers (AT&T, US Steel and Standard Oil of California among others) to make large lump-sum cash payments to its minority employees for past discrimination and caused these firms to start affirmative action programs to prevent future abuses.

STATE STATUTES

Thirty-nine states now have statutes outlawing discrimination in hiring, firing and compensation. These laws not only affect employers but also employment agencies and unions. They are generally administered by a "Fair Employment Practices Commission".

In most of these states a person who feels he has been unlawfully discriminated against may file a complaint with the local fair employment commission, and it will conduct an investigation and then issue a certificate which states there is probable cause to believe the complaint or dismiss it entirely. If there is probable cause, the commission will attempt to conciliate and persuade the parties to reach an amicable agreement. If conciliation and persuasion fail, a hearing officer will hear the case publicly. If he finds that there has been unlawful discrimination, he will issue a cease and desist order. If the discriminating employer refuses to obey this order, the commissioin may institute contempt proceedings, which can end with a possible jail sentence and/or a fine.

FEDERAL FAIR EMPLOYMENT LEGISLATION

The federal government entered the fair employment field in 1964 with the establishment of the Equal Employment Opportunity Commission (EOC), which investigates complaints of discrimination involving businesses in interstate commerce with over 25 employes. The procedures to implement this Act are similar to those of the state fair employment practices commissions. The federal laws also prohibit unlawful discrimination among private employers who work on federal projects or finance their businesses through federal loans or grants. Discrimination has also been defined as an unfair labor practice in federal laws controlling union activities.

WOMEN

Most fair employment cases have involved discrimination because of race, religion or national origin. The Fourteenth Amendment also prohibits unlawful, irrational discrimination on the basis of sex, and most fair employment practice legislation protects women from unlawful hiring, firing and compensation practices. However, discrimination against women is so deeply rooted in our customs that it will take years to eradicate it.

Women were long discriminated against as a matter of official policy. As late as 1966, three states prohibited women from serving as jurors. (The Supreme Court ruled this practice unconstitutional.) The Court has ruled that any state action which irrationally discriminates between the sexes is unconstitutional, but the question of what is irrational depends on the circumstances of each individual case. The last major decision in this field occurred in 1972 when the Court ruled out an Idaho law prohibiting women from serving as executors of estates. Many states still restrict married women in matters of contracts, management of property and establishment of legal residence. The constitutionality of these statutes is in doubt.

There is a proposed constitutional amendment which has been passed by both houses of the Congress which would prohibit any type of public or private discrimination against women. This amendment, if passed by the required number of state legislatures, will wipe out any laws which discriminate against women—it will also remove laws which have been enacted for their protection (such as limits on the weight which they can lift at work or limits on work hours.)

By 1970 only 25 states had fair employment laws which fully covered discrimination on the basis of sex, although 40 states prohibit discrimination between males and females in the area of rate of compensation for equal work. Congress entered the field with the Civil Rights Act of 1964, which prohibits discrimination on the basis of sex by employers, labor organizations and employment agencies exept where gender is a bona fide occupational qualification reasonably necessary to the operation of a business. The burden is on the employer to show rational grounds. (Women with children of pre-school age can be discriminated against because the women's position as a mother may prevent her from devoting full time to her job.)

Employers can dismiss pregnant employees only by proving the pregnancy affected their work. This allows each woman to be judged on her own individual merit, and not be placed in the broad classification of "a pregnant woman". However, women who leave work because of a normal pregnancy are not entitled to state disability benefits because this condition is not considered a disability unless there is a complication.

The proposed Twenty-Seventh Amendment states "Equality of rights under the law shall not be abridged by the United States or by any state on account of sex." Legal scholars differ on the precise effect of this amendment if it becomes law. Generally, however, it would no longer restrict married women in matters of contracts, management of property and establishment of legal residences.

AGE

There is an Age Discrimination in Employment Act, (enacted in 1967) which prohibits employers from firing or discriminating against employees between the ages of 40 and 64 on the basis of their age. If you feel that you have been unlawfully discriminated against on the basis of age, contact either the EOC or the Department of Labor, or you can sue the employer through a private attorney.

QUOTAS

The same quotas which were mentioned in Section II of this chapter on education are used in employment situations. The Supreme Court has successfully avoided making a decision in the area of employment as it has done in the field of education.

HOUSING

The Constitution does not guarantee us the right to be housed and there is no provision against discrimination in housing on the basis of race, religion, national origin, or sex on the part of private individuals. The Fourteenth Amendment only protects us from discrimination from "state action", but that term has been broadly interpreted for the protection of the individual. There are also many federal laws and state fair housing laws which protect us from housing discrimination.

Prior to 1948, many restrictive covenants were attached to real property deeds which purchasers had to sign before they could buy homes. These agreements provided that an owner could not resell his property to a non-Caucasian. In 1948 the Supreme Court ruled that such covenants could not be enforced in state courts, as this was state action in furtherance of unlawful racial discrimination. The decision was used to invalidate racial discrimination on public property including public housing projects and, later, the Civil Rights Act of 1964 forbade segregation in public accommodations. The federal government also prohibits private discrimination in housing through directives to federal agencies which have a direct effect on private housing.

For instance, the Federal Housing Administration (FHA) cannot guarantee loans on projects which discriminate against persons on the basis of race or sex, and the Department of Housing and Urban Development (HUD) will not authorize housing or redevelopment projects which would allow unlawful discrimination.

HUD and the federal courts also protected the rights of persons who have been displaced by new public housing or redevelopment projects - they must be provided with suitable replacement housing, and sometimes they get cash settlements to pay for the new housing. Citizens may also contest the redevelopment projects in their neighborhoods.

Many states and local communities have adopted fair housing legislation, which makes it illegal for a private individual to discriminate on the basis of race in sales or rentals. Most states have commissions which act on complaints. They generally stress conciliation or persuasion, but their cease and desist orders are enforced by the courts.

GLOSSARY OF LEGAL TERMS

ABANDONMENT: Giving up of a legal right without the intention of reclaiming it at a later date, as in the abandonment of property or children.

ABATE: To decrease or destroy, as in the abatement of an environmental nuisance.

ABDUCTION: The taking away of a child without consent or the taking away of a female, usually under age, for prostitution or marriage, or both.

AB INITIO: This is one of the few Latin terms still left in the law, and it means "from the beginning." For instance, a marriage which is void ad initio is a marriage which is void from its beginning.

ABORTION: The destruction of a human fetus.

ABUSE OF DISCRETION: An unjustified act by a judge where he has discretion to act.

ABUSE OF PROCESS: A tort which is committed by the malicious use of legal proceedings which are used to annoy, vex or harass another.

ACCEPTANCE: The legal meaning of this term is that one receives something with the intention of retaining it so that the acceptance is a binding act. For instance, the acceptance of an offer makes a binding contract.

ACCESSORY: A person who is involved in the commission of a felony, although he may not be personally present at the time the felony is committed. An *accessory before the fact* is a person who advises or encourages someone else to commit the felony. An *accessory after the fact* is someone who conceals this knowledge or protects or assists the person who has committed the felony.

ACCOMPLICE: A person who actually participates in the commission of a crime.

ACCORD AND SATISFACTION: A settlement agreement after a dispute. One party usually must accept less than what he had originally bargained for as a means of compromise.

ACCOUNT STATED: An account rendered by a creditor to a debtor.

ACCUSED: A person charged with a crime, felony or misdemeanor.

ACQUITTAL: The release of criminal charges after a trial.

ACTION: A judicial proceeding.

ACTIONABLE: A term used to describe circumstances which are grounds for maintaining a lawsuit.

AD HOC: This is a Latin term which means "for this." For instance, ad hoc committees are committees which are formed expressly for one particular purpose.

ADJUDGE: A judicial decision or settlement.

ADJUSTER: A person employed by an insurance company to investigate and settle personal injury and property damage claims.

ADMINISTRATION OF ESTATES: The management and settlement of an estate of a deceased or incompetent person.

ADMINISTRATOR: A person appointed by a probate court to administer an estate.

ADMIRALTY LAW: Law of the seas and maritime affairs.

ADOPTION: The legal substitution of parents; the taking of another's child into one's own family and giving the child all the rights and obligations of a natural child.

ADULT: One who has reached the age of majority and full legal responsibility.

ADULTERY: Sexual intercourse between a married person and unmarried person.

ADVERSARY PROCEEDING: A judicial proceeding between disputing parties.

ADVERSE POSSESSION: The continuing defiant possession of real property by a trespasser who is attempting to establish ownership rights on a piece of real property.

AFFIANT: A person who swears to the facts stated in an affidavit.

AFFIDAVIT: A statement of facts which is sworn to, under oath, by the person declaring the facts.

A FORTIORI: The Latin term which means "by a stronger reason."

AGENCY: The relationship of one person acting for another.

AGGRAVATED ASSAULT: A particularly brutal assault.

ALIBI: This is a Latin word which literally means "elsewhere." In criminal law alibi is a defense which a defendant can use to show that he was some place other than the scene of the crime.

ALIEN: A foreign-born person who is not a citizen of the United States.

ALIENATION OF AFFECTION: Intentionally causing a wife to withdraw her affection from her husband, and vice versa. This is a tort for which a victim can collect damages, but this tort has been abolished in most states.

ALIMONY: The money allowance one spouse must pay another by order of a court after or during a divorce action.

AMBULANCE CHASER: A lawyer who unlawfully and unethically solicits accident injury cases.

AMENDMENT: Alteration of a law or resolution.

AMICUS CURIAE: A Latin term which means "friend of the court." Many times attorneys, who do not actually represent litigants, will submit legal argument in briefs as friends of the court.

AMNESTY: A general pardon granted by the government to all persons guilty of a criminal offense.

AMORTIZATION: The payment of a debt by installments.

ANCILLARY: Auxillary or subsidiary.

ANNEXATION: The addition of new territory.

ANNUITY: A specific yearly sum paid on a periodic basis.

ANNULMENT: The voiding of an act (marriage).

ANSWER: The pleading of a defendant in response to a plaintiff's complaint.

ANTENUPTIAL AGREEMENT: A contract between a man and a woman before their marriage to declare each other's rights and interests in property.

ANTITRUST LAWS: The laws to protect businesses and consumers from monopolies and illegal restraints of trade.

APPEAL: The review of a court case by a court of higher jurisdiction.

APPELLANT: A person appealing a court judgment.

APPELLATE COURT: A court which hears appeals from a court of lower jurisdiction.

APPORTIONMENT: The separation of respective interests in the subject matter of litigation.

APPRAISAL: The estimated value of property.

APPREHENSION: Arrest.

ARBITRATION: The settling of a disputed matter between opposing parties by a private person chosen by the disputing parties.

ARRAIGNMENT: The formal advisement to a criminal defendant of the specific charges against him.

ARREARS: An overdue debt.

ARREST: To seize and hold a person by legal authority.

ARSON: The intentional burning of a home or other building.

ASSAULT: An intentional threat or attempt to do violent harm to another person.

ASSESSMENT: The setting of a value on property.

ASSETS: The property which one possesses.

ASSIGNMENT: The transferring of property; the person assigning the property is called the *assignor,* and the person receiving the property is called the *assignee.*

ATTACHMENT: The taking of persons or property into custody by a peace officer.

ATTEMPT: The intent to commit a crime coupled with some movement to actually commit the crime. An attempt may constitute a crime, even though a crime was never committed or completed.

ATTESTATION: The act of witnessing the signing of a document and further declaring in the document that the signing was witnessed.

ATTORNEY AT LAW: A person who is formally licensed to give legal advice and try cases in court. In the United States the term attorney at law is synonymous with lawyer, counselor at law, and barrister.

ATTORNEY IN FACT: The person who is given authority to act in another's place. The authority is given by a written power of attorney.

ATTRACTIVE NUISANCE: A condition or instrumentality which is dangerous to young children and attracts them to it.

AUDIT: An official examination of an account.

AWARD: A judgment, sentence, or final decision.

BAIL: Financial security which is given to obtain the release of a person from police custody to assure he will appear at any and all later court appearances.

BAIL BOND: A form of financial security given by an insurance surety company.

BAILIFF: A court attaché whose duty it is to keep order in the court and guard the jury.

BAILMENT: The delivery of goods by one person to another, but ultimately to be redelivered to the owner. The person who gives the property is called the *bailor,* and the person who receives the property is the *bailee.*

BANKRUPTCY: A judicial determination that one is insolvent and his property is subject to distribution among his creditors according to the bankruptcy laws.

BAR: (1) A place in the court where a person stands to plead his case; (2) the members of the legal profession.

BASTARD: A child born out of wedlock.

BATTERY: The unlawful touching of another person.

BEARER: A person in possession of a bill, note, check, draft or other negotiable instrument which is payable to the bearer.

BENCH: The court.

BENCH WARRANT: A warrant issued by a judge for the arrest of a person who has failed to appear before the judge after being ordered to do so.

BENEFICIARY: A person who receives benefits, profits or proceeds of an estate or insurance policy.

BEQUEST: A gift of personal property in a will; technically the word devise means a gift of real property in a will, but bequest is often used synonymously with devise.

BIGAMY: The criminal offense of entering into a marriage before one's previous marriage is legally dissolved.

BILL OF RIGHTS: The first ten Amendments to the United States Constitution.

BINDER: A contract of insurance providing temporary protection until a formal written policy is issued.

BLACKMAIL: The extortion of money or other valuable property through intimidation.

BLUE LAW: Laws which regulate personal conduct on Sundays.

BLUE RIBBON JURY: A jury composed of citizens who have a higher station in life and education than the average citizen.

BLUE SKY LAW: Laws enacted to regulate the sale of stocks and other securities to protect investors from fraud.

BONA FIDE: A Latin phrase which means "in good faith."

BOOKMAKING: The registering of wagers.

BREACH OF CONTRACT: The failure to perform a condition of a contract.

BREACH OF THE PEACE: A crime which is committed when disorderly behavior disturbs members of the public.

BREACH OF WARRANTY: The failure of a manufacturer, distributor or seller of goods to meet his promise relating to the quality of goods.

BRIBERY: The crime of giving something of value to a public official to influence his decision on a public matter.

BRIEF: A written document prepared by an attorney to argue his case.

BROKER: A middleman who earns a commission for negotiating contracts.

BURDEN OF PROOF: The obligation of a litigant to prove his case.

BURGLARY: At common law, it was the breaking and entering of a dwelling at night with the intent to commit a felony. Burglary has been extended by statute to now include the breaking and entering at any time of any building or automobile with the intent to commit a crime.

BYLAWS: A set of rules for the running of an association or corporation.

CAPITAL GAIN: Profit from the sale of property.

CAUSE OF ACTION: The ground on which a lawsuit can be sustained.

CAVEAT EMPTOR: A Latin phrase which means "let the buyer beware." This doctrine is supposed to warn the purchaser against any latent defects of a product.

CHAIN OF TITLE: Succession of transfers pertaining to a particular piece of real property.

CHANGE OF VENUE: The change of a place of a trial.

CHARITABLE TRUST: A trust set up for public or charitable benefit.

CHATTEL: A piece of personal property.

GLOSSARY OF LEGAL TERMS

CHATTEL MORTGAGE: The mortgage of a piece of personal property to secure payment of a debt.

CHECK: A written order to a bank to pay money upon demand to the bearer of the check.

CIRCUMSTANTIAL EVIDENCE: Facts which furnish reasonable belief for inferring the existence of other related facts.

CITATION: A court approved summons ordering a person to appear at a judicial tribunal at a particular time on a particular day.

CLAIM: The demand of a right.

CLAIMANT: The person who makes a claim.

CLASS ACTION: A lawsuit brought by one or more persons on behalf of an entire class of persons who are similarly situated or wronged.

CLOSED CORPORATION: A business in which the stock is owned by a few persons.

CLOUD ON TITLE: A claim against a person's real property interests.

CODICIL: A supplement to a will.

CO-EXECUTOR: A person named with one or more persons or corporations in a will to perform the duties of execution of the terms of the will.

COHABITATION: The act of living together as husband and wife.

COLLATERAL: Accompany; additional; not directly connected with.

COLLECTIVE BARGAINING: Negotiations between employers or groups of employers and the representatives of a group of employees.

COLLUSION: A secret combination or concerted action between two or more persons for deceitful or unlawful purposes.

COMITY: Courteous action, as in judicial comity which refers to the courts of one state giving full faith and credit to the laws and judicial decisions of another state.

COMMON LAW: The principles of law which have been derived through the years from the law of England and embodied in court decisions, to be distinguished from statutory or codified law.

COMMON LAW MARRIAGE: Living together as husband and wife without the benefit of marriage ceremony.

COMMUNITY PROPERTY: Generally the property acquired by either a husband or wife during their marriage. Community property is only recognized in eight states.

COMMUTATION: Reduction of a judicial sentence.

COMPARATIVE NEGLIGENCE: A legal doctrine which takes into account the negligence of the plaintiff as well as the defendant to determine damages.

COMPETENCE: Legally qualified to act in a specified capacity, as in competence to execute a will or contract.

COMPLAINT: A document which states a plaintiff's grievance against a defendant.

COMPOUND OF FELONY: To drop criminal charges or refuse to prosecute in return for money or other consideration.

COMPROMISE: An out of court settlement of a dispute.

COMPULSORY ARBITRATION: Arbitration of a dispute which is binding on all disputing parties.

CONCEALMENT: Hiding, suppressing or withholding an important fact.

CONCURRENT JURISDICTION: A situation where two or more judicial bodies have the authority to act.

CONDEMNATION: A proceeding where private property is taken for public use without the consent of the property owner but with payment of just compensation. Just compensation is determined by the courts if no settlement figure can be arrived at by the parties.

CONDITIONAL SALE: A sale which can be completed upon the happening of a contingency or condition.

CONDOMINIUM: An apartment house in which each apartment is owned by an individual.

CONDONATION: The forgiveness of a spouse of acts which could constitute grounds for divorce.

CONFIDENTIAL COMMUNICATION: A communication which cannot be divulged because of some overriding public policy which protects the communication.

CONFLICT OF LAWS: A disagreement between the laws of different jurisdictions.

CONFRONTATION: The face-to-face meeting between the criminally accused and the person who is accusing him of commission of a crime. Confrontation takes place in the courtroom, and it is exercised through cross-examination of accusing witnesses by the attorney for the defendant.

CONSANGUINITY: The relation of persons descended from a common ancestor or blood relationship.

CONSCIENTIOUS OBJECTION: Opposition to war on the basis or religious or moral principles.

CONSIDERATION: The inducement given for entering into a contract.

CONSIGNMENT: Placing of goods in the care of another to be sold or returned to the owner if a sale cannot be accomplished.

CONSORTIUM: The right of a husband or wife to the affection and company of the other spouse; what every spouse should theoretically expect from a marriage relationship.

CONSPIRACY: An agreement between two or more persons to commit illegal acts.

CONSTITUTION: The basic law of a sovereign nation or state.

CONSTRUCTIVE: A legal status which does not fit within the strict definition or rule, but which is assumed or inferred by a legal interpretation. For instance, a constructive trust is created when a court orders a freeze on funds which were unlawfully obtained.

CONTEMPT OF COURT: A willful disregard of the order, authority or dignity of a court.

CONTINGENT FEE: A fee which is payable to an attorney only if he achieves a certain result, as in the settlement of a personal injury lawsuit.

CONTINUANCE: A postponement of judicial proceedings to another time and day.

CONTRABAND: Goods which are illegal to possess, as heroin, stolen property, or machine guns.

CONTRACT: A legally enforceable promise between two or more persons.

CONTRIBUTION: The reimbursement of a person who has paid a debt or judgment of others who are also responsible for its payment.

CONVERSION: The wrongful appropriation or use of another's personal property.

CONVEY: To transfer or pass property.

COOPERATIVE ASSOCIATION: A jointly owned operation which operates for the mutual benefit of its members, as a cooperative apartment house.

GLOSSARY OF LEGAL TERMS

COPYRIGHT: (1) A common law copyright is the right of an author to protect the benefits of his unpublished literary and artistic endeavors; (2) a statutory copyright is provided by the United States Congress for the protection of an author's exclusive right to the benefit of his literary and artistic products if he meets with the provisions of specific copyright statutes.

CORAM NOBIS: A writ which seeks a judicial review on the grounds of an error in the proceeding.

CORRESPONDENT: A person charged with having committed adultery with a defendant in a divorce suit.

CORONER: A public official whose function is the determination of cause of death where the circumstances of death are suspicious.

CORPORATION: A legally sanctioned, artificial entity with the capacity to conduct business as a natural person.

CORPUS DELICTI: This is a Latin phrase which means "the body of the crime." It means that certain essential facts must be shown before one can be charged with the commission of a crime.

CORROBORATE: To strengthen or give further credibility to evidence.

COSTS: Legal costs which one incurs in the prosecution or defense of a lawsuit. The winner of a lawsuit is entitled to reimbursement of legal costs from the loser; legal costs consist of filing fees, deposition fees, witness fees, and the charges for process servers; legal costs do not include attorney fees.

COUNSEL: A lawyer.

COUNTERLCAIM: A claim by a defendant which diminishes or offsets the claim against a defendant by a plaintiff.

COURT OF LAST RESORT: A court from which there is no further right of appeal.

CONVENANT: A written agreement.

CREDITOR: A person to whom money is owed.

CRIME: An act or omission to act for which the state proscribes, in the name of the society, a punishment.

CRIMINAL INSANITY: A deranged or diminished mental capacity which deprives a person of the necessary comprehension and responsibility of his actions. The traditional test for criminal insanity is the ability of the criminal defendant to distinguish right from wrong at the time of the commission of the act, although the test for criminal insanity can differ from state to state.

CROSSCLAIM: A claim brought by a defendant against a plaintiff concerning matters brought up in the plaintiff's complaint.

CROSS-EXAMINATION: The examination of a witness on behalf of the party against whose interest the witness was originally called to testify.

CURFEW: A regulation keeping people off the streets after a designated time.

CURTESY: The right of a husband to take part of his deceased wife's estate.

CUSTODY: The physical care and keeping of person or property.

CY PRES: A French term meaning "as near as possible." It is used in the law of trusts when a gift may not be used exactly as a testator has stated, but the courts will attempt to follow the testator's instructions as near as possible to his intention.

DAMAGES: Reparations in money.

DEBENTURE: A bond which is not secured by any specific property.

DEBT: A specified sum which is owed by one person to another.

DEBTOR: A person who owes money.

DECEDENT: A deceased person.

DECEIT: A fraudulent misrepresentation.

DECISION: A written judgment of a court which decides a dispute.

DECLARATORY RELIEF: A judgment which declares the status or rights of disputing parties.

DECREE: A judicial decision which is often synonymously used with the term judgment.

DEDICATION: The setting aside of private property for public use.

DEED: A written instrument transferring an interest in property.

DE FACTO: A Latin expression which means "in fact." It means a condition which exists in fact although the condition may not exist as a matter of law. For instance, de facto segregation is segregation which exists as a matter of fact, not as a matter of the law of a state or school board.

DEFAMATION: The injury to a person's character or reputation by false statements.

DEFAULT: The failure to meet a legal obligation.

DEFENDANT: The person denying or defending the claim of a lawsuit.

DE JURE: A Latin expression which means "by law." It is used to denote a condition which exists in accordance with the laws of a particular jurisdiction.

DELINQUENT: A person who fails to perform a duty or a person who commits some public offense.

DEMAND NOTE: A note payable on demand of the creditor.

DEMISE: death.

DEMURRER: An objection to the legal basis of a lawsuit even if the facts, as stated in the complaint, are true and correct.

DEPENDENT: A person who must depend on another for support.

DEPONENT: A person whose deposition is being taken.

DEPOSITION: The testimony of a witness through the question and answer process, which testimony is taken under oath by a shorthand reporter.

DEPRECIATION: A loss in value on account of deterioration or age.

DERIVATIVE ACTION: A suit brought by stockholders on behalf of a corporation which suit is brought when the management of a corporation has failed to act.

DESCENDANT: The heir of an ancestor.

DESCENT: The passing of an estate by inheritance through a will or the laws of intestate succession.

DESERTION: Willful abandonment.

DEVISE: To give real property by will.

DICTUM: An incident or collateral remark made by a judge in a written decision.

DILIGENCE: Personal care in the handling of one's affairs.

DIRECT EXAMINATION: The first examination of a witness.

DISABILITY: The legal or physical incapacity to act.

DISBAR: To revoke an attorney's license to practice law.

DISCHARGE: (1) To satisfy an obligation; (2) the release of a bankrupt from his financial obligations after he has been adjudicated a bankrupt.

DISCOVERY: The various legal processes which allow litigants to discover important facts about an opponent's position in a lawsuit.

GLOSSARY OF LEGAL TERMS

DISCRIMINATION: The favoring of one class of persons over another.

DISENFRANCHISE: To deprive a person of his right to vote.

DISINHERIT: To prevent an heir from obtaining possession of one's property after death.

DISMISSAL WITH PREJUDICE: The termination of a lawsuit without the ability to reinstate the claim at a later date.

DISORDERLY CONDUCT: A vague term which generally means conduct that tends to disturb the peace or shock the public sense of decency and morality.

DISSENT: The disagreement of the minority of judges on a court with a decision of the majority.

DISSOLUTION: The breaking up of a legal entity.

DISTRIBUTION: In probate this is the apportioning of property as per the will, estate plan or intestate succession.

DIVIDEND: A sum of money which is paid to shareholders of a corporation from the corporate profits.

DIVORCE: Judicial severence of the bonds of matrimony.

DOCKET: A list of cases to be heard by a court.

DOE: A fictitious name used to identify a party whose real name is unknown.

DOMICILE: A person's permanent residence.

DONEE: The recipient of a gift.

DONOR: The giver of property.

DOUBLE JEOPARDY: The subjection of a person to a criminal trial for the same offense for which he has already been tried.

DOWER: The share of a deceased husband's estate that is given to his widow by law.

DRAFT: (1) A check; (2) a preliminary version of what is destined to be a formal written document.

DRAWEE: A person who must pay a check or honor a negotiable instrument.

DRAWER: A person who writes a check or negotiable instrument.

DUE PROCESS OF LAW: A term which refers to the fundamental rights and principles of justice which limit the power of the government.

EASEMENT: The privilege or right to the limited use of another's real property.

EJECTMENT: This is a common law action to determine who has legal possession of real property.

ELECTION: Pertaining to the law of wills, election is the choice of a widow to accept the bequest made to her in her husband's will or to disregard the will and elect to take the amount to which she is entitled because of the state's dower or community property laws.

EMANCIPATION: The independence of a minor from parental control and custody, which independence gives the minor the legal status of an adult.

EMBEZZLEMENT: The converting of money or goods for his own use by one who is entrusted with the property.

EMINENT DOMAIN: Power of the state to take private property for public use, providing the state make reasonable compensation for the property.

ENCUMBRANCE: A claim or lien on real or personal property.

ENDORSEMENT: The writing of one's name on the back of a negotiable instrument.

ENJOIN: To prohibit some action by court order.

ENTRAPMENT: A legal defense to a criminal prosecution which occurs when a criminal defendant has been induced by the police to commit a crime he had not contemplated so that the person will be prosecuted for the offense.

EQUAL PROTECTION OF THE LAWS: This phrase comes from the Fourteenth Amendment of the Constitution, and it requires every state to give all persons equal treatment and protection under the law; anything less than equal treatment is unconstitutional.

EQUITY: (1) A system of justice which was administered at common law to make up for the inadequacies of common law. Courts of equity could force persons to act or prohibit them from acting; (2) the amount of principal one has put into property which he is buying on time.

ESCHEAT: The reversion of property to the state when no legal heir or qualified persons can be found to claim the property.

ESCROW: Money, property, or a document held by a third person for delivery to another upon the occurrence or performance of conditions; the title to the property does not pass until all of the conditions are fulfilled.

ESTATE: (1) The property in which a live person has rights or interests; (2) the property left by a deceased person or a bankrupt.

ESTOPPEL: A condition which prevents a person from claiming legal rights because of his prior misleading conduct.

EVICTION: The dispossession of a tenant of his dwelling by processes of the law.

EVIDENCE: Any matter which furnishes proof at a trial.

EXECUTION: (1) The fulfilling of any and all legal requirements necessary to make a legal document valid; (2) the enforcement of a legislative or judicial decree or judgment.

EXECUTOR (m.) or EXECUTRIX (f.): A person who is appointed by a testator to execute the terms and provisions of the testator's will.

EXEMPTION: A privilege or immunity from an obligation.

EX PARTE: "In the interest of one side"; an ex parte order is one granted at the request of one party without notification to the other involved parties.

EXPERT WITNESS: A specialist in a field beyond the normal competence and comprehension of a layman.

EX POST FACTO: "After the fact"; an ex post facto law makes certain actions a crime when these actions were not punishable by law at the time they were committed.

EXTORTION: Blackmail.

EXTRADITION: The surrender of an accused criminal by a foreign country or state to the place in which a crime was allegedly committed by the accused.

EXTREME CRUELTY: Serious misconduct by one spouse toward the other, which misconduct is grounds for a divorce.

FAIR COMMENT: The privilege of making false statements on matters of public interest if the statements are made without malice and with the general belief that they are true.

FAIR MARKET VALUE: The price which property could be bought and sold under ordinary circumstances.

FALSE ARREST: (1) False imprisonment; (2) unlawful detention of one person by another.

GLOSSARY OF LEGAL TERMS

FALSE PRETENCES: Willful misrepresentations made in order to cheat another person.

FAMILY CAR DOCTRINE: A legal doctrine which is based on the theory that a parent is liable for any member of his family who drives the family car.

FEE SIMPLE: Absolute ownership of real property.

FELONY: A grave crime punishable by heavy fine and long imprisonment.

FIDELITY BOND: An insurance policy which indemnifies a business for losses caused by the dishonesty of an employee.

FIDUCIARY: A person who handles another's money or property in a way which involves confidence and trust.

FINE: Money required to be paid as a penalty for the commission of a criminal offense.

FIXTURE: A piece of personal property affixed to real property.

FORCIBLE ENTRY AND DETAINER: A legal action to recover possession of real property.

FORECLOSURE: The taking and selling of mortgaged property to enforce payment of debt which was secured by the property.

FOREMAN: A member of a jury who presides over the jury when it deliberates.

FORENSIC MEDICINE: The application of medical knowledge to law.

FORGERY: A crime which is committed when a check or other negotiable instrument is materially altered or changed with fradulent intent to pass it as a genuine instrument.

FRAUD: An act of deceit or misrepresentation which is perpetrated to deprive another of valuable property.

FULL FAITH AND CREDIT: A phrase from the United States Constitution which provides that each state must recognize and adhere to the public acts, records and judicial proceedings of other states.

FORNICATION: Sexual intercourse; some states still have fornication laws on their books which make sexual intercourse between unmarried persons a crime. These laws are unconstitutional, but they have not been tested lately in a higher court because district attorneys refuse to attempt to prosecute them.

GARNISHMENT: The notice to a person holding money or other property (a bank holding a bank account or an employer holding a paycheck) not to turn the property over to the person entitled to it.

GIFT: The transfer of property from one person to another without any contract or consideration.

GRAND JURY: A group of citizens called (1) to hear accusations of the commission of crimes and file indictments where it believes there is probable cause that an accused has committed a crime, and (2) to investigate governmental functions and agencies.

GRANT: The formal transfer of real property; the *grantor* is the person giving the grant, and the *grantee* is the person to whom the grant is made.

GUARANTY: A promise to be responsible for the legal obligation of another person in case of his default.

GUARDIAN: The person who is legally responsible for the care of the person and/or property of another who is incompetent to act for himself, such as a minor or an insane adult.

GUARDIAN AD LITEM: The person appointed by a court to represent an incompetent person in litigation.

HABEAS CORPUS: "You have the body"; a writ commanding the person detaining another (generally the warden of a prison or officer of the law) to produce him and submit to a decision on the legality of his detention.

HEARING: A trial or other adversary proceeding where both sides present evidence.

HEARSAY: Second hand evidence.

HEIR: A person who inherits property.

HOLDOVER TENANT: A tenant who remains in possession of property after the term of a lease.

HOLOGRAPHIC WILL: A will entirely in the handwriting of the testator.

HOMESTEAD: A family home which is exempt from execution by general creditors.

HOMICIDE: The killing of one human being by another; a homicide may be a crime or justifiable or excusable.

HUNG JURY: A jury which is so divided in number that it cannot reach a verdict.

HYPOTHECATE: To pledge property as security.

i.e.: "That is."

ILLEGITIMATE CHILD: A child whose parents were not married when it was born.

IMMUNITY: Freedom from penalty or obligation.

IMPEACH: (1) To discredit a witness; (2) to officially charge a public official with a crime in office.

IMPOTENCE: Incapacity for sexual intercourse. Impotence is a ground for divorce in many states.

IN CAMERA: "In a room." In Camera proceedings are heard in a judge's private chambers or in a courtroom which has been cleared of all spectators.

INCEST: Sexual intercourse between a man and woman so closely related by blood that the state forbids them to have sexual intercourse; incest is a crime, and it is grounds for divorce and annulment in many states.

INCOMPETENCE: A person unfit or unable to manage his own affairs and discharge his responsibilities.

INCRIMINATE: To associate another or one's self to a crime or tort.

INCUMBRANCE: Encumbrance.

INDEMNITY: To promise or to actually make reimbursement to one for an actual or anticipated loss.

INDENTURE: A properly executed legal document between two or more persons.

INDEPENDENT CONTRACTOR: A person who contracts to do work on his own as a separate and distinct business entity as opposed to an employee.

INDICTMENT: A formal written charge by a grand jury accusing a person of the commission of a serious crime.

INFORMATION: An accusation, similar to an indictment, filed by a prosecuting officer.

INFRACTION: A breach of the law.

INFRINGMENT: A violation of a legal right.

INHERITANCE: The passing of real or personal property after death.

INJUNCTION: A court order directing a person or organization to take action or refrain from taking action.

IN LOCO PARENTIS: A Latin phrase which means "in the place of a parent."

IN PARI DELICTO: "Equal in guilt"; in the law of contracts neither party to an illegal contract can enforce the contract in the courts because both are in pari delicto.

IN PERSONAM: "Against the person"; lawsuits in personam are against the person as opposed to lawsuits in rem — against the property.

INQUEST: The investigation of the coroner as to the cause of death under suspicious circumstances.

IN RE: "In the case or matter of."

IN REM: See in personam.

INSANE: Legal incapacity to perform a specified act because of a diseased or deranged mind.

INSTRUMENT: A formal written document.

INSOLVENCY: The financial condition of a person or business which is unable to pay its debts as they become due.

INSURABLE INTEREST: An interest in a person or property which an insurance company protects for a premium.

INTER ALIA: "Among other things."

INTEREST: (1) The price for borrowing money; (2) a part of the ownership of property.

INTERLOCUTORY: Provisional; an interloctory decree of divorce is only provisional until it becomes final with the passage of time.

INTERPLEADER: A legal proceeding for a person, who has money or goods claimed by two or more other persons, to ask the court for direction on how and to whom to disburse the money or goods.

INTERROGATORIES: A series of written questions which must be answered in writing under oath.

INTER VIVOS: "Between the living"; an inter vivos trust is a trust which is established by a living person for a living person.

INTESTATE: Dying without a will.

INVOLUNTARY MANSLAUGHTER: The unintentional, but unjustified and inexcusable killing of one person by another.

IPSO FACTO: "By the facts itself."

ISSUE: (1) A point of contention between disputing parties; (2) a direct descendent — child, grandchild, etc.

JOINT AND SEVERAL: The individual and collective responsibility of a defendant to pay damages.

JOINT TENANCY: Property owned by two or more persons, all of whom have the right to automatically succeed to the ownership interest of a joint tenant who dies.

JUDGMENT: The final determination by a court of the rights of disputing parties to a lawsuit.

JUDICIARY: The courts of law.

JURISDICTION: The extent of the power of a court to exercise authority and power.

JURISPRUDENCE: The philosophy of law and legal principles.

JURY: A body of men and women who must determine questions of fact according to the law and the evidence before them.

KIDNAPPING: A crime which is committed by the seizure and detention of a person by force, usually for the purpose of a ransom for the safe return of the person.

LACHES: An unreasonable delay in asserting a legal right.

LANDLORD: The owner of real estate who rents to another for a specific period.

LAPSE: The termination of a right.

LARCENY: The unlawful taking away of the personal property of another; stealing.

LAST CLEAR CHANCE: A legal doctrine which states that a person who has the last obvious chance to avoid injury to another person is liable if he does not exercise this opportunity.

LATENT: Hidden; concealed.

LAW: A rule of conduct decreed by a judicial tribunal or a formal enactment by a legislative or executive body.

LAWYER: Attorney; barrister; counselor.

LEASE: A contract for the use of property for a specific period of time. The *lessor* is the landlord and the *lessee* is the tenant.

LEGACY: A gift of personal property in a will.

LEGAL AID SOCIETY: A group of lawyers who provide free legal advice and representation to persons who are too poor to afford a lawyer.

LEGITIMATE: Lawful; authorized by law.

LEGITIMATE CHILD: A child born to parents who were married or an illegitimate child made legitimate by subsequent legitimation.

LESSEE: A tenant with a lease.

LESSOR: A landlord who rents under a lease.

LETTERS OF ADMINISTRATION: A probate court document authorizing a person to act as administrator of an estate.

LETTERS TESTAMENTARY: A probate court document authorizing a person to act as the executor of a will.

LEVY: The seizure of property by a sheriff, marshall or other court officer under a writ of execution.

LIABILITY: The responsibility to answer for another's damages.

LIBEL: A written or published defamatory statement.

LICENSE: Permission to do some act which would be illegal without the authority of a license.

LIEN: A claim on property to secure a debt.

LIFE ESTATE: The right of a person to use property for the duration of his life or for the duration of another's life.

LIQUID ASSETS: Cash or assets which can be easily converted into cash.

LITIGATION: A lawsuit.

LIVING TRUST: An intervivos trust; a trust created during the lifetime of the person creating the trust.

MAGISTRATE: The judge of a court of limited jurisdiction.

MALFEASANCE: The commission of an unlawful act by affirmative action.

MALICE: The intention to hurt another by deliberately perpetrating a wrongful act.

MALICIOUS MISCHIEF: A crime which is committed by the willful damaging of another's property.

MALICIOUS PROSECUTION: A tort which is committed when one instigates civil or criminal litigation without probable cause or justification.

MALPRACTICE: Negligent conduct by a professional person.

MANDAMUS: "We command"; a writ of mandamus is a court order directed to public officials ordering them to perform or not perform specific acts.

MANSLAUGHTER (voluntary): The taking of a human life by another as a result of the heat of passion or the diminished mental capacity of the killer.

MARITAL DEDUCTION: A deduction which is given widows and widowers in computing the taxes on the estate passing to the surviving spouse.

MARTIAL LAW: Temporary rule by military forces or executive fiat.

MAYHEM: A felony crime which is committed by violently injuring or maiming a person's body.

MECHANICS LIEN: A lien which attaches to real property and buildings for the benefit of an artisan in constructing or repairing the building to insure payment for the artisan's work.

MERGER: The combining of two or more businesses into one.

METES AND BOUNDS: Boundary lines of land.

MINOR: A young person who does not have all the rights and obligations of an adult.

MISDEMEANOR: Criminal offenses less serious than felonies but punishable by a fine and/or imprisonment, usually not more than one year in a local jail.

MISFEASANCE: Negligence; the improper method of performance of an act.

MISREPRESENTATION: A false statement.

MISTRIAL: A trial which comes to no conclusion because of the jurors' inability to agree or because of some error in the conduct of the trial.

MITIGATE: To reduce.

MONOPOLY: The exclusive power over an industry.

MORAL TURPITUDE: Immoral or depraved behavior.

MORTGAGE: A pledge of property to secure the payment of a debt or the performance of an obligation. The person who gives his property for security is the *mortgagor,* and the person who lends the money is the *mortgagee.*

MOTION: An application to a court for an order.

MUNICIPAL CORPORATION: A public corporation which is formed for the running of local civil government.

MURDER: Intentional killing of one person by another with malice aforethought. Malice aforethought is defined as a murder which is perpetrated with premeditation or during the commission of a dangerous felony (burglary, robbery, rape, kidnapping and mayhem). Murder in the second degree is generally defined as murder which is committed without premeditation or in the commission of a non-dangerous felony.

MUTUALITY: Reciprocal obligations.

NATURALIZATION: The adopting of a foreigner into a nation as a citizen and giving him all of the rights of a natural born citizen.

NECESSITY OF LIFE: Those material things which are indispensible to the maintenance of a decent life.

NEGLIGENCE: The failure to exercise the due care which an ordinary, reasonable person would exercise in similar circumstances; carelessness.

NEGOTIABLE INSTRUMENT: A draft, check, note, bill of lading, bill of exchange or other written document which can be transferred by a written endorsement and delivery. The holder of the negotiable instrument is entitled to receive the full amount on the face of the instrument from the person or organization on whom it is drawn.

NET: The gross amount of assets, recovery or income less expenses.

NOLO CONTENDERE: A Latin term which means "I will not contest it." It is a plea which can be used by a defendant in a criminal case which plea is tantamount to a plea of guilty. A plea of nolo contendere is not admissable against the defendant in a subsequent civil lawsuit.

NOMINAL: Trivial or negligible.

NON COMPOS MENTIS: A Latin phrase which means "insane."

NONFEASANCE: The failure to perform an act which one should perform.

NONSUIT: A judgment against a plaintiff because he cannot carry his burden of proof.

NOTARY PUBLIC: A person who is empowered to administer oaths and witness signatures.

NOVATION: Substitution of one contract for another.

NUISANCE: A condition which annoys, harms or damages another. A nuisance may be private and affect one person or a small group of persons, or a nuisance may be public and affect a large segment of a population.

NULLITY: No legal effect.

NUNC PRO TUNC: A Latin phrase which means "now for then"; for instance, a final judgment of divorce may be entered nunc pro tunc, which means that, although the final judgment is entered at a particular date, it is valid from some time previous to the actual entry of the judgment.

NUNCUPATIVE WILL: An oral will.

OATH: A solemn affirmation to tell the truth. The intentional breaking of the oath can result in prosecution for perjury.

OFFER: A proposal to make a binding contract.

OFFSET: A claim which balances or cancels another person's claim.

OMBUDSMAN: A person who is designated to investigate, report and act upon grievances of citizens against the government.

OPEN SHOP: A business which employs union and non-union labor.

OPINION: A written statement by a court which statement expresses the reasons and principles a judge has used to reach a decision.

ORAL: Spoken; verbal.

ORDER: A court-imposed direction to a person to act or refrain from acting in a certain way.

ORDINANCE: A law enacted and promulgated by a municipal government.

OVERT: Open.

PARAMOUNT: Superior. For instance, paramount title is title which is superior to all others who may claim title to property.

PARDON: To release a person from criminal punishment after he has been convicted for a crime.

PAROL: Spoken; oral.

PAROLE: The release of a convict from part of a sentence under specific conditions.

PARTITION: A dividing of property between owners.

PARTNERSHIP: A business association between two or more persons.

PARTY WALL: A single wall which is shared in common by two adjoining buildings.

PAR VALUE: The stated value of a share of stock or bond.

PATENT: The exclusive right to commercially exploit an invention; the exclusivity is granted by the government.

PENDENTE LITE: "Pending litigation" for instance, alimony pendente lite is alimony which is awarded pending any final determination of a divorce suit.

PEREMPTORY: Arbitrary; for instance, a peremptory challenge to a juror is the challenge an attorney may make to the service of a juror without giving any reason for the challenge.

PERJURY: Lying under oath.

PER SE: "By itself."

PER STIRPES: "By roots"; in the law of wills, it is taking property by right of representation by a group whose ancestor would have inherited the property if he had not died.

PETITION: A formal application requesting judicial action.

PLAINTIFF: A person who starts a lawsuit.

PLEA: An answer to charges.

PLEADING: (1) Advocating one's cause in court; (2) a formal written document which frames the issues of a lawsuit.

PLEDGE: The deposit of personal property with a creditor as security for a debt.

POLICE POWER: The power of the government to promulgate laws for the welfare of its citizens.

POLL TAX: A tax levied on one who is exercising his right to vote.

POSTHUMOUS: After death.

POSTMORTEM: An event occurring after death.

POWER OF APPOINTMENT: The power bestowed by one person to another to name still a third person to receive an interest in the property of the first person.

POWER OF ATTORNEY: A written document which gives one the authority to act as another's agent. The power of attorney may be general, in which case the agent can act in all respects for the principal; or the power of attorney may be special in which case the agent can only act in limited circumstances for the principal.

PRECEDENT: A judicial decision which is used to decide subsequent cases which present the same or similar legal problems.

PRELIMINARY HEARING: A hearing presided over by a judge or magistrate to determine if there is reasonable and probable cause to hold an accused person to answer for a felony in a court of general trial jurisdiction.

PREMEDITATION: Weighing the gravity and ramifications of an act and then performing it.

PREPONDERANCE OF EVIDENCE: The persuasive evidence which is necessary to prove one's case in a civil lawsuit.

PRIMA FACIE: "At first view."

PRIMOGENITURE: At common law the right of the eldest son of a family to inherit the property or title of a parent to the exclusion of his younger brothers and sisters.

PRINCIPAL: (1) A person who gives authority to an agent to act for him; (2) property as opposed to interest.

PRIVILEGE: (1) A benefit which is not the right of all to enjoy; (2) an exemption based on some overriding social policy.

PRIVITY: The link between negotiating parties to a contract.

PROBABLE CAUSE: In criminal law it is a state of facts which would lead a reasonable person of ordinary intelligence to believe that an accused has committed a crime.

PROBATE: (1) The judicial process which proves a will and oversees its execution; (2) the court which oversees the administration of the estates of persons who are legally incompetent — minors, incompetents, and the dead.

PROBATION: The release from incarceration on a promise of good behavior usually under the supervision of a probation officer.

PROCEEDING: Some judicial business.

PRO FORMA: "As a matter of form."

PROHIBITION: A judicial writ which commands an inferior court to cease and desist from acting in a certain manner.

PROMISSORY NOTE: A written promise to pay a debt at a specified time.

PROPERTY: Any tangible or intangible item which may be owned or possessed.

PROPRIETARY: Belonging to an owner.

PRO RATA: In proportion.

PROSECUTOR: A district attorney or state's attorney; the person who conducts criminal proceedings on behalf of the state.

PROXIMATE CAUSE: The direct cause of an injury.

PROXY: An agent authorized to act or vote for his principal at a meeting.

PUNITIVE DAMAGES: Damages awarded to a plaintiff against the defendant because of the defendant's fraudulent, oppressive or malicious behavior; exemplary damages; damages intended to punish and make an example of.

PURCHASE MONEY MORTGAGE: A mortgage given to secure the unpaid balance of the purchase price of a piece of real property.

RECIDIVIST: An habitual criminal.

REDEMPTION: The regaining of property.

REFEREE: A court officer who investigates pending cases and reports on them to a judge.

RELEASE: The relinquishment of a claim or privilege.

REMAND: To send back.

REPLEVIN: A legal action to regain possession of personal property.

RESCIND: Cancel.

RESIDENCE: Home.

RESIDUE: The remainder of an estate after all specific bequests and debts of the estate have been paid.

RES IPSA LOQUITUR: A Latin phrase which means "the thing speaks for itself." This term is used in negligence cases to infer negligence against a defendant when the instrumentality which caused an injury was under the exclusive control of the defendant, when accidents of the kind which injured the plaintiff do not ordinarily occur in the absence of negligence, and when there is not contributory negligence attributable to the action of the plaintiff.

RES JUDICATA: "The matter is decided"; if an issue between the same two parties has been decided before by another court, then it is res judicata and a new court will not alter the prior decision.

PUTATIVE: Alleged; supposed; reputed.

QUASH: To set aside.

QUASI: Appearing as.

QUID PRO QUO: "Something for something."

QUITCLAIM DEED: A deed to real property which contains no warranty or guarantee of title.

RAPE: A crime which is the unlawful carnal knowledge of a woman against her will by a man.

RATIFY: To approve; sanction; validate.

RE: In the matter of.

REAL PROPERTY: Land and whatever is affixed to it.

REASONABLE DOUBT: That doubt which a reasonable man might entertain to make him disbelieve an allegation.

GLOSSARY OF LEGAL TERMS

REBATE: A valuable return of money or other property after a sale has been consummated.

REBUT: To contradict.

RECEIVER: A court-appointed official whose duty it is to take custody and management of property of a litigant pending the litigant's legal action.

RECEIVING STOLEN PROPERTY: A crime which is committed by the possession of stolen property with the knowledge that the property has been unlawfully obtained. This crime can be a misdemeanor or a felony depending on the value of the goods and the disposition of the district attorney.

RESPONDENT: The party responding to an original lawsuit or an appeal.

RESTITUTION: The restoration of property to a person who has been the victim of a wrongful act to put the victim in the same economic circumstances as he was before the act.

RESTRAINT OF TRADE: Business agreements which are designed to eliminate competition and obstruct normal business activity.

RETAINER: The employment of an attorney.

RETROACTIVE LAW: A law which affects activities which occurred before the law was enacted.

REVERSE: To revoke a court judgment.

RIDER: An addition to an insurance policy or other contract.

RIGHT OF WAY: (1) Pertaining to motor vehicles, the right of a driver to cross in front of the path of another driver; (2) in real property law, the right to pass over another person's land.

RIOT: A crime which occurs when there is a disturbance of the peace by three or more persons acting in concert.

RIPARIAN: Pertaining to a person whose real property borders on a water course.

ROBBERY: A felony crime which is committed by the taking of personal property of another by fear or force.

SANCTION: Penalty.

SANCTUARY: A place where a fugitive from justice might flee to avoid the long arm of the law.

SEARCH AND SEIZURE: Police examination of a person or his premises to find contraband or other evidence of guilt of a crime.

SEARCH WARRANT: A judicial order allowing a peace officer to search a specified enclosed area for specific items.

SECURED CREDITOR: A creditor who holds a lien on the property of his debtor to secure payment of the debt.

SECURITY: (1) Stocks and bonds; (2) property pledged to guarantee payment of a debt.

SEDUCTION: Inducing a woman into sexual intercourse by peaceful persuasion or bribery.

SENTENCE: The penalty for the commission of a crime.

SEPARATION AGREEMENT: An agreement between a husband and wife who have stopped living together, which agreement may provide for child support, alimony, child visitation, and distribution of property.

SERVICE OF PROCESS: The legal notification of the existence of a lawsuit to a defendant.

SIMULTANEOUS DEATH: Pertaining to the law of wills, the death of two or more persons in the same accident under circumstances which make it impossible to determine who died first.

SLANDER: An oral statement which defames another person's reputation.

SOLVENCY: The ability to pay one's debts as they arise.

SOUND MIND: A healthy mind which can grasp the importance of entering into a legally binding situation.

SOVEREIGN IMMUNITY: The immunity of governments from being sued.

SPECIFIC PERFORMANCE: A legal remedy, which if decreed by a court, forces a party to perform a certain act in a specified way. For instance, a judgment for specific performance to sell property would force an owner of property to convey his real estate to a person to whom he previously promised to sell it.

SPENDTHRIFT TRUST: A trust which provides for an imprudent beneficiary to prevent his creditors from garnishing any of the trust.

STARE DECISIS: A Latin phrase which means "to stand by decided matters." It is the judicial policy of following the precedents set forth by previous courts.

STATE'S EVIDENCE: Testimony of an accomplice to a crime which testimony incriminates others in the commission of the crime.

STATES' RIGHTS: The Constitutional power of the states to govern themselves in areas not regulated by the federal government.

STATUTE: A law duly enacted by a legislature.

STATUTE OF FRAUDS: A law requiring certain contracts be in writing to be effective and enforceable.

STATUTE OF LIMITATIONS: A law which places a time limit on the rights of a party to file a lawsuit.

STATUTORY RAPE: A crime which is committed by a male who has sexual relations with a female who is under the age of consent.

STAY: A suspension of a party's right to enforce a judgment.

STIPULATION: An agreement.

SUBCONTRACTOR: A person who contracts with a general or a principal contractor to do some phase of the work which the general contractor has agreed to complete.

SUBDIVIDE: To divide a plot of land into lots or parcels for easier sale and improvement.

SUBLEASE: A lease given by one who is already a lessee to take all or part of the lessee's place on the premises.

SUBORNATION OF PERJURY: The crime of persuading another person to commit perjury.

SUBPOENA: An order to appear in court at a certain time to give testimony.

SUBPOENA DUCES TECUM: An order to appear in court with a particular document directed to one who has control over the particu'ar document.

SUBSCRIBE: To write one's name at the end of a document.

SUCCESSION: Acquiring property from an estate.

SUFFRAGE: The right to vote.

SUMMARY JUDGMENT: A judgment which is entered in favor of one party without a trial, as there are no real triable issues of fact.

GLOSSARY OF LEGAL TERMS

SUMMONS: A court document directing a litigant to appear in court to answer a lawsuit or suffer the risk of a default judgment.

SURETY: A person who agrees to be responsible for the debt of another.

SURROGATE: A judge who has control over a probate court.

SYNDICATE: A business association formed to accomplish a particular commercial purpose.

TARIFF: A tax levied for the privilege of importing goods from outside the United States.

TAX SALE: The sale of one's property to pay for his delinquent taxes.

TENANCY: The period of time which a tenant is legally entitled to possess real estate.

TENANT: A renter of real property.

TENDER: An offer to perform.

TESTAMENT: A will.

TESTAMENTARY: Pertaining to a will or an act which plans for the orderly passing of property at one's death.

TESTATOR (m.) or TESTATRIX (f.): A person who makes a will.

TITLE: Legal ownership of property.

TORT: A wrongful act or ommission to act which causes damage to another.

TRADEMARK: A distinctive name or symbol which is used by a businessman to identify and distinguish his goods or services from others.

TREASON: An overt attempt to overthrow the government by a citizen of the government.

TREATY: A formal agreement between two or more nations.

TRESPASS: An unlawful entry or interference with the property of another.

TRIAL: A judicial hearing which decides the dispute between litigating parties.

TRIBUNAL: A court of justice.

TRUST: The holding, managing, protecting and disbursing property by one person *(trustee)* for the benefit of another person *(beneficiary)*. The person who creates the trust is called the *trustor* or a *settlor*.

ULTRA VIRES: A Latin phrase which means "beyond the powers." It is used in the law of corporations, and it denotes acts of corporate officers which are beyond the powers given to them by the corporate bylaws or the laws of the state of incorporation.

UNCONSTITUTIONAL: An act which is in violation of the Constitution and, therefore, void.

UNDUE INFLUENCE: That amount of improper influence which overpowers the will of another and induces him to act according to the wishes of the person who is exercising the undue influence.

UNILATERAL: Binding on one party only.

UNLAWFUL ASSEMBLY: A misdemeanor crime which is committed when three or more persons gather together to assist each other in the execution of an unlawful act.

UNLAWFUL DETAINER: The unlawful retention or possession of real property.

UNLIQUIDATED: Unascertained.

USURY: A crime which is committed by the charging of interest for a loan beyond the rate that is allowable by law.

VACATE: To set aside; to move out.

VAGRANT: A person who has no visible means of support, no fixed home, and lives on the charity of others. Most vagrancy laws are unconstitutional because they unlawfully discriminate against the poor.

VALID: Legally binding.

VENDEE: A buyer.

VENDOR: A seller.

VENUE: The geographical area where a cause of action arises and where a trial must be held.

VERDICT: The decision of a jury.

VERIFICATION: A sworn statement attesting to the truth of a document.

VESTED INTEREST: A fixed and immediate right to the use and enjoyment of property.

VOID: No legal force or validity.

VOIR DIRE: An examination of a person to test his qualifications.

WAIVER: The voluntary relinquishment of a privilege or a right.

WARD: A person who is the subject of a guardianship.

WARRANT: A writ or document which authorizes and directs the performance of a certain act (arrest, search or the payment of money).

WARRANTY: An express or implied assurance of the quality of goods by the seller of those goods.

WASTE: An injury to property by a person who is in lawful possession of it.

WILL: A declaration, usually written, to show a person's intent as to the passing of his property at his death.

WRIT: The written order of a court.

The Constitution

of the

United States of America

Preamble

We the people of the United States, in order to form a more perfect union, establish justice, insure domestic tranquility, provide for the common defense, promote the general welfare, and secure the blessings of liberty to ourselves and our posterity, do ordain and establish this Constitution for the United States of America.

ARTICLE I.

SECTION 1. All legislative powers herein granted shall be vested in a Congress of the United States, which shall consist of a Senate and House of Representatives.

SECTION 2. The House of Representatives shall be composed of members chosen every second year by the people of the several states, and the electors in each state shall have the qualifications requisite for electors of the most numerous branch of the state legislature.

No person shall be a representative who shall not have attained to the age of 25 years, and been seven years a citizen of the United States, and who shall not, when elected, be an inhabitant of that state in which he shall be chosen.

Representatives and direct taxes shall be apportioned among the several states which may be included within this union, according to their respective numbers, which shall be determined by adding to the whole number of free persons, including those bound to service for a term of years, and excluding Indians not taxed, three-fifths of all other persons. The actual enumeration shall be made within three years after the first meeting of the Congress of the United States, and within every subsequent term of ten years, in such manner as they shall by law direct. The number of representatives shall not exceed one for every 30,000, but each state shall have at least one representative; and until such enumeration shall be made, the state of New Hampshire shall be entitled to choose three, Massachusetts eight, Rhode Island and Providence Plantations one, Connecticut five, New York six, New Jersey four, Pennsylvania eight, Delaware one, Maryland six, Virginia ten, North Carolina five, South Carolina five, and Georgia three.

When vacancies happen in the representation from any state, the executive authority thereof shall issue writs of election to fill such vacancies.

The House of Representatives shall choose their

speaker and other officers; and shall have the sole power of impeachment.

SECTION 3. The Senate of the United States shall be composed of two senators from each state, chosen by the legislature thereof, for six years; and each senator shall have one vote.

Immediately after they shall be assembled in consequence of the first election, they shall be divided as equally as may be into three classes. The seats of the senators of the first class shall be vacated at the expiration of the second year, of the second class at the expiration of the fourth year, and of the third class at the expiration of the sixth year, so that one-third may be chosen every second year; and if vacancies happen by resignation, or otherwise, during the recess of the legislature of any state, the executive thereof may make temporary appointments until the next meeting of the legislature, which shall then fill such vacancies.

No person shall be a senator who shall not have attained to the age of 30 years, and been nine years a citizen of the United States, and who shall not, when elected, be an inhabitant of that state for which he shall be chosen.

The vice-president of the United States shall be president of the Senate, but shall have no vote, unless they be equally divided.

The Senate shall choose their other officers, and also a president pro tempore, in the absence of the vice-president, or when he shall exercise the office of president of the United States.

The Senate shall have the sole power to try all impeachments. When sitting for that purpose, they shall be on oath or affirmation. When the president of the United States is tried, the chief justice shall preside: And no person shall be convicted without the concurrence of two-thirds of the members present.

Judgment in cases of impeachment shall not extend further than to removal from office, and disqualification to hold and enjoy any office of honour, trust or profit under the United States; but the party convicted shall nevertheless be liable and subject to indictment, trial, judgment and punishment, according to law.

SECTION 4. The times, places and manner of holding elections, for senators and representatives, shall be prescribed in each state by the legislature thereof; but Congress may at any time by law make or alter such regulations, except as to the places of choosing senators.

The Congress shall assemble at least once in every year, and such meeting shall be on the first Monday in December, unless they shall by law appoint a different day.

SECTION 5. Each house shall be the judge of the elections, returns and qualifications of its own members, and a majority of each shall constitute a quorum to do business; but a smaller number may adjourn from day to day, and may be authorized to compel the attendance of absent members, in such manner, and under such penalties as each house may provide.

Each house may determine the rules of its proceedings, punish its members for disorderly behaviour, and, with the concurrence of two-thirds, expel a member.

Each house shall keep a journal of its proceedings, and from time to time publish the same, excepting such parts as may in their judgment require secrecy; and the yeas and nays of the members of either house on any question shall, at the desire of one-fifth of those present, be entered on the journal.

Neither house, during the session of Congress, shall, without the consent of the other, adjourn for more than three days, nor to any other place than that in which the two houses shall be sitting.

SECTION 6. The senators and representatives shall receive a compensation for their services, to be ascertained by law, and paid out of the treasury of the United

Every order, resolution, or vote to which the concurrence of the Senate and House of Representatives may be necessary (except on a question of adjournment) shall be presented to the president of the United States; and before the same shall take effect, shall be approved by him, or, being disapproved by him, shall be re-passed by two-thirds of the Senate and House of Representatives, according to the rules and limitations prescribed in the case of a bill.

SECTION 8. The Congress shall have the power to lay and collect taxes, duties, imposts, and excises, to pay the debts and provide for the common defence and general welfare of the United States; but all duties, imposts and excises shall be uniform throughout the United States:

To borrow money on the credit of the United States:

To regulate commerce with foreign nations, and among the several states, and with the Indian tribes:

To establish an uniform rule of naturalization, and uniform laws on the subject of bankruptcies throughout the United States:

To coin money, regulate the value thereof, and of foreign coin, and fix the standard of weights and measures:

To provide for the punishment of counterfeiting the securities and current coin of the United States:

To establish post-offices and post-roads:

To promote the progress of science and useful arts, by securing for limited times to authors and inventors the exclusive rights to their respective writings and discoveries:

To constitute tribunals inferior to the supreme court:

To define and punish piracies and felonies committed on the high seas, and offences against the law of nations:

To declare war, grant letters of marque and reprisal, and make rules concerning captures on land and water:

States. They shall in all cases, except treason, felony and breach of the peace, be privileged from arrest during their attendance at the session of their respective houses, and in going to and returning from the same; and for any speech or debate in either house, they shall not be questioned in any other place.

No senator or representative shall, during the time for which he was elected, be appointed to any civil office under the authority of the United States, which shall have been created, or the emoluments whereof shall have been increased during such time; and no person holding any office under the United States, shall be a member of either house during his continuance in office.

SECTION 7. All bills for raising revenue shall originate in the House of Representatives; but the Senate may propose or concur with amendments as on other bills.

Every bill which shall have passed the House of Representatives and the Senate, shall, before it becomes a law, be presented to the president of the United States; if he approve, he shall sign it, but if not, he shall return it, with his objections, to that house in which it shall have originated, who shall enter the objections at large on their journal, and proceed to reconsider it. If after such reconsideration, two-thirds of that house shall agree to pass the bill, it shall be sent, together with the objections, to the other house, by which it shall likewise be reconsidered, and if approved by two-thirds of that house, it shall become a law. But in all such cases the votes of both houses shall be determined by yeas and nays, and the names of the persons voting for and against the bill shall be entered on the journal of each house respectively. If any bill shall not be returned by the president within ten days, (Sundays excepted) after it shall have been presented to him, the same shall be a law, in like manner as if he had signed it, unless the Congress by their adjournment prevent its return, in which case it shall not be a law.

To raise and support armies, but no appropriation of money to that use shall be for a longer term than two years:

To provide and maintain a navy:

To make rules for the government and regulation of the land and naval forces:

To provide for calling forth the militia to execute the laws of the union, suppress insurrections and repel invasions:

To provide for organizing, arming and disciplining the militia, and for governing such part of them as may be employed in the service of the United States, reserving to the states respectively, the appointment of the officers, and the authority of training the militia according to the discipline prescribed by Congress:

To exercise exclusive legislation in all cases whatsoever, over such district (not exceeding ten miles square) as may, by cession of particular states, and the acceptance of Congress, become the seat of the government of the United States, and to exercise like authority over all places purchased by the consent of the legislature of the state in which the same shall be, for the erection of forts, magazines, arsenals, dock-yards, and other needful buildings:

And,

To make all laws which shall be necessary and proper for carrying into execution the foregoing powers, and all other powers vested by this constitution in the government of the United States, or in any department or officer thereof.

SECTION 9. The migration or importation of such persons as any of the states now existing shall think proper to admit, shall not be prohibited by the Congress prior to the year 1808, but a tax or duty may be imposed on such importation, not exceeding 10 dollars for each person.

The privilege of the writ of *habeas corpus* shall not be suspended, unless when in cases of rebellion or invasion the public safety may require it.

No bill of attainder or *ex post facto* law shall be passed.

No capitation, or other direct tax shall be laid unless in proportion to the census or enumeration herein before directed to be taken.

No tax or duty shall be laid on articles exported from any state.

No preference shall be given by any regulation of commerce or revenue to the ports of one state over those of another; nor shall vessels bound to, or from, one state, be obliged to enter, clear, or pay duties in another.

No money shall be drawn from the treasury, but in consequence of appropriations made by law; and a regular statement and account of the receipts and expenditures of all public money shall be published from time to time.

No title of nobility shall be granted by the United States: And no person holding any office of profit or trust under them, shall, without the consent of Congress, accept of any present, emolument, office, or title, of any kind whatever, from any king, prince or foreign state.

SECTION 10. No state shall enter into any treaty, alliance, or confederation; grant letters of marque and reprisal; coin money; emit bills of credit; make any thing but gold and silver coin a tender in payment of debts; pass any bill of attainder, *ex post facto* law, or law impairing the obligation of contracts, or grant any title of nobility.

No state shall, without the consent of Congress, lay any imposts or duties on imports or exports, except what may be absolutely necessary for executing its inspection laws; and the net produce of all duties and imposts, laid by any state on imports or exports, shall be for the use of the treasury of the United States; and all such laws shall be subject to the revision and control of the Congress.

No state shall, without the consent of Congress, lay any duty on tonnage, keep troops, or ships of war in time of peace, enter into any agreement or compact with another state, or with a foreign power, or engage in war, unless actually invaded, or in such imminent danger as will not admit of delay.

ARTICLE II.

SECTION 1. The executive power shall be vested in a president of the United States of America. He shall hold his office during the term of four years, and, together with the vice-president, chosen for the same term, be elected as follows:

Each state shall appoint, in such manner as the legislature thereof may direct, a number of electors, equal to the whole number of senators and representatives to which the state may be entitled in the Congress; but no senator or representative, or person holding an office of trust or profit under the United States, shall be appointed an elector.

The electors shall meet in their respective states, and vote by ballot for two persons, of whom one at least shall not be an inhabitant of the same state with themselves. And they shall make a list of all the persons voted for, and of the number of votes for each; which list they shall sign and certify, and transmit sealed to the seat of the government of the United States, directed to the president of the Senate. The president of the Senate shall, in the presence of the Senate and House of Representatives, open all the certificates and the votes shall then be counted. The person having the greatest number of votes shall be president, if such number be a majority of the whole number of electors appointed; and if there be more than one who have such majority, and have an equal number of votes, then the House of Representa-

tives shall immediately choose by ballot one of them for president; and if no person have a majority, then from the five highest on the list, the said House shall, in like manner, choose the president. But in choosing the president, the votes shall be taken by states, the representation from each state having one vote; a quorum for this purpose shall consist of a member or members from two-thirds of the states, and a majority of all the states shall be necessary to a choice. In every case, after the choice of the president, the person having the greatest number of votes of the electors shall be the vice-president. But if there should remain two or more who have equal votes, the Senate shall choose from them by ballot the vice-president.

The Congress may determine the time of choosing the electors, and the day on which they shall give their votes; which day shall be the same throughout the United States.

No person except a natural born citizen, or a citizen of the United States, at the time of the adoption of this constitution, shall be eligible to the office of president; neither shall any person be eligible to that office, who shall not have attained to the age of 35 years, and been 14 years a resident within the United States.

In case of the removal of the president from office, or of his death, resignation, or inability to discharge the powers and duties of the said office, the same shall devolve on the vice-president, and the Congress may by law provide for the case of removal, death, resignation, or inability, both of the president and vice-president, declaring what officer shall then act as president, and such officer shall act accordingly, until the disability be removed, or a president shall be elected.

The president shall, at stated times, receive for his services, a compensation, which shall neither be increased nor diminished during the period for which he shall have been elected, and he shall not receive within that period any other emolument from the United States, or any of them.

Before he enter on the execution of his office, he shall take the following oath or affirmation:

"I do solemnly swear (or affirm) that I will faithfully execute the office of president of the United States, and will to the best of my ability, preserve, protect and defend the constitution of the United States."

SECTION 2. The president shall be commander in chief of the army and navy of the United States, and of the militia of the several states, when called into actual service of the United States; he may require the opinion, in writing, of the principal officer in each of the executive departments, upon any subject relating to the duties of their respective offices, and he shall have power to grant reprieves and pardons for offences against the United States, except in cases of impeachment.

He shall have power, by and with the advice and consent of the Senate, to make treaties, provided two-thirds of the senators present concur; and he shall nominate, and by and with the advice and consent of the Senate, shall appoint ambassadors, other public ministers and consuls, judges of the supreme court, and all other officers of the United States, whose appointments are not herein otherwise provided for, and which shall be established by law. But the Congress may by law vest the appointment of such inferior officers, as they think proper, in the president alone, in the courts of law, or in the heads of departments.

The president shall have power to fill up all vacancies that may happen during the recess of the Senate, by granting commissions, which shall expire at the end of their next session.

SECTION 3. He shall, from time to time, give to the Congress information of the state of the union, and recommend to their consideration, such measures as he shall judge necessary and expedient; he may, on extraordinary occasions, convene both houses, or either of them, and in case of disagreement between them, with respect to the time of adjournment, he may adjourn them to such time as he shall think proper; he shall receive ambassadors and other public ministers; he shall take care that the laws be faithfully executed, and shall commission all the officers of the United States.

SECTION 4. The president, vice-president, and all civil officers of the United States shall be removed from office on impeachment for, and conviction of, treason, bribery, or other high crimes and misdemeanors.

ARTICLE III.

SECTION 1. The judicial power of the United States, shall be vested in one supreme court, and in such inferior courts as the Congress may, from time to time, ordain and establish. The judges, both of the supreme and inferior courts, shall hold their offices during good behaviour, and shall, at stated times, receive for their services a compensation, which shall not be diminished during their continuance in office.

SECTION 2. The judicial power shall extend to all cases, in law and equity, arising under this constitution, the laws of the United States, and treaties made, or which shall be made under their authority; to all cases affecting ambassadors, other public ministers and consuls; to all cases of admiralty and maritime jurisdiction; to controversies to which the United States shall be a party: to controversies between two or more states, between a state and citizens of another state, between citizens of different states, between citizens of the same state, claiming lands under grants of different states, and between a state, or citizens thereof, and foreign states, citizens or subjects.

In all cases affecting ambassadors, other public ministers and consuls, and those in which a state shall be party, the supreme court shall have original jurisdiction. In all the other cases before-mentioned, the supreme court shall have appellate jurisdiction, both as to law and fact, with such exceptions, and under such regulations as the Congress shall make.

The trial of all crimes, except in cases of impeachment, shall be by jury; and such trial shall be held in the state where the said crimes shall have been committed; but when not committed within any state, the trial shall be at such place or places as the Congress may by law have directed.

SECTION 3. Treason against the United States shall consist only in levying war against them, or in adhering to their enemies, giving them aid and comfort. No person shall be convicted of treason unless on the testimony of two witnesses to the same overt act, or on confession in open court.

The Congress shall have power to declare the punishment of treason, but no attainder of treason shall work corruption of blood, or forfeiture, except during the life of the person attainted.

ARTICLE IV.

SECTION 1. Full faith and credit shall be given in each state to the public acts, records and judicial proceedings of every other state. And the Congress may by general laws prescribe the manner in which such acts, records and proceedings shall be proved, and the effect thereof.

SECTION 2. The citizens of each state shall be entitled to all privileges and immunities of citizens in the several states.

A person charged in any state with treason, felony, or other crime, who shall flee from justice, and be found in another state, shall, on demand of the executive authority of the state from which he fled, be delivered up, to be removed to the state having jurisdiction of the crime.

No person held to service or labour in one state, under the laws thereof, escaping into another, shall, in consequence of any law or regulation therein, be discharged from such service or labour, but shall be delivered up on claim of the party to whom such service or labour may be due.

SECTION 3. New states may be admitted by Congress into this union; but no new state shall be formed or erected within the jurisdiction of any other state, nor any state be formed by the junction of two or more states, or parts of states, without the consent of the legislatures of the states concerned, as well as of the Congress.

The Congress shall have power to dispose of and make all needful rules and regulations respecting the territory or other property belonging to the United States; and nothing in this constitution shall be so construed as to prejudice any claims of the United States, or of any particular state.

SECTION 4. The United States shall guarantee to every state in this union, a republican form of government, and shall protect each of them against invasion; and on application of the legislature, or of the executive (when the legislature cannot be convened), against domestic violence.

ARTICLE V.

The Congress, whenever two-thirds of both houses shall deem it necessary, shall propose amendments to this constitution, or on the application of the legislatures of two-thirds of the several states, shall call a convention for proposing amendments, which, in either case, shall be valid to all intents and purposes, as part of this constitution, when ratified by the legislatures of three-fourths of the several states, or by conventions in three-fourths thereof, as the one or the other mode of ratification may be proposed by the Congress: Provided, that no amendment which may be made prior to the year 1808, shall in any manner affect the first and fourth clauses in the ninth section of the first article; and that no state, without its consent, shall be deprived of its equal suffrage in the Senate,

ARTICLE VI.

All debts contracted and engagements entered into, before the adoption of this constitution, shall be as valid against the United States under this constitution, as under the confederation.

This constitution, and the laws of the United States which shall be made in pursuance thereof; and all treaties made, or which shall be made, under the authority of the United States shall be the supreme law of the land; and the judges in every state shall be bound thereby, any thing in the constitution or laws of any state to the contrary notwithstanding.

The senators and representatives before-mentioned, and the members of the several state legislatures, and all executive and judicial officers, both of the United States and of the several states, shall be bound by oath or affirmation, to support this constitution; but no religious test shall ever be required as a qualification to any office or public trust under the United States.

ARTICLE VII.

The ratification of the conventions of nine states, shall be sufficient for the establishment of this constitution between the states so ratifying the same.

Done in convention, by the unanimous consent of the states present, the 17th day of September, in the year of our Lord 1787, and of the independence of the United States of America the 12th. In witness whereof we have hereunto subscribed our names.

[Names omitted]

Articles of Amendment

AMENDMENT 1.

Congress shall make no law respecting an establishment of religion, or prohibiting the free exercise thereof; or abridging the freedom of speech or of the press; or the right of the people peaceably to assemble, and to petition the government for a redress of grievances.

AMENDMENT 2.

A well-regulated militia being necessary to the security of a free state, the right of the people to keep and bear arms shall not be infringed.

AMENDMENT 3.

No soldier shall, in time of peace, be quartered in any house without the consent of the owner, nor in time of war but in a manner to be prescribed by law.

AMENDMENT 4.

The right of the people to be secure in their persons, houses, papers, and effects, against unreasonable searches and seizures, shall not be violated, and no warrants shall issue but upon probable cause, supported by oath or affirmation, and particularly describing the place to be searched, and the persons or things to be seized.

AMENDMENT 5.

No person shall be held to answer for a capital or other infamous crime unless on a presentment or indictment of a grand jury, except in cases arising in the land or naval forces, or in the militia, when in actual service, in time of war or public danger; nor shall any person be subject for the same offence to be twice put in jeopardy of life or limb; nor shall be compelled in any criminal case to be a witness against himself, nor be deprived of life, liberty, or property, without due process of law; nor shall private property be taken for public use without just compensation.

AMENDMENT 6.

In all criminal prosecutions, the accused shall enjoy the right to a speedy and public trial, by an impartial jury of the state and district wherein the crime shall have been committed, which district shall have been previously ascertained by law, and to be informed of the nature and cause of the accusation; to be confronted with the witnesses against him; to have compulsory process for obtaining witnesses in his favor, and to have the assistance of counsel for his defense.

AMENDMENT 7.

In suits at common law, where the value in controversy shall exceed twenty dollars, the right of trial by jury shall be preserved, and no fact tried by a jury shall be otherwise re-examined in any court of the United States than according to the rules of the common law.

AMENDMENT 8.

Excessive bail shall not be required, nor excessive fines imposed, nor cruel and unusual punishments inflicted.

AMENDMENT 9.

The enumeration in the constitution of certain rights shall not be construed to deny or disparage others retained by the people.

AMENDMENT 10.

The powers not delegated to the United States by the constitution, nor prohibited by it to the states, are reserved to the states respectively, or to the people.

AMENDMENT 11.

The judicial power of the United States shall not be construed to extend to any suit in law or equity, commenced or prosecuted against one of the United States, by citizens of another state, or by citizens or subjects of any foreign state.

AMENDMENT 12.

The electors shall meet in their respective states, and vote by ballot for President and Vice-President, one of whom at least shall not be an inhabitant of the same state with themselves; they shall name in their ballots the person voted for as President, and in distinct ballots the person voted for as Vice-President; and they shall make distinct lists of all persons voted for as President, and of all persons voted for as Vice-President, and of the number of votes for each, which lists they shall sign and certify, and transmit, sealed, to the seat of the government of the United States directed to the president of the Senate; the president of the Senate shall, in the presence of the Senate and House of Representatives, open all the certificates, and the votes shall then be counted; the person having the greatest number of votes for President shall be the President, if such number be a majority of the whole number of electors appointed; and if no person have such majority, then from the persons having the highest numbers not exceeding three, on the list of those voted for as President, the House of Representatives shall choose immediately, by ballot, the President. But in choosing the President, the votes shall be taken by states, the representation from each state having one vote; a quorum for this purpose shall consist of a member or members from two-thirds of the states, and a majority of all the states shall be necessary to a choice. And if the House of Representatives shall not choose a President, whenever the right of choice shall devolve upon them, before the fourth day of March next following, then the Vice-President shall act as President, as in the case of the death or other constitutional disability of the President. The person having the greatest number of votes as Vice-President shall be the Vice-President, if such number be a majority of the whole number of electors appointed, and if no person have a majority, then from the two highest numbers on the list the Senate shall choose the Vice-President; a quorum for the purpose shall consist of two-thirds of the whole number of senators, and a majority of the whole number shall be necessary to a choice. But no person constitutionally ineligible to the office of President shall be eligible to that of Vice-President of the United States.

AMENDMENT 13.

SECTION 1. Neither slavery nor involuntary servitude, except as a punishment for crime whereof the party shall have been duly convicted, shall exist within the United States, or any place subject to their jurisdiction.

SECTION 2. Congress shall have power to enforce this article by appropriate legislation.

AMENDMENT 14.

SECTION 1. All persons born or naturalized in the United States, and subject to the jurisdiction thereof, are citizens of the United States and of the state wherein they reside. No state shall make or enforce any law which shall abridge the privileges or immunities of citizens of the United States; nor shall any state deprive any person of life, liberty, or property without due process of law; nor deny to any person within its jurisdiction the equal protection of the law.

SECTION 2. Representatives shall be apportioned among the several States according to their respective numbers, counting the whole number of persons in each state, excluding Indians not taxed. But when the right to vote at any election for the choice of electors for President and Vice-President of the United States, representatives in Congress, the executive and judicial officers of a State, or the members of the legislature thereof, is denied to any of the male members of such state being of twenty-one years of age, and citizens of the United States, or in any way abridged, except for participation in rebellion or other crime, the basis of representation therein shall be reduced in the proportion which the number of such male citizens shall bear to the whole number of male citizens twenty-one years of age in such state.

SECTION 3. No person shall be a senator or representative in Congress, or elector of President and Vice-President, or hold any office, civil or military, under the United States, or under any state, who, having previously taken an oath, as a member of Congress, or as an officer of the United States, or as a member of any state legislature, or as an executive or judicial officer of any state, to support the Constitution of the United States, shall have engaged in insurrection or rebellion against the same, or given aid and comfort to the enemies thereof. But Congress may, by a vote of two-thirds of each House, remove such disability.

SECTION 4. The validity of the public debt of the United States, authorized by law, including debts incurred for payment of pensions and bounties for services in suppressing insurrection or rebellion, shall not be questioned. But neither the United States nor any state shall assume or pay any debt or obligation incurred in aid of insurrection or rebellion against the United States, or any claim for the loss or emancipation of any slave; but all such debts, obligations, and claims shall be held illegal and void.

SECTION 5. The Congress shall have power to enforce, by appropriate legislation, the provisions of this article.

AMENDMENT 15.

SECTION 1. The right of citizens of the United States to vote shall not be denied or abridged by the United States or by any state, on account of race, color, or previous condition of servitude.

SECTION 2. The Congress shall have power to enforce this article by appropriate legislation.

AMENDMENT 16.

The Congress shall have power to lay and collect taxes on incomes, from whatever source derived, without apportionment among the several States, and without regard to any census or enumeration.

AMENDMENT 17.

The Senate of the United States shall be composed of two senators from each state, elected by the people thereof for six years; and each senator shall have one vote. The electors in each state shall have the qualifications requisite for electors of the most numerous branch of the state legislatures.

When vacancies happen in the representation of any state in the Senate, the executive authority of such state shall issue writs of election to fill such vacancies; provided, that the legislature of any state may empower the executive thereof to make temporary appointments until the people fill the vacancies by election as the legislature may direct.

This amendment shall not be so construed as to affect the election or term of any senator chosen before it becomes valid as part of the Constitution.

AMENDMENT 18.

SECTION 1. After one year from the ratification of this article the manufacture, sale, or transportation of intoxicating liquors within, the importation thereof into, or exportation thereof from the United States and all territory subject to the jurisdiction thereof, for beverage purposes is hereby prohibited.

SECTION 2. The Congress and the several states shall have concurrent power to enforce this article by appropriate legislation.

SECTION 3. This article shall be inoperative unless it shall have been ratified as an amendment to the Constitution by the legislatures of the several states, as provided in the Constitution, within seven years from the date of submission hereof to the states by the Congress.

AMENDMENT 19.

The right of the citizens of the United States to vote shall not be denied or abridged by the United States or by any state on account of sex.

Congress shall have power to enforce this article by appropriate legislation.

AMENDMENT 20.

SECTION 1. The terms of the President and Vice-President shall end at noon on the 20th day of January, and the terms of senators and representatives at noon on the 3rd day of January, of the year in which such terms would have ended if this article had not been ratified; and the terms of their successors shall then begin.

SECTION 2. The Congress shall assemble at least once in every year, and such meeting shall begin at noon on the 3rd day of January, unless they shall by law appoint a different day.

SECTION 3. If, at the time fixed for the beginning of the term of President, the President elect shall have died, the Vice-President elect shall become President. If a President shall not have been chosen before the time fixed for the beginning of his term, or if the President elect shall have failed to qualify, then the Vice-President elect shall act as President until a President shall have qualified; and the Congress may by law provide for the case wherein neither a President elect nor a Vice-President elect shall have qualified, declaring who shall then act as President, or the manner in which one who is to act shall be selected, and such person shall act accordingly until a President or Vice-President shall have qualified.

SECTION 4. The Congress may by law provide for the case of the death of any of the persons from whom the House of Representatives may choose a President, whenever the right of choice shall have devolved upon them, and for the case of the death of any of the persons from whom the Senate may choose a Vice-President, whenever the right of choice shall have devolved upon them.

SECTION 5. Sections 1 and 2 shall take effect on the 15th day of October following the ratification of this article.

SECTION 6. This article shall be inoperative unless it shall have been ratified as an amendment to the Constitution by the legislatures of three-fourths of the several states within seven years from the date of its submission.

SECTION 1. The eighteenth article of amendment to the Constitution of the United States is hereby repealed.

SECTION 2. The transportation or importation into any state, territory, or possession of the United States, for delivery or use therein of intoxicating liquors, in violation of the laws thereof, is hereby prohibited.

SECTION 3. This article shall be inoperative unless it shall have been ratified as an amendment to the Constitution by conventions in the several states, as provided in the Constitution, within seven years from the date of the submission hereof to the states by the Congress.

AMENDMENT 22.

No person shall be elected to the office of the President more than twice, and no person who has held the office of President, or acted as President, for more than two years of a term to which some other person was elected President shall be elected to the office of the President more than once. But this Article shall not apply to any person holding the office of President when this Article was proposed by the Congress, and shall not prevent any person who may be holding the office of President, or acting as President, during the term within which this Article becomes operative from holding the office of President or acting as President during the remainder of such term.

AMENDMENT 23.

SECTION 1. The District constituting the seat of Government of the United States shall appoint in such manner as the Congress may direct:

A number of electors of President and Vice-President equal to the whole number of Senators and Representatives in Congress to which the District would be entitled if it were a State, but in no event more than the least populous State; they shall be in addition to those appointed by the States, but they shall be considered, for the purpose of the election of President and Vice-President, to be electors appointed by a State; and they shall meet in the District and perform such duties as provided by the twelfth article of amendment.

SECTION 2. The Congress shall have power to enforce this article by appropriate legislation.

AMENDMENT 24.

SECTION 1. The right of citizens of the United States to vote in any primary or other election for President or Vice-President, for electors for President or Vice-President, or for Senator or Representative in Congress, shall not be denied or abridged by the United States or any State by reason of failure to pay any poll tax or other tax.

SECTION 2. The Congress shall have power to enforce this article by appropriate legislation.

AMENDMENT 25.

SECTION 1. In case of the removal of the President from office or of his death or resignation, the Vice-President shall become President.

SECTION 2. Whenever there is a vacancy in the office of the Vice-President, the President shall nominate a Vice-President who shall take office upon confirmation by a majority vote of both Houses of Congress.

SECTION 3. Whenever the President transmits to the President pro tempore of the Senate and the Speaker of the House of Representatives his written declaration that he is unable to discharge the powers and duties of his office, and until he transmits to them a written declara-

tion to the contrary, such powers and duties shall be discharged by the Vice-President as Acting President.

SECTION 4. Whenever the Vice-President and a majority of either the principal officers of the executive departments or of such other body as Congress may by law provide, transmit to the President pro tempore of the Senate and the Speaker of the House of Representatives their written declaration that the President is unable to discharge the powers and duties of his office, the Vice-President shall immediately assume the powers and duties of the office as Acting President.

Thereafter, when the President transmits to the President pro tempore of the Senate and the Speaker of the House of Representatives his written declaration that no inability exists, he shall resume the powers and duties of his office unless the Vice-President and a majority of either the principal officers of the executive departments or of such other body as Congress may by law provide, transmit within four days to the President pro tempore of the Senate and the Speaker of the House of Representatives their written declaration that the President is unable to discharge the powers and duties of his office. Thereupon Congress shall decide the issue, assembling within forty-eight hours for that purpose if not in session. If the Congress, within twenty-one days after receipt of the latter written declaration, or, if Congress is not in session, within twenty-one days after Congress is required to assemble, determines by two-thirds vote of both Houses that the President is unable to discharge the powers and duties of his office, the Vice-President shall continue to discharge the same as Acting President; otherwise, the President shall resume the powers and duties of his office.

AMENDMENT 26.

SECTION 1. The right of citizens of the United States who are eighteen years of age or older, to vote shall not be denied or abridged by the United States or by any State on account of age.

SECTION 2. The Congress shall have power to enforce this article by appropriate legislation.

INDEX